D1213140

THE GARDEN AND THE CITY

1 Crayon painting of Pope, *c.* 1743. By William Hoare

The GARDEN and the CITY

Retirement and Politics in the
Later Poetry of Pope
1731-1743

Maynard Mack

University of Toronto Press

© University of Toronto Press 1969

Manufactured in the United States of America
for University of Toronto Press
Toronto and Buffalo

SBN 8020 5209 6

Published in Great Britain by
Oxford University Press

For
Pam and Cuyler
Sari and George
Kathie and Sandy

Who is a poet? He whose life is symbolic.

THOMAS MANN

Preface

This is a book about Pope at Twickenham in the last phase of his poetical career, as represented by the satires and epistles of the 1730's and the final *Dunciad* of 1742–43. I like to think that in some of its implications it is also a book about the mythopoeic imagination, a faculty that when I was a young man growing up Pope and his fellow artists of the eighteenth century were not usually allowed to have. Though that situation has changed, perhaps there is yet room for a modest effort to show how one eighteenth-century writer, at any rate, managed to fashion from his personal experience and the literary past an enabling myth for himself and his work.

Among other limitations that the reader will discover in this essay, there are two that I wish especially to stress. First of all, it is not, primarily, an exercise in criticism. Criticism in the case of literary figures is never entirely separable from literary history and biography; yet it is more or less separable, and the merit of this book, if it has any, lies in the two latter areas. If I am judged to be right about the profoundly political orientation of most of Pope's poems of the 30's and about there being a certain emblematic quality in his way of life at Twickenham whose shaping influence is also felt inside the poems, here may be an additional complexity of texture which criticism will wish to take into account. But this is by the way. My findings do not deeply affect the poetic integrity of Pope's satires and epistles, even if (as I hope) it be allowed that I have supplied a more satisfying existential and personal context in which to read those poems than we have hitherto had.[1]

Second, this is a frankly speculative work. Much that it suggests can never be proved. I have tried to supply the reader, especially through the plates and appendices, with such contemporary and near-contemporary factual records of Pope's domain at Twickenham as today survive. But I have not hesitated to ask questions of the evidence, and to leap from fact to inference, sometimes, I suspect, extracting more inference than the facts will strictly bear. About people whom we have known for a very long time, shapes of likelihood and probability insistently emerge before our consciousness—the likelihood that this action entails that intention, the probability that a particular sort of stimulus will give rise to this response but not that. These shapes are our own subjective creations, yet we sense at the same time that they answer to something in the person, constitute at least a plausible image of his mystery, even if they can never pluck out its heart. Such an image (and only such an image) my account of Pope in these pages aspires to be. It is by no means the rounded biography of the man that I hope eventually to write.

Chapters I–III and the Epilogue were delivered as the Alexander Lectures before an exceptionally gracious audience at University College, Toronto, during the second week of March 1963. Our particular host—I say "our," because my

---

1/To give "readings" of the satires and epistles in the ordinary sense has therefore been foreign to my purpose. For these, the reader may consult: E. R. Wasserman, *Pope's Epistle to Bathurst: A Critical Reading with an Edition of the Manuscripts* (Johns Hopkins University Press, 1960); Thomas Edwards, *This Dark Estate: A Reading of Pope* (University of California Press, 1963); Thomas E. Maresca, *Pope's Horatian Poems* (Ohio State University Press, 1966); Jay Levine, "Pope's *Epistle to Augustus*, Lines 1–30," *Studies in English Literature*, VII (1967), 427–51; and the articles listed in the section on the Horatian Imitations in *Essential Articles for the Study of Alexander Pope*, 2d. ed. rev. and enl. (Archon Books), 1968).

I regret that I met with Peter Dixon's *The World of Pope's Satires* (1968) and Isaac Kramnick's *Bolingbroke and His Circle* (1968) too late to profit from them. Mr. Dixon addresses himself to some of the topics I have touched on in the three essays published earlier (Chaps. I–III here), often from a larger perspective, and Mr. Kramnick offers a fresh and valuable interpretation of the nature of Bolingbroke's hold on the Opposition and of the causes of their antipathy to Walpole.

I am grateful to Alfred A. Knopf, Inc., for permission to quote from Wallace Stevens' *Opus Posthumous* (below, p. 214); and to Harcourt, Brace and World, Inc., and Faber and Faber, Ltd., for permission to quote from T. S. Eliot's *Waste Land* (below, p. 217).

wife was also a beneficiary of his kindness—was the late A. S. P. Woodhouse, who held us for three days enchanted by the same medicines that Hal is alleged to have administered to Falstaff, with the result that, though we had never seen the man before, we ended by loving him—as had countless others. To all who contributed of their time, patience, or substance to the joyousness of those occasions, I register our warm thanks. Chapters I–III were later published as individual essays in considerably altered form, and have been again expanded and revised for their appearance here. Chapters IV–VI have evolved in the meantime from what in the original oral presentation occupied only a few pages. As in all imaginable worlds, the garden anticipated the city, which first sprang up nearby and then encroached.

For reading the entire manuscript and suggesting notable improvements, I am grateful to my friends and colleagues, Louis L. Martz and William K. Wimsatt, both of whom have an unerring eye for discriminating hawks from handsaws even when the wind is not southerly. I have a debt of a similar sort to Michael J. O'Loughlin, some of whose contributions are acknowledged individually later on. To Annetta Bynum, I am obliged for heroic assistance in preparing the manuscript for the printer, and to Wilda Hamerman, Ann Lincoln (*qui pro republica non pro sua obsonat*), Grace Michele, Doris Pfuderer, and Edith Rylander for generosity and patience while this consuming task proceeded. At an earlier stage, the impeccable typing of Alice Whitham was a blessing gratefully received. My wife, as usual, I can thank only by implication; this is her book in more ways than she herself will guess.

Apart from these immediate debts, I should like to acknowledge here my sense of a longstanding obligation to two men whom I have always, with some temerity, regarded as my masters: the late Chauncey Brewster Tinker of Yale and the late George Sherburn of Chicago, Columbia, and Harvard. In eighteenth-century studies, their mark is visible throughout this country and abroad: *Si monumentum requiris, circumspice.*

I dedicate this book to my three children and those to whom they are married. I do so partly because all six of them are teachers, holders of or candidates for graduate degrees—a circumstance that makes every family reunion (God save the mark!) a miniature session of the ACLS, even to congestion in the bathrooms; partly because they are of a forgiving nature and can be counted on to be tolerant of its faults, as they have always been tolerant of my own; and chiefly because I like them.

M.M.

Yale University
April 1968

Contents

Abbreviations

CLIFFORD-LANDA: *Pope and His Contemporaries*, ed. J. L. Clifford and L. A. Landa (Oxford, 1949).

CORRESPONDENCE: *The Correspondence of Alexander Pope*, ed. George Sherburn (5 vols., Oxford, 1956).

CRAFTSMAN: Caleb D'Anvers, The *Craftsman* (14 vols., London, 1737).

EGMONT: Earl of Egmont, *Manuscripts of the Earl of Egmont: Diary* (3 vols., London, 1920–23).

HERVEY: John, Lord Hervey, *Some Materials Towards Memoirs of the Reign of King George II*, ed. Romney Sedgwick (3 vols., London, 1931).

KILLANIN: Lord Killanin, *Sir Godfrey Kneller and His Times, 1646–1723* (London, 1948).

LEES-MILNE: James Lees-Milne, *Earls of Creation: Five Great Patrons of Eighteenth-Century Art* (London, 1962).

PERCIVAL: Milton Percival, ed., *Political Ballads Illustrating the Administration of Sir Robert Walpole* (*Oxford Historical and Literary Studies*, VIII, 1916).

PIPER: David Piper, *Catalogue of Seventeenth-Century Portraits in the National Portrait Gallery, 1625–1714* (Cambridge, 1963).

PLUMB I: J. H. Plumb, *Sir Robert Walpole: The Making of a Statesman* (London, 1956).

PLUMB II: J. H. Plumb, *Sir Robert Walpole: The King's Minister* (London, 1960).

SPENCE: Joseph Spence, *Observations, Anecdotes, and Characters of Books and Men*, ed. James M. Osborn (2 vols., Oxford, 1966).

STEPHENS: Frederic George Stephens and M. Dorothy George, *Catalogue of*

Prints and Drawings in the British Museum, Division 1: *Political and Personal Satires* (6 vols., London, 1870–1919).

TE: The Twickenham Edition of Pope's *Poetical Works* (vols. I–VI: the original poems, London, 1938–61; vols. VII–X: the Homer translations, London, 1967).

WALPOLE: *The Correspondence of Horace Walpole*, ed. Wilmarth S. Lewis (New Haven, 1937 ——).

WIMSATT: William K. Wimsatt, *The Portraits of Alexander Pope* (New Haven, 1965).

List of Plates

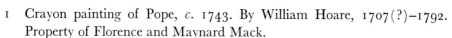

1 Crayon painting of Pope, *c.* 1743. By William Hoare, 1707(?)–1792. Property of Florence and Maynard Mack.

2 A view of Twickenham, with identification of several houses, 1756. By J. H. Müntz, active *c.* 1755–75. Engraved by John Green. Courtesy of W. S. Lewis, Farmington, Connecticut.

3 Pope's house, *c.* 1750, with identification of some of his neighbors. Pen and wash, artist unknown. Courtesy of Sir John Murray, London.

4 A sketch said to be of Twickenham village, probably by Pope. Courtesy of Major S. V. Christie Miller, Clarendon Park, Salisbury.

5 A view of Twickenham village showing St. Mary's, *c.* 1748. By Augustin Heckell, *c.* 1690–1770. The Ionides Collection. Courtesy of the Greater London Council.

6 A view of Richmond Hill from Strawberry Hill, in 1772, showing Pope's house. By William Pars, 1742–82. Courtesy of W. S. Lewis, Farmington, Connecticut.

7 A view from Richmond Hill looking southwest toward Twickenham. By Antonio Joli, 1700(?)–77. Courtesy of the Greater London Council.

8 Pope's house after Sir William Stanhope's enlargements, *c.* 1760–72. By Samuel Scott, 1710(?)–72. Courtesy of W. S. Lewis, Farmington, Connecticut.

9 Pope's house in 1795, twelve years before it was torn down. By Joseph Farington, 1747–1821. Engraved by J. C. Stadler (active 1780–1812) for the Boydells. Courtesy of W. S. Lewis, Farmington, Connecticut.

10 Vases said to have been designed for Pope by William Kent. Courtesy of the Trustees of the British Museum.

11 Pope's obelisk to his mother's memory. From an engraving in Edward Ironside's *History and Antiquities of Twickenham* (London, 1797), reprinted in John Nichols, *Miscellaneous Antiquities, In Continuation of the Biblioteca Topographica Britannica*, vol. x., opposite p. 40. Courtesy of Yale University Library.

THE GARDEN AND THE CITY

Chapter 1

A Poet in His Landscape

Paradise, and groves
Elysian, Fortunate Fields—like those of old
Sought in the Atlantic Main—why should they be
A history only of departed things,
Or a mere fiction of what never was?
            —Wordsworth, *The Recluse*

I

Pope's poetry, like the book he was accustomed to call Scripture, begins with a garden and ends with a city. To be sure, the city in Revelation is a holy city, whereas the city in the *Dunciad* of 1743 is a version of Augustan London. Yet both are in an important sense visionary, and beyond the *Dunciad's* city looms another that is more abiding: the eternal City of man's recurring dream of the civilized community, only one of whose names is Rome.

As for the garden, so far as we have evidence today, Pope's quasi-Horatian *Ode on Solitude*, celebrating the quiet life of the gentleman-gardener-farmer, was "the first fruit ... of his poetical genius."[1] Nor is anyone today ignorant of the poet's early and lasting association with settings horticultural and rural. First Binfield, then Chiswick, then the villa at Twickenham, and throughout his life,

---

1/Owen Ruffhead, *The Life of Alexander Pope, Esq.* (London, 1769), p. 22. The poem is quoted below, pp. 104–5.

at home and on summer rambles, the landscaping and planting carried on by
himself and his aristocratic friends.[2] It is curious that this side of his personality
and work should have gone almost unnoticed by nineteenth-century critics, who,
following Warton, usually consigned him to the outer darkness of artificial and
urban poets. Considering that he was a lifelong gardener of some renown; considering that he chatters repeatedly in his letters about broccoli and pineapples,
about prospects and wildernesses; considering that he left behind him a sub-
stantial body of verse having to do with the natural scene, and was among the
leaders of a landscaping movement which so modified the character of rural England that "in a sense," says E. K. Waterhouse, "the greatest English landscapes of
the century are not the works of Lambert or Wilson or Gainsborough, but the
gardens of Rousham (as they once were) and of Stourhead (as they are
today),"[3] the oversight of the Romantic critics seems at first glance extraordinary. But only at first glance. Pope's interest in landscape was not their interest.
His landscape had plenty of room for espaliers and kitchen-gardens, as theirs had
not, and no room whatever for Helvellyn or caverns measureless to man—a circumstance that seems to have rendered it unsuitable to Romantic needs and
perhaps almost unrecognizable as "real" landscape. There, clearly enough, lies
the crux of the matter. "As is the Gardener, so is the Garden," runs the adage
set down by Thomas Fuller the physician in his *Gnomologia*,[4] summarizing an
ancient *topos* that may be applied to periods as well as to men. The landscape
that could mirror the sensibility of the Romantic generation tended in Renato
Poggioli's phrase to be "as wild and boundless as the romantic view of the
self"—[5] though Keats is an obvious exception. They could hardly be expected to
thrill at the *paysages humanisés* of Rousham or Stourhead or even Stowe.

Furthermore, up to a point, the Romantic critics are right about Pope. He *is* a
city poet, not simply in the obvious ways they saw, but in deeper ways they failed
to see. His poetry has apocalyptic mutterings in it from his earliest years; it shapes
itself again and again in patterns that exhibit loss converting into triumph or,
for satiric ends (as in the fourth *Dunciad* and the first dialogue of the *Epilogue
to the Satires*), triumph that in fact is loss. And always in Pope the thing that is

---

2/On Pope's activities as a gardener and landscaper, and his wide interests in sculpture,
architecture, and painting, see Morris Brownell's *Alexander Pope, Virtuoso: A Poet and the
Sister Arts*, to be published in 1969 by the Clarendon Press.

3/E. K. Waterhouse, *Painting in Britain: 1530–1790* (Pelican History of Art, 1953), p. 115.

4/Thomas Fuller, *Gnomologia: Adagies and Proverbs, Wise Sentences and Witty Sayings,
Ancient and Modern, Foreign and British* (London, 1732), no. 701.

5/Renato Poggioli, "The Pastoral of the Self," *Daedalus*, LXXXVIII (1959), 699.

being lost, or lost and recovered, or lost and recovered and lost again, is a vision of the civilized community, the City. To illustrate briefly: the *Essay on Criticism* moves from the glories of the past, through the errors and dissensions caused by pride, to the long line of "true" critics, in whom, each carrying like an Olympic torch-bearer his own portion of the "One *clear, unchang'd* and *Universal* Light" (69), a way is shown that can reunite the critical and creative functions, the individual with tradition. *Windsor Forest* gives this pattern, based again on the loss and restoration of the good community, a larger scope. Beginning in "Peace and Plenty" because a Stuart reigns, the poem reverts to times of terror and desolation when usurpers ruled the land. These usurpers are the Norman Williams, but half-concealed in their shadow stands what Pope evidently regarded with the Jacobite half of his being as a more recent "usurpation," the accession of William III.[6] Then we return by way of a leisurely survey of native kings to "the great figure of the present, Anne, whose armies and fleets have won world-wide dominion, and whose ministers have brought about a Peace to which Pope attributes all the blessings of a Saturnian age of gold."[7]

This pattern became deeply rooted in Pope's thought; fragments and variants of it recur throughout his career. Particularly interesting, to my mind, is the form it takes in the *Epistle to Dr. Arbuthnot*. This poem begins, harried and breathless, as everyone remembers, with the figure of the tired literary lion bedeviled by his own success, totally caught up in a passing show that goads him into angry postures and tart replies. Gradually the argument expands to include considerations of far greater moment than "poetry and prate," reaching its climax in the juxtaposition of the slanderous and fawning Sporus with the staunch, firmly vertebrate, unflinching Satirist:

> Not proud, nor servile, be one Poet's praise
> That, if he pleas'd, he pleas'd by manly ways. (336–37)

The conclusion of the poem, which speedily follows this, brings a scene of

---

6/J. R. Moore, "Windsor Forest and William III," *Modern Language Notes*, LXVI (1951), 451–54. Perhaps a further clue to Pope's private view of William emerges unconsciously (?) in the echo in *Imitations of Horace, Ep.* II ii 62–63:

> Hopes after Hopes of pious Papists fail'd,
> While mighty WILLIAM's thundring Arm prevail'd

of Dryden's lines in *Palamon and Arcite*, III 669–70:

> So laugh'd he, when the rightful *Titan* fail'd,
> And *Jove*'s usurping Arms in Heav'n prevail'd.

7/Aubrey Williams, Introduction to *Pastoral Poetry and An Essay on Criticism*, TE, I 142.

2 A view of Twickenham, with identification of several of Pope's neighbors,
1756. By J. H. Müntz, active *c.* 1755–75

restored perspective, where the poet recaptures in memory the solid virtues and
natural pieties of his father's world at Binfield:

> Born to no Pride, inheriting no Strife,
> Nor marrying Discord in a Noble Wife,
> Stranger to Civil and Religious Rage,
> The good Man walk'd innoxious thro' his Age.
> No Courts he saw, no Suits would ever try,
> Nor dar'd an Oath, nor hazarded a Lye:
> Un-learn'd, he knew no Schoolman's subtle Art,
> No Language, but the Language of the Heart.
> By Nature honest, by Experience wise,
> Healthy by Temp'rance and by Exercise:
> His Life, tho' long, to sickness past unknown,
> His Death was instant, and without a groan.   (392–403)

Mrs Hathaway's.   Edwards,   Pope's.
                      Fisherman.

3 Pope's house, c. 1750, with identification of the houses of some of
his nearest neighbors. Pen and wash, artist unknown

He recaptures these values in memory and by his prayer invokes their attendance upon his own future life at Twickenham: "Oh grant me thus to live, and thus to die!" (404) In this way the epistle ends on a note of renewal and benediction, the child becoming father of the man in a sense that Wordsworth would have understood and approved as well as in the very literal sense that summons the poet at this moment "To rock the Cradle of reposing Age" (409).

The *Epistle to Dr. Arbuthnot* is, of course, an urban poem by Romantic standards, and, like all Pope's works, it is ultimately about the City. Yet the evocation of Binfield at its end and the image of the invaded garden at its beginning—

> They pierce my Thickets, thro' my Grot they glide,
> What Walls can guard me, or what Shades can hide?
> By land, by water, they renew the charge—   (7–9)

together with all those other glimpses of garden, countryside, and landscape that come and go in the mature satires, remind us of a vein in Pope that his Romantic critics overlooked and our own critics have so far largely ignored.[8] In this chapter and the two following, I have attempted a brief exploratory sounding of this vein, in the hope of somewhat clarifying its nature and its use.

To deal with it fully, one would need to speak at length of those characteristics of Pope's interpretation of the natural world that seem to have as much in common with Renaissance conceptions as with the so-called century of Newton; one would have to note the extraordinary animism of nature in his poems; its continuing importance to him as a book of truths to be read, as a mirror reflecting human character and institutions; and the principles of reciprocity, retribution, and rehabilitation that in his poetry still govern its relationships with men, as it heals the wounds they make in it and brings good out of the evil they do. One would also need to speak at length of Pope the man, of his youthful experiences in Windsor Forest, of the love of country scenes recorded so often in his letters, and of the landscaping innovations, already mentioned, which partly through his precepts and partly through his example helped modify the face of England and eventually half Europe.[9]

Though I shall have occasion to glance briefly at all or most of these matters in the ensuing argument, my initial concern in this study is with the poet's small estate at Twickenham. There, as it seems to me, in the famous garden, grotto, and villa, he evolved over the years a setting that expressed him and at the same time helped nourish in his consciousness the dramatic personality who speaks to us from the satires and epistles of the 1730's—a personality who is at once the historical Alexander Pope and the fictive hero of a highly traditional confrontation between virtuous simplicity and sophisticated corruption. I have written elsewhere of the relation of this figure to the conventions of formal satire.[10] Here I propose to consider some of the ways in which the semi-rural Twickenham situation, with all its emblems of philosophical and poetic "retreat," afforded a clarifying and defining focus for that figure and those conventions in Pope's individual case. Chapters I and II seek to construct, so far as space and evidence

---

8/A happy exception to this is Geoffrey Tillotson's *Pope and Human Nature* (Oxford University Press, 1958), ch. vii.

9/On the influence of Pope's gardening, see especially Miles Hadfield, *Gardening in Britain* (London, 1960), pp. 185–94.

10/"The Muse of Satire," *Yale Review*, XLI (1951), 80–92; reprinted in *Studies in the Literature of the Augustan Age*, ed. R. C. Boys (Ann Arbor, Mich., 1952, 1966). See also John Butt, "Pope: The Man and the Poet," *Of Books and Humankind: Essays and Poems Presented to Bonamy Dobrée* (London, 1964), pp. 69–79.

allow, a reliable account of the Twickenham house and grotto, with particular attention to what each may have contributed to the poet's sense of himself as spokesman for an idealized community, a way of life, a point of view. Chapter III is given to examining some of the forms under which this sense materializes and finds expression in the poems of the 30's, with particular reference to traditional postures of retirement. In Chapters IV–V it is argued that these poems contain other postures, postures of political action and aggression, which are pervasive in them to a degree not hitherto appreciated and, in fact, extremely difficult to assess, owing to the ambiguous nature of the instrument that political censorship required the Opposition writers to use. These postures, as Chapter VI attempts to show, collaborate in Pope's poetry of the period to effect a confrontation of the actual world of Augustan England with a country of the mind.

In the Epilogue, I venture to suggest that Pope's "creation" of Twickenham constituted an act of the mythopoeic imagination and (to borrow a phrase from the manuals of religious meditation) a "composition of place" without which he could not have written his mature poems as we have them.

II

It was in the late winter of 1719 that Pope settled at Twickenham, having leased on Thames-side a small house, together with a modest plot of land, most of it divided from the house by the main road between Hampton Court and Richmond. He had been toying for some months with the notion of building a "*palozzotto*" in London (his friend Bathurst's term and spelling), but was at last dissuaded—we may suppose by several considerations of common sense. One no doubt was expense, of which Bathurst warns him in an amusing letter of August 1718, observing how "the noise of saws and hammers," then audible on his own estate at Cirencester, is "apt to melt money" in ways that the natural philosophy of neither Aristotle nor Descartes can explain.[1]

1/Pope's earliest mention of "building a house in town" in the surviving correspondence occurs in a letter to Caryll of June 1718 (I 475). Bathurst's objection on the grounds of expense comes in August of that year (I 488). On 11 October (I 516), Pope tells Burlington that the only reason he has not built this past summer "in that piece of ground behind Burlington house (which is the Situation I am fond of to the last degree)" is the expense of "Mr Campbell's Proposal." This is Colin Campbell, author of *Vitruvius Britannicus* (3 vols., 1715–25), whom Burlington was employing in 1718–19 to remodel Burlington House. In a further letter of February 1719, Pope informs Burlington that he is ready to "resign the piece of ground intended for me, as not being yet prepared to build, & absolutely unwilling to retard the progress of the rest who are" (II 2). On Pope's site, the present no. 32 Old Burlington

A further consideration necessarily was health. London, already complained of for "Sootie Ayre" in 1645,[2] and by this time in a fair way to assuming all winter long its "sea-coal canopy," as Byron would call it—

> A huge dun cupola, like a foolscap crown
> On a fool's head—(*Don Juan* X lxxxii)

was no place for a respiratory system like Pope's. Nor for his nervous system either, now that his reputation was made and his time beginning to be subject to all the vexations he would enumerate in due course in the *Epistle to Dr. Arbuthnot*. He could not command in London the privacy needed for a writing career; even Chiswick had failed badly on that count.[3] Besides, he had been reared among country scenes, needed them for exercise and relaxation; had grown up under a father who was a dedicated gardener, praised by his neigh-

---

Street was soon after built by Colin Campbell for himself, though it appears he never lived in it. See Sheppard's *Survey of London*, vol. XXXII: *The Parish of St. James, Westminster; part* II: *North of Piccadilly* (London, 1963). In the Homer MSS (Brit. Mus. Add. MS. 4808, leaf 30, verso) there are some crude sketches which may, as Professor Sherburn pointed out (*Correspondence*, I 488n), show Pope toying with designs for his "palozzotto"; but they are not very revealing, and since they have no discernible relationship with Pope's Twickenham villa, I have not reproduced them.

The first dated letter clearly directed to Pope at Twickenham is of June 1719 (II 6–7). February letters to Burlington and Broome suggest that by this date he has taken the Twickenham house but is not yet living in it, doubtless owing to necessary renovations. In the autumn (9 November: II 18), he tells Thomas Dancastle that he has added "2 Acres of land last week." I infer this to be an enlargement of the plot across the London-Hampton Court road, which divided the house from its future garden. That the total holding came to (approximately?) five acres is attested on several occasions by Horace Walpole. (To Mann, 20 June 1760, and 23 August 1781: XXI 417, and, for the second letter, not yet published in the edition by W. S. Lewis, the Toynbee edition (ed. Mrs. Paget Toynbee [Clarendon Press, 1904]), XII, 41. See also his *History of the Modern Taste in Gardening*, ed. I. W. U. Chase [Princeton University Press 1943], p. 28). On the other hand, the visitor who described Pope's house and garden for *The Newcastle General Magazine, or Monthly Intelligencer* in 1747 estimated the garden at "not much over or under two Acres of Ground" (below, Appendix A). If he is accurate, Pope's reference in the Dancastle letter must be to the *whole* plot across the Hampton Court road, and his garden will then have to be reckoned much smaller than we had supposed. But perhaps Pope's own statement, even though "poetical," may be allowed to decide the matter: "Than in five acres now of rented land" (*Imit. Hor., Sat.* II ii 136, below p. 109).

2/Dudley North, *A Forest of Varieties* (1645), p. 68. See also Evelyn's *Fumifugium: or, the Inconvenience of the Aer, and Smoake of London Dissipated* (1661).

3/George Sherburn, *The Early Career of Alexander Pope* (Clarendon Press, 1934), p. 215. Cf. Pope's complaints to Caryll, 11 August 1718 (I 484): "... at my own house I have no peace from visitants, and appointments of continual parties of pleasure ..."; and to Thomas Dancastle, 7 August 1716 (I 352): "I have been in a constant Course of Entertainments and Visits ever since I saw you. ..."

bors for his "Hartichokes";[4] and lately, when he had himself engaged, at the instance of wealthy friends, in the planning of plantations and buildings going forward on their estates, he had found in the work intense satisfaction. A letter to the Blount sisters from Lord Bathurst's on 8 October [1718], where he had been enjoying this satisfaction for some time, shows clearly the impulses now prevailing with him to abandon the idea of a city "palace" for a residence where more gardening and life out-of-doors could be expected: "I write an hour or two every morning, then ride out a hunting upon the Downes, eat heartily, talk tender sentiments with Lord B. or draw Plans for Houses and Gardens, open Avenues, cut Glades, plant Firrs, contrive waterworks, all very fine and beautiful in our own imagination. ... I like this course of life so well that I am resolvd to stay here, till I hear of some body's being in towne that is worth my coming after." (I 515)

Some five months after this, he relinquished the ground Lord Burlington had been reserving for him and moved to the village on the Thames which has become inseparable from his name.[5]

III

Twickenham in 1719 was an attractive spot. Far enough from London to be semi-rural, not so far as to be inaccessible, its cluster of houses and historic church rested gracefully in a broad bow of the river as it curled down through its "matchless vale" (the phrase is Thomson's; *Summer*, 1425) from Hampton Court toward Kew and Chiswick, past what was then reputed one of the finest views in England, the prospect from Richmond Hill.[1] From Richmond—England's "Frescaty," as John Macky would spell it in his *Journey Through England* in 1722,[2] alluding to the fashionable resort outside Rome—as far downstream as Chelsea, the riverside was "bespangled with Villages; ... those Villages, fill'd

---

4/Trumbull to Pope, 15 June 1706 (I 17).

5/A further motive for his decision may have been the rule forbidding Roman Catholics to live within ten miles of Westminster—a rule that often slept on the books but could be reanimated embarrassingly at any moment.

1/Often painted in the eighteenth and early nineteenth centuries—e.g. by Samuel Scott, Antonio Joli, and J. M. W. Turner. See Plate 7. Pope refers to the view in his *Alley*, 53–54 (TE, VI 44):

> Ne *Richmond*'s self, from whose tall Front are ey'd
> Vales, Spires, meandring Streams, and *Windsor*'s tow'ry Pride.

2/*A Journey Through England. In Familiar Letters from a Gentleman Here, To His Friend Abroad* (1722), 4th ed., 1724, p. 62.

4 A sketch said to be of Twickenham village,
probably by Pope

with [noble] Houses, and the Houses surrounded with Gardens, Walks, Vistos, Avenues, representing all the Beauties of Building, and all the Pleasures of Planting." So reads the revised edition of Defoe's *Tour* in 1738 (I 238). In the opposite direction, upstream from Richmond to Twickenham, Teddington, Ham, and Petersham, the neighborhood where, to quote Thomson again, "the silver Thames first rural grows" (*Summer*, 1416), the prospect was more open, comprising mainly field and wood as far as Hampton Court, between which and Twickenham John Macky could find nothing requiring notice.

At Twickenham village itself, the riverside was notably inviting. Across, on the curving Surrey shore, lay Hamwalks, a mixture of meadow and grove in which the Blount sisters "often walked" during the second summer of Pope's habitation in Twickenham, he no doubt with them; and which the following December, in time of severe flood, he looked out to see "coverd with Sails."[3]

3/Pope to Teresa Blount, 11 December 1720 (II 59). There are two good maps showing

5 A view of Twickenham village showing St. Mary's, *c.* 1748.
By Augustin Heckell, *c.* 1690–1770

In the river, just off the village, rose some picturesque islets or "aits." "Twicken-ham Ait" (better known to Victorians as Eel-Pie Island, mentioned by Dickens in *Nicholas Nickleby* and by Jerrold in *Mrs. Caudle's Curtain Lectures*, objec-tive of many a cockney summer outing) was situated approximately opposite the church. Another ait lay a few hundred yards upstream, where eventually the proprietor of Strawberry Hill would look out upon haymaking at sunset and be reminded of the coloring of Claude Lorrain.[4]

The village itself stretched along the Middlesex bank, flanked on either end by a succession of estates large and small, almost reaching in the upriver direction the site of the future Strawberry Hill and downriver as far as Marble Hill. Marble Hill, an elegant Palladian mansion, was erected in the fields toward

eighteenth-century Twickenham and its environs, one by Jean Rocque (often referred to as John Rocques), 1746 (Plate 20), the other by Samuel Lewis, 1784.

4/Horace Walpole to Mary and Agnes Berry, 16 September 1791 (XI 351).

6 A view of Richmond Hill from Strawberry Hill, in 1772, showing
Pope's house. By William Pars, 1742–82

Richmond a very few years after Pope's arrival by his friend Henrietta Howard,
mistress to the Prince of Wales, the future George II, whose own domicile lay
across the river at Richmond Lodge.[5] It contributed "largely," according to

5/The design of Marble Hill is credited to Henry Herbert, ninth Earl of Pembroke, whose
professional collaborator was Roger Morris. Swift's note to his amusing *Pastoral Dialogue
between Richmond-Lodge and Marble-Hill* (*Poems*. ed. Sir Harold Williams, 2nd ed.
[Clarendon Press, 1958], II 407) states: "*Mr. Pope was the Contriver of the Gardens, Lord*
Herbert *the Architect, and the Dean of St. Patrick's chief Butler, and Keeper of the* Ice
House." The house was said to be finished save "only for its roof" in a letter of 1724 (Pope to
Fortescue, 17 September: II 257), but Roger Morris's bills for "finishing the principal story"
and "for the finnishing all workes done ... at Marble Hill" are dated 1728 and 1729. The
finishing obviously continued for some years after Mrs. Howard had taken up residence (Lees-
Milne, pp. 80 ff.). Pope was engaged in planning and superintending work on the Marble Hill
gardens from 1723 (Peterborough to Pope, undated: II 197).

Marble Hill still stands, and recent restorations by the Greater London Council have brought
it almost to its former elegance.

7 A view from Richmond Hill looking southwest toward Twickenham.
By Antonio Joli, 1700(?)–77

Letitia Hawkins, "to give Twickenham the epithet of *classic*,"[6] but there were other supporters of that reputation. Macky tells us that the villa of Lady Ferrers, Pope's close neighbor, whose summer-house may be seen in several of the engravings of his own villa (see Plate 2), "would pass in *Italy* for a delicate Palace," and he singles out for additional praise the house which in Pope's time belonged to James Johnston, Pope's "Scoto,"[7] former Secretary of State for Scotland—which he describes as being "exactly after the Model of the Country-Seats in *Lombardy*," and as making—"for the Elegancy and Largeness" of its gardens,

6/*Anecdotes, Biographical Sketches, and Memoirs*, I (1822), 88–89. Peacock refers to Twickenham's "classic shores" in his *Genius of the Thames* (*Works*, ed. Brett-Smith [London, 1924–34], VI 147).

7/*Epistle to Cobham*, 158 ff. Johnston was not one of Pope's favorites: see his *Alley*, 50 and note (TE, VI 44–45); *Correspondence* (II 316, III 272 and note); and the reading of l. 363 in the first edition of the *Epistle to Dr. Arbuthnot* (TE IV 122).

its "*Terrace* on the River," and its "Situation"—"much the brightest Figure" in "a Village remarkable for abundance of curious Seats."[8]

Pope's own venture in the Anglo-classic style was of course far more modest. Horace Walpole thought it "small and bad."[9] Yet one observer in 1747 found it "not of so large or magnificent a Structure, as a lightsome Elegance and neat Simplicity in its Contrivance"—[10] terms which Pope would certainly have relished.[11] We do not know what the house was like when Pope leased it in 1719, but it emerged from his extensive alterations, some of which were designed for him by James Gibbs,[12] a dwelling of three storeys and some ten or twelve rooms, whose plan and ornamentation recall in a general way the classicism of Inigo Jones, Palladio, and the north Italian villa. It consisted of a central block, with slightly recessed and lowered wings, the north wing fitted with bow windows framed in Ionic pilasters. The center block rose from grotto-entrance in the basement storey to a balustraded platform at the level of the *piano nobile*, then to a balustraded balcony supported on Tuscan pillars at the chamber-level, and so to a highly decorated cornice topped by a hipped roof (Plate 45 and n.) Niched into the bank of the Thames, it had in front of it a handsome grass plot

---

8/Macky, p. 60. For Johnston's house, see Plate 7 and n.; also R. S. Cobbett, *Memorials of Twickenham* (London, 1872), pp. 214–15; *Victoria County Histories: Middlesex*, III, ed. Susan Reynolds (London, 1962), p. 150. Only the detached Octagon Room, said to have been built by Johnstone to entertain Queen Caroline, now stands.

9/To Mann, 20 June 1760 (XXI 417).

10/It is so described by "T," whose letter "To Mr. P—— T—— in Newcastle," dated 18 March 1747, is published in *The Newcastle General Magazine* (above, p. 9, n. 1, and below, Appendix A).

11/Though Pope himself deprecates the house—"(which you know is nothing)"—in a letter to Ralph Allen (7 April [1736]: IV 9), this is hardly surprising in view of the opulence Allen was used to and would soon start consolidating in stone at Prior Park. See Benjamin Boyce, *The Benevolent Man: A Life of Ralph Allen of Bath* (Harvard University Press, 1967), ch. vi.

12/A letter of Gibbs to Pope about "designes" in 1719 (?) may refer either to Pope's proposed house in London or to alterations of the Twickenham villa, as Sherburn remarks (*Correspondence*, II 4 and note). There is, however, in Gibbs's memoir of himself (now in the possession of Sir John Soane's Museum) an unamplified reference to his additions to "Alexander Pope's villa." See Bryan Little, *The Life and Work of James Gibbs* (London, 1955, p. 85; and H. M. Colvin, *A Biographical Dictionary of British Architects, 1660–1840* (London, 1954).

Gibbs, who designed St. Mary-le-Strand, St. Martin-in-the-Fields, the Radcliffe Camera at Oxford, and many other public and private buildings of distinction, belonged to the circle of Pope's friend Edward Harley, second Earl of Oxford, and was in general, as Summerson puts it, the "favourite architect of the Tory party" (*Architecture in Britain, 1530–1830* [London, 1954], p. 210. Though influenced by the fashionable Palladianism, which was to some extent a Whiggish phenomenon, he kept his balance and independence—much like Pope himself.

bounded by high walls of verdure sloping to the river, and, behind it, across the public road beneath which ran the famous grotto, the equally famous garden.

Such was Twickenham in the early 1720's, on the threshold of its fame. It had already literary associations: with Bacon, Donne, Suckling, Richard Corbet, and Clarendon of the great History.[13] But its reputation as an artistic and social resort, home of the Muses and Graces together, begins around the time of Pope's arrival and extends through Horace Walpole's lifetime, though by no means all of its renown was owing to them. For varying periods and at various dates during the next hundred years, Twickenham would be home not only to Pope, but to Fielding and Lady Mary Wortley Montagu; to Paul Whitehead and Sir John Hawkins; to Walpole and Richard Owen Cambridge (the former often visited by Gray, who said he knew no "more *laughing* Scene" in England than the neighborhood of Twickenham);[14] to Mrs. Pritchard and Kitty Clive the actresses; to the painters Godfrey Kneller, Thomas Hudson, Samuel Scott, and J. M. W. Turner; and to a host of lesser celebrities in the arts as well as many great celebrities in the world of fashion.[15]

Some sense of the coloration of the place at its peak of popularity in the century's middle years, when already Pope was becoming a legend, his house a shrine,[16] and Walpole's Strawberry Hill one of the great show-places of England, may be gathered from a pamphlet published anonymously in 1760 by Mrs.

13/Bacon had tenure of Twickenham Park during much of the 1590's and is said to have received Queen Elizabeth there. A later occupant of this seat was Lucy, Countess of Bedford, whose garden is celebrated in Donne's *Twicknam Garden*. Suckling had a house at neighboring Whitton. Bishop Corbet's father seems to have conducted a horticultural nursery in the area. York House, which still stands, belonged to Clarendon during the 1660's; according to Pepys (*Diary*, 6 December 1667), the morning after his escape to the Continent "his coach, and people about it, went to Twittenham, and the world thought that he had been there." Information on the residency of these and other prominent figures may be had from Edward Ironside, *The History and Antiquities of Twickenham* (London, 1797); Cobbett (cited above); and the *Victoria County History of Middlesex* (also cited above).

14/To Wharton, 18 September 1754 (*Correspondence*, ed. Toynbee-Whibley [1935], I 407).

15/F. C. Hodgson, *Thames-Side in the Past* (London, 1913); G. S. Maxwell, *The Authors' Thames* (New York, 1924). Later, Dickens and Tennyson were short-time residents.

16/Pope's house remained a shrine until its demolition in 1807 by the Baroness Howe, who purchased it in that year, and is said to have demolished it on the ground that she was "tired of these intrusions on her privacy." See "The Literary Suburb of the Eighteenth Century," *Fraser's Magazine*, LXI (1860), 553. Even by 1760, however, Pope's successor in the property, Sir William Stanhope, had much changed the appearance of the house by adding wings, and in Horace Walpole's opinion had mutilated the garden past recognition (to Mann, 20 June 1760: XXI 417). Most eighteenth-century views of the house show it with Stanhope's alterations. See Plate 9 and n.

8 Pope's house after Sir William Stanhope's enlargements, c. 1760–72. By Samuel Scott, 1710(?)–72

9 Pope's house in 1795, twelve years before it was torn down.
By Joseph Farington, 1747–1821

Henrietta Pye.[17] She prefaces her *Short Account of the Principal Seats and Gardens in and about Richmond and Kew* with a brief discourse on Twickenham, which she describes as if she were a voyager bringing news of a far-off clime. This "little *Kingdom*," she says, is

situated on the Banks of the *Thames*; its Soil Gravelly, its Air balmy, clear, and healthful: The whole Place is one continued Garden. Plenty and Pleasure are the Ideas convey'd by its large Fields of Corn and its verdant Meadows; 'tis govern'd by a King [here a footnote specifies that the king is R. O. Cambridge], whom Arts (not

17/London, 1760. It was also published with this title and a Brentford imprint, without date; as *A Short View of the Principal Seats and Gardens in and about Twickenham* (London, 1767); and as *A Peep into the Principal Seats and Gardens in and about Twickenham* (*The Residence of the Muses*) ... *To which is added, A History of a little Kingdom on the Banks of the Thames, and its Present Sovereign, his Laws, Government, etc.* (London, 1775). The 1775

Arms) recommend to the Dignity, the Government not being Hereditary: He is pro-
claim'd by a Muse, and acknowledged by the People. Their last Monarch [here
another footnote specifies that the "last Monarch" was Pope] was the Terror of
Fools and Knaves, and the Darling of the Learned and Virtuous: He reigned long
over them, belov'd and well establish'd, and was succeeded by their present Sovereign, whom God grant long to reign! ...

The Genius of the Inhabitants inclines not towards Commerce, Architecture
seems their chief Delight, in which if any one doubts their excelling, let him sail up
the River and view their lovely Villas beautifying its Banks; Lovers of true Society,
they despise Ceremony, and no Place can boast more Examples of domestic Happiness. Their Partiality for their Country [i.e., Twickenham, their "kingdom"] rises
to Enthusiasm; and what is more remarkable, there is scarce any Instance of a
Stranger's residing for a few Days among them, without being inspir'd by the same
rapturous Affection for this Earthly *Elesium*. Their Laws and Customs are dictated
by Reason, and regulated by social Love. Happy! thrice happy they, to whom it is
permitted to spend their Lives in such a Country, such Society, and under such a
Government; possest of

> An elegant Sufficiency; Content,
> Retirement, rural Quiet, Friendship, Books,
> Progressive Virtue, and approving *HEAV'N*.[18]

I quote Mrs. Pye at length, partly because her description is not widely known,
partly because it illustrates the extent to which Virgil's great paean to the
happiness of the Italian farmer in his second *Georgic* is ever-present in the
eighteenth century even to the most ordinary sensibility. There were reasons for
this which went beyond the mere veneration of Virgil as a classic. He had evoked
in the *Georgics* the simple virtues, the hardihood, and the pieties joining man to
man and man to nature, which had brought Rome to its Augustan greatness. An
evocation nostalgic in tone, as if the verse already foretold the decline of these
virtues even at the instant of their triumph, it struck a sympathetic chord in an
age becoming conscious that Augustus's *Pax Romana* might be paralleled by a

---

edition is somewhat revised. My quotation is from the undated Brentford edition, pp. 3–4, 5–6.
Horace Walpole thought the pamphlet "most inaccurate, superficial, blundering" (to Cole,
25 April 1775: 1 367); but he is not perhaps an unbiased witness. He may have felt (with some
justification) that the proprietor of Strawberry Hill made a more suitable successor to Pope's
throne than R. O. Cambridge.
18/Thomson, *Spring*, 1161–62, 1164.

Pax Britannica, and already anxious, at least in some of its more sensitive minds, both Whig and Tory, lest the post-Augustan chapters of Roman history be repeated too.[19]

IV

Despite the reputation of Pope's garden with his friends and contemporaries, we have surprisingly little detailed information about it, still less about what it meant to him. We may properly say "what it meant," because, as a number of recent studies have shown, gardens and the pursuits associated with them could at this period "mean" a great deal.[1] They had been associated variously, during the hundred years from James I to George I, with the life of unspotted felicity, with ethical self-mastery, with "hortulan" saintship, with an innocent epicureanism, and with physico-theological "O-altitudinizing."[2] Garden imagery and garden situations, in poems of all genres by poets of all persuasions—Jonson, Herrick, Herbert, Waller, Denham, Cowley, Vaughan, Marvell, Milton, to mention only a few—had been made the vehicle for some of the deepest feelings of the age and some of its shrewdest comments on the human condition. Moreover, the relevant classical texts, all those passages in the Roman writers glorifying the retired life— its simplicity, frugality, self-reliance, and independence—had been so often culled, so often translated, paraphrased, and imitated that they had become part of the mind of England, and indeed of Europe. In mishmashes like Pomfret's *Choice*, where the fibre of Stoic tradition was replaced by sentimentality, they would soon become part of its fantasy life as well.

As if quickened by this tide of literary association, the English countryside itself brought forth ruins, arches, urns, obelisks, gods, goddesses, temples—all

---

19/See L. I. Bredvold, "The Gloom of the Tory Satirists," in Clifford-Landa, pp. 1–19; A. D. McKillop, *The Background of Thomson's Liberty* (*Rice Institute Pamphlets*, xxxviii, 1951); and chs. iv–vi, below.

1/See, for example, Hadfield (cited above, p. 8, n. 9); Christopher Hussey, *The Picturesque* (London, 1927), his introductions to Margaret Jourdain's *The Work of William Kent* (London, 1948) and Dorothy Stroud's *Capability Brown* (London, 1950, rev. ed. 1957), and his *English Gardens and Landscapes, 1700–1750* (London, 1967); B. Sprague Allen, *Tides in English Taste* (2 vols., Harvard University Press, 1937); I. W. U. Chase, *Horace Walpole, Gardenist* (Princeton University Press, 1943); Laurence Whistler, *The Imagination of Vanbrugh and His Fellow Artists* (London, 1954); Edward Malins, *English Landscaping and Literature, 1660–1840* (Oxford University Press, 1966); and a fascinating essay by Kenneth Woodbridge entitled "Henry Hoare's Paradise," in *The Art Bulletin*, xlvii (1965), 83–116.

2/See Maren-Sofie Røstvig, *The Happy Man: Studies in the Metamorphoses of a Classical Ideal* (2 vols., Oslo, 1954, 1958)—a pioneering work of first importance.

that "quarry above ground"[3] of which remnants may be seen in many an English park and garden today. It arranged itself in "scenes" to remind the traveler and virtuoso of Rome, Arcadia, and Elysium; of Praeneste, Daphne, and Tempe; of Poussin, Rosa, and Lorrain. It teased out "openings" on distant prospects, raised up hanging terraces and cascades, built mounts, grottos, theatres, canals. And since it was rarely forgotten in the eighteenth century for whom the earth had been (even if not exclusively) created, there was assigned to every romantic "view" a rustic bower or seat—"from whence," Pope writes of one such seat in Lord Digby's gardens at Sherborne, using a verb that might be more easily taken for granted a century later, "you lose your eyes upon the glimmering of the Waters under the wood, & your ears in the constant dashing of the waves."[4]

Altogether, landscape and garden at this period assume some of the functions of album and commonplace book, philosophical *vademecum* and *memento mori*.[5] They serve as aids to reflection—or to recollection, introspection, and worship, giving us, says Addison, "a great Insight into the Contrivance and Wisdom of Providence" and suggesting "innumerable Subjects for Meditation."[6] They serve as memorials of friendship and virtue, secular incitements to holy living and holy dying, like the Temple of British Worthies at Stowe,[7] or the

---

3/The phrase was used by the Duke of Shrewsbury of Vanbrugh's Blenheim, according to an undated letter of Pope's to an unnamed lady (1 432); Pope applies it to Timon's Villa in the *Epistle to Burlington*, 110.

4/To Martha Blount, 22 June [1724] (II 238). The large mount in Pope's own garden had its "Forest Seat" (Appendix A, p. 241).

5/Shaftesbury, in the *Characteristicks* (4th ed., 1732), III 184–85n.), had dwelt at length on the imaginable similarities, but (too often) actual contrasts between the harmony achieved on princely estates and that neglected in princes' souls:

What Pains! Study! Science!—Behold the Disposition and Order of these finer sorts of Apartments, Gardens, *Villas*!—The kind of Harmony to the Eye, from the various Shapes and Colours agreeably mixt, and rang'd in Lines, intercrossing without confusion, and fortunately co-incident.—A *Parterre*, Cypresses, Groves, Wildernesses.—Statues, here and there, of *Virtue*, *Fortitude*, *Temperance*.—*Heroes*-Busts, *Philosophers*-Heads; with sutable Mottos and Inscriptions.—Solemn Representations of things deeply natural.—*Caves, Grottos, Rocks.*—*Urns* and *Obelisks* in retir'd places, and dispos'd at proper distances and points of Sight; with all those Symmetrys which silently express a reigning *Order, Peace, Harmony*, and *Beauty*!—But what is there answerable to this, in the MINDS of the *Possessors*?—What *Possession* or *Propriety* is theirs? What *Constancy* or *Security* of Enjoyment? What *Peace*, what *Harmony* WITHIN?

6/*Spectator*, no. 477 (6 September 1712).

7/Among other buildings and areas at Stowe of associative and psychic intent were the "Elysian Fields," the "Gothic Building," the "Grecian Valley," the "Garden of Venus," the "Temple of Ancient Virtue," the "Temple of Concord and Victory." Some of these remain today and may be seen pictured in Margaret Jourdain's *William Kent* (above, p. 21, n. 1). Descriptions will be found in Whately (below, n. 8), pp. 213 ff.

commemorative urns that lined Shenstone's walks at The Leasowes.[8] They
present themselves to be read as epitomes of recent history, or psychological
states, or human life in general, as by Marvell in *The Garden* and *Upon Appleton House*;[9] or of politics and the relationship of social classes, as by Denham in
Cooper's Hill;[10] or of the *concordia discors* that ties the universe together, as in
both *Cooper's Hill* and *Windsor Forest*. And sometimes they are felt as *horti
conclusi*, enclosing, if not the tamed unicorn of the mediaeval tapestries, or even
the lost footprints of the classical Astraea fleeing earth,[11] at any rate some linger-
ing traces of that ancient animism whose ebbing before a new dispensation had
so stirred Milton's imagination in his *Nativity Ode*:

> The lonely mountains o're,
> And the resounding shore,
> > A voice of weeping heard, and loud lament;
> From haunted spring, and dale
> Edg'd with poplar pale,
> > The parting Genius is with sighing sent,—
> With flowre-inwov'n tresses torn
> The Nimphs in twilight shade of tangled thickets mourn.
>
> > > > (181–88)

It is usually thought that by Pope's time the Nymphs have departed, leaving
no addresses; but this judgment is not altogether correct. The "Genius" that
Milton sees "parting," Pope sees persisting as a "Genius of the Place,"[12] who

---

8/Thomas Whately rates these "among the principal ornaments" of The Leasowes (*Observations on Gardening*), 2d ed. [1770], p. 170).

9/See, especially, J. H. Summers, "Marvell's 'Nature'," *ELH*, xx (1953), 121–35; D.C.
Allen, *Image and Meaning: Metaphoric Traditions in Renaissance Poetry* (Johns Hopkins
University Press), 1960, ch. vii; Harry Berger, "Marvell's 'Upon Appleton House': An Inter-
pretation," *Southern Review* [Australia], 1 (1965); H. E. Toliver, *Marvell's Ironic Vision*
(Yale University Press, 1965), ch. iii; and J. M. Wallace, *Destiny His Choice: The Loyalism
of Andrew Marvell* (Cambridge University Press, 1968), ch. vi.

10/See Earl Wasserman, *The Subtler Language* (Baltimore, 1959), ch. iii.

11/*Georgics*, ii 473–74:
> ... extrema per illos
> Iustitia excedens terris vestigia fecit.
> ("... among them, as she quitted the earth,
> Justice planted her latest steps.")

In quoting from classical authors in this book, I have used the texts and translations of the
Loeb Library, unless otherwise stated.

12/*Epistle to Burlington*, 57 ff.

continues to embody that intuition of a mysterious life in things which for
another two hundred years his descendants will also embody, in a succession of
changing forms, from ancient mariner and old leech-gatherer to scholar gypsy,
Mr. Apollinax, and the cartoons of Charles Addams.

Though the weight of the Christian dispensation had tended to despiritualize
garden and landscape in this respect, it had helped to respiritualize them in another. The memory of the first garden was never far away from the minds of those
who worked in gardens, or wrote about them, in the seventeenth and eighteenth
centuries. The individual gardener in his garden was acclaimed heir to all the
innocence and felicity of Eden, and to the pagan paradises that anticipated it.
"Talke of perfect happinesse or pleasure," says Gerard in his *Herbal* of 1597,
"and what place was so fit for that, as the garden place where *Adam* was set, to
be the Herbarist? Whither did the Poets hunt for their syncere delights, but into
the gardens of *Alcinous*, of *Adonis*, and the orchards of *Hesperides*? Where did
they dreame that heaven should be, but in the pleasant garden of *Elysium*?"[13]
Addison writes less exuberantly in 1711, but to the same effect: "A Garden was
the Habitation of our First Parents before the Fall. It is naturally apt to fill the
Mind with Calmness and Tranquility, and to lay all its turbulent Passions at
rest."[14]

At the same time, it was never forgotten that the individual gardener was
Eden's heir in another sense, and faced therefore a task of reparation and improvement, psychic and moral as well as horticultural. Here again the continuity
of the doctrine is impressive. Evelyn, in a letter to Sir Thomas Browne of 1658,
announces his desire to form "a society of ... *paradisi cultores*, persons of antient
simplicity, Paradisean and Hortulan saints"; he intends to show soon in print,
he writes, "how caves, grotts, mounts, and irregular ornaments of gardens do
contribute to contemplative and philosophicall enthusiasme; how *elysium, an-
trum, nemus, paradysus, hortus, lucus*, etc., signifie all of them *rem sacram et
divinam*; for these expedients do influence the soule and spirits of man, and
prepare them for converse with good angells."[15] In a changed idiom, the professional gardener Stephen Switzer is still saying much the same thing in 1715.
"Paradise," he writes, in his preface to *The Nobleman, Gentleman, and Gardener's Recreation* (pp. iii, iv):

... properly signifies *Gardens of Pleasure*, the Residence of Angelick and Happy

---

13/"To the courteous and well-willing Readers."
14/*Spectator*, no. 477 (above, p. 22, n. 6).
15/28 January. See Browne's *Works*, ed. Simon Wilkin (London, 1836), I 375–76.

Souls, unsullied with Guilt, and of Duration equal with Time: And tho' the Original Compact between God and Man was after that invalidated and broke, yet we may gather from After-History, how great a Share Gard'ning and the Pleasures of the Country had in the Minds and Practice of the most Virtuous in all the successive Centuries of the World. ...

And 'tis from the Admiration of these [i.e., "Rural Delights"] that the Soul is elevated to unlimited Heights above, and modell'd and prepar'd for the sweet Reception and happy Enjoyment of Felicities, the durablest as well as happiest that Omniscience has created.

Edward Young's inscription in his garden at Welwyn was presumably intended to remind him, and his visitors, of the Eden situation at both its poles: *Ambulantes in horto audierunt vocem Dei.*[16]

V

Seen against this context and habit of mind, certain aspects of Pope's abode and life at Twickenham become luminous with implication. The site was obviously first chosen for its practical advantages, being in the country but also near London; yet the developments and improvements he carried out there over a period of twenty-five years, and the increasing reference to one or other aspect of it in the mature poems, suggest that it was gradually transformed in his imagination by associations similar in kind to those we have been examining. These were whimsical in part no doubt. He drew amusement from considering himself a minuscule inhabitant of a world tailored to fit him. He is "Homer in a nutshell," to use the phrase he appropriated from Bishop Atterbury, who had thus described his appearance when driving his little "chariot."[1] He is "as busy in three inches of Gardening, as any man can be in threescore acres ... like the fellow that spent his life in cutting the twelve apostles in one cherry stone."[2] He is prepared, if need be, to live yet more diminutively than he does, shrinking back to his "Paternal cell":

> A little House, with Trees a-row,
> And like its Master, very low. (*Imit. Hor. Ep.* i vii 77–78)

16/*Life and Letters of Edward Young*, ed. H. C. Shelley (Boston, 1914), p. 282. I have corrected Mr. Shelley's "docem" to "vocem."
1/To Atterbury, 19 March 1722 (ii 110).
2/To the Earl of Strafford, 5 October [1725] (ii 328).

The Lilliputian scale of the poet's domain at Twickenham, reflecting his own proportions, became particularly a subject of jest between him and Lord Bathurst, whose holdings at Cirencester in Gloucestershire were vast. If you will agree to visit me, Bathurst writes on one occasion in 1730, mixing playful bribe with threat:

I'll cutt you off some little corner of my Park (500 or 1000 acres) which you shall do what you will with, & I'll immediately assign over to you 3 or 4 millions of plants out of my Nursery to amuse your self with. if you refuse coming I'll immediately send one of my wood-Carts & bring away your whole house & Gardens, & stick it in the midst of Oakly-wood [this was a part of Bathurst's estate] where it will never be heard off any more, unless some of the Children find it out in Nutting-season & take possession of it thinking I have made it for them. (19 September 1730: III 134)

Pope alludes in the foregoing couplet on his "Paternal cell" to a favorite *topos* of the classical poets, which identifies a man's house with its owner. This analogy has relevance to his works at Twickenham as a whole, on which he impresses an image of himself as sharply as he impressed the head of Homer on the wax with which he sealed his letters. Horace Walpole gives a description of the poet's garden that is revealing in this respect. "It was a singular effort of art and taste," Walpole says, "to impress so much variety and scenery on a spot of five acres. The passing through the gloom from the grotto to the opening day, the retiring and again assembling shades, the dusky groves, the larger lawn, and the solemnity of the termination at the cypresses that lead up to his mother's tomb"—Walpole evidently means the obelisk erected in his mother's memory—"are managed with exquisite judgement."[3] We have only to retain Walpole's principal value-terms ("effort," "art," "taste," "variety," "exquisite judgement"), and substitute literary equivalents for the operations of gardening, to arrive at a statement that could be applied to the effects Pope achieves in his best poetry: packed couplets, graceful transitions, effective contrasts, and easy but diversified crescendoes leading to climaxes either small or large. Indeed, Walpole drew the analogy himself in a letter of 1760 to Mann, describing the garden before the poet's successor, William Stanhope, had spoiled it: "... it was a little bit of ground of five acres, enclosed with three lanes and seeing nothing. Pope had twisted and twirled and rhymed and harmonized this, till it appeared two or three sweet little lawns opening and opening beyond one another, and the whole surrounded with thick impenetrable woods" (20 June: XXI 417).

3/*A History of the Modern Taste in Gardening* (above, p. 9, n. 1), pp. 28–29. For the obelisk, see Plates 11 and 19.

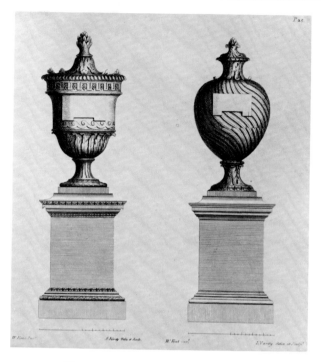

10 Vases said to have been designed for Pope
by William Kent

Walpole's insistence on the amount of "scenery" Pope had managed to in-
corporate in his five acres is seconded by a remark of Bolingbroke's at the
beginning of a philosophic letter addressed to Pope. "All I dare promise you is,
that my thoughts ... shall be communicated to you just as they pass thro my mind,
just as they use to be when we converse together on those, or any other subjects;
when we saunter alone, or as we have often done with good ARBUTHNOT,
and the jocose dean of St. Patrick's among the multiplied scenes of your little
garden."[4] Bolingbroke's "multiplied scenes" obviously refers to the poet's cunning
disposition of the garden into areas and features—a grotto, three mounts (one of
these quite large), some quincunxes, groves, a wilderness, an orangery, a vineyard, a kitchen garden, a bowling green, a shell temple, and an obelisk;[5] more

4/*Works* (1754), III 318.
5/The features mentioned here are indicated by Searle in his *Plan of Mr. Pope's Garden*

especially, it must refer to his striking use of openings, walks, and vistas, each terminating on a point of rest, supplied by urn or statue.[6] With a curious foresight, Pope had discussed this practice and related it to poetry in his "Essay on Homer's Battles" in 1716. Defending Homer's bardic repetitions—for instance, the use of the same similes in the same words—he had protested: "But may not one say Homer is in this like a skilful Improver, who places a beautiful Statue in a well-disposed Garden so as to answer several Vistas, and by that Artifice one single Figure seems multiply'd into as many Objects as there are Openings whence it may be viewed?"[7] Pope's comment, like the intricate and ingenious garden he was soon to fashion on its principles, corresponds better with his own poetic practice than with Homer's. The artifice he praises in the disposition of a single figure to answer several points of view has more affinities with pun and zeugma than with bardic repetition, and is a species of economy and polysemousness wholly characteristic of his mode.

VI

Walpole's description of the garden is interesting in a further respect. It indicates that the poet's obelisk to the memory of his mother was in fact the point of visual and emotional climax for the observer in the garden that it appears to be in

---

(below, p. 29 and n.), with the exception of the quincunxes, which may, however, be the actual form of the groves he depicts. Pope refers to "my Quincunx" in *Imit. Hor., Sat.* II i 130; Spence (no. 602) speaks of "two quincunx groves."

6/Searle indicates urns and statues in his *Plan*, but does not distinguish them. Some of the urns were given Pope by the Prince of Wales in the spring of 1739. Lyttelton, Pope's friend and the Prince's secretary, writes to the poet: "You may have six small ones for your Laurel Circus, or two large ones to terminate points, as you like best" (*c.* April: IV 170). The language Pope uses in a letter to Allen that spring (18 May: IV 181) suggests, though it does not prove, that he chose the six small urns. The inventory (Appendix B) taken of Pope's goods after his death lists, "In the Garding," i.e., garden, four "Lead Urns" and sixteen "Stone Urns and Pedestals." It also lists "a Venus with Stone Pedestall," possibly the one referred to by Curll; "a Mercury with a Wood Pedestall," "a Stone Statue with a Wood Pedestall," and "4 Busstos Antike with Stone Termes." An attack on Pope in 1732—*Of Good Nature: An Epistle Humbly Inscrib'd to His G [race] the D [uke] of C [handos]* mentions "Niches" with "Deities" in his grounds, specifying a Jove and a Hercules. Some leaden urns now preserved in the gardens at Mapledurham House, seat of the Blount family, are presumed to have come from Pope's villa by way of Martha Blount, his legatee. (See further note to Plate 45.)

7/This essay prefaces his *Iliad*, II (1716). See also the note (his? or Broome's?) at *Odyssey*, XIII 502. The analogy of garden and poem (especially epic poem) is of course a commonplace from classical times on.

John Searle's *Plan*.[1] We need not read far in Pope's correspondence of any period to see that not only was he a very good son, but that good sonship occupied, in his case, a position of some importance in that more or less edifying conception of the self by which we all live; it was a salient point of reference for his imagination as well as for his daily life.[2] After his mother's death, his friend Richardson painted a picture, now lost, of "Pope in a mourning gown with a strange view of the garden to shew the obelisk as in memory to his mothers Death,"[3] a picture one would give a good deal to recover. Certainly the key position of the obelisk, as Walpole describes it, signalizes not only the gravity of Pope's sense of loss but also, with an aptness of which he himself was probably not fully conscious, his repossession of her beyond "the solemnity ... of the cypresses": topographically —for the obelisk formed the principal point of rest in a garden of memory and meditation;[4] psychologically—for she was one of the chief *dramatis personae* in that continuing drama about the meaning of his life which we may watch both the historical Pope and the figure who speaks to us from the poems of the 30's weave in his inner consciousness. "This," says the author of the *Short Account of the Principal Gardens in and about Richmond and Kew*, referring to Pope's obelisk and regard for his mother, "is a Circumstance of more Credit to him than all his Works; for the Beauties of Poetry are tasted only by a few, but the Language of the Heart is understood by all."[5] Today we incline to smile at such statements, and when we read in the poet's letters that he thinks he would rather be known for a good man than a good poet, we suspect him of posturing, or of a

---

1/*A Plan of Mr. Pope's Garden, As it was left at his Death: With a Plan and Perspective View of the Grotto* (1745). See Plate 21. Searle was Pope's gardener. The text accompanying his *Plan* is given below in Appendix c.

2/Possibly his early and long saturation in Homer's world of profound filial pieties between sons and fathers, and, in the *Odyssey*, between a son and his mother, colored his attitudes from childhood. Homer touched Pope deeply, but in ways not easy to formulate. See the Introduction to the Homer translations, TE VII, ccxxiv–ccxxxiv.

3/Kent to Burlington, 28 November 1738 (IV 150).

4/Henry Hoare erected an obelisk to his father in his gardens at Stourhead, where the viewer was led on a quasi-symbolic journey among scenes with pronounced psychic overtones. See the essay by Kenneth Woodbridge cited above at p. 21, n. 1.

5/P. 11. Mrs. Pye may have been remembering Pope's own phrase as he pays tribute to Cowley in the *Epistle to Augustus*, 78: "But still I love the language of his Heart;" and to his father in the *Epistle to Dr. Arbuthnot*, 398–99:

> Un-learn'd, he knew no Schoolman's subtle Art,
> No Language, but the Language of the Heart.

See below, pp. 106–7, 113–15.

11 Pope's obelisk to his mother's memory.
From an engraving appearing in 1797

lack of self-knowledge. We may be wrong. Perhaps the will to virtue in Pope was genuine, only the act a slave to limit—as in many before and since. One of the strengths of the eighteenth century was that for all its superficial yet sometimes genuine elegance it could not forget certain linsey-woolsey truths. This may have been one of the strengths of its best poet too.

Friendship was another force in Pope's life that left its mark on the Twicken-ham design. Pope's capacity for making and keeping friends amounted to genius, as is clear from the forty years of his correspondence that we possess; and like the care of his mother, this also occupied a position of importance in his conception of himself. He likes to imagine his house "an Inn," himself a patriarch living by the side of the road and "receiving all comers"[6]—a figure along the lines of

6/To Hugh Bethel, 9 August 1726; to Caryll [1726]; to Fortescue, 23 August 1735 (II 387, 380; III 486). See also the Introduction to the Homer translations, TE VII, ccxxvi–ccxxix.

Menelaus in the Odyssey, whose capacity to welcome the coming, speed the going guest he claims for himself in his imitation of Horace's second satire of the
Second Book (lines 157–60). Though he was not so indifferent as he liked to
think to other sorts of eminence, he was right in believing that circumstances had
fitted him peculiarly to cherish friends. "Nature, temper, and habit, from my
youth," he writes to Gay in 1730, "made me have but one strong desire; all other
ambitions, my person, education, constitution, religion, &c. conspir'd to remove
far from me. That desire was to fix and preserve a few lasting, dependable
friendships" (October: III 138). Ten years later he had commemorated to a
degree unmatched in literature every person he knew and loved: father, mother,
Gay, Swift, Arbuthnot, Fortescue, Bathurst, Burlington, Ralph Allen, Martha
Blount – the list could be extended to great length.[7]

This aspect of Pope's nature also attained to visible expression in the Twickenham estate. Though it seems unlikely that he ever actually placed over his gate
the motto he told Fortescue would be suitable: *"Mihi & Amicis ...*; & indeed,
Plus Amicis quam Meipsi,"*[8] the effect of his lifelong orientation to friendship
can be seen in the inventory of his goods taken after his death in 1744.[9] Apart
from some expected and quite modest furnishings, his villa was like his poems a
memorial to friends. On the bedroom storey, "in the Chince Room fronting
the Thames," there were portraits of Wycherley, Betterton, Peterborough, his
mother, and Martha Blount; in "the next Room fronting the Thames," portraits
of Bolingbroke, Swift, Atterbury, Gay, Arbuthnot, Parnell, Prior, and Burlington; in "the Best Room fronting ye Thames," portraits of Martha Blount,
Bathurst, Molly Lepell, Henrietta Howard, Lady Mary Wortley Montagu,
Bolingbroke, and Dr. Garth. The *piano nobile* was furnished on the same lines.
The "Little Parlor" had Lord Bolingbroke, and the Earl of Oxford; "Mr. Popes
Roome" had Hugh Bethel (a portrait Pope had obtained shortly before his
death);[10] and "the Great Parlor" had (besides his father, mother, three aunts,
and some likenesses of himself) Prior, Betterton, the Duchess of Hamilton, the
Duchess of Montagu, Lady Mary Wortley Montagu, Judith Cowper, and

---

7/Lamb held Pope's verse compliments "the finest ... ever paid by the wit of man. Each
of them is worth an estate for life—nay, is an immortality." After reading some of them aloud,
"his voice totally failed him, and throwing down the book, he said, 'Do you think I would
not wish to have been friends with such a man as this?' " (Hazlitt, "Of Persons One Would
Wish To Have Seen," *Selected Essays*, ed. Geoffrey Keynes [London, 1930], pp. 530–31).

8/21 September [1736] (IV 34). He does, however, write Marchmont on 10 October 1741
of the "motto ... I am putting over my Door at Twitnam, Libertati & Amicitiae" (IV 365).

9/*Notes and Queries*, 6th series, V (1882), 363–65. See Appendix B.

10/To Hugh Bethel, 20 February [1744] (IV 500).

Martha and Teresa Blount. Besides these, there were in the best room at the third storey the Duchess of Buckingham, Craggs, Digby, Shrewsbury—

> Oft in the clear, still Mirrour of Retreat,
> I study'd SHREWSBURY, the wise and great,[11]

and Walsh—"the Muse's Judge and Friend."[12] In no other small house of which we have records—as in no other poetry—can there be found such concentration on a single theme.[13]

VII

It is possible that Pope's house expressed its owner in other ways as well. During the years when the original alterations were being made, he was studying Palladio.[1] Here he would meet with an insistence on architectural responsibility, such as we see him inculcating later in his *Epistle to Burlington*: that an architect must not so much mind what his patrons "can afford to lay out as the quality of the building that is proper for them"; that the *pian terreno* of a dwelling should contain its "pantries, kitchens, servants-halls, wash-houses, ovens," not, as at Timon's villa (apparently), its master's study; that church buildings ideally should be round, to figure forth the divine strength, capacity, uniformity, equality, simplicity, and infinity, and so become—if this may be legitimately taken as one meaning of the phrase in the *Epistle to Burlington*—(198) "worthier of the God"; that where there are paintings in a place of worship, those "will not be proper, which by their signification alienate the mind from the contemplation of divine things," like the sprawling "Saints" on the ceiling of Timon's chapel.[2]

11/*Epilogue to the Satires: Dial.* ii 78–9.

12/*Essay on Criticism*, 729.

13/That Pope was fully conscious how much a man's walls expressed their owner, we may gather from his remark to Ralph Allen (30 April [1736]: IV 13): "A Man not only shews his Taste but his Virtue, in the Choice of such Ornaments: And whatever Example most strikes us, we may reasonably imagine may have an influence upon others, so that the History itself (if wellchosen) upon a Rich-mans Walls, is very often a better lesson than any he could teach by his Conversation. In this sense, the Stones may be said to speak, when Men cannot, or will not."

1/To Digby, 20 July 1720 (II 50). According to the inventory cited above, Pope's library contained busts of both "Poladio" and "Indigo Jones." It would be a plausible guess that these were copies of the ones made by Rysbrack for Chiswick House. See M. I. Webb, *Michael Rysbrack, Sculptor* (London, 1954), figs. 36–37.

2/*The Four Books of Andrea Palladio's Architecture*, tr. Isaac Ware, rev. by Burlington (1738), pp. 37–38, 81–82.

12 A view of Pope's house, 1747–48.
The Newcastle General Magazine

Pope would also encounter in Palladio practices of mathematical proportioning in room design which have their ultimate theoretical basis in Pythagorean doctrine about the music of the spheres[3] and reflect the same theories of cosmic harmony that he had appealed to in his *Essay on Man*. These practices were still being warmly advocated as the great secret of the ancients by Pope's fellow townsman, the architect Robert Morris, in 1734.[4]

Nature has taught Mankind in *Musick* certain Rules for Proportion of Sounds, so *Architecture* has its Rules dependant on those Proportions, or at least such Propor-

---

3/See Rudolf Wittkower, *Architectural Principles in the Age of Humanism*, 2d ed., (London, 1952), pp. 63–66, and part iv: "The Problem of Harmonic Proportion in Architecture."

4/They had been followed to the letter by Lord Pembroke and Robert Morris's kinsman, Roger, in the design of rooms at Marble Hill. See Lees-Milne, pp. 86–89.

tions which are Arithmetical Harmony; and those I take to be dependant on Nature. The Square in *Geometry*, the Unison or Circle in *Musick*, and the Cube in *Building*, have all an inseparable Proportion; the Parts being equal, and the Sides, and Angles, *etc.* give the Eye and Ear an agreeable Pleasure; from hence may likewise be deduc'd the Cube and half, the Double Cube; the Diapason, and Diapenté, being founded on the same Principles in *Musick*.[5]

In *Musick* are only seven distinct Notes, in *Architecture* likewise are only seven distinct Proportions, which produce all the different Buildings in the Universe, *viz.* The Cube,—the Cube and half,—the Double Cube,—the Duplicates of 3, 2, and 1,—of 4, 3, and 2,—of 5, 4, and 3,—and of 6, 4, and 3, produce all the Harmonick Proportions of Rooms.[6]

We know that Pope was familiar with this kind of doctrine in its cosmological form. It was in fact a commonplace of the age:

> From Harmony, from heav'nly Harmony
> This universal Frame began:
> From Harmony to Harmony
> Thro' all the compass of the Notes it ran,
> The Diapason closing full in Man.[7]

Through Shaftesbury, if no one else, he must also have been familiar with its ethical extensions:

Shou'd a Writer upon *Musick*, addressing himself to the Students and Lovers of the Art, declare to 'em, "That the Measure or Rule of HARMONY was *Caprice* or *Will*, *Humour* or *Fashion*"; 'tis not very likely he shou'd be heard with great Attention, or treated with real Gravity. For HARMONY is Harmony *by Nature*, let Men judg ever so ridiculously of Musick. So is *Symmetry* and *Proportion* founded still *in Nature*, let Mens Fancy prove ever so barbarous, or their Fashions ever so *Gothick*

5/*Lectures on Architecture* (London, 1734), p. 74.

6/*Ibid.*, p. 94. Morris was the theorist of the neo-Palladian movement, as John Summerson notes (*Architecture in Britain: 1530–1830* [Pelican History of Art, 1954], pp. 219–20). The subtitle of his *Essay in Defence of Ancient Architecture* (1728), an attack on the baroque principles of Hawksmoor and Vanbrugh, reveals its tendency: "a Parallel of the ancient Buildings with the modern, shewing the Beauty and Harmony of the Former, and the Irregularity of the Latter." So does the subtitle of his *Lectures on Architecture*: "Consisting of Rules Founded upon Harmonick and Arithmetical Proportions in Building." His *Select Architecture* of 1755 had considerable influence in the American Colonies as well as at home.

7/Dryden, *Song for St. Cecilia's Day*, 11–15. This phase of the doctrine is discussed in John Hollander's *The Untuning of the Sky* (Princeton University Press, 1962).

13 A view of Pope's house, 1749.
By Augustin Heckell, c. 1690–1770

in their Architecture, Sculpture, or whatever other designing Art. 'Tis the same case, where *Life* and MANNERS are concern'd. *Virtue* has the same fix'd Standard. The same *Numbers*, *Harmony*, and *Proportion* will have place in MORALS; and are discoverable in the *Characters* and *Affections* of Mankind; in which are laid the just Foundations of an Art and Science, superior to every other of human Practice and Comprehension.[8]

Was Pope familiar, like his fellow townsman Morris, with the long history of this doctrine in architecture? Had he applied the harmonic proportions in any of the reconstructions of his villa—in, say, that "great room" (a double cube room?) about which his friend Digby inquires in 1723?[9] or the "New Room" of which he

8/*Characteristicks* (4th ed., 1732), I 353. See Pope, *Imit. Hor.*, *Ep.* II ii 202–5.
9/14 August (II 192).

tells the Countess of Burlington in 1733?[10] And did this sort of thing still carry with it a tingle of Pythagorean and Platonic association? A man like Daniele Barbaro, Rudolf Wittkower suggests (alluding to the Venetian philomath and commentator on Vitruvius for whom Palladio built the magnificently "harmonic" Villa Maser at Asolo), could perhaps experience "under a Renaissance dome ... a faint echo of the inaudible music of the spheres."[11] Could an eighteenth-century poet and Palladian experience, or imagine that he experienced, in the great salon at Marble Hill, or possibly in the interior of his own dwelling, if not so metaphysical an echo, at least an exhilarating access of confidence that all things are One? It is impossible to say. All we may safely say is that Pope and all the rest of the neo-Palladians shared their master's conviction (summed up in Wittkower's words) that "the practice of good architecture is ... a moral faculty, and architecture ... one emanation of the unity of the sciences and arts which together constitute the idea of *virtus*."[12] It would not have surprised Pope to think that the pleasure of the eye in the proportions of a "Cube and half" or a "Double Cube" sprang from a principle of concord which also moved the sun and other stars, and might therefore be registered on that inner sense which is attuned to ditties of no tone.

> What tho' nor real voice nor sound
> Amid their radiant orbs he found?
> In Reason's ear they all rejoice,
> And utter forth a glorious voice. ...[13]

This would not have surprised Pope, and it would have pleased him. Many things in his surroundings at Twickenham, like many things in his poems, indicate that his associative instinct was profound. In contemplating his "Tuscan portico" and "Ionic pilasters," he must have felt at the very least the same deep stirrings of identification with an admired tradition as those which impelled him to keep about him in his library the busts of Homer, Spenser, Shakespeare, Milton, Dryden, and to plan for his grass-plot at the river's edge the extraordinary ornament described by Spence in 1743.

10/13 January (III 341).
11/*Architectural Principles* (cited above, p. 33, n. 3), p. 124.
12/*Ibid.*, p. 57. See the engraved title in Ware's translation of the *Four Books*.
13/Addison, *Spectator*, no. 465 (23 August 1712).

VIII

His design for this, Spence tells us (no. 620)

was to have a swan, as flying into the river, on each side of the landing-place, then the statues of two river gods reclined on the bank between them and the corner seats, or temples[,] with

Hic placido fluit amne Meles

on one of their urns, and

Magnis ubi flexibus errat Mincius

on the other. Then two terms in the first niches in the grove-work on the sides with the busts of Homer and Virgil, and higher, two others with those of Marcus Aurelius and Cicero.

This is a more elaborate work of the associative instinct than at first appears. Like some of the allusions in Pope's verse, it spreads in circles of analogy that one hardly knows how far to follow. The first of the two inscriptions comes from Politian's *Ambra*, whose title is itself a reference to a villa by a stream at which Lorenzo the Magnificent and his circle, Politian being one, met to carry on their philosophical studies and conversations. Are we meant to see here an allusion to Bolingbroke and Pope, and "good ARBUTHNOT, and the jocose dean of St. Patrick's," who, as we have earlier seen, roamed the Twickenham garden engaging in similar pursuits? Probably not—though it is difficult to be sure. As for the inscription itself, this is taken from a passage in the *Ambra* which describes the river Meles as follows: "Here softly flows the Meles, and silent in its deep grottos listens to its singing swans."[1] This accounts for the stone swans Pope proposed, and reminds us of all those other "swans"—from Chaucer down—whose singing the Thames has heard, and in whose number Pope makes one. But the widening circle of analogy extends far beyond this. Politian's point in referring to the Meles is to introduce the particular poet with whom that river has immemorially been associated: "This region," the *Ambra* goes on, "first bore that excellent poet. An Aonian deity, patron of the dance and even able to contend on equal terms

---

1/Ll. 211–12 (translation mine):
Hic placido fluit amne Meles, auditque sub altis
Ipse tacens antris meditantes carmina cycnos.
For what may be the product of a similarly associative instinct, see Plate 14.

14 A pastiche of Pope's house and its surroundings.
By Joseph Nickolls(?), c. 1755–60(?)

with Apollo, had filled beautiful Critheis with a secret child. Hence sprang that mighty genius" [Homer].[2]

Pope's other river-god to be assimilated to the Thames is that of Virgil's river, the Mincius. The inscription for *his* urn—"Where the Mincius wanders with great windings"—brings us once again to the *Georgics*: specifically to that famous passage in the third *Georgic*, where Virgil states a goal for himself which was to kindle many a Renaissance mind to like effort, but which Pope is the last major poet of England to take seriously: the goal of enlarging and enriching the national culture by causing to be poured into it the great works of classical antiquity:

> primus Idumaeas referam tibi, Mantua, palmas
> et viridi in campo templum de marmore ponam
> propter aquam, tardis ingens ubi flexibus errat
> Mincius et tenera praetexit harundine ripas.   (12–15)

Dryden states the program with suitable resonance in his translation.

> I, first of *Romans*, shall in Triumph come
> From conquer'd *Greece*, and bring her Trophies home,
> With Foreign Spoils adorn my native place,
> And with *Idume's* palms, my *Mantua* grace.
> Of *Parian* Stone a Temple will I raise,
> Where the slow *Mincius* through the Vally strays. ...   (II 15ff.)

Thus, as by a conqueror, the Greek Muses are to be secured for Italy; Mantua is to flourish with Palestinian palms (as in Pope's *Windsor Forest* English oaks bear amber and balm); and a great temple is to be erected in verse, which in commemorating the victory will at the same time constitute it.

Here was a pattern, it must have occurred to Pope, which epitomized his own career. Had not he also brought home the Greek Muses for his country, adorned his "native place" with spoils from many literatures, and in the body of his work as a whole, nourished by the classics and dedicated to their honor, raised another votive temple beside another stream? Only some such thoughts, I am inclined to

---

2/Ll. 215–19:

> Pater, aonii deus incola luci,
> Ductare assuetus thiasos sacrisque sororum
> Responsare choris et par contendere Phœbo,
> Furtivo pulchram implerat Critheida fœtu.
> Inde capax nato ingenium, ...

think, can have inspired his curious juxtaposition of the *Ambra* with the third *Georgic*, the Meles and the Mincius with the Thames, a passage on the birth of Homer with a passage on the poetical conquest of Greece, and conceivably, though this may very well be pursuing the edge of analogy too far, Virgil's imaginary "temple in marble beside the water" (*templum de marmore ... propter aquam*) with a Florentine villa beside a stream and a villa at Twickenham on the Thames. Horace Walpole spoke wittily, but also with a fine sense of what I suspect Pope's villa meant to its occupant, when he referred to it in a letter to Horace Mann as "that fragment of the rock Parnassus" (20 June 1760: XXI 417).

Chapter 2

The Shadowy Cave

Had he still continued there,
Made that lonely wondrous cave
Both his palace and his grave,
Peace and rest he might have found
(Peace and rest are underground).
> —Lady Winchilsea, *Petition for an Absolute Retreat*

I

In the preceding chapter, I have drawn attention to some of the elements that went into the making of Pope's Twickenham "landscape," literal and psychological. Within this ambience he viewed himself for a quarter of a century. And the evidence suggests, I think, that there was traffic in both directions: as he impressed an image of himself upon his works at Twickenham, they answered with an image that merged with and somewhat colored and enlarged the first. We may see this best if we turn to the one detail of the Twickenham landscape of which so far little has been said: the grotto.[1] If we let our imaginations linger for a moment there, I believe we catch a glimmering of some of the ways in which, not only for Pope but for other poets, and indeed in a degree for all of us, reality and dream converge and blur, each determining yet helping to transform the other.

1/For discussions of the grotto with a different end in view, see Helen S. Hughes, "Mr. Pope

Our earliest account of the grotto at Twickenham occurs in a letter of 2 June 1725, five years or thereabouts after Pope had begun work on it—the first of many occasions when he mistakenly believed that he had "put the last Hand to my works of this kind." He has found a spring in the grotto, he writes to Edward Blount, "which falls in a perpetual Rill, that echoes thro' the Cavern day and night (II 296)." This is an arresting circumstance, I think, because it comes from the man who had written from Lord Digby's gardens at Sherborne of losing his ears in the sound of water (above, p. 22) and had placed among his Eloisa's aids to meditation in her convent "The grots that eccho to the tinkling rills" (158). One notices, therefore, with some interest that by 1740 he is able to speak of having conveyed into the grotto "three falls of water," which "murmur in a Cavern till they run out of sight."[2] One notices too that our correspondent who reports on the grotto to the *Newcastle General Magazine*, only three years after the poet's death, dwells ecstatically upon its waterworks: "Here it gurgles in a gushing Rill thro' fractur'd Ores and Flints; there it drips from depending Moss and Shells; here again, washing Beds of Sand and Pebbles, it rolls in Silver Streamlets; and there it rushes out in Jets and Fountains; while the Caverns of the Grot incessantly echo with a soothing Murmur of aquatick Sounds (I 26. See below, Appendix A).

Some of the possibilities of Pope's grotto as accessory to his Muse begin in these words dimly to emerge. Did its "soothing murmur" help induce in him, when solitary, states of concentration like those we know from the testimony of other poets—when one is "laid asleep" in body to become a "living soul," or sinks so deep in hearing music

> That it is not heard at all, but you are the music
> While the music lasts?

I am inclined to think it did.[3] Pope was familiar with such states, as his correspondence shows. "Like a witch," he says, describing one such experience to his friend Caryll's son in his younger days,

---

on His Grotto," *Modern Philology*, XXXIII (1930), 100–4; R. D. Altick, "Mr. Pope Expands His Grotto," *Philological Quarterly*, XXI (1942), 427–30; R. W. Babcock, "Pope's Grotto Today," *South Atlantic Quarterly*, XLII (1943), 289–95; Frederick Bracher, "Pope's Grotto: The Maze of Fancy," *Huntington Library Quarterly*, XII (1949), 141–62; Benjamin Boyce, "Mr. Pope, in Bath, Improves the Design of his Grotto," *Restoration and Eighteenth Century Literature: Essays in Honor of A. D. McKillop* (1963), pp. 143–53.

2/To Fortescue, 17 September 1740 (IV 267).

3/According to Evelyn Underhill (*Mysticism*, 6th ed. [London, 1916], p. 361, running water is among the objects to be concentrated on in inducing a mystical condition.

15 Pope at work in the grotto. By William Kent or Dorothy Boyle,
Countess of Burlington

whose Carcase lies motionless on the floor, while she keeps her airy Sabbaths &
enjoys a thousand Imaginary Entertainments abroad, in this world, & in others, I
seem to sleep in the midst of the Hurry, even as you would swear a Top stands still,
when 'tis in the Whirle of its giddy motion. 'Tis no figure, but a serious truth I tell
you when I say that my Days & Nights are so much alike, so equally insensible of any
Moving Power but Fancy, that I have sometimes spoke of things in our family as
Truths & real accidents, which I only Dreamt of; & again when some things that
actually happen'd came into my head, have thought (till I enquird) that I had
only dream'd of them.[4]

4/To John Caryll, Jr., 5 December 1712 (1 163). Cf. 1 243 (To Jervas, 16 August 1714):
"I have the greatest proof in nature at present of the amusing power of Poetry, for it takes me
up so intirely that I scarce see what passes under my nose, and hear nothing that is said
about me."

Though the passage lacks Wordsworth's and Eliot's cathedral tone, its striking references to a seeming sleep that is actually profound agitation and to a turning wheel whose centre is repose suggest that the natural history of poetic meditation may be in all ages much the same.

II

The next sentences in the letter to Blount equally deserve attention. The poet speaks first of the fact that his grotto permits an unbroken vista between his garden, which lies on one side of the public road dividing his property, and his parterre and the river Thames, which lie on the other. Then he turns to the chiaroscuro effects to be obtained by closing the grotto's doors and to the quite different effects when, with the doors still closed, he illuminates the interior with an alabaster lamp. The passage has been often quoted, but will bear repeating:

From the River *Thames* you see thro' my Arch up a Walk of the Wilderness to a kind of open Temple, wholly compos'd of Shells in the Rustic Manner; and from that distance under the Temple you look down thro' a sloping Arcade of Trees [lining the walk to the grotto on the garden side], and see the Sails on the River passing suddenly and vanishing, as thro' a Perspective Glass.[1] When you shut the Doors of the Grotto, it becomes on the instant, from a luminous Room, a *Camera obscura*; on the Walls of which the objects of the River, Hills, Woods, and Boats, are forming a moving Picture in their visible Radiations:[2] And when you have a mind to light it up, it affords you a very different Scene; it is finished with Shells interspersed with Pieces of Looking-glass in angular forms; and in the Cieling is a Star of the same Material, at which when a Lamp (of an orbicular Figure of thin Alabaster) is hung in the Middle, a thousand pointed Rays glitter and are reflected over the Place.[3]

1/A view through the grotto to a sailboat on the river is shown in Plate 16.

2/II 296–97. Cf. *Spectator*, no. 414 (25 June 1712): "The prettiest Landskip I ever saw, was one drawn on the Walls of a dark Room, which stood opposite on one side to a navigable River, and on the other to a Park. The Experiment is very common in Opticks. Here you might discover the Waves and Fluctuations of the Water in strong and proper Colours, with the Picture of a Ship entering at one end, and sailing by Degrees through the Whole Piece. On another there appeared the Green Shadows of Trees, waving to and fro with the Wind, and Herds of Deer among them in Miniature, leaping about upon the Wall."

3/Defoe's Robinson Crusoe had anticipated Pope in this pleasurable experience. Having crawled into a cave and lighted two candles, he exclaims (ch. vii): "... Never was such a glorious Sight seen on the island, I dare say, as it was to look round the Sides and Roof of this Vault, or Cave; the Walls reflected 100 thousand Lights to me from my two Candles; what was in the Rock, whether Diamonds, or any other precious Stones, or Gold, ... I knew not.

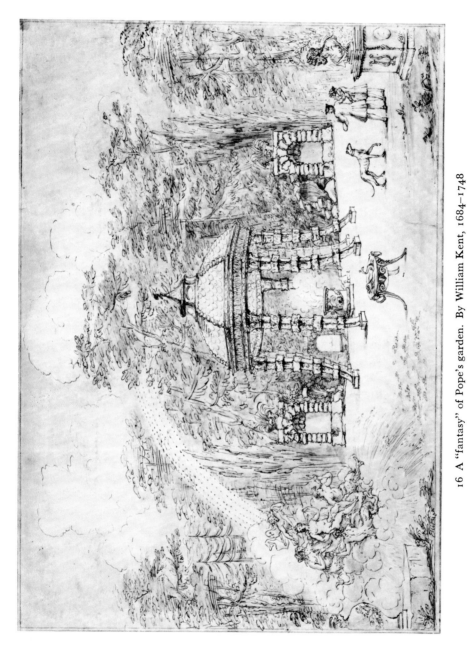

16 A "fantasy" of Pope's garden. By William Kent, 1684–1748

This creation was obviously well suited to bring pleasure to one who is perhaps the acutest observer of effects of light among the English poets. Pope's eye loved light, and was capable of the most delicate discernments of it.[4] His poems know the difference between effulgence and refulgence; between the "mild Lustre" of spring mornings and the peculiarly "Purple Light" of autumn sunsets; between the "glitter" of ice, the "Gleam" of water, the flame and "blaze" of diamonds, the "shine" of fruits, the "glow" of flowers. They know how armor "beams" in lamplight, "flashes" in firelight. They know how moonlight on foliage yields a yellow radiance, on stone a silver. They know how, on a bright day when the sun is darkened by a passing cloud, the landscape momentarily loses its features, discomposes, "decays." They know too that what we see depends as much upon the optics seeing as the object seen: that the pheasant's breast "flames" most when we feel the pathos of its extinction, the sun "glares" most when we are weary of it, the lustres of a chandelier "double" and "dance" chiefly when we have had too much to drink.[5] And they know the telescope and microscope, the mirror and prism: how the obliquity of the latter can break a ray of light;[6] how the reflections in a mirror may falsify reality[7] or discover it;[8] and how with the right kind of instruments, optical, dioptrical, and catoptrical, one may so manipulate a beam that it enlarges, multiplies, contracts, inverts, to say nothing of coloring, with "ten thousand dyes," all that we see.[9]

If we may believe the observer from Newcastle, the effects of this kind in Pope's grotto were even more spectacular than the waterworks. Just following the passage quoted earlier, he adds:

To multiply this Diversity, and still more increase the Delight, Mr. *Pope's* poetick Genius has introduced a kind of Machinery, which performs the same Part in the Grotto that supernal Powers and incorporeal Beings act in the heroick Species of Poetry: This is effected by disposing Plates of Looking glass in the obscure Parts of the Roof and Sides of the Cave, where a sufficient Force of Light is wanting to dis-

---

4/For the delicacy of Pope's discernments of color, a different but related topic, see "Mr. Alexander Pope: Painter," in Norman Ault's *New Light on Pope* (London, 1949), ch. v.

5/The words and phrases quoted are, in succession, from *Spring*, 74; *Autumn*, 14; *Dunciad*, I 75 (cf. *Temple of Fame*, 54); *Windsor Forest*, 215; *Temple of Fame*, 94 (cf. *Essay on Man*, IV 10, *Epistle to Cobham*, 98); *Autumn*, 73; *Epistle to Burlington*, 83 (cf. *Spring*, 31, *Odyssey*, V 94); *Epistle to Augustus*, 319; *Iliad*, VIII 705; *ibid.*, 693; *ibid.*, 694 (cf. *Imit. Hor.*, *Sat.* II vi 192); *Temple of Fame*, 20; *Epistle to Cobham*, 32; *Windsor Forest*, 118; *Epistle to a Lady*, 256; *Imit. Hor.*, *Sat.* II i 48.

6/*Essay on Man*, III 231.

7/*Ibid.*, IV 393.

8/*One Thousand Seven Hundred and Thirty-Eight*, Dial. ii 78.

9/*Epistle to Cobham*, 25–29 (cf. *Temple of Fame*, 132–34).

cover the Deception, while the other Parts, the Rills, Fountains, Flints, Pebbles, & c. being duly illuminated, are so reflected by the various posited Mirrors, as, without exposing the Cause, every Object is multiplied, and its Position represented in a surprizing Diversity. Cast your Eyes upward, and you half shudder to see Cataracts of Water precipitating over your Head, from impending Stones and Rocks, while saliant Spouts rise in rapid Streams at your Feet: Around, you are equally surprized with flowing Rivulets and rolling Waters, that rush over airey Precipices, and break amongst Heaps of ideal Flints and Spar. Thus, by a fine Taste and happy Management of Nature, you are presented with an undistinguishable Mixture of Realities and Imagery.[10]

III

This subterranean dark chamber, where, when the doors are shut, the outer world throws moving shadows on the walls and, when the lamp is lit, light sets all the contents glittering in "an undistinguishable Mixture of Realities and Imagery," is, of course, teasing to the modern imagination. On its dark side, reflecting images from elsewhere, it would appear to have analogues with Plato's cave and Locke's "dark room" of the understanding—"a closet," says Locke, "wholly shut from light, with only some little openings left, to let in external visible resemblances, or ideas of things without."[1] But viewed as possessing a lamp of its own that startles all it touches into "Imagery," it would appear to fall in equally with Plotinus's notion that the mind is a power, not simply a reflector, giving "a radiance out of its own store."[2] The latter notion is very much in keeping with Pope's recurrent figuring of all forms of creativity as light derived from heaven, which "*Clears*, and *improves* whate'er it shines upon."[3]

How many, if any, of these analogies were savored or intended by the poet himself, we shall never know. One supposes he cannot have been oblivious of the associations between consciousness and caverns that are indicated in his own Cave of Spleen, Cave of Poetry, and Cave of Truth.[4] One supposes he was alert to the position his grotto occupied in the minds of his contemporaries, as a place "sacred" to poetry, dwelling place of his Muse. And one supposes that the long tradition that made grots and caverns the haunt of frugal virtue, philosophy, and true wisdom had not escaped the attention of one who could rally Queen Caroline

---

10/*Newcastle General Magazine*, I 26. Below, Appendix A.
1/*Essay Concerning Human Understanding*, II xi 17.
2/*Enneads*, tr. Stephen MacKenna, IV vi 3.
3/*Essay on Criticism*, 316.
4/*Rape of the Lock*, IV; *Dunciad*, I 34 and IV 641.

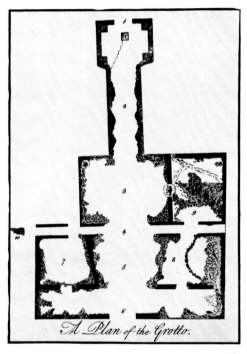

17 John Searle's diagram of the grotto, in his
Plan of Mr. Pope's Garden (1745)

on the incongruity of placing a bust of the courtly Dr. Samuel Clarke in her "Hermitage" at Richmond.[5] The tradition of the Sage in the holy cave was in any case widespread and so powerful that it persisted well into the nineteenth century. Coleridge in 1809 is impelled to make substantially the same point about Idoloclastes Satyrane, the hero of his *Tombless Epitaph*—

> Yea, oft alone
> Piercing the long-neglected holy cave,
> The haunt obscure of old Philosophy,
> He bade with lifted torch its starry walls
> Sparkle, as erst they sparkled to the flame
> Of odorous lamps tended by Saint and Sage—   (28–33)

5/*Epistle to Burlington*, 78.

A Perspective View of the Grotto.

18 John Searle's "Perspective View" of the grotto,
in his *Plan of Mr. Pope's Garden* (1745)

as Robert Dodsley had made in 1743 about future generations of visitors to the
"Cave of Pope":

> Grateful Posterity, from Age to Age,
> With pious Hand the Ruin shall repair:[6]
> Some good old Man, to each enquiring Sage
> Pointing the Place, shall cry, the Bard liv'd there, ...
>
> With aweful Veneration shall they trace
> The Steps which thou so long before hast trod;

6/Dodsley was unduly sanguine. If posterity has been grateful, it has not chosen to show it
by repairing the grotto, which has been much mutilated and is now almost past restoration. See
Plate 28.

19 The obelisk today, in the park
at Penn House

With reverend Wonder view the solemn Place,
From whence thy Genius soar'd to Nature's God.[7]

With his "odorous lamps" and "sparkling walls" Coleridge might almost be
describing a visit to the Twickenham grotto itself.

Leaving all this aside, as we must, we may recognize nevertheless that there was
a fine propriety for a poet in the grotto's character and situation. Between the
ever-moving river with its transient scenes and figures and the garden with its
quiet temple, the poet in his cave—whatever that cave may have represented to
him—was intermediary. On the garden side, he had assembled all the instruments and emblems of the life of contemplation: his shell temple; his "Mount"
with its "Forest Seat or Chair,"[8] overlooking his small domain; his serpentine

7/*The Cave of Pope: A Prophecy*, 9–12, 21–24. Below Appendix E.
8/*Newcastle General Magazine*, I 27. Below, Appendix A.

walks leading in and out of "Wildernesses"; and, from 1735, the obelisk to his mother—"a plain Stone Pillar resting upon a Pedestal," incised:

AH EDITHA!

MATRUM OPTIMA.

MULIERUM AMANTISSIMA.

VALE.[9]

On the other side lay the traffic of the river, the great world seen in a passing show—"as thro' a perspective glass," says the letter to Edward Blount; the Heraclitean flowing away of all things; and, at a modest distance downstream, emblem of these and other impermanent delights: London.

IV

In constructing his Twickenham surroundings, Pope may have been influenced by the design of the classical *locus amoenus*.[1] This usually consisted of a grove, a spring, sometimes a meadow, and more often than not, an overhanging rock or cave like the one inhabited by Calypso in the fifth book of the *Odyssey* or the one sacred to the naiads in the thirteenth book, both of which Pope had described in his translation of Homer[2] at about the same time that he was building his own cave at Twickenham and by which it is not impossible that his view of its significance was influenced. What is interesting for our purpose about the classical poets' *locus amoenus* is that it appears to have been, at least for Pope, a major source and sanction of the new "natural" style in gardening, advocated in his writings and illustrated at Twickenham. In his early paper "On Gardens" for the *Guardian*,[3] where he took the influential stand against topiary and "other Fantastical Operations of Art" that he was to return to thirty years later in the picture of Timon's villa ("Trees cut to Statues, Statues thick as trees"; "Grove nods at grove, each Alley has a brother")[4], his examples of "the amiable simplicity of unadorned Nature" are all, and I think significantly, descriptions from

9/*Ibid*. See Plate 11.

1/E. R. Curtius has some informative pages on this in *European Literature and the Latin Middle Ages* (London, 1953), ch. x.

2/William Kent's headpiece to Book v of the *Odyssey* illustrating Calypso's grotto (1725) has some interesting affinities with the "Perspective" of Pope's grotto published by Searle in his *Plan* (1745). See Plates 17, 18, 25, and nn. See also TE VII ccxxiv–ccxxvi.

3/No. 173, 29 September 1713.

4/*Epistle to Burlington*, 120, 117.

the classical poets. First, Martial's account of the villa of Faustinus (III lviii)—containing, Martial says, no "idle myrtle beds" or "clipped clumps of box," but presenting itself as a true country retreat, "honest and artless," and very like Pope's own house at Binfield, according to the "particular Friend" (perhaps Rowe) cited at the beginning of the paper. Second, Virgil's account in the *Georgics* (II 130–33) of the old Corycian, who had a few acres unsuited for farming, grazing, or the vine:

> hic rarum tamen in dumis olus albaque circum
> lilia verbenasque premens vescumque papaver
> regum aequabat opes animis, seraque revertens
> nocte domum dapibus mensas onerabat inemptis.

("Yet, as he planted herbs here and there among the bushes, with white lilies about, and vervain, and slender poppy, he matched in contentment the wealth of kings, and returning home in the late evening, would load his board with unbought dainties.")

And third, Homer's lines on the gardens of Alcinous, of which Pope then and there supplies the translation that twelve years later he was to use in the *Odyssey* unchanged:

> Close to the Gates a spacious Garden lies,
> From Storms defended, and inclement Skies:
> Four Acres was th' allotted Space of Ground,
> Fenc'd with a green Enclosure all around.
> Tall thriving Trees confest the fruitful Mold;
> The red'ning Apple ripens here to Gold,
> Here the blue Figg with luscious Juice o'erflows,
> With deeper Red the full Pomegranate glows,
> The Branch here bends beneath the weighty Pear,
> And verdant Olives flourish round the Year.
> The balmy Spirit of the Western Gale
> Eternal breathes on Fruits untaught to fail:
> Each dropping Pear a following Pear supplies,
> On Apples Apples, Figs on Figs arise:
> The same mild Season gives the Blooms to blow,
> The Buds to harden, and the Fruits to grow.
>   Here order'd Vines in equal Ranks appear
> With all th' United Labours of the Year,

Some to unload the fertile Branches run,
Some dry the black'ning Clusters in the Sun,
Others to tread the liquid Harvest join,
The groaning Presses foam with Floods of Wine.
Here are the Vines in early Flow'r descry'd,
Here Grapes discolour'd on the sunny Side,
And there in Autumn's richest Purple dy'd.
    Beds of all various Herbs, for ever green,
In beauteous Order terminate the Scene.
Two plenteous Fountains the whole Prospect crown'd;
This thro' the Gardens leads its Streams around,
Visits each Plant, and waters all the Ground:
While that in Pipes beneath the Palace flows,
And thence its Current on the Town bestows;
To various Use their various Streams they bring,
The People one, and one supplies the King.[5]

The character of these scenes, as of most others by the classical poets, is determined by two norms which became central to Pope's thinking about gardening
and landscaping (as well as about life) throughout his career. One was utility.
This he exemplified on his own small estate by orchard, vineyard, orangery, and
kitchen garden, not to mention his "stoves" for wintering tender plants like pineapples; and this he never tired of affirming in his poems as the true principle of
creative ownership. The other was "naturalness," understood in the sense that
the visitor from Newcastle had in mind when he praised the "unaffected Simplicity" of Pope's landscaping, which "wanders so much from all common Forms
and stated Fashions, that a Wood or a Forest doth not deviate much more from
Rule":

It is not here,
That—Grove nods at Grove, each Alley has a Brother,
        And half the Platform just reflects the other,
But—Pleasing Intricacies intervene,
        And artful Wildness to perplex the Scene.

Near the Bounds of the Garden, the Trees unite themselves more closely together,
and cover the Hedges with a thick Shade, which prevents all prying from without,

---

5/VII 142–75 (TE IX 242–44). The text given here, however, follows that of the *Guardian*
in accidentals.

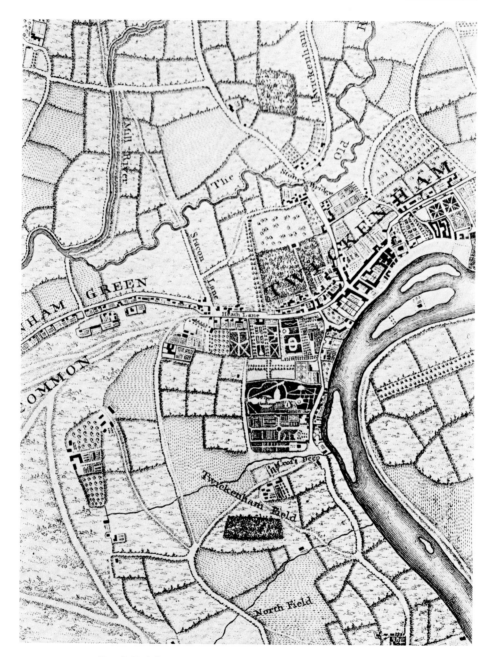

20 Pope's Twickenham situation as shown on John Rocque's map of
the environs of London, *c.* 1746

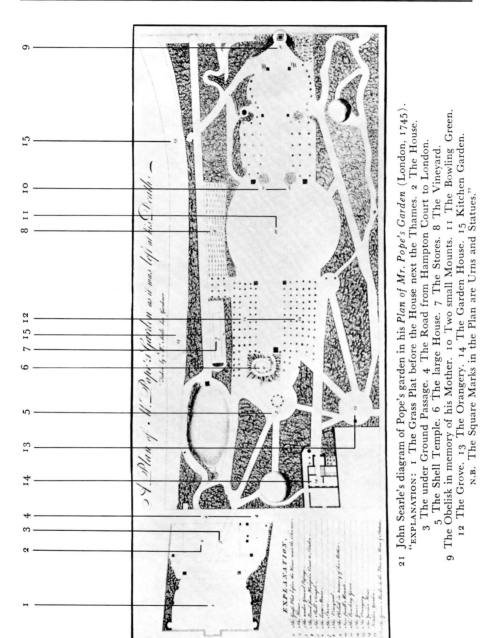

21 John Searle's diagram of Pope's garden in his *Plan of Mr. Pope's Garden* (London, 1745). "EXPLANATION: 1 The Grass Plat before the House next the Thames. 2 The House. 3 The under Ground Passage. 4 The Road from Hampton Court to London. 5 The Shell Temple. 6 The large House. 7 The Stores. 8 The Vineyard. 9 The Obelisk in memory of his Mother. 10 Two small Mounts. 11 The Bowling Green. 12 The Grove. 13 The Orangery. 14 The Garden House. 15 Kitchen Garden. N.B. The Square Marks in the Plan are Urns and Statues."

and preserves the Privacy of the interior Parts. These Wilderness-Groves are either
Quincunces, or cut thro' by many narrow serpentine Walks; and as we recede from
the Boundary and approach towards the Center, the Scene opens and becomes less
entangled; the Alleys widen, the Walks grow broader, and either terminate in small
green Plots of the finest Turf, or lead to the Shell Temple. The Middle of the
Garden approaches nearest to a Lawn or open Green, but is delightfully diversified
with Banks and Hillocks; which are entirely cover'd with Thickets of Lawrel, Bay,
Holly, and many other Evergreens and Shrubs, rising one above another in beautiful
Slopes and Intermixtures, where Nature freely lays forth the Branches, and disports
uncontroul'd; except what may be entirely prun'd away for more Decency and
Convenience to the surrounding Grass-plots, for no Shear-work or Tonsure is to be
found in all the Scene. Towards the South side of the Garden is a Plantation of
Vines curiously disposed and dress'd; it adjoins the Wilderness, and is in the same
Taste, but opener to the Sun, and with more numerous interveening Paths. Among
the Hillocks on the upper Part of the open Area, rises a Mount much higher than
the rest, and is composed of more rude and indigested Materials; it is covered with
Bushes and Trees of a wilder Growth, and more confused Order, rising as it were
out of Clefts of Rocks, and Heaps of rugged and mossy Stones; among which a
narrow intricate Path leads in an irregular Spiral to the Top; where is placed a
Forest Seat or Chair, that may hold three or four Persons at once, overshadowed
with the Branches of a spreading Tree. From this Seat we face the Temple, and
overlook the various Distribution of the Thickets, Grass-plots, Alleys, Banks, &c.
Near this Mount lies the broadest Walk of the Garden, leading from the Center to
the uppermost Verge; where, upon the gentle Eminence of a green Bank, stands an
Obelisk, erected by Mr *Pope* to the Memory of his Mother. ... As this Obelisk
terminates the longest Prospect of Mr *Pope*'s Garden, it shall also put a Period to
my Description; which is not of a Place that bears the high Air of State and
Grandeur, that surprizes you with the vastness of Expence and Magnificence; but
an elegant Retreat of a Poet strongly inspired with the Love of Nature and Retirement; and shews you, with respect to these Works, what was the Taste of the finest
Genius that this or any other Age has produced.[6]

The "naturalness" here is of course naturalness in an Augustan not a nineteenth-
century sense: not oppressively trammeled or corseted by man, yet always
conspicuously responding, as Ruskin would eventually point out of all classically
arranged landscapes, to human pleasure and human need.

6/*Newcastle General Magazine*, I 27–28. Below, Appendix A.

In this perspective, I believe, Pope's innovations in English gardening are best understood. His influential "natural" or "open" style, like his Palladianism in architecture, has its deepest roots in a disposition to be more rather than (as has sometimes been argued) less classical. He is moved by his reading in the admired ancients and possibly also in Shaftesbury, their interpreter, and in Milton, their heir, to seek a truer, more "primitive" classicism by reaching behind the overlay of time and custom, notably in this instance Italian and French custom, in much the same way that his age, in all fields of enquiry, was given to reaching behind the alleged "corruptions" of contemporary practice in the hope of establishing contact with that which, since it was in the beginning, must be closer to "nature." In the *Guardian* already mentioned, as he prepares to cite the magic names of Virgil and Homer before attacking the current fashion, he observes:

There is certainly something in the amiable Simplicity of unadorned Nature, that spreads over the Mind a more noble Sort of Tranquility, and a loftier Sensation of Pleasure, than can be raised from the nicer Scenes of Art.

This was the Taste of the Ancients in their Gardens, as we may discover from the Descriptions [that] are extant of them. The two most celebrated Wits of the World have each of them left us a particular Picture of a Garden; wherein those great Masters, being wholly unconfined, and Painting at Pleasure, may be thought to have given a full Idea of what they esteemed most excellent in this way. ...

How contrary to this Simplicity is the modern Practice of Gardening; we seem to make it our Study to recede from Nature, not only in the various Tonsure of Greens into the most regular and formal Shapes, but even in monstrous Attempts beyond the reach of the Art it self: We run into Sculpture, and are yet better pleas'd to have our Trees in the most awkward Figures of Men and Animals, than in the most regular of their own. ...

I believe it is no wrong Observation that Persons of Genius, and those who are most capable of Art, are always most fond of Nature, as such are chiefly sensible, that all Art consists in the Imitation and Study of Nature.

V

With this point of view Pope's grotto was also, as he viewed it, explicitly in keeping, and in the course of his work on it after 1725 he made it more so. The figure of the rocky cave had acquired early in its literary history a predisposition toward the side of Nature in that running debate about the relations of Nature and Art which preoccupied the Roman writers and afterward those of the Renaissance.

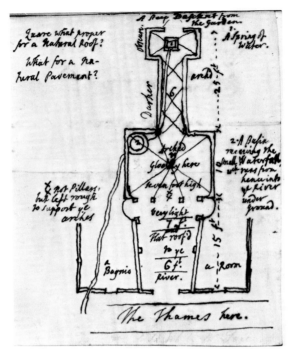

22 Pope's drawing of his grotto,
14 January 1740

"In its most secret nook there was a well-shaded grotto, wrought by no artist's hand. But Nature by her own cunning had imitated art, for she had shaped a native arch of the living rock and soft tufa. A sparkling spring with its slender stream babbled on one side. ..."[1] So wrote Ovid, in what is probably the most influential grotto passage in literature. "A cave, made as it should seem by Nature in despite of Arte," Sidney writes in the *Arcadia* (ed. 1598, p. 37), echoing Ovid but anticipating in a number of features Pope's cave at Twickenham as it came in time to be:

1/*Metamorphoses*, III 157–61:
>   cuius in extremo est antrum nemorale recessu
>   arte laboratum nulla: simulaverat artem
>   ingenio natura suo; nam pumice vivo
>   et levibus tofis nativum duxerat arcum;
>   fons sonat a dextra tenui perlucidus unda. ...

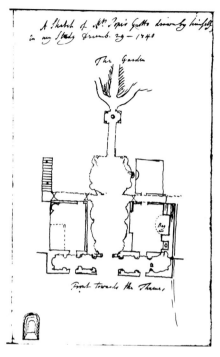

23 Pope's drawing of his grotto,
29 December 1740

so fitlie did the rich-growing marble serve to beautifie the valt of the first entrie. Underfoot the ground seemed minerall, yeelding such a glistering shew of gold in it, as they say the river *Tagus* caries in his sandy bed. The cave framed out into many goodly spacious roomes. ... There ran through it a litle sweet river, which had left the face of the earth to drowne her self for a small way in this darke, but pleasant mansion.

Unlike Sidney, Pope was not content that the floor alone should glister, and before his death he had three streams in his cave, not one; but his grotto, though framed by art, was intended, like Ovid's and Sidney's, to be a show-piece of nature, framed on the principle that "nature is made better by no mean   But nature makes that mean"—as his letters repeatedly make clear. "I wish you were here to bear Testimony how little it owes to Art, either the Place itself, or the Image I give of it," he says in his letter of 1725 to Blount. This statement antedates more considerable applications of art by which his cavern was extended to several rooms and its walls were lined with minerals from all parts of Britain and many parts of the world.[2] Yet his notion of what he is about never essentially alters. He will be proud if he seems to "have imitated Nature well," he tells Allen in 1740.[3] His "great Business" of late, he tells Bolingbroke at about the same time, "has been to patch up a Grotto (the same You have so often sate in the Sunny part of under my house,) with all the varieties of Natures works under Ground—Spars Minerals & Marbles."[4] He tells Borlase he would have "the Place resemble Nature in all her workings,"[5] and Dr. Oliver that he expects it may be "the best Imitation of Nature" he has ever made, since Nature is so much easier to understand "in these sort of works ... than in her Animal, much less in her Rational Productions."[6] In this way the grotto increasingly became, it has been well said, a "shrine for great Nature—Pope's metaphysical Goddess."[7] Yet at the same time, and necessarily, it became a monument of art—in fact, a realization in stone of Augustan convictions about art—an exemplum, whether conscious or not, of the conviction that "nature" is discovered in (and also brought to) her perfection only by the means of art.[8]

Thus what the poet's imagination is to accomplish in the grotto, as he muses between the garden and the river, catching in his art's mirror nature's "moving Pictures," is already objectified in what the grotto itself is. *Nihil in carmine*, we might say—paraphrasing the tag of the sensationalist philosophers but not forgetting that every proper poet's-cave has, like Pope's, both a lamp and a mirror in it, both imagination and memory—*nisi quod prius in antro.*

VI

That the grotto was related in some special way to Pope's life and work as poet was instinctively understood by his contemporaries. Dr. Oliver, for instance,

---

2/Many of the minerals, with their places of origin, are recorded by Searle in the list accompanying his *Plan*. Below, Appendix c.

3/[? August, 1740] (IV 254).

4/3 September 1740 (IV 261).

5/9 March 1740 (IV 228).

6/10 March [1740] (IV 229).

7/H. F. Clark, "Eighteenth Century Elysiums," *Journal of the Warburg and Courtauld Institutes*, VI (1943), 168.

8/Jonson gives a classic statement of the classic view in *Timber* (*Discoveries*, ed. Maurice Castelain [Paris, 1906], p. 127), translating Stobaeus: "... Without Art, Nature can nere bee perfect; & without Nature, Art can clayme no being."

offering to send more "Marble Spar or Diamonds," remarks that he is sure every diamond already sent "has acquired new Lustre from it's artful Disposition."[1] "Artful disposition" was precisely the skill for which Pope's poetry was most admired, and Oliver intends the analogy he hints at between grotto-building and poem-building to be noticed.[2] Swift too grasps intuitively a poetic affiliation of the grotto. He tells Pope that he has heard from Ford about the "Subterranean Passage" to the garden whereby Pope has "turned a blunder into a beauty which is a Piece of Ars Poetica."[3] Johnson seems to be recalling this comment when he observes in the *Life of Pope*: "[His] excavation was requisite as an entrance to his garden, and, as some men try to be proud of their defects, he extracted an ornament from an inconvenience, and vanity produced a grotto where necessity enforced a passage."[4]

Johnson shows here his characteristic lack of sympathy with the *furor rusticus*, but his fine intelligence catches in passing at an ethical analogy that is highly characteristic of him and contains an important truth about Pope. Much in Pope's career, I think we must agree, *was* determined by an effort to extract ornament from inconvenience of a rather painful kind—to find, or make, some ground for pride in all too visible "defects." But had Johnson written "defects and deprivations," his remark would have touched a profounder truth. This comfortable estate at Twickenham, famous for its gardens, its grotto, and its distinguished visitors, famous particularly for its occupant, the man who was, in every sense of the phrase he had himself applied to the indwelling powers of nature, "the Genius of the Place"[5]—what was it all if not an exercise in extracting ornament from inconvenience? Barred by his religion from the ordinary routes to advancement and the normal kinds of patronage, largely self-educated, a retired merchant's son, physically a dwarf—barred too, by his deformity and by his acute sense of the ridiculous (as well as by the filial duty owed his mother), from the ordinary comforts of spouse and children—he had plunged the more passionately into the hurly-burly of literary London, bested the university-trained wits on their own classic ground, and, like another country boy a century and a quarter earlier, made his fortune. Indeed, he had made much more than his

---

1/15 October 1740 (IV 281).

2/Cf. Warburton's observation in his note to Pope's verses on the grotto (*Works* [1751], VI 77) that "the beauty of his poetic genius, in the disposition and ornaments of this romantic recess, appears to as much advantage as in his best contrived Poems."

3/29 September 1725 (II 325–26).

4/*Lives of the English Poets*, ed. G. B. Hill (Clarendon Press, 1905), III 135.

5/*Epistle to Burlington*, 57.

fortune: he was now one of whom it could be said that "His word alone gave Infamy or Fame,"[6] and of whom, though he lacked place or patron, Envy had to "own, I live among the Great."[7] Yet he had always, though he had friends on both sides, belonged more to the Outs than to the Ins. In the beginning, the Roman Catholic families of Binfield and its neighborhood. Later, his first literary advisers and well-wishers, all luminaries of the "last" age—Trumbull, Walsh, Wycherley, Sheffield, Cromwell, Congreve. Then the close friends of his young manhood and maturity, men sooner or later cast away by the government and court, driven into geographical or at least spiritual exile—Bolingbroke, Harley, Atterbury, Arbuthnot, Swift, Gay. And finally, even his latest friends, the new youth—Wyndham, Marchmont, Murray, Lyttelton, and the rest—who counted themselves on the side of the Patriot Opposition till the fall of Walpole in 1742.

Hence the poet who declared himself "TO VIRTUE ONLY and HER FRIENDS, A FRIEND"[8] had for his friends, in fact, and particularly during his formative years at Binfield, mostly alienated men—quite literally "Chiefs, out of War, and Statesmen, out of Place."[9] The communities he had known best were communities seeking to "dignify Disgrace" by retreat to "the silent Shade,"[10] to the country and the garden, to books and study and (inevitably) self-conscious virtue, the mind telling itself that it had served the world no worse, perhaps better, than the run of mankind, yet the world, with its famed ingratitude, no longer having use for it:

> AWAKE, my ST. JOHN! leave all meaner things
> To low ambition, and the pride of Kings.[11]

For more than two hundred years of European and English history, as old causes crumbled, this plangent refrain had been recurring and would recur. John Evelyn, writing in 1658 and urging the satisfaction to be found in gardens now that "brutish and ambitious persons seeke themselves in the ruines of our miserable yet dearest country,"[12] sounds substantially the same note as Justus Lipsius in his *De Constantia*, written when Lipsius was fleeing from his own war-ravaged country in the preceding century.[13] Likewise, Henry Vaughan, who published

---

6/Dodsley, *The Cave of Pope*, 16. Cf. *Correspondence*, IV 245, n. 3.
7/*Imit. Hor., Sat.* II i 133.
8/*Ibid.*, 121.
9/*Ibid.*, 126.
10/*Epistle to Oxford*, 30, 28.
11/*Essay on Man*, I 1–2.
12/28 January 1658. Cited also above, p. 24, n. 15.
13/*Two Books of Constancie*, tr. Stradling (1594), II iii.

his *Flores Solitudinis* in 1654, "*to bee*," he tells us, "*a companion of those wise Hermits, who have withdrawne from the present generation, to confirme them in their solitude, and to make that rigid* necessity *their pleasant* Choyse,"[14] says no more than Pope was to say again in the following century in the address to Bolingbroke in the *Essay on Man*. Vaughan's final phrase, in fact, is simply another way of putting the Senecan sentiment that Pope is reputed to have applied to his work on his grotto—and not, one may venture to fancy, without reference to wider issues—"What we cannot *overcome* we must *undergo*."[15]

VII

Pope's Twickenham estate, then presents itself in two lights. On the one hand, it was evidence in its way of what a Roman Catholic, not to mention a hunch-backed, poet in Pope's society must undergo: the exclusions to which he might be subject at a moment's notice (for example, the ten-mile rule)[1] and the aliena-tions he might feel. To live secluded in this manner, to appear only on his own terms, as carefully arranged as when he sat for bust or portrait,[2] was one way of meeting the problem of his ugly body, to which he was keenly sensitive, particu-larly when women were concerned. Seclusion likewise afforded a way of dealing with the practices of his religion, which, strictly speaking, were forbidden. He was not, to be sure, a devout man, and Augustan Catholic culture, cut away from its Continental root, would perhaps not have satisfied his sophisticated imagina-tion if he had been so.

But the old usages must certainly to an extent have been kept up, at the very least while his mother lived, and there are indications in his grotto of the same resolution not to shrink from the consequences of his professed faith that he had shown in his reply to Atterbury when asked why he did not become an Anglican. An incised stone still surviving, affixed to the grotto's ceiling at the point where it is entered from the river side, represents one element of the *arma Christi*, the Crown of Thorns; another incised stone, three feet away, immediately above the entrance to the main passage, represents the Five Wounds.[3] These appear to be

---

14/"To the Reader," Leaf A6, verso.

15/*Autobiography, Letters, and Literary Remains of Mrs. Piozzi*, ed. A. Hayward (London, 1861), II 154. Mrs. Piozzi's marginal note is not altogether unambiguous: it is possible she intends to assign the witticism to Johnson.

1/See above, p. 11, n. 5.

2/See Wimsatt, xxix–xxvi.

3/See Plates 24, 28. On the history and use of the *arma Christi*, there is valuable informa-

24 Entrance to Pope's grotto, showing
the *arma Christi* (1964)

of stonework older than the grotto and were, one must suppose, made originally
for some other situation, perhaps chapel or church, and contributed to the grotto
by a Catholic friend or friends, as the spars and lignites were contributed by other
friends. Their devotional significance should not be exaggerated.[4] Yet their
presence in this prominent position is not the work of one who would evade
acknowledgment of his creed, and they may have served to remind Pope (as
well as those who visited him) of the many circumstances that separated him
from the ordinary pursuits and pastimes of the world. "All the beneficial circumstances of life, and all the shining ones," he had said in his reply to Atterbury,
"lie on the part you would invite me to. But if I could bring myself to fancy,
what I think you do but fancy, that I have any talents for active life, I want health
for it; and besides it is a real truth, I have less Inclination (if possible) than
Ability. Contemplative life is not only my scene, but it is my habit too."[5]

On the other hand—and this, as I have suggested, must have been the light
in which Pope oftenest saw the matter himself—the Twickenham villa was visible
and enormous proof of his success in overcoming what had to be undergone,
extracting the ornament from the inconvenience. Here, in his own modern
Tusculum, he could dispose of an affluence and independence that enemies might
mock but must acknowledge:

> SAWNEY, a mimick Sage of huge Renown,
> To *Twickenham* Bow'rs retir'd, enjoys his Wealth,
> His Malice and his Muse: In Grottos cool,
> And cover'd Arbours dreams his Hours away.[6]

Here he could receive his friends and, in language that may in fact spring from
a conscious and whimsical evocation of the traditions of the philosopher-king

---

tion in Rudolf Berliner's "Arma Christi," *Münchener Jahrbuch der bildenden Kunst*, Dritte
Folge, Band VI (1955), 35–152, and R. Wildhaber's "Der Feiertagschristus als ikono-
graphischer Ausdruck der Sonntagsheiligung," *Zeitschrift für schweizerische Archäologie und
Kunstgeschichte*, XVI (1956), 1–34. I owe these references to my friend Joseph Trapp of the
Warburg Institute.

4/In his "Postscript" to the *Odyssey* (TE, X 390), Pope compares the occasional use of "old
work" in translating to "the working old Abbey stones into a building, which I have sometimes
seen to give a kind of venerable air, and yet not destroy the neatness, elegance, and equality
requisite to a new work." His *arma Christi* may have meant no more than this—but with
Pope one is uncertain.

5/20 November 1717 (I 454).

6/James Ralph, *Sawney* (1728), p. 1.

(the recluse whose kingdom is in his mind or lies all about him in nature),[7] could introduce them to the marvels of his realm: to the "triumphal arch, under which you shall be led into my garden,"[8] to the Large Mount, "in a point of view to shew you the glory of my little kingdom,"[9] to the new coat of stucco on "my palace, which you may now more truly style *Little Whitehall* than when last you saw it."[10] Here he could live at his sweet will, like those Eastern Kings to whom he has a habit of referring—

> I sought no homage from the Race that write;
> I kept, like *Asian* Monarchs, from their sight—[11]

and could set against the world beyond the thicket which hedged his property (the world of stratagem and compromise and money-grubbing and self-interest —into which he often entered because he had to and because it answered to the vein of stratagem and compromise and self-interest in his own nature), an imagined ideal community of patriarchal virtues and heroic friends: a community of the garden and the "grot." He pictures this community in one of the best-known passages of his first Horatian Imitation:

7/A tradition with an interesting history, but so far little studied. For some of the changes that have been rung on it in lyric poetry, see Edward Dyer's "My Mind to Me a Kingdom Is," John Norris's "The Retirement," and Cowper's "Verses Supposed To Be Written by Alexander Selkirk" (which repudiate it). It coalesces at times with the tradition studied in Maren-Sofie Røstvig's *The Happy Man*, but is not idential with it. Pope's portrait of his father in the *Epistle to Dr. Arbuthnot* (above, p. 6) alludes to it in a final couplet:

> Oh grant me thus to live, and thus to die!
> Who sprung from Kings shall know less joy than I—

which compresses the content of two of Dyer's:

> Lo! thus I triumph like a king,
> My mind content with anything. (23–24)
> Thus do I live, thus will I die,—
> Would all did so as well as I! (35–36)

8/To Caryll, 20 March 1733 (III 358).
9/To Atterbury, 19 March 1722 (II 109).
10/To Caryll, 19 April [1734] (III 406).
11/*Epistle to Dr. Arbuthnot*, 219–20. Cf. also l. 198, and "Elegy to the Memory of an Unfortunate Lady," 21–22:

> Like Eastern Kings a lazy state they keep,
> And close confin'd to their own palace sleep.

The notion of the good man as "king", especially in his true home the country, is of course also found in Horace (*Epist.* 1 i 59–60 and 1 x 8). Pope paraphrases the former passage in his imitation of that poem as "Virtue, brave boys! 'tis Virtue makes a King"—a view that seems also to permeate the passage from his first Horatian Imitation that I am about to quote in the text.

25 Headpiece of Book v of Pope's quarto *Odyssey*, showing the grotto
of Calypso. By William Kent, 1684–1748

TO VIRTUE ONLY and HER FRIENDS, A FRIEND,
The World beside may murmur, or commend.
Know, all the distant Din that World can keep
Rolls o'er my *Grotto*, and but sooths my Sleep.
There, my Retreat the best Companions grace,
Chiefs, out of War, and Statesmen, out of Place.
There *St. John* mingles with my friendly Bowl,
The Feast of Reason and the Flow of Soul:
And He, whose Lightning pierc'd th' *Iberian* Lines,
Now, forms my Quincunx, and now ranks my Vines,
Or tames the Genius of the stubborn Plain,
Almost as quickly, as he conquer'd *Spain*.[12]

12/*Sat.* II i 121–32: To Mr. Fortescue. Pope doubtless intends a criticism of Walpole's

26 Pope at work in the grotto, with grotesques.
By William Kent or Dorothy Boyle

We must not neglect the contemporary dimension here, of which there is much to be said on a later page. But the full weight of the passage, even when its political allusions have been penetrated, falls elsewhere. The *ultimate* object of its indictment is not Walpole's ministry, but "a Land of Hectors, / Thieves, Supercargoes, Sharpers, and Directors," of which Walpole is only a symptom, and behind that, "the way of the world," against which poets have always warred. Likewise, the indictment draws its strength less from the actual little cripple who lived at Twickenham than from a poet's generous vision of a possible true community. It is a community degreeless and heroic, where companions

peace policy. The man who had mastered Spain before, his friend Lord Peterborough, had been notably "out of war" under Walpole. By 1733 there was great unrest among the City merchants owing to Spanish depredations. *Fog's Weekly Journal* advertises a ballad on Captain Jenkins's ear as early as 25 December 1731.

confer "grace" by their very presence—unlike the companions of the Garter and the Bath; where—as among philosopher-kings—the taking of food has the dignity of a "Feast," the taking of drink the dignity of a "friendly Bowl" (both actions so transfigured by collations of another sort as to compose a "Feast of Reason" and a "Flow of Soul"); and where the same man, like that famous Roman Cincinnatus of the plow, now wields his battle "Lightning" like a Jove, now wrestles with and tames a lesser godhead—"the Genius of the stubborn Plain."[13]

Swift perhaps spoke better than he knew when he compared the grotto to a piece of *ars poetica*. It was to become a place where not only had a beauty been snatched from blunder once, but where the world, having thrown its shadow on the walls, was continuously transformed by art into "an undistinguishable Mixture of Realities and Imagery." Actual great men came there, actual impassioned conversations about the commonweal were evidently held there; but all that happened there was translated by the poetic imagination (of which it was itself the handiwork and possibly the conscious symbol) out of history into dream.

VIII

This is the case in the lines at which we have just been looking, and it is notably the case in the lines which follow, based on the ancient formula of *Siste, viator*: Pope's *Verses on a Grotto by the River Thames at Twickenham, composed of Marbles, Spars, and Minerals*:

> Thou who shalt stop, where *Thames'* translucent Wave
> Shines a broad Mirrour thro' the shadowy Cave;
> Where lingering Drops from Mineral Roofs distill,
> And pointed Crystals break the sparkling Rill,
> Unpolish'd Gemms no Ray on Pride bestow,
> And latent Metals innocently glow:
> Approach. Great NATURE studiously behold!
> And eye the Mine without a Wish for Gold.
> Approach: But aweful! Lo th' Ægerian Grott,
> Where, nobly-pensive ST. JOHN sate and thought;

13/For possible colorings from Homer on the way Pope sees Bolingbroke and Peterborough in this passage, see TE VII, ccxxxiii–ccxxxiv.

> Where *British* Sighs from dying WYNDHAM stole,
> And the bright Flame was shot thro' MARCHMONT's Soul.
> Let such, such only, tread this sacred Floor,
> Who dare to love their Country, and be poor.[1]

These are not among Pope's best lines. They are too much on the stretch in sense, and somewhat pompous in gait. But they illustrate nonetheless well the operation of that skill in multiplying and reflecting by which he achieved—in his grotto, as the Newcastle correspondent noticed, and also in a body of poetry adjusted to the norms of common speech—effects analogous to those performed in epic discourse by a machinery of "Superior Powers and uncorporeal Beings." The phrase "*Ægerian* Grott," like one of those "posited Mirrors" in the actual grotto, flashes upon the pensive figures of Bolingbroke, Wyndham, and Marchmont the almost archetypal image of the virtuous philosopher—"Saint and Sage"[2]— meditating in his cave, and also the particular variant of this image emanating from the legend of King Numa, who was credited with receiving from the nymph Egeria[3] the moral instruction that made his government memorable. As Livy has it: "There was a grove watered by a perpetual spring which flowed through the midst of it, out of a dark cave. Thither Numa would often withdraw, without witness, as if to meet the goddess; so he dedicated the grove to the Camenae [a mysterious group of deities formerly identified with the Muses], alleging that they held council there with his wife Egeria." (I xxi 3)

Plutarch's version of this story knows nothing of Egeria as wife to Numa, but is equally clear about the function of the Muses. He argues that as the gods very probably approve men of virtue we should not judge it incongruous that "a like spirit" should be presumed to have visited Minos, Zoroaster, Lycurgus, and Numa, "the controllers of kingdoms, and the legislators of commonwealths."

Numa spoke of a certain goddess or mountain nymph that was in love with him, and met him in secret ...; and professed that he entertained familiar conversation with the Muses, to whose teaching he ascribed the greatest part of his revelations. ...[4]

1/The *Verses* were circulated in many versions and transcripts. They were published in *The Gentleman's Magazine* for January 1741, and October 1743, and separately as a small-quarto pamphlet on 13 October 1743. As sent to Bolingbroke in a letter of 3 September 1740 (IV 262), ll. 9–10 read less clumsily:

> Awful as Plato's Grove or Numa's Grot
> Here nobly-pensive St John sat & thought.

2/From Coleridge's *Tombless Epitaph*, 33.

3/According to Searle's list (below, Appendix C), Pope's grotto contained "a Fine Piece of Marble from the grotto of *Egeria* near *Rome*, from the Reverend Mr. *Spence*."

And on a later page (91), he adds:

His reign ... [was] a living example and verification of that saying which Plato, long afterwards, ventured to pronounce, that the sole and only hope of respite or remedy for human evils was in some happy conjunction of events which should unite in a single person the power of a king and the wisdom of a philosopher, so as to elevate virtue to control and mastery over vice.

Numa's reign, in this notion of it, impressively anticipates much that Boling-broke asks of his ideal monarch in his essay *On the Idea of a Patriot King*, a footnote in the long history of Plato's idea of philosopher-kings which Pope so admired that he had it privately printed.[5] Numa's deriving wisdom and inspiration from the Muse(s) likewise anticipates in its way the function that the younger Patriots in the late 30's and early 40's sought to assign Pope himself vis-à-vis the Prince of Wales (their wan hope of that era) and in fact vis-à-vis the whole movement of reform. Thus Lyttelton writes to him in late 1738, speaking of the Prince:

Be therefore as much with him as you can, Animate him to Virtue, to the Virtue least known to Princes, though most necessary for them, Love of the Publick; and think that the Morals, the Liberty, the whole Happiness of this Country depends on your Success. If that Sacred Fire, which by You and other Honest Men has been kindled in his Mind, can be Preserv'd, we may yet be safe." ... (25 October: IV 138–39)

Three years later he expands upon the theme:

I wish he [Bolingbroke] was in England upon many accounts, but for nothing more than to Exhort and Animate You not to bury your excellent Talents in a Philo-sophical Indolence, but to Employ them, as you have so often done, in the Service of Virtue. ... I believe they wou'd be of great Present Benefit; some sparks of Publick Virtue are yet Alive, which such a Spirit as Your's might blow into a flame, among the Young men especially. ... (7 November 1741: IV 369)

All this is comical enough now, as the politics of a past age is always comical if it escapes being tragic. Pope and his Muse in the role of Egeria, well-head of

---

4/"Numa," in *Lives*, tr. Dryden-Clough, Modern Library ed., p. 80.

5/Cf. Fannie E. Ratchford, *Pope and the Patriot King*, "University of Texas Studies in English", no. 6 (1926), pp. 157–77.

inspiration to a political movement that was no more disinterested than such movements always are, presents a hilarious picture of naïveté all around. Yet the conviction that the pursuits of every day should be shot through with the idealism and detachment of poetry, the arts of government lit by the imagination, intuition, and grace of heaven which we represent in the poet's Muse: there is nothing absurd in that. If we have come to think so, it is because we have lost the confidence that widely disparate areas of experience and instruments of knowing may interpenetrate to their mutual advantage.

IX

Pope had by no means lost this confidence, as two further allusions in the *Verses* show. One is to Virgil. The last two lines—

> Let such, such only, tread this sacred Floor,
> Who dare to love their Country, and be poor—

were, I think rightly, seen by Gilbert Wakefield as intended to evoke the episode of Evander's house in the eighth *Aeneid*. This is an episode which exemplifies unforgettably the fruitful interpenetration of areas of experience and ways of knowing, the fusion of poetic imagination with political realism. Aeneas is instructed by Tibernus, god of the Tiber (and poetic forebear of that Father Thames who prophesies for Pope in *Windsor Forest*), that he must not be dislodged from faith in the success of his great mission by the hostility of the Latins. Instead, he must turn now for help to Evander, king of Arcadia, a fellow Danaan by descent. Going to Arcadia, Aeneas is cordially received by King Evander, and we learn that his land is both the ancient abode of Saturn, under whose reign were "the golden ages men tell of," and the site of future Rome. The theme of Pope's allusion appears in the last lines of the description of Evander's dwelling —to which, we are told (as to Pope's grotto, in the grotto *Verses*), the great of the past and future come, and are known for what they are, when they pass not a politician's but a poet's test:

> Talibus inter se dictis ad tecta subibant
> pauperis Euandri, ...
> ut ventum ad sedes, "haec," inquit, "limina vitor
> Alcides subiit, haec illum regia cepit.

> aude, hospes, contemnere opes et te quoque dignum
> finge deo. ..."[1]

("So talking, they drew near the house of the poor Evander. ... As they reached his dwelling, he exclaimed: 'This house, victorious Alcides stooped to enter; this lowly "palace" welcomed him. Dare, my guest, to scorn riches and make yourself like him worthy of divinity'." [Translation mine])

The other allusion is to Juvenal.[2] In identifying his grotto with Egeria and distinguishing its visitors as those who dare to love their country and be poor, Pope can hardly have been ignorant that he was recalling Juvenal's third satire. At the opening of this poem, the honest Umbricius, unable longer to survive in a Rome given over to knavery, Greekish *arrivistes*, and feverish pursuit of wealth, pauses at the Porta Capena to deliver to his friend Juvenal a diatribe against the city. Together they turn aside near the shrine of Egeria, just outside the city walls, and the poet by his description of the place and what has happened to it in recent times sets the stage for Umbricius's remarks. In Professor Gilbert Highet's words: "He and his friend hate the city so much that they will not even stop to talk within its walls, but turn their backs on it and look for the quiet of nature; and the only spot they can find has been ruined by foreigners, by greed, by tasteless extravagance, and by the destruction of fine old traditions":[3]

> Now while my Friend just ready to depart,
> Was packing all his Goods in one poor Cart;
> He stopp'd a little at the Conduit-Gate,
> Where *Numa* modell'd once the *Roman* State,
> In Mighty Councels with his Nymph retir'd:
> Though now the Sacred Shades and Founts are hir'd
> By Banish'd Jews, who their whole Wealth can lay
> In a small Basket, on a Wisp of Hay;
> Yet such our Avarice is, that every Tree
> Pays for his Head; not Sleep it self is free:

1/Lines 359ff. Dryden translates (477–80):
> Mean as it is, this Palace, and this Door,
> Receiv'd *Alcides*, then a Conquerour.
> Dare to be poor: accept our homely Food
> Which feasted him; and emulate a God.

2/I owe this suggestion to my student, colleague, and friend, Michael O'Loughlin.

3/*Juvenal the Satirist*: *A Study* (Oxford University Press, 1962), p. 69.

27 A sketch of the view from the grotto,
c. 1760–70(?)

Nor Place, nor Persons now are Sacred held,
From their own Grove the Muses are expell'd.
Into this lonely Vale our Steps we bend,
I and my sullen discontented Friend:
The Marble Caves, and Aquæducts we view;
But how Adult'rate now, and different from the true!
How much more Beauteous had the Fountain been
Embellish't with her first Created Green,
Where Crystal Streams through living Turf had run,
Contented with an Urn of Native Stone![4]

Pope's grotto, as his imagination plays over it in the *Verses*, clearly defines
itself as a point of proud resistance to the corrupt values associated by Juvenal's

---

4/Juvenal, III 10–20. Dryden's translation, 17–36.

28 The remains of Pope's grotto today (1965)

poem with modern Rome, and by his own poems with modern London and the
Court of George II. Here beside the Thames is an Egerian grot that is still
unspoiled; its springs are pure, its gems and metals are innocent, its Muse is in
residence, its grove is not for sale. He who "stops" to inspect it, as Umbricius and
Juvenal stop to inspect its Roman original, will find not pedlars but the memories
of great men—St. John, Wyndham, Marchmont—and instead of "Adult'rate"
marble splendors a shrine to "Great Nature," which, like the arrangement of
sculpture planned for his river front, is at the same time a shrine to poetry's
transforming power.

Chapter 3

Secretum Iter

'Tis to create, and in creating live
A being more intense, that we endow
With form our fancy, gaining as we give
The life we image. ...
—Byron, *Childe Harold*, III 6

I

Egeria, counselor to philosophers and kings in Plutarch and Livy, and in Juvenal the neglected representative of a humane world consumed by the indifferent and commercial city, is not the only nymph Pope chose to associate with his grotto. In the letter to Edward Blount above, p. 44, he refers to another. "It wants nothing to compleat it", he tells Blount at the close of his description of the grotto, "but a good Statue with an Inscription, like that beautiful antique one which you know I am so fond of." He then sets down four Latin verses, followed by his own translation:

Hujus Nympha loci, sacri, custodia fontis,
Dormio, dum blandae sentio murmur aquae.
Parce meum, quisquis tangis cava marmora somnum
Rumpere, seu bibas, sive lavere, tace.

29 Sleeping nymph in the grotto at Stourhead, with Pope's verses
("Nymph of the Grot") inscribed beneath

> Nymph of the Grot, these sacred Springs I keep,
> And to the Murmur of these Waters sleep;
> Whoe'er thou art, ah gently tread the Cave,
> Ah Bathe in silence, or in silence lave.[1]

By the time these Latin verses reached Pope, they and the nymph whose sleeping figure they purported to explain had had a fascinating history. A classical sculpture of a sleeping girl, probably in origin an exhausted Maenad rather than a nymph, had attracted to itself in the later fifteenth century the anonymous

---

1/In the editions of his letters from 1737 on, Pope translates the last two verses more accurately:

> Ah spare my Slumbers, gently tread the Cave!
> And drink in silence, or in silence lave!

unclassical inscription which Pope translates. The combination so far captivated the Renaissance imagination that sleeping nymphs of stone, accompanied by these verses, were given residence beside fountains and in grottos all over Europe during the following two centuries; made their way into paintings by Dürer, Cranach, Claude; were popularized in engraved collections of ancient monuments, and in the long run became familiar garden-ornaments, to be numbered, like Keats's rainbow, in the dull catalogue of common things. Yet as the historian who has traced this theme shrewdly remarks, they never altogether lost their power of suggestion for the imagination: "A silence, one might almost say a religious mood, makes itself felt. True, a certain playfulness and antiquarian learning proudly displayed are always present, but at the same time, something of the awe surrounding pagan sanctuaries of the nymphs has been preserved. *Nullus enim fons non sacer.*"[2]

II

We do not know whether Pope actually placed the figure of a sleeping nymph in his grotto. Since the Newcastle visitor in 1747 says nothing about her, I am inclined to think that he did not.[1] But her presence in his imaginings of the spot, indicated in the letter of 1725, can serve to focus for us in a figure antithetical to the politically sophisticated Egeria all those predispositions which attracted him to the point of view that Professor E. M. W. Tillyard has called the "retirement myth".[2] Already in his first published letter, printed in the *Spectator* of 16 June 1712, we find him debating the question of "action" versus "retreat" and inclining to retreat. Neither way of life is tenable in the extreme, he allows—

> in the former Men generally grow useless by too much Rest,
> and in the latter are destroy'd by too much Precipitation.

Yet there is a "sort of People who seem design'd for Solitude," and he places himself among them:

2/Otto Kurz, "Huius nympha loci," *Journal of the Warburg and Courtauld Institutes,* XVI (1952), 177.

1/During the ownership of Sir William Stanhope, Pope's grotto contained the statue of a nymph (not, however, sleeping), which may yet be seen. I suspect it was a contribution by Stanhope to help accommodate the reality of the grotto to the expectation of the tourist. Henry Hoare placed a sleeping nymph in his own grotto at Stourhead with the verses from Pope's letter to Blount inscribed. This too may still be seen (Plate 29).

2/*Some Mythical Elements in English Literature* (London, 1961), ch. v.

As for my own Part, I am one of those of whom *Seneca* says, *Tam Umbratiles sunt,*
ut putent in turbido esse quicquid in luce est. Some Men, like Pictures, are fitter for
a Corner than a full Light; and I believe such as have a natural Bent to Solitude,
are like Waters which may be forc'd into Fountains, and exalted to a great Height,
may make a much nobler Figure and a much louder Noise, but after all run more
smoothly, equally, and plentifully, in their own natural Course upon the Ground.[3]
The Consideration of this would make me very well contented with the Possession
only of that Quiet which *Cowley* calls the Companion of Obscurity.[4]

We know of course that this was not consistently Pope's view. He was to show
himself in due course a busy manager of fame and fortune, as artful in mani-
pulating his auctorial world of booksellers and printers as Walpole in Parliament;
an opener of doors and promoter of benefactions; a political rallying point; a
gregarious acquaintance and tireless friend. Yet the notion that he belongs to
those "designed for Solitude" never dims in him. In part it motivates his retirement to Twickenham. It starts up on page after page of his correspondence,
often cheek by jowl with the acknowledgment (not always distinguishable from

---

3/This interesting contrast, derived from the various possible applications of water in land-
scape-gardening, was to reappear two decades later in Pope's characterization of the Man of
Ross, whose inner nature finds expression in his characteristic use of outward nature:

> Who hung with woods yon mountain's sultry brow?
> From the dry rock who bade the waters flow?
> Not to the skies in useless columns tost,
> Or in proud falls magnificently lost,
> But clear and artless, pouring thro' the plain
> Health to the sick, and solace to the swain.
> (*Epistle to Bathurst*, 253–58)

See also the letter to Atterbury, quoted earlier, p. 65.

4/The influence of Cowley's "Several Discourses By Way of Essays, in Verse and Prose,"
published posthumously in the *Works* (1668), on the dissemination of retirement attitudes
generally and on Pope particularly, is very considerable. These eleven informal essays, whose
collective import may be gathered from their titles ("Of Liberty," "Of Solitude," "Of
Obscurity," "Of Agriculture," "The Garden," "Of Greatness," "Of Avarice," "The Dangers
of an Honest Man in Much Company," "The Shortness of Life and Uncertainty of Riches,"
"The Danger of Procrastination," "Of Myself"), together with the poems and translations
accompanying them, give graceful and sometimes powerful expression to that whole body of
convictions, *exempla*, and images concerning the priority of ethical and aesthetic self-cultivation—far from the madding crowd of courts and cities—which the seventeenth and eighteenth
centuries in England inherited from the Roman poets. The reader of these essays and poems
will be struck by the frequency with which some part of them seems to have lingered in Pope's
mind.

The phrase Pope quotes in the *Spectator* letter is from Cowley's translation of the second
chorus of Seneca's *Thyestes* (appended to his essay "Of Obscurity"). See below, pp. 104, 115.

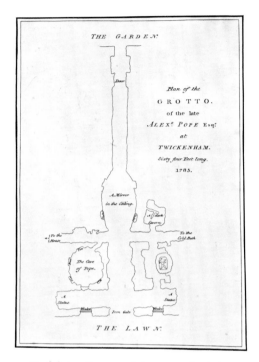

30 A later diagram of the grotto (1785),
showing Stanhope's alterations

a boast) that he is harassed by more "business" than any mortal should allow
himself to be. And it plays, I believe, rather a larger role than has been appreciated in the complex of attitudes, reminiscences, assumptions, and value symbols
(everything that constitutes a sensibility and habit of mind) on which his poems
of the 30's draw. The voice that Pope's editors and critics have listened to with
most discernment is the voice of the man whose restless appetite for "some new
thing" is recorded in the proper names we annotate and who tells us, in the
characteristic epic-like tones of the *vita activa,*

> Yes, I am proud; I must be proud to see
> Men not afraid of God, afraid of me.
>
> (*Epilogue to the Satires: Dial.* ii, 208–9)

We have listened less attentively to another voice that speaks from this same
poetic personality and calls on a tradition and vocabulary of retirement literature

31 A later "perspective view" of the grotto,
with statues

which was as "available" to his contemporaries, and as fully charged with
imaginative meanings, as the traditions of satire or epic. Though I cannot give
more in this chapter than a sketch of so large a subject, I hope to make clear that
retirement attitudes and retirement idiom together contribute a dimension to
Pope's work that it is unwise to ignore.

III

I begin with some passages whose connection with the literature of retirement
has not been noticed, or at least not stressed. They serve to indicate the extent to
which the vocabulary of this tradition was present to the poet's mind and should
therefore be present to ours, though the specific source of the vocabulary, in any
given instance, may escape us. The following lines from the imitation of Donne's
second satire, for instance, make their point adequately if we observe that they

define hospitality, in the Tudor sense of manorial and parochial responsibility, as an act whose basis is religious and whose continuance is as inseparable from the well-being of the nation as the maintenance of the Vestal fire at Rome.

> We see no new-built Palaces aspire,
> No Kitchens emulate the Vestal Fire. (111–12)

It is not imperative, in other words, that we see behind the Vestal allusion, which is Pope's addition to his original, a reminiscence of Cowley's paraphrase of Martial (x xlvii) on the happy retired life:

> Let constant Fires the Winters fury tame;
> And let thy Kitchens be a Vestal Flame.[1]

Yet once we recognize it, this echo of one of the great set pieces of Roman retirement literature, coming through Cowley, himself an influential spokesman of *beatus ille* sentiment, adds a certain weight to Pope's expressed concern in the poem for the right use of wealth, and associates it, as in so many of his other poems, to a particular way of life.

Something similar may be said of these lines in the *Epistle to Cobham*:

> Court-virtues bear, like Gems, the highest rate,
> Born where Heav'n's influence scarce can penetrate:
> In life's low vale, the soil the virtues like,
> They please as Beauties, here as Wonders strike. (93–96)

Here it is enough to catch the general reference to retired innocence, and to mark the characteristic gulf that poetry in this vein always places between court or city and "the soil the virtues like." Yet in any account of the genesis of the passage, we should have to note that Pope possibly remembers in its third verse an image from Cowley's paraphrase of Virgil's *O fortunatos nimium*: "In Life's cool vale let my low Scene be laid" (*Essays*, p. 47). If so, the Virgilian passage masses behind Pope's contrast of court and country the most authoritative of all literary precedents:

> si non ingentem foribus domus alta superbis
> mane salutantum totis vomit aedibus undam,
> nec varios inhiant pulchra testudine postis
> inlusasque auro vestis Ephyreiaque aera,

1/*Cowley's Essays*, eds. J. R. Lumby and Arthur Tilley (Cambridge University Press, 1923), p. 113. Hereafter referred to as *Essays*.

alba neque Assyrio fucatur lana veneno,
nec casia liquidi corrumpitur usus olivi:
at secura quies et nescia fallere vita,
dives opum variarum, at latis otia fundis,
speluncae vivique lacus et frigida Tempe
mugitusque boum mollesque sub arbore somni
non absunt; illic saltus ac lustra ferarum,
et patiens operum exiguoque adsueta iuventus,
sacra deum sanctique patres: extrema per illos
Iustitia excedens terris vestigia fecit.[2]

("What though no stately mansion with proud portals disgorges at dawn from all its halls a tide of visitors, though they never gaze at doors inlaid with lovely tortoise-shell or at raiment tricked with gold or at bronzes of Ephyra, though their white wool be not stained with Assyrian dye, or their clear oil's service spoiled by cassia? Yet theirs is repose without care, and a life that knows no fraud, but is rich in treasures manifold. Yea, the ease of broad domains, caverns, and living lakes, and cool vales, the lowing of the kine, and soft slumbers beneath the trees—all are theirs. They have woodland glades and the haunts of game; a youth hardened to toil and inured to scanty fare; worship of gods and reverence for age; among them, as she quitted the earth, Justice planted her latest steps.")

Cowley's paraphrase of Virgil is one of several verse appendices to his prose essay "Of Agriculture." The essay itself may easily lurk somewhere in the genetic background of Pope's lines, its theme being precisely the superiority of country to court or city as a nourisher of virtues. "We walk here," Cowley writes (contrasting dark and light in a way that may have helped father Pope's contrast of gem mine and country vale in the *Epistle to Cobham*), "in the light and open wayes of the Divine Bounty; we grope there in the dark and confused Labyrinths of Human Malice" (*Essays*, p. 37); and a little later (p. 41), referring to the poets' traditional fondness for retreat, he shifts from prose to verses that perhaps also lingered in Pope's mind, though the horticultural image is of course a commonplace:

2/*Georgics*, II 461–74. I quote at some length, not because Pope's phrase necessarily demands or calls up a context so extensive, but because the dream to which Virgil here gives form haunts the imagination of the eighteenth century and colors much of its life, art, and thought. Above, p. 20; below, pp. 100–15.

> As well might Corn as Verse in Cities grow;
> In vain the thankless Glebe we Plow and Sow,
> Against th' unnatural Soil in vain we strive;
> 'Tis not a Ground in which these Plants will thrive.

Such passages, one supposes, show at most reminiscence, not allusion. We move somewhat closer to the latter (though without quite reaching it) in the couplet that begins Pope's description of a visit to Timon's villa in the *Epistle to Burlington*:

> At Timon's Villa let us pass a day,
> Where all cry out, "What sums are thrown away!" (99–100)

Turn from this to William Temple's essay "Upon the Gardens of Epicurus," and we find the following:

The perfectest figure of a garden I ever saw ... was that of Moor Park in Hertford-shire, when I knew it about thirty years ago. It was made by the Countess of Bedford, esteemed among the greatest wits of her time, and celebrated by Doctor Donne; and with very great care, excellent contrivance, and much cost; but *greater sums may be thrown away without effect or honour, if there want sense in proportion to money,* or *if Nature be not followed; which I take to be the great rule in this, and perhaps in everything else ... And whether the greatest of mortal men should attempt the forcing of Nature,* may best be judged, by observing how seldom God Almighty does it himself, by so few, true and undisputed miracles ... For my own part, *I know not three wiser precepts for the conduct either of princes or private men, than—*
    Servare modum, finemque tueri, Naturamque sequi.[3]

It would be rash to claim that Pope's account of Timon's villa insists on our remembering Temple's paragraph. We are given sufficient indication without it that the poet speaks in the guise of the Twickenham garden-philosopher who understands and respects nature, and who therefore knows, as we have seen, that the criterion of true possession is not ownership but enjoyment. Yet quite evidently we have in the paragraph an important instance of the body of opinion with which the speaker of the poem allies himself and even possibly the germ of

---

3/*The Gardens of Epicurus*, ed. A. F. Sieveking (London, 1908), p. 50. Italics mine, except those of the Latin. Pope had imitated this famous tag (Lucan, *Pharsalia*, II 381–82) in his portrait of the happy man in *Windsor Forest* (below, pp. 105–6). The theme of his portrait of Timon, and of the *Epistle to Burlington* generally, is in part a version of this sentiment.

his references to "sums ... thrown away," the priority of "Sense" over "Expence," and the error of forcing rather than following nature. Moreover, the picture of the foolish Timon's villa stands out with added clarity if we allow ourselves to glimpse beyond it the "perfectest figure of a garden I ever saw"—made by one who was among "the greatest wits" of her time, who esteemed poetry and poets, and knew how to treat them (as Timon does not), and who, though building with much cost, did not throw her "sums" away.

IV

A more complicated instance, involving allusion unmistakably, occurs in the *Epistle to Bathurst*. Here, at several points, Pope's commentary on the corrupting power of gold echoes with recollections of one of the primary classical texts in praise of rural innocence and simplicity—Horace's sixteenth ode of the Third Book:

> aurum per medios ire satellites
> et perrumpere amat saxa, potentius
> ictu fulmineo: concidit auguris
>   Argivi domus, ob lucrum
>
> demersa exitio; diffidit urbium
> portas vir Macedo et subruit aemulos
> reges muneribus; munera navium
>   saevos inlaqueant duces.
>
> crescentem sequitur cura pecuniam
> maiorumque fames. ...
>
> contemptae dominus splendidior rei,
> quam si, quidquid arat impiger Apulus,
> occultare meis dicerer horreis,
>   magnas inter opes inops.
>
> purae rivus aquae silvaque iugerum
> paucorum et segetis certa fides meae
> fulgentem imperio fertilis Africae
>   fallit sorte beatior.
>
>   ... multa petentibus
> desunt multa; bene est, cui deus obtulit
>   parca quod satis est manu.   (9–18, 25–32, 42–44)

("Gold loves to make its way through the midst of sentinels and to break through rocks, for 'tis mightier than the thunderbolt. 'Twas for the sake of gain that the house of the Argive prophet plunged to destruction and fell in ruins. 'Twas by gifts of gold that the Macedonian burst open gates of cities and overthrew rival kings; gifts ensnare bluff admirals, too. Yet as money grows, care and greed for greater riches follow after ... [I am] a more glorious master of the wealth I spurn than were I said to hide within my barns the produce of all the acres that the sturdy Apulian ploughs, a beggar in the midst of mighty wealth. My stream of pure water, my woodland of few acres, and sure trust in my crop of corn bring me more blessing than the lot of the dazzling lord of fertile Africa, though he know it not. ... To those who seek for much, much is ever lacking; blest is he to whom the god with chary hand has given just enough.")

Much of what Pope has to say about the wrong and right use of riches in the *Epistle to Bathurst* could be regarded as (in a general way) an inspired application of these attitudes and of the rhetoric of paradox in which they are expressed: *magnas inter opes inops* ("a beggar in the midst of mighty wealth"), *multa petentibus desunt multa* ("To those who seek for much, much is ever lacking"), *contemptae dominus splendidior rei* ("a more glorious master of the wealth I spurn"), and so on. The Horatian phrases point precisely to the two worlds of Pope's epistle: that which contains Bathurst, Oxford, and the Man of Ross, on the one hand, and that which contains Cotta, Villiers, Hopkins, Cutler, and all the rest who manifest "Want with a full ... purse," on the other. Possibly there are also links of a more explicit sort between what Horace says about the power of gold to pierce all barriers and Pope's apostrophe to "Blest paper-credit," which corrupts closer home than Horace's Greek cities:

> Gold imp'd by thee, can compass hardest things,
> Can pocket States, can fetch or carry Kings;
> A single leaf shall waft an Army o'er,
> Or ship off Senates to a distant Shore: ...
> Pregnant with thousands flits the Scrap unseen,
> And silent sells a King, or buys a Queen.   (71–74, 77–78)

Such analogies with Horace's ode may well belong more to the genesis of Pope's *Epistle* than to its meaning. Not so, however, when we come to the story of Balaam. Here Pope's "Tempter," who failed with Job, and therefore nowadays "tempts by making rich, not making poor," pours wealth on his victim:

> 'Till all the Daemon makes his full descent,
> In one abundant show'r of Cent. per Cent.,
> Sinks deep within him, and possesses whole.   (371–73)

The allusion to Zeus's possession of Danaë is clear enough without Horace, but the application of this ancient story to the seductions of money directs our attention squarely to the ode we have been discussing, where, in two stanzas I have so far left unquoted, Horace makes this application his introduction to praise of the retired life:

> Inclusam Danaën turris aënea
> robustaeque fores et vigilum canum
> tristes excubiae munierant satis
>   nocturnis ab adulteris,
>
> si non Acrisium virginis abditae
> custodem pavidum Iuppiter et Venus
> risissent: fore enim tutum iter et patens
>   converso in pretium deo.   (1–8)

("Tower of bronze, doors of oak, and the strict guard of watch-dogs had quite protected imprisoned Danaë from nocturnal lovers, had not Jupiter and Venus laughed at Acrisius, anxious keeper of the hidden maiden. For they knew that the way would be safe and open, when the god had turned to gold.")

Horace's *converso in pretium deo* ("when the god had turned to gold") obviously anticipates the metamorphosis of Satan in Pope's poem. It also anticipates the materialism of Balaam's worship. Beginning by "solemnizing" the Lord's Day with "an added pudding," then salving his conscience for theft by going to church twice on Sunday, he is presently vouchsafed the "full descent" of the Satanic Comforter, whereupon he arrogates the role of Providence to himself:

> What late he call'd a Blessing, now was Wit,
> And God's good Providence, a lucky Hit—   (377–78)

translates the observances of worship to his counting-house;

> Things change their titles, as our manners turn:
> His Compting-house employ'd the Sunday-morn—   (379–80)

and by a predictable progression eventually curses God and dies. Through the Danaë analogue, Pope makes a comment in sexual terms on the perversion implicit in Balaam's possession not by a god but by his own wealth. By deliberately vulgarizing the greatest spiritual drama of the Old Testament into a mercantile success story, he makes a comment on perversions of a deeper and more inclusive kind. To these he adds through Horace the constructive perspectives of the literature of retirement, as earlier in the poem he had set beside his gallery of wealth-abusers the figure of the Man of Ross. In the context of the Roman allusion, we are invited to hear not simply the voice of Horace but the authority implicit in a long tradition of philosophical self-cultivation, telling us there are less costly ways than Balaam's to the discovery that

> multa petentibus
> desunt multa; bene est, cui deus obtulit
> parca quod satis est manu.

V

Easily the most insistent of Pope's overt allusions to the idiom of retirement literature in these poems of the 30's occurs in his imitation of the fourth satire of Donne. Pope's poem, like Donne's, comes to a point about midway when the speaker's narrative of his visit to court is punctuated by his longed-for escape from an impertinent courtier and his return home. There—in a "trance," as Donne has it; Pope's word is "vision"—he relives his visit as if it were a glimpse of hell, experiencing yet stronger repugnance at what he sees.

In Donne, the flight from court is simply a flight to the poet's house, accomplished to the accompaniment of mock pity:

> At home in wholesom solitariness
> My piteous soul began the wretchedness
> Of suiters at court to mourn, and a Trance
> Like his, who dream't he saw hell, did advance
> It self o're me: Such men as he saw there
> I saw at Court, and worse, and more. ... (155–60)

In Pope the escape from court to solitude is marked more sharply. It is signaled by a break from narrative to apostrophe, and it brings into play a *mise-en-scène* wholly characteristic of retirement literature, inhabited by characteristic figures:

> Bear me, some God! oh quickly bear me hence
> To wholesome Solitude, the Nurse of Sense:

> Where Contemplation prunes her ruffled Wings,
> And the free Soul looks down to pity Kings.
> There sober Thought pursu'd th' amusing theme
> Till Fancy colour'd it, and form'd a Dream.
> A *Vision* Hermits can to Hell transport,
> And force ev'n me to see the Damn'd at Court.
> Not *Dante* dreaming all th' Infernal State,
> Beheld such Scenes of *Envy, Sin,* and *Hate.*   (184–93)

Pope's alteration of Donne's "At home" to a special habitat of retirement virtues is interesting, partly because, like all his other changes, it sharpens the attack on court life, but chiefly because of its ancestry. The place where Contemplation prunes ruffled wings and the free Soul looks down has probably its antecedent in those medieval gardens where the souls of the just are represented by birds, though it is by no means clear that Pope knew this. What he surely did know is that this garden situation is the normal habitat of that bird-of-the-soul which materializes so often in seventeenth-century poetry, most familiarly in Marvell's "The Garden"—

> There like a Bird it sits, and sings,
> Then whets, and combs its silver Wings;
> And, till prepar'd for longer flight,
> Waves in its Plumes the various Light—   (53–56)

and which has reappeared in our time in versions (and gardens) as different as those of *Burnt Norton* and the palace of the emperor of Byzantium.

Pope's personified "Solitude," "Sense," and "Contemplation" pruning ruffled wings also have a history, as his editors point out. They look directly back to the speech of the elder brother in *Comus* on the integrity and security of virtue even when most exposed:

> Virtue could see to do what virtue would
> By her own radiant light, though Sun and Moon
> Were in the flat Sea sunk. And Wisdom's self
> Oft seeks to sweet retired Solitude,
> Where with her best nurse Contemplation
> She plumes her feathers, and lets grow her wings
> That in the various bussle of resort
> Were all to-ruff'd, and sometimes impair'd.
> He that has light within his own clear brest
> May sit i'th centre, and enjoy bright day.   (373–82)

The allusion to *Comus*, clearly one we are not meant to overlook, marshals beside the figure of Pope's garden-sage, whose free soul is proof against the corruption of courts, the particular image of Milton's virtuous Lady, who as easily resists Comus' seduction and for the same reason: "Thou canst not touch the freedom of my mind" (662). The inclination of Pope's "Soul" to look down and pity "Kings" (specifically) no doubt owes more to the teachings of platonized stoicism he had rendered recently in the *Essay on Man* (and perhaps to his view of the House of Brunswick)—

> AWAKE, my ST. JOHN! leave all meaner things
> To low ambition, and the pride of Kings—   (1 1–2)

than to Milton or seventeenth-century garden mysticism. But Solitude, Contemplation, and the bird-of-the-soul are another matter.[1] These make a background for the ensuing vision of the court as hell that could hardly be improved on, and remind us how profoundly Pope's mind is penetrated by the conceptions of the century into which he was born.

VI

To think of the century into which Pope was born is to think of a network of values and assumptions in his poetry of the 30's which are almost as elusive as they are allusive. That they are inherited assumptions does not make them less deeply felt—quite the contrary: Pope's most powerful vein is often elegiac. Their genealogy can be traced in the work of Jacobean and Stuart poets, particularly those who wrote celebrating English country-houses and the landscape and way of life of which such houses were at their best a centre. Mr. G. R. Hibbard has written eloquently on this subject, locating in certain poems of Jonson's, Carew's, and Herrick's, and in parts of Marvell's *Upon Appleton House*, a body of poetry "truly Augustan in the sense that it voices and defines the values of a society conscious of its own achievement of a civilized way of living, and conscious also

---

1/Pope's "free Soul" and the general character of his apostrophe to "some God" suggest that, whether or not he is remembering Marvell, he is remembering Dryden's

> my free Soul, aspiring to the Height
> Of Nature, and unclouded Fields of Light;

and also his

> Some God conduct me to the sacred Shades ...
> Or lead me to some solitary Place
> And cover my Retreat from Human Race—

in his translation of Virgil's *O fortunatos nimium* (*Georgics*, II, 686, 692, 696–97). If so, the passage has a further link with retirement literature.

of the forces that threatened to undermine and overthrow that achievement."[1]
He concedes that the period in which such poetry could be written was brief,
terminated by changes in domestic architecture and social organization each of
which mutually hastened the other; but argues that the poetry remained influential because of its high quality, and that the attitudes it inculcated survived into
the next century, remarkably, and to some extent, uniquely, in Pope. "Pope's
conception of what the great house should be," he concludes (p. 174), referring
to the *Epistle to Burlington*: "was, of course, different from that of Ben Jonson
and his successors, in the purely architectural sense. Where they set up the traditional Elizabethan house in opposition to the baroque, Pope set up the classical
designs of Palladio. But underneath this surface difference he is wholly in agree-
ment with them that the right and proper end of building is use, not show; and
that the proper aim of the individual should be the subordination of himself to
the service of the community, not exploitation of the community for his own
personal ends."

Mr. Hibbard is surely right in associating Pope with this tradition. If not
strictly in the main current of seventeenth-century retirement literature, it incorporates nevertheless the same values and derives from the same classical texts;
and Pope draws from it, I think, many of the predispositions that gleam unstated
behind his criticism of such phenomena as Timon's villa in the *Epistle to Burlington*. The absurd Brobdingnagian grandeur of that place—

> To compass this, his building is a Town,
> His Pond an Ocean, his parterre a Down—   (105–6)

recalls not only the conspicuous consumption of certain contemporary Whig
magnates, but equally the stress laid by Jonson, Carew, Herrick, and Marvell
on dwellings built for use not show, each one "arisen, as it were, out of the earth
it stands on" (p. 164) to be a true home to its "lord":

> Now, PENSHURST, they that will proportion thee
> With other edifices, when they see
> Those proud, ambitious heaps, and nothing else,
> May say, their lords have built, but thy lord dwells.[2]   (99–102)

1/"The Country House Poem of the Seventeenth Century," *Journal of the Warburg and
Courtauld Institutes*, XIX (1956), 159.

2/See the close of "Upon the Duke of Marlborough's House at Woodstock," variously
attributed to Swift, Pope, Abel Evans, and William King.

> I find, by all you have been telling,
> That 'tis a house, but not a dwelling.

See also below, pp. 210–11.

Marvell, too, proposes in his opening lines on Appleton House an antitype—an anti-dwelling, so to speak—which incorporates some of the eccentricities of Timon's villa, as well as other follies recorded in the *Epistle to Burlington*:

> Within this sober Frame expect
> Work of no Forrain *Architect*;
> That unto Caves the Quarries drew,
> And Forrests did to Parterres hew.   (1–4)

Marvell's "Architect" clearly belongs in the ancestry of Timon, who has made his house "a labour'd Quarry above ground," and also probably in that of Sabinus' son, who cut away all the trees in which Sabinus had taken joy:

> His Son's fine Taste an op'ner Vista loves,
> Foe to the Dryads of his Father's groves,
> One boundless Green, or flourish'd Carpet views,
> With all the mournful family of Yews;
> The thriving plants ignoble broomsticks made,
> Now sweep those Alleys they were born to shade.   (93–98)

Marvell's query about the proportionableness of his anti-dwelling to its owner—

> What need of all this Marble Crust
> T'impark the wanton Mote of Dust?—   (21–22)

exhibits the same concern that Pope feels for right relations between house and man:

> Who but must laugh, the Master when he sees,
> A puny insect, shiv'ring at a breeze!   (107–8)

Marvell's comic vision of the house as a palace filled, like Aeolus's, with draughts—

> But He, superfluously spread,
> Demands more room alive then dead.
> And in his hollow Palace goes
> Where Winds as he themselves may lose—   (17–20)

if it has not inspired, at any rate looks forward to Pope's emphasis on impractical grandeur:

> Greatness, with Timon, dwells in such a draught
> As brings all Brobdignag before your thought—   (103–4)

and on the general propensity of such grandeur to favor appearance against comfort, calling even

> the winds thro' long Arcades to roar,
> Proud to catch cold at a Venetian door.   (35–36)

Altogether, the contrast that Marvell establishes between his hypothetical grandee, dwarfed by his showy house, and Fairfax, whose unpretentious dwelling barely contains his greatness—

> Height with a certain Grace does bend,
> But low Things clownishly ascend—   (56–60)

has the same ethical base as that which Sidney had established with respect to Kalander's house:

The house it selfe was built of faire and strong stone, not affecting so much any extraordinarie kind of finenesse, as an honourable representing of a firme state-linesse. The lights, doores and staires, rather directed to the use of the guest, then to the eye of the Artificer.[3]

Pope moves on exactly the same grounds in his distinction between the architecture of "Imitating Fools" and the architecture of Burlington, who shows us "Rome was glorious, not profuse" (23). Pope's criticism of contemporary ostentation speaks here from a long and (in the best sense) "classical" tradition.

VII

Much else in Pope's role as spokesman for a "country" point of view becomes clearer when we see it in the light of the seventeenth-century conventions and conceptions to which he was immediate heir. Digressing for a moment to his earlier work, we are helped to understand the lines in *Windsor Forest* which have been so often misread[1] if we call to mind their Elizabethan, Jacobean, and Stuart antecedents:

> Not proud *Olympus* yields a nobler Sight,
> Tho' Gods assembled grace his tow'ring Height,

3/*Arcadia* (ed. 1958), p. 7.
1/E.g., in Bernard Groom's "Some Kinds of Poetic Diction," *Essays and Studies by Members of the English Association*, xv (1929).

Than what more humble Mountains offer here,
Where, in their Blessings, all those Gods appear.
See *Pan* with Flocks, with Fruits *Pomona* crown'd,
Here blushing *Flora* paints th' enamel'd Ground,
Here *Ceres'* Gifts in waving Prospect stand,
And nodding tempt the joyful Reaper's Hand,
Rich Industry sits smiling on the Plains,
And Peace and Plenty tell, a STUART reigns.   (33–42)

Pope's description follows the convention of Tudor and Stuart allegorical painting, where monarchs regularly lead and control figures of "Peace and Plenty,"
together with more orthodox members of the classical Pantheon. Behind his
tableau lies also, we may guess, the tradition of emblematic pageants (this is a
Windsor landscape after all, and the monarch is its climax) such as were acted
at court and put on for royal progresses in the reigns of Elizabeth and James. In
addition, *To Penshurst* and other poems like it have contributed to these lines
their vision of an English countryside so profoundly oriented toward man that
its fruits and living creatures are emulous to feed him,[2] as the grain in Pope's lines
seems consciously to "tempt" the reaper's hand. Especially to be noticed is the
characteristically Renaissance way of understanding the presence of pagan gods
in a modern setting. Pope dwells upon a relation of near-identity between the
gifts of those gods and their "apparition" or theophany: "Where, in their Blessings, all those Gods appear," Carew, Pope's anticipator and perhaps model in
this, sees mainly a contrast between the gods' gifts and their icons:

> *Amalthea's* Horne
> Of plentie is not in Effigie worne
> Without the gate, but she within the dore
> Empties her free and unexhausted store.
> Nor, croun'd with wheaten wreathes, doth *Ceres* stand
> In stone, with a crook'd sickle in her hand:
> Nor, on a Marble Tunne, his face besmear'd
> With grapes, is curl'd uncizard *Bacchus* rear'd.
> We offer not in Emblemes to the eyes,
> But to the taste those usefull Deities.
> (*To My Friend G. N., from Wrest*, 57–66)

2/Cf. *To Penshurst*, 29–38, and Carew's *To Saxham*, 19–30.

What is true of *Windsor Forest* remains true, *mutatis mutandis*, in the poems of the 30's. They are unmistakably Augustan, yet the pressure of the preceding age often swells visibly beneath the contemporary surface. The expression of responsibilities and pieties remains patriarchal in its feeling for the relation between master and dependents:

> Where are those Troops of poor, that throng'd of yore
> The good old Landlord's hospitable door?
>> (*The Second Satire of Dr. John Donne*, 113–14)

The land continues to be seen as a locus of invisible presences:

> The woods recede around the naked seat,
> The Sylvans groan. ...
>> (*Epistle to Bathurst*, 209–10)

The objects of satire have an Elizabethan and Jacobean substance for all their contemporary dress: they are to a large extent, as in the preceding century, lawyers, embezzlers, extortionists, courtiers, affected females, royal favorites, Italianate returned travellers—and what is equally significant in this connection is that Pope chose to paraphrase two satires by Donne and contemplated paraphrasing one of Hall's.

One's attention is especially struck in these poems by the old-fashioned notions of what constitutes national and individual virtue, and the emotions which reverberate in the verse whenever such virtue is mentioned. These attitudes have long roots, often reaching as far back as Rome, but all seem to be nourished and extended in Pope's case by his wide reading in the seventeenth-century poets. Essentially, it is *their* vision of his country that he makes his own—the new Eden, the new Jerusalem, the new Rome. It is their feeling for the life of considerate use that pulses behind much of his social criticism, though the immediate vehicle be Horace. Their picture of the country gentleman living on his estate and so far as possible by it, seeking no city gain or court preferment, radiating through the land practices of provident abundance, occupying a great house "rear'd with no man's ruin, no man's groan," caring for his tenants and so loved by them that:

> all come in, the farmer, and the clowne:
> And no one emtpy-handed, to salute
> [The] lord, and lady, though they have no sute—
>> ("To Penshurst," 48–50)

this is Pope's picture, too, whenever in the satires he allows the positive ideals underlying his criticism to emerge:

His Father's Acres who enjoys in peace,
Or makes his Neighbours glad, if he encrease;
Whose chearful Tenants bless their yearly toil,
Yet to their Lord owe more than to the soil;
Whose ample Lawns are not asham'd to feed
The milky heifer and deserving steed;
Whose rising Forests, not for pride or show,
But future Buildings, future Navies grow:
Let his plantations stretch from down to down,
First shade a Country, and then raise a Town.

(*Epistle to Burlington*, 181–90)

This passage is highly characteristic of Pope. Yet its deep sense of reciprocities between man and man and man and nature, eventuating in a whole whose every part is responsive to every other (where tenants "bless," soil can be "owed" a debt, lawns are "not asham'd," forests rise but not for "pride," etc.), is a sense rare among eighteenth-century poets. It belongs in outlook, though not in phrasing, to the Renaissance.

When Pope thinks of hospitality, it is invariably again a highly traditional picture, Homeric, Biblical, with Tudor-Stuart colorations, that comes to his mind.[3] Like Jonson and his successors he sees a gate which turns no one away, homebred fare, a host who gives himself along with the meal. In his imitation of Horace's second satire of the Second Book, Horace's own passing references to the hospitality of Ofellus are intensified by Pope, first, with an allusion to a well-known turbot in Satire IV of Juvenal (37 ff.), and then with a proud specificity as to the homebred character of the meal he offers, the pride belonging as fully to seventeenth-century English housekeeping attitudes as to Horatian Rome.

'Tis true, no Turbots dignify my boards,
But gudgeons, flounders, what my Thames affords.
To Hounslow-heath I point, and Bansted-down,
Thence comes your mutton, and these chicks my own:
From yon old wallnut-tree a show'r shall fall;
And grapes, long-lingring on my only wall,
And figs, from standard and Espalier join:
The dev'l is in you if you cannot dine.   (141–48)

3/See his *Correspondence*, II 386, III 125, and the Introduction to the TE Homer, VII ccxxvi ff.

The stress in Pope's original is on the sufficient though simple character of the meal, which did not require "fish sent from town." Pope incorporates within this a notably seventeenth-century English sense of proprietorship and place.[4]

Or if it is manorial hospitality which comes to Pope's mind, he thinks of the great halls celebrated by an earlier age, where lord, tenants, neighbors, guests, travelers, and poor were alike welcome and shared alike from a bounteous table. His portrait of Cotta in the *Epistle to Bathurst* consists precisely in inverting this:

> Old Cotta sham'd his fortune and his birth,
> Yet was not Cotta void of wit or worth:
> What tho' (the use of barb'rous spits forgot)
> His kitchen vy'd in coolness with his grot?
> His court with nettles, moats with cresses stor'd,
> With soups unbought and sallads blest his board.
> If Cotta liv'd on pulse, it was no more
> Than Bramins, Saints, and Sages did before;
> To cram the Rich was prodigal expence,
> And who would take the Poor from Providence?
> Like some lone Chartreux stands the good old Hall,
> Silence without, and Fasts within the wall;
> No rafter'd roofs with dance and tabor sound,
> No noontide-bell invites the country round;
> Tenants with sighs the smoakless tow'rs survey,
> And turn th' unwilling steeds another way:
> Benighted wanderers, the forest o'er,
> Curse the sav'd candle, and unop'ning door;
> While the gaunt mastiff growling at the gate,
> Affrights the beggar whom he longs to eat.   (179–98)

We do less than justice to such lines if we do not imagine, crowding in behind them, like the disapproving ghosts who haunt the tent of Shakespeare's Richard III the night before Bosworth Field, the Sidneys of Penshurst, the Wroths of Loughton House and Durrants, the Crofts of Saxham, the Greys of Wrest, the Pembertons of Rushden, the Fairfaxes of Nunappleton, and all those others who took seriously in their time the responsibilities of rank and wealth. Old Cotta's cold kitchen and miser's view of "barb'rous spits" are to be seen against the "liberall board" of Penshurst, flowing "With all that hospitalitie doth know" (60), or the great hall of Wrest:

4/One may notice Dryden's "homebred plenty," in *Georgics*, II 657, his own insertion.

> Where at large Tables fill'd with wholsome meates
> The servant, Tennant, and kind neighbour eates,
> > (Carew, *To My Friend G.N., from Wrest*, 35–36)

or, especially, the mighty kitchen at Rushden:

> The fat-fed smoking Temple, which in
> The wholsome savour of thy mighty Chines
> > Invites to supper him who dines,
> Where laden spits, wrap't with large Ribbs of Beefe,
> > Not represent, but give reliefe
> To the lanke-Stranger, and the sowre Swain;
> > Where both may feed, and come againe. ...
> > (Herrick, *A Panegyrick to Sir Lewis Pemberton*, 6–12)

Cotta's "soups unbought and sallads," as has often been pointed out, cross his image ironically with that of the old Corycian in Virgil's fourth *Georgic*, the figure typifying contentment with little, noticed in the preceding chapter; but they further cross it with the seventeenth-century English countryman's pride in self-sufficiency, expressed in Carew's praise of Wrest, where grow

> Such native Aromatiques, as we use
> No forraigne Gums, nor essence fetcht from farre— (14–15)

and Jonson's of Robert Wroth:

> [Thou] canst, at home, in thy securer rest,
> Live, with un-bought provision blest.
> > (*To Sir Robert Wroth*, 13–14)

When Cotta leaves the poor to "Providence," we are to recall those who acted by another code—for instance, the Greys of Wrest, who did not fill their dining room with "statues" but with "living men" (33–34), and the Fairfaxes, whose "open Door" was adorned with "a stately Frontispiece of Poor" (65–67); and we are also to recall their successors in Pope's own day, the Oxfords, Bathursts, Burlingtons, all who carry on the tradition of wealth applied to social ends, among whom "English Bounty," like *Iustitia* among the *O fortunatos nimium* of the second Georgic,

> yet a-while may stand,
> And Honour linger ere it leaves the land.
> > (*Epistle to Bathurst*, 247–48)

Even Cotta's gaunt mastiff, who gives solid expression to the philosophy of "sav'd candle" and "unop'ning door," has possibly among his literary ancestors a figure whose absence is dwelt on in seventeenth-century descriptions of country houses properly run. In Jonson, it is the officious waiter, who is not to be found at Penshurst:

> Here no man tells my cups; nor, standing by,
> A waiter, doth my gluttony envy;
> But gives me what I call, and lets me eat.   (67–69)

In Carew, it is the surly porter who does not guard the gate at Saxham:

> Thou hast no Porter at thy doore
> T' examine, or keep back the poore;
> Nor locks, nor bolts: thy gates have bin
> Made onely to let strangers in;
> Untaught to shut, they do not feare
> To stand wide open all the yeare.
>
> ("To Saxham," 49–54)

In Herrick, it is both porter and waiter, neither of whom is employed at Rushden:

> For no black-bearded *Vigil* from thy doore
>   Beats with a button'd-staffe the poor: ...
> Thus, like a *Roman Tribune*, thou thy gate
>   Early setts ope to feast, and late:
> Keeping no *currish Waiter* to affright,
>   With blasting eye, the appetite.
>
> (*A Panegyrick to Sir Lewis Pemberton*, 13–14, 45–48)

VIII

The end product of the influence of retirement literature on Pope's poems of the 30's is the ingratiating semi-rural figure whose value-system colors them all, and whose personality and vocabulary are impressed at some point on most. Essentially, this is the figure of the *beatus vir* of literary tradition, a composite of Roman outlines shaped to English seventeenth-century and Augustan circumstances, or, to restate the matter in rhetorical terms, a collecting of traditional *topoi* into something like an identifiable physical presence by the voice of a speaker who is at once Pope of Twickenham and a universal type.

In the tradition on which Pope draws, this figure normally speaks from a small

homestead of inherited land—his *rura paterna*, as Horace has it in the second
Epode (1.3)—about which he has feelings of the kind expressed by the elder
shepherd in Shakespeare's *Winter's Tale*:

> To die upon the bed my father died,
> To lie close by his honest bones.   (IV, iv, 456–57)

Here the happy man was born, and here he stays. For in the words of Claudian's
De Sene Veronensi, one of the main Latin sources of the figure:

> Felix, qui propriis aevum transegit in arvis,
> ipsa domus puerum quem videt, ipsa senem.   (1–2)

("Happy he who has passed his whole life mid his own fields, he of whose birth and
old age the same house is witness.")

Partly he is bound to his birthplace by natural pieties of the sort Vaughan praises
in his man of "constancy" (in his translation of Casimir Sarbiewski), who can
contentedly

> *dine* and *sup*
> Where his *old parents* bred him up.
> (*Lib. 4. Ode 15,* 29–30)

Partly he is bound by the conviction that "Fair quiet" and Innocence her "Sister
dear" are best sought after elsewhere than "In busie Companies of Men."[1]
Jonson had stated the point memorably in his verses to Lady Aubigny, subsequently recalled by Gray:

> In single paths, dangers with ease are watch'd:
> Contagion in the prease is soonest catch'd.
> This makes, that wisely you decline your life,
> Farre from the maze of custome, error, strife,
> And keepe an even, and unalter'd gaite ...
> (*To Katherine, Lady Aubigny,* 57–61)

The *beatus vir* therefore shuns "the Forum's madness,"[2] never on any account
goes to law,[3] cherishes independence like all who, having learned "the Great Art

---

1/Marvell, "The Garden," 10–12.

2/*Georgics*, II 502: *insanumque forum*; cf. Cowley's "The Wrangling Barr" in "Of Myself"
(*Essays*, p. 112). This is the *beatus vir*'s usual view of law courts, and may account for Pope's
rendering Donne's "the termes of law" as "the bawling Bar" (*Imit. Donne*, IV 55).

3/Martial, II xc 10: *sit nox cum somno, sit sine lite dies* ("Let me have night with sleep, have
day without a lawsuit").

of cheerful Poverty,"[4] "can endure to stoop"[5] as they enter their humble door-ways, and hugs himself that he has got free of the world and its ways:

> Let others trust the seas, dare death and hell,
> Search either *Inde*, vaunt of their scarres and wounds;
> Let others their deare breath (nay silence) sell
> To fools, and (swoln, not rich) stretch out their bounds
> By spoiling those that live, and wronging dead;
> That they may drink in pearl, and couch their head
> In soft, but sleeplesse down; in rich, but restlesse bed.[6]

His conscience is quiet. His sleep at night is unbroken by fears or cares.[7] His health is sound because his diet is spare and got by labor or hunting:

> ... all the Rivers, and the Forests nigh,
> Both Food and Game, and Exercise supply.[8]

He keeps a warm ever-blazing hearth,[9] values his friends, has a wife (if he has a wife at all) who is a paragon of chastity,[10] reverences his ancestors, worships his God, and bridles his will. He neither fears the approach of death nor longs for it,[11] but when it comes, "Serenely as he liv'd, resigns his breath."[12]

The essential features of this portrait remained recognizable for nearly two millenia. This we may see by placing the following versions of it side by side. First, the Virgilian version, in which preference oscillates between the life of the happy farmer and that of the retired poet-sage:

4/Cowley's translation of *patiens operum exiguoque adsueta* (*Georgics*, II 472), in his rendering of *O fortunatos nimium* at the close of his essay "Of Agriculture" (*Essays*, p. 46).

5/Martial, II liii 8: "si tua non rectus tecta subire potes" ("if you can endure to stoop as you enter your dwelling"). This gesture became a standard emblem in retirement literature, probably owing in part to the great stress laid on it in Virgil's episode of Evander's house (*Aeneid*, VIII 362ff; above, pp. 72–73) Shakespeare puts a version of it into the mouth of Belarius in *Cymbeline*, III iii 1ff.

6/Phineas Fletcher's adaption of *O fortunatos nimium* (II 503–6) in the *Purple Island*, canto 1, st. xxvi.

7/Cf. for example Horace, *Epist.*, I x 18: *est ubi divellat somnos minus invida Cura?* ("Is there any place where envious Care less distracts our slumber?").

8/Cowley's rendering of *illic saltus ac lustra ferarum* (*Georgics*, II 471) in his version of *O fortunatos nimium* in "Of Agriculture" (*Essays*, p. 46).

9/Martial, x xlvii 4: *focus perennis*.

10/*Ibid.* 10: *non tristis torus et tamen pudicus* ("a wife not prudish and yet pure"); *Georgics*, II 524: *casta pudicitiam servat domus* ("his unstained home guards its purity").

11/Martial, x xlvii 13: *summum nec metuas diem nec optes*.

12/George Granville, "An Imitation *of the second* Chorus *in the second* Act *of* Seneca's *Thyestes*," 29.

O happy, if he knew his happy State!
The Swain, who, free from Business and Debate,
Receives his easy Food from Nature's Hand. ...
Give me the Ways of wandring Stars to know:
The Depths of Heav'n above, and Earth below.
Teach me the various Labours of the Moon,
And whence proceed th' Eclipses of the Sun.
Why flowing Tides prevail upon the Main,
And in what dark Recess they shrink again. ...
But if my heavy Blood restrain the Flight
Of my free Soul, aspiring to the Height
Of Nature, and unclouded Fields of Light:
My next Desire is, void of Care and Strife,
To lead a soft, secure, inglorious Life.
A Country Cottage near a Crystal Flood,
A winding Vally, and a lofty Wood. ...
Happy the Man, who, studying Nature's Laws,
Thro' known Effects can trace the secret Cause. ...
And happy too is he, who decks the Bow'rs
Of Sylvans, and adores the Rural Pow'rs:
Whose Mind, unmov'd, the Bribes of Courts can see.[13]

Next, Martial's epigram *Ad Seipsum* (X xlvii), as Englished by Ben Jonson:

The Things that make the happier life, are these,
Most pleasant Martial; Substance got with ease,
Not labour'd for, but left thee by thy Sire;
A Soyle, not barren; a continewall fire;
Never at Law; seldome in office gown'd;
A quiet mind; free powers; and body sound;
A wise simplicity; freindes alike-stated;
Thy table without art, and easy-rated:
Thy night not dronken, but from cares layd wast;
No sowre, or sullen bed-mate, yet a Chast;
Sleepe, that will make the darkest howres swift-pac't;
Will to bee, what thou art; and nothing more:
Nor feare thy latest day, nor wish therfore.

13/Dryden's translation: *Georgics*, II 639–41, 677–82, 685–91, 698–99, 702–4.

Third, part of Seneca's second chorus in *Thyestes* in Cowley's rendering at the close of his essay "Of Obscurity":

> Upon the slippery tops of humane State,
> The guilded Pinnacles of Fate,
> Let others proudly stand, and for a while
> The giddy danger to beguile,
> With Joy, and with disdain look down on all,
> Till their Heads turn, and down they fall.
> Me, O ye Gods, on Earth, or else so near
> That I no Fall to Earth may fear,
> And, O ye gods, at a good distance seat
> From the long Ruines of the Great.
> Here wrapt in th' Arms of Quiet let me ly;
> Quiet, Companion of Obscurity.
> Here let my Life, with as much silence slide,
> As Time that measures it does glide.
> Nor let the Breath of Infamy or Fame,
> From town to town Eccho about my Name.
> Nor let my homely Death embroidered be
> With Scutcheon or with Elegie.
> An old *Plebean* let me Dy,
> Alas, all then are such as well as I.
> To him, alas, to him, I fear,
> The face of Death will terrible appear:
> Who in his life flattering his senceless pride
> By being known to all the world beside,
> Does not himself, when he is Dying know
> Nor what he is, nor Whither hee's to go.

Fourth, Pope's ode *On Solitude*, probably his first poem, an Augustan landmark in this tradition:

> Happy the man, whose wish and care
> A few paternal acres bound.
> Content to breathe his native air,
> In his own ground.
>
> Whose herds with milk, whose fields with bread,
> Whose flocks supply him with attire,

> Whose trees in summer yield him shade,
>> In winter fire.

> Blest! who can unconcern'dly find
> Hours, days, and years slide soft away,
> In health of body, peace of mind,
>> Quiet by day,

> Sound sleep by night; study and ease
> Together mix'd; sweet recreation,
> And innocence, which most does please,
>> With meditation.

> Thus let me live, unseen, unknown;
> Thus unlamented let me dye;
> Steal from the world, and not a stone
>> Tell where I lye.

Fifth, the version of the type-figure which Pope adopts for *Windsor Forest*, compressing in one Virgil's alternatives of happy rural innocent and retired philosopher, but with a heavy bias toward the latter:

> Happy ... who to these Shades retires,
> Whom Nature charms, and whom the Muse inspires,
> Whom humbler Joys of home-felt Quiet please,
> Successive Study, Exercise and Ease.
> He gathers Health from Herbs the Forest yields,
> And of their fragrant Physick spoils the Fields:
> With Chymic Art exalts the Min'ral Pow'rs,
> And draws the Aromatick Souls of Flow'rs.
> Now marks the Course of rolling Orbs on high;
> O'er figur'd Worlds now travels with his Eye.
> Of ancient Writ unlocks the learned Store,
> Consults the Dead, and lives past Ages o'er.
> Or wandring thoughtful in the silent Wood,
> Attends the Duties of the Wise and Good,
> T' observe a Mean, be to himself a Friend,
> To follow Nature, and regard his End.

> Or looks on Heav'n with more than mortal Eyes,
> Bids his free Soul expatiate in the Skies,
> Amid her Kindred Stars familiar roam,
> Survey the Region, and confess her Home!　(237–56)

Finally, a passage we have seen before—not usually associated with the tradition, but obviously dependent on it:

> Born to no Pride, inheriting no Strife,
> Nor marrying Discord in a Noble Wife,
> Stranger to Civil and Religious Rage,
> The good Man walk'd innoxious thro' his Age.
> No Courts he saw, no Suits would ever try,
> Nor dar'd an Oath, nor hazarded a Lye:
> Un-learn'd, he knew no Schoolman's subtle Art,
> No Language, but the Language of the Heart.
> By Nature honest, by Experience wise,
> Healthy by Temp'rance and by Exercise:
> His Life, tho' long, to sickness past unknown,
> His Death was instant, and without a groan.
> Oh grant me thus to live, and thus to die!
> Who sprung from Kings shall know less joy than I.
> 　　　　　　　　(*Epistle to Dr. Arbuthnot*, 392–405)

What is especially interesting about Pope's portrait of his father here is its fusion of reality with something else, which we are now in a position to understand. The lines give us a true character of the elder Mr. Pope, so far as we can judge from the evidence we have; this is certainly how Pope felt about him, as letters to Caryll show: "I have lost one whom I was even more obliged to as a friend, than as a father"; "I heartily beg of God to give me just such a death, on condition he will in his mercy allow me just such a life."[14] Yet the portrait which the poet actually creates follows in every essential detail the type-figure of the happy man and rounds it off with a well-placed echo of Virgil's praise of the old Corycian: "he matched in contentment the wealth of kings."[15]

14/[28 October 1717], 6 November 1717 (I 448–49).

15/*Georgics*, IV 132: "regum aequabat opes animis," For a much more detailed account of the attributes of the type-figure than I have had occasion to give here, see Maren-Sofie Røstvig's *The Happy Man* (above, p. 21, n. 2).

Painters, it has been pointed out, are as often prone to see what they know how to draw as to draw what they see.[16] Something of the sort is also true of poets: Pope sees his father, in poetry, through the lens of a convention, very much as Shakespeare sees his kings in poetry through another convention, that of the sleepless head which wears a crown.

IX

When Pope looks at himself through this convention, the image that confronts him does not correspond at every point with the one we have just examined, for the poet is a man of affairs and fame, as his father was not; nor are the traditional features of the *beatus vir* represented equally in every poem. Yet there is an identifiable poet-speaker in all the poems of the 30's who incorporates a large number of the *topoi* with which we have here been concerned.

Beneficiary of a true old-fashioned education, this figure has been "bred up at home" and taught "to know the good from bad" by a father who can bear injustice without repining or wavering from principle:

> For Right Hereditary tax'd and fin'd,
> He stuck to Poverty with Peace of Mind;
> And me, the Muses help'd to undergo it;
> Convict a Papist He, and I a Poet.
>
> (*Imit. Hor., Ep.* II ii, 64–67)

Son and father, subscribing to a faith that costs something—in the son's case, poetry as well as popery—have stood necessarily withdrawn in a world to which the Old Religion is as alien as old-fashioned costumes or scruples,[1] and in which lust of gain drives peeress and butler to the same gaming table.[2] In the son's case, a competence of means has been reached, "thanks to *Homer*," which enables him to "piddle" along happily on "Broccoli and mutton," entertaining his "ancient friends," now ceremonially with "Feast" and "Bowl,"[3] now simply, like a good bourgeois, with "Beans and Bacon":

16/See especially on this theme E. H. Gombrich, *Art and Illusion* (London, 1960), p. 86, and the whole chapter.

1/*Imit. Donne*, II 121–24; *Imit. Hor. Ep.* II ii 116–26; *Epilogue to the Satires: Dial.* i 39–40.

2/*Epistle to Bathurst*, 137 ff.

3/The quotations are from *Ep.* II ii 68; *Sat.* II ii 137–39; and *Sat.* II i 127–28.

32 POETA ANGLUS, 1741. Copper medal
by Jacques Antoine Dassier

My Friends above, my Folks below,
Chatting and laughing all-a-row,
The Beans and Bacon set before 'em,
The Grace-cup serv'd with all decorum.
(*Imit. Hor., Sat.* II vi, 35–38)

In either case the diet is staunchly homebred like himself and serves as index
and metaphor of a way of life where duties to neighbors, friends, parents, and
one's Creator are cheerfully carried out: "And, what's more rare, a Poet shall say
Grace."[4] True, he knows the tug of nostalgia for a time when there was no double
taxing of Roman Catholics, when no "Laws, by Suff'rers thought unjust" were
on the statute books: "My lands are sold, my Father's house is gone"; but the

4/*Sat.* II ii 150. Cf. *Georgics*, II 473: "sacra deum sanctique patres."

33 The laureated poet, 1734. By Jonathan Richardson,
1665–1745

proper response to this—"I'll hire another's, is not that my own?"—cannot be long in occurring to a mind schooled to the full implications of the retirement creed: "Fix'd to no spot is Happiness sincere."[5] Though he had formerly somewhat more of this world's goods, he was then no better off:

> In *South-sea* days not happier, when surmis'd
> The Lord of thousands, than if now *Excis'd*;
> In Forest planted by a Father's hand,
> Than in five acres now of rented land.
>
> (*Imit. Hor., Sat.* II ii, 133–36)

And though he should lose much of what he has, he would be no worse off: he could shrink back to his "Paternal Cell," following again his father's example.

5/The quotations are from *Ep.* II ii 60; *Sat.* II ii 155, 156, and *Essay on Man,* IV 15.

> There dy'd my Father, no man's Debtor,
> And there I'll die, nor worse nor better.
>
> (*Ibid., Ep.* I vii, 79–80)

For the true test of ownership, at Twickenham as at Penshurst, Wrest, and Rushden, is use:

> Well, if the Use be mine, can it concern one
> Whether the Name belong to Pope or Vernon?
>
> (*Ibid., Sat.* II ii, 165–66)
>
> Delightful *Abs-court*, if its Fields afford
> Their Fruits to you, confesses you its Lord;
>
> (*Ibid., Ep.* II ii, 232–33)

and the true use of what one owns is to keep one free. Free of the penalties exacted by the world of those who are at its mercy:

> South-sea Subscriptions take who please,
> Leave me but Liberty and Ease.
> 'Twas what I said to Craggs and Child,
> Who prais'd my Modesty, and smil'd.
> Give me, I cry'd, (enough for me)
> My Bread, and Independency!
>
> (*Ibid., Ep.* I vii, 65–70)

And free of the worse penalties exacted by the inner world of desire, when not taught to remember that "*Man?* and *for ever?*" (*Ibid.*, II ii 252) have no connection in the natural scheme of things:

> Grac'd as thou art, with all the Pow'r of Words,
> So known, so honour'd, at the House of Lords;
> Conspicuous Scene! another yet is nigh,
> (More silent far) where Kings and Poets lye.
>
> (*Ibid.*, I vi, 48–51)

In this autobiographical figure of the 30's, a variety of strains merge. It is a Roman figure, derived from many works and authors, of whom Horace is only one. It is also a recognizable seventeenth-century figure, hero of a thousand poems in praise of virtuous retirement, sprung up in part from the political and social stresses dramatized by the Civil Wars, and from the abyss sensed between one vision of England and another which was to be institutionalized after 1688.

And it is very plainly a version of the historical Alexander Pope. Its effectiveness is precisely in its seamlessness, as we may see from two further expressions of it, one having to do with the poet's life, the other with his works.

Over the entrance to his grotto, Pope inscribed the words: *Secretum iter et fallentis semita vitae* ("a secluded journey along the pathway of a life un-noticed"). The inscription was obviously suitable to the place and, as eighteenth-century practitioners of retirement go, to the man who placed it there: it had a personal valency, as we have seen. This same sentiment, however, is Cowley's theme in his essay "Of Obscurity," and its flavor perfectly suits many a well-known poet and poem of that age. Thus it has an historical valency too, pointing to a long tradition of self-seclusions, some of them partly engendered by political exclusions, like Pope's own situation at Twickenham. Finally, the inscription is an Horatian tag, with a philosophical valency of sorts, bringing to the reader a context from Horace's eighteenth epistle of Book I that could serve as epigraph equally for the ethical teaching of his satires and epistles as a group or that of the *Essay on Man*:

> Inter cuncta leges et percontabere doctos,
> qua ratione queas traducere leniter aevum,
> num te semper inops agitet vexetque cupido,
> num pavor et rerum mediocriter utilium spes,
> virtutem doctrina paret Naturane donet,
> quid minuat curas, quid te tibi reddat amicum,
> quid pure tranquillet, honos an dulce lucellum,
> an secretum iter et fallentis semita vitae.   (96–103)

("Amid all this you must read and question the wise, how you may be able to pass your days in tranquillity. Is greed, ever penniless, to drive and harass you, or fears and hopes about things that profit little? Does wisdom beget virtue, or Nature bring her as a gift? What will lessen care? What will make you a friend to yourself? What gives you unruffled calm—honour, or the sweets of dear gain, or a secluded journey along the pathway of a life unnoticed?")

Roman ethical culture, the tradition of withdrawal from political action inspired by seventeenth-century British history, the personal tastes of Pope of Twicken-ham on one side of his nature: all are joined together in the consensus of a line from Horace.

My other example comes from Pope's imitation of Horace's second epistle of Book II:

> Well, on the whole, *plain* Prose must be my fate:
> Wisdom (curse on it) will come soon or late.
> There is a time when Poets will grow dull:
> I'll e'en leave Verses to the Boys at school!
> To Rules of Poetry no more confin'd,
> I learn to smooth and harmonize my Mind,
> Teach ev'ry Thought within its bounds to roll,
> And keep the equal Measure of the Soul.   (198–205)

This is pure Horace, one is obliged to confess, particularly the conception of life as a poem to be "formed." But it is pure "moral philosophy," too, of a kind often enunciated in seventeenth-century *vade-mecums*. And it is likewise pure Pope, sealed as his by the wry grimace, the easy diction, the formidable rhythms, and the immediately ensuing lines which tie Horace's undifferentiated speaker to a specifically realized Twickenham setting:

> Soon as I enter at my Country door,
> My Mind resumes the thread it dropt before;
> Thoughts, which at Hyde-Park-Corner I forgot,
> Meet and rejoin me, in the pensive Grott.
> There all alone, and Compliments apart,
> I ask these sober questions of my Heart. ...   (206–11)

The lines are also sealed as Pope's by the personal concern which we know from other sources invested this problem for him. He raises it in the *Epistle to Dr. Arbuthnot*:

> Heav'ns! was I born for nothing but to write?[6]
> Has Life no Joys for me? or (to be grave)
> Have I no Friend to serve, no Soul to save?   (272–74)

In his letters it concerns him repeatedly. The young man's acknowledgment of the price of his art, stated in the early days as a discovery lately made—"To follow Poetry as one ought, one must forget father and mother, and cleave to it alone"—[7] deepens as time wears on into "sober questions" about perfection of the life or of the work:

To write well, lastingly well, Immortally well, must not one leave Father and Mother

---

6/See also *Ep.* II ii 32: "D'ye think me good for nothing but to rhime?"
7/To Jervas, 16 August 1714 (I 243).

and cleave unto the Muse? Must not one be prepared to endure the reproaches of Men, want and much Fasting, nay Martyrdom in its Cause. 'Tis such a Task as scarce leaves a Man time to be a good Neighbour, an useful friend, nay to plant a Tree, much less to save his Soul.[8]

And in still another moving letter filled with harassments—the poet has been looking after repairs to Fortescue's house before rushing off to see Peterborough in his last illness—there comes a question at the close, in words belonging obviously to the retirement tradition yet having in them the home-felt pressure of the individual case:

... when shall you & I sit by a Fireside, without a Brief or a Poem in our hands, & yet not idle, not thoughtless, but as Serious, and more so, than any Business ought to make us, except the great Business, that of enjoying a reasonable Being, & regarding its End. The sooner this is our case, the better: God deliver you from Law, me from Rhime![9]

Here too, Pope of Twickenham, seventeenth-century Christian humanism, and Horatian and other Roman precedents speak with a single voice.

X

For a final instance of the way in which the retirement tradition moves always under the surface of Pope's consciousness and may at any time break out, we may look again at the *Epistle to Dr. Arbuthnot*. The eloquent shape of this poem comes in large part, as we saw, from the poet's tying his "Bill of Complaint"[1] against others to a progressive enlargement of vision in himself. This takes him from amused self-centered harassment at the opening to outward-looking serenity at the close, and the proud commemorative portrait of his father, quoted above in the sequence of retirement figures, marks the final stage in a process of sloughing off distraction and detraction and other vanities of worldly fame to reach a single-minded vision of true innocence. This way of life the poet then identifies with his own best longings—"Oh grant me thus to live, and thus to die!"—and, in the final prayerful lines for Arbuthnot and his mother, seems to make his own for the days to come. To put the progress of the poem in another way, at its beginning the poet's known personal ill-health is seen in part as the

---

8/To Bolingbroke, 9 April 1724 (II 227).
9/To Fortescue, 23 August 1735 (III 486). Cf. *Windsor Forest*, 252; above, p. 105.
1/Pope's phrase in the poem's *Advertisement*.

"disease" of worldly success, a "Plague" no "*Drop* or *Nostrum*" can cure, which makes the address to the physician Arbuthnot a stroke of imagination as well as friendship.[2] At its end, the speaker, now identified with a father whose life excluded all such "sickness," has in a sense changed places with the physician; he is possessed of "lenient Arts" of his own for smoothing the "Bed of Death" and for "extending" the breath of the living (earlier, l. 27, it was Arbuthnot who "prolonged" life), and it is he who is given the final healing prayer for the physician's preservation and well-being, as well as his own.

To this extent, the poem's debt to retirement attitudes is obvious. There may, however, have been a more circumstantial debt. One of the many classic delineations of the *beatus vir* is found in the closing portion of the second chorus of Seneca's *Thyestes*, a favorite passage with Pope, often referred to in his correspondence;[3] and one of the most influential imitations of Seneca's lines is Cowley's rendering, already quoted (p. 104). It may be that thinking about his father in connection with the tribute he wished to pay him in the epistle put Pope in mind of the Senecan passage, and that this reminded him of Cowley's essay "Of Obscurity," to which these lines formed the afterpiece.[4] It may be that Pope was put in mind of Cowley's essay by his own reference to it in his letter of 1712 to the *Spectator*, which he would perhaps have been going over at about the time he was composing the epistle, with an eye to the publication of his literary correspondence in 1735. It may be that occasionally Pope took down his copy of Cowley to reread, and had done so near the time of writing *Arbuthnot*. Or it may be that there is no connection whatever between the epistle and the passages I am about to quote, that the resemblances are coincidental.

What will be striking in any case, to a reader who has just come from a close perusal of the structure of the *Epistle to Dr. Arbuthnot*, is that Cowley's essay begins with an analysis of the Horatian line that Pope adopted for the archway

---

2/See E. F. Mengel, Jr., "Patterns of Imagery in Pope's *Arbuthnot*," *Publications of the Modern Language Association*, LXIX (1954), pp. 189–97.

3/To Atterbury, 19 March 1722 (II 109). In this instance Pope quotes from Granville's version of the Senecan lines: (see above, p. 102, n. 12), to Caryll, 26 October [1722] (II 14); to Broome, 29 June [1725] (II 302).

4/One detail in the portrait of his father ("Death ... without a groan"), not to be found in Seneca's Latin except by inference, may possibly be a reminiscence of Marvell's version of this chorus (8–11):

> Thus when without noise, unknown,
> I have liv'd out all my span,
> I shall dye, without a groan.
> An old honest Country man.

But see below, p. 115, the passage from Cowley's "Of Obscurity," where this detail is also found.

of his grotto: *Secretum iter et fallentis semita vitae*—a line eminently calculated to remind Pope of his father and of his own (occasional) desires for himself. The essay then proceeds rapidly to words of counsel that it is easy to suppose were tumbling in Pope's brain when he reached the important realization that his poem must begin from a position of invaded privacy.

If we engage into a large Acquaintance and various familiarities, we set open our gates to the Invaders of most of our time: we expose our life to a *Quotidian Ague* of frigid impertinencies, which would make a wise man tremble to think of.

Not only the invasion but the disease image is here, crying out to be elaborated.
    The sentence just quoted leads immediately to further counsel about staying out of the world's view:

> (I sought no homage from the Race that write;
> I kept, like *Asian* Monarchs, from their sight ...)

and about avoiding all fame but that of virtue:

> (Curst be the Verse, how well soe'er it flow,
> That tends to make one worthy Man my foe. ...)

Then comes the most striking resemblance of all: Cowley's prose sketch of the stock retirement figure, in which it would certainly have been hard for Pope *not* to recognize his father, and again, one aspect of himself:

Upon the whole matter, I account a person who has a moderate Minde and Fortune, and lives in the conversation of two or three agreeable friends, with little commerce in the world besides, who is esteemed well enough by his few neighbours that know him, and is truly irreproachable by any body, and so after a healthful quiet life, before the great inconveniences of old age, goes more silently out of it then he came in, (for I would not have him so much as Cry in the *Exit*)—This Innocent Deceiver of the world, as *Horace* calls him, this *Muta persona*, I take to have been more happy in his Part, then the greatest Actors that fill the Stage with show and noise. ...

The essay continues with the chorus from *Thyestes*.
    Perhaps a stricter relevance than we had thought lies behind the tribute Pope paid, less than three years after the *Epistle to Dr. Arbuthnot*, in the *Epistle to Augustus* (75–78):

> Who now reads Cowley? if he pleases yet,
> His moral pleases, not his pointed wit;
> Forgot his Epic, nay Pindaric Art,
> But still I love the language of his Heart.

Chapter 4

Galling the Horsemen

How safe, methinks, and strong, behind
These Trees have I incamp'd my Mind;
Where Beauty, aiming at the Heart,
Bends in some Tree its useless Dart;
And where the World no certain Shot
Can make, or me it toucheth not.
But I on it securely play,
And gaul its Horsemen all the Day.

—Marvell, *Upon Appleton House*

I

In the same body of poems in which the little "squire" of Twickenham, as he was beginning in the 30's to be called, nourished the self-image of retired leisure that we have been considering, he also mounted, as everyone knows, a satirical campaign of some intensity against the court of George Augustus and the ministry of Robert Walpole. We must look into that campaign at this point, for it represents the other boundary of our theme—the pursuit of politics from the vantage of retirement. The supporting evidence is necessarily bulky, and I have therefore placed it for the most part in the notes, which the reader who has no special interest in the political journalism of the period will be well advised to sample with restraint.[1] I must also ask the reader to bear in mind that the political

---

1/For invaluable hints on the intrigues of the 1730's, political and otherwise, I want to express my thanks to Mrs. Lois Morrison, whose forthcoming work on Eustace Budgell seems certain to light up some exceptionally dark corners.

dimension I seek to delineate in Pope's later work exists side by side, and in the same poems, with the retirement attitudes which we have just examined. I have separated the two elements in writing about them here so that each may be seen more clearly; but they are not separable in the poems, where they create a systole and diastole that I hope will become evident in the sixth chapter and the Epilogue.

We can only guess now at the influences and motives that initially led Pope to make politics a major poetic theme—presumably one aspect of what he was to describe in the *Epistle to Dr. Arbuthnot* (341) as stooping to truth and moralizing his song. They must, however, have been compelling to attract into the orbit of political warfare one whose "situation" (as Swift had summed it up in a letter of 1 June 1728 following two long visits to Twickenham [II 497]), "hath made all parties and interests indifferent to you, who can be under no concern about high and low-church, Whig and Tory, or who is first Minister." Swift might have added that as a known friend of prominent Jacobites like Atterbury, by this time openly serving the Pretender abroad, and as a defiant eulogist of discredited statesmen like Robert Harley, as well as the imminent target of a horde of Grub Street hacks now that the *Art of Sinking* and the first *Dunciad* had been published, Pope would be well advised to cling to his status of political detachment indefinitely.

Among the causes that may be supposed to have precipitated the change, two or three spring instantly to mind. First and foremost would be his admiration of Bolingbroke.[2] Chief theorist of the Opposition and one of the principal contributors to the *Craftsman*, Bolingbroke had vigorously initiated by 1727 the acrid polemicism against Walpole that would characterize the reign of George II; and, if the *Vision of Camilick*[3] is his, had established the stock image and allegory of the nature of Walpole's power which was to unfold in the imagination of poets and engravers, playwrights and ballad-makers, pamphleteers and magazine writers, in hundreds of mutations and adaptations, for the next fifteen years.[4]

2/Bolingbroke's political ideas, long dismissed as merely the expedient devices of a mind bent exclusively on power, are today, in some quarters, regarded with more respect. See Harvey C. Mansfield, Jr., *Statesmanship and Party Government: A Study of Burke and Bolingbroke* (University of Chicago Press, 1965); Jeffrey Hart, *Viscount Bolingbroke: Tory Humanist* (University of Toronto Press, 1965); Robert Shackleton, "Montesquieu, Bolingbroke, and the Separation of Powers," *French Studies* (Oxford) III (1949) 25–38; J. H. Burns, "Bolingbroke and the Concept of Constitutional Government," *Political Studies*, x (1962), 264–76.

3/Published in the *Craftsman*, 27 January 1727.

4/Both Bolingbroke and the *Craftsman* owed a good deal, however, to the example set by Philip Duke of Wharton's *The True Briton*, published between 3 June 1723 and 17 February 1724, just at the period of Bolingbroke's pardon and return to English politics.

34 To the Glory of the Rt Honble Sr Robert Walpole.
"F. Doumouchel Delin. P. Foudrinier Sculp." June (?) 1737

The Vision of Camilick, vaguely Oriental in its coloring like the "Visions" in the *Spectator*, tells a crude tale of a continuing Armageddon between the supporters of political freedom and the supporters of arbitrary sway, from which emerges in due course a "large *Roll* of Parchment," a "sacred Charter"—obviously the Magna Carta. This has the happy faculty of floating above the armies of freedom and bringing new inspiration to all who look up at it. As time passes, its celestial influence is able to reconcile even the hostile hosts themselves, with the result that (as an earlier Bolingbroke had put it in Shakespeare's *1 Henry IV*) they "now in mutual well-beseeming ranks March all one way."

At last the long contention ceas'd: I beheld both Armies unite and move together under the same divine influence. I saw one King twelve times bow down before the bright Phaenomenon, which from thence forward spread a light over the whole land, and descending nearer to the Earth, the beams of it grew so warm as it approach'd, that the hearts of the inhabitants leap'd for joy. The face of war was no more. The same Fields, which had so long been the scene of death and desolation, were now cover'd with golden harvests. The Hills were cloath'd with sheep; the Woods sung with gladness; Plenty laugh'd in the Valleys; Industry, Commerce, and Liberty danc'd hand in hand thro' the Cities.

While I was delighting myself with this amiable Prospect, the scene entirely chang'd; The fields and armies vanish'd, and I saw a large and magnificent Hall, resembling the great *Divan* or Council of the Nation: at the upper end of it, under a canopy, I beheld the *Sacred Covenant*, shining as the Sun. ... In the midst ... enter'd a man ... with a purse of gold in his hand. He threw himself forward into the room, in a bluff, ruffianly manner. A Smile, or rather a Snear, sat on his countenance. His Face was bronz'd over with a glare of Confidence. An arch malignity leer'd in his eye. Nothing was so extraordinary as the effect of this person's appearance. They no sooner saw him, but they all turn'd their faces from the Canopy, and fell prostrate before him. He trod over their backs, without any ceremony, and march'd directly up to the Throne. He open'd his Purse of Gold, which he took out in Handfuls, and scattered amongst the Assembly. While the greater Part were ingaged in scrambling for these Pieces, He seiz'd, to my inexpressible surprise, without the least Fear, upon the sacred *Parchment* it self. He rumpled it rudely up, and cramm'd it into his pocket. Some of the people began to murmur. He threw more Gold, and they were pacified. No sooner was the *Parchment* taken away, but in an instant I saw half the august Assembly in Chains.[5]

5/It has not, I think, been sufficiently understood that the Opposition use of "gold" for Walpole's emblem was not merely the usual politician's attack upon corruption in the other

Though flat as satire, *The Vision of Camilick* anticipated a great deal that was to come. Numberless other "Visions," including that of Vice Triumphant in Pope's first dialogue of *One Thousand Seven Hundred and Thirty Eight*, and that of the "Wizard old," in *Dunciad* IV, whose "Cup," more powerful than Circe's, "takes away the mind, and leaves the human shape" (528n.) would spring in future from the same motifs. From them Gay would build in the *Beggar's Opera* and *Polly* his comic-opera versions of a society for sale or sold, and Thomson, Mallet, and Brooke their stereotypes of Wicked Ministers in *Edward and Eleonora, Mustapha*, and *Gustavus Vasa*.[6] Generations of balladeers would also ring the changes on them—for example, in pieces of advice like the following, which a ballad called *The Chelsea Monarch* (after Walpole's town house in Chelsea) puts into the mouth of the Great Man himself:

> D'ye Lustre affect, d'ye wish to be Great,
> Have ye fix'd your Desire, on a Post or a Wife;
> Would ye shine in the Church, would ye rise in the State,
> Make Money the End, and the Aim of your Life.
> > Be it all your Design,
> > To grasp at the Coin,

---

party, and not merely the traditional moralist's attack on the effects of luxury and greed, though both these motives were present. It represented too a more specific alarm at what was felt by many in the opposition to be a new and highly dangerous phenomenon—a growing group of "moneyed men," who derived their wealth not from land but from investment in the stocks of the great trading companies or in the Bank of England and the national debt. In one way of looking at the situation, the government could be understood to draw its revenues from the landed class by the land tax and to pay them out again in tax-free interest on the national debt to the moneyed class.

6/In *Gustavus Vasa* (1739) Trollio, minister to the usurper Cristiern; in *Mustapha* (1740), Rustan, accomplice of a strong queen in turning a weak king against his son. In *Edward and Eleonora* (1739), there is no single wicked minister, but Prince Edward, in Palestine on a Crusade, is advised to hurry home to save his father "from his Ministers, from those Who hold him captive in the worst of Chains." Subsequently, Edward is informed by dispatches that his father is dead and bursts out (p. 50) with a lament amazingly prophetic of one mouthed piously by Opposition circles in Thomson's own time:

> O my deluded Father! Little Joy
> Had'st thou in Life, led from thy real Good
> And genuine Glory, from thy People's Love,
> That noblest Aim of Kings, by smiling Traitors.
> Is there a Curse on human Kind so fell,
> So pestilent, at once, to Prince and People,
> As the base servile Vermin of a Court,
> Corrupt, corrupting Ministers and Favourites?

> For the want then of Nothing, you need to repine;
> As I told you at first, it is Gold that's held dear,
> And whate'er Rules elsewhere—it is Gold that Rules HERE.[7]

If the author of *The Vision of Camilick* was in fact Bolingbroke, there is a striking propriety in the circumstance that it was also he who was Pope's closest confidant during the composition of the epistles to Burlington and Bathurst, and who, picking up a volume of Horace from the poet's table in early 1733, set him upon the *Imitations of Horace*.[8]

II

A second impulse that drew Pope toward increasing political involvement may have been (by 1731–32) his own personal feelings about the Walpole government and the court of George II. His strong sympathies with Harley, Swift, Atterbury, Bolingbroke, and Mrs. Howard, were bound to prevent his personal intercourse with the Minister from amounting to more than a wary armed truce, however warmly it may have been forwarded by Fortescue and for a time in the late 20's supported by affabilities on both sides.[1] By 1730, at the latest 1731, these meetings had ceased, for reasons nowhere clarified in the correspondence but perhaps not hard to surmise. Walpole, we are told by his latest biographer, had early tired of Pope and "the Twickenham set": "They were too complicated, their wit was too acid, their loyalty too suspect."[2] Even more suspect, of course, was their attachment to the chief minister and to his conceptions of a healthy political state. Partly it was the old case of fire and water. A hard-bitten realist and pragmatist, without a shred of either wishful thinking or idealism in his make-up, preoccupied on every hand with the fear, greed, and general cussedness of human beings in political situations and reveling in his mastery of their motives, Walpole did not have it in his nature to acknowledge any City

---

7/See Percival, 50–53. The ballad was published in May, 1731, and with similar attacks was brought before a Grand Jury in July.

8/Spence, nos. 321, 321*a*.

1/Pope seems to have met Walpole through Fortescue, and with Fortescue, or more rarely alone, attended occasionally at Walpole's Sunday dinners in the late 1720's (Correspondence, II 276, 294, 323, 368, 441, 530; III 11, 53, 85, 91n, 112n, 113, 139). The available evidence does not seem to me to support J. H. Plumb's statement that he was "most assiduous" in his attendance (II 175).

2/Plumb, *ibid*. To this must be added what Plumb says on an earlier page (131)—that "Walpole never relished intellectual society."

more abiding than the one whose merchants were always at him to declare war on France or Spain; or to entertain any architectural intentions for "England's green and pleasant land" beyond that of completing Houghton. Most poets—at least when their singing-robes are on—have other views. Walpole assumed, no doubt, that they could all be had for a price. But as he was never willing to test his theory—in fact, went out of his way to offend them all by the absurdity of his offer to Gay[3]—no one will ever know the truth of the matter. Suffice it to say that by his position as outsider, for whatever reasons cherished, Pope gained a moral purchase on public opinion without which his later work is unimaginable.

There were more immediate vexations too. Though we lack evidence on the point, it is probably safe to guess that Walpole was furious when he discovered, presumably after the fact, that Mr. Pope's *Dunciad Variorum*, which he had been serviceable enough to present officially to the King and Queen on 12 March 1729, contained in its very first lines one reference which could be read as a slur on George II as well as George I,[4] together with praise of Swift for his dissection of the English Court in *Gulliver* and his victory over the same Court in the matter of Wood's halfpence.[5] Elsewhere in the poem, Walpole would be told, further anti-government innuendoes were scattered—equally infuriating because no one could "resent" them without acknowledging, and thus in a sense (so the poet's defenders might argue) creating them. Was it a coincidence, for example, that among the writers pilloried in that poem as Mr. Pope's enemies so many were his own government employees?

Two years later, in December 1731, when the *Epistle to Burlington* was published, a similar question had to be asked—if not by Walpole himself, at least by those in his entourage who kept track of such matters. With its powerful ridicule of ostentation and prodigality, climaxing in a character whose very name ("Timon") seemed calculated to suggest a politician of great wealth fated to lose it and with it his former "friends"—at whom was this aimed?[6] True, there were several touches in the description of Timon's estate not to be found at Houghton, though some—the absence of water, for instance—were widely

---

3/Of the post of Gentleman-Usher to the two-year-old Princess Louisa, which Gay had dignity enough to refuse. See Pope to Gay, 16 October 1727 (II 453–54).

4/"Still Dunce the second reigns like Dunce the First" (I 6).

5/See I 21–22 and Pope's note.

6/Professor Kathleen Mahaffey has argued, in my view rightly, that Timon and his villa were calculated to suggest Walpole and Houghton, at least to contemporaries capable of reading between the lines ("Timon's Villa: Walpole's Houghton," *Texas Studies in Literature and Language*, IX (1967), 193–222). I add some further details to the argument in Appendix F.

That Pope calls Timon's vast dwelling a "villa" is part of the joke: see below, p. 208.

known and came close home.[7] True also, that only a very few would catch an allusion to the King's minister (was any intended?) in "the wealthy fool" cited earlier in the poem—

> Heav'n visits with a Taste the wealthy fool,
> And needs no rod but Ripley with a Rule—   (17–18)

since very few would know that Houghton, planned by Colin Campbell, and later Kent, had actually been built by Thomas Ripley—who, in any case, had built for others too. Was this earlier allusion, if it were such, a guarantee that the later portrait was *not* the King's minister? or was it meant to alert readers to the identity of the portrait, as a small charge fuses a great one? And what exactly did this recent letter in the *Post-Boy* (22 December) imply—purporting to come from one of Mr. Pope's friends,[8] but without doubt written by himself—which in denying that "Timon" was aimed at the Duke of Chandos carefully stopped short of denying that it was in some way personal, and concluded: "I know no good Man who would be more concerned, if he gave the least Pain or Offense to another; *and none who would be less concerned, if the Satire were challenged by any one at whom he would really aim it. If ever that happens, I dare engage he will own it, with all the Freedom of a Man whose Censures are just, and who sets his Name to them.*"[9] Could this by any chance be a challenge by a ridiculous little hunchback to the mightiest officer in the land?

III

From Pope's point of view during these years, the evidence suggests that there were like irritations. He can hardly have helped asking himself how much of the outcry against the *Epistle to Burlington*, accusing its author of the basest ingratitude to Chandos, was the inspired work of Walpole's hirelings. Leonard Welsted, whom Pope believed to be one of the chief instruments of the indictment,[1] and

---

7/See the article cited in the preceding note and the imprecations uttered in the *Vision of Camilick* against every destroyer of English liberties, with special reference to Walpole: "Let that man be cut off from the earth ... let his palaces be destroy'd; let his gardens be as a desart, having no water," and so on.

8/In the editions of Pope's letters from 1737 on, it is attributed to William Cleland.

9/*Correspondence*, III 256–57. Italics mine.

1/See the *Epistle to Dr. Arbuthnot*, 375n (TE, IV 123), where Pope says of Welsted: "This Man had the Impudence to tell in print, that Mr. *P.* had occasion'd a *Lady's death*. ... He also publish'd that he had libell'd the Duke of *Chandos*; with whom (it was added) that he had liv'd in familiarity, and receiv'd from him a Present of *five hundred pounds*." Welsted, besides

John Henley, earliest of its promulgators (in *The Hyp-Doctor*, 22 December),
were on the government payroll,[2] and the list of those whom the poet names in
his *Master Key to Popery*[3] as purveyors of the lie that "Timon" was Chandos
includes also Concanen, Cibber, and Sir William Yonge, all creatures of Walpole,
and Hervey, Dodington, and Lady Delorain, all courtly gossips who could be
counted on to take the administration line. Though the *Master Key* itself remained unpublished, the poet had perhaps already hinted at the nature of his
suspicions in the *Post-Boy* letter. "No wonder those who know Ridicule belongs
to them, find an inward Consolation in removing it from themselves as far as they
can; and it is never so far, as when they can get it fixt on the *best Characters*."[4]
For those of Pope's readers who had been nourished for some years on the oblique
style of the *Craftsman*, the allusion here may have been plain—as plain as such
allusions dared to be at a time when they could cause an offending work along
with its author to be seized and brought before a grand jury. Who else but
Walpole with his army of paid writers and court minions would be represented as
capable of "removing" a satire from himself and fixing it on another? Who else

---

earlier attacks, had published in 1732 *Of Dulness and Scandal. Occasioned by the Character
of Lord Timon, in Mr. Pope's Epistle to the Earl of Burlington* and *Of False Fame; an Epistle
to the Right Honourable the Earl of Pembroke*—both savage denunciations of Pope, though
neither refers specifically to Chandos or Pope's ingratitude to him. It seems clear that in his
note Pope intends a distinction between "tell in print" and "publish'd," using the latter term
in the sense of make public or disseminate. For a detailed account of his relations with Welsted
throughout his career (though one that is somewhat marred by a fictionalizing style of presentation), see D. A. Fineman, *Leonard Welsted: Gentleman Poet of the Augustan Age* (1950),
esp. ch. vii.

2/Welsted was clerk in the office of the Secretary of State, then in the Ordinance office, and
also "one of the commissioners for managing the State-lottery." (See TE, IV 393 and Welsted's
Works, ed. John Nichols (1787), pp. xi–xii). Henley seems to have served Walpole in various
ways, among them by his writings in the *Hyp-Doctor*. See *Dunciad* (1743), III 199n (TE, V
444); and *Craftsman*, 25 September 1731, where Walpole is represented as saying: "I think,
Doctor *Hyp*, you are the only Gentleman in this Assembly, who hath any Reason to complain of
Neglect; but I am sensible of your Services and will reward them. ... I will put you upon my
list of *private Pensioners*. ..."

3/Printed for the first time by John Butt in Clifford-Landa, pp. 41–57; reprinted in TE, III
ii, Appendix c.

4/*Correspondence*, III 255–56. If Walpole did in fact suspect that the objectives of the
Timon portrait included Houghton and himself, his public response shrewdly took the form
proposed by Molière's Uranie: "Pour moi, je me garderai bien de m'en offenser et de prendre
rien sur mon compte de tout ce qui s'y dit. Ces sortes de satires tombent directement sur les
mœurs, et ne frappent les personnes que par réflexion. Toutes les peintures ridicules ... sont
miroirs publics, ou il ne faut jamais témoigner qu'on se voie." (*La Critique de L'Ecole des
Femmes*, scene vi).

could easily be recognized (in the right quarters) as an ultimate "worst," between whom and "the *best Characters*" the distance was absolute—"never so far"?

Two months later, when Welsted's *Of False Fame* appeared, containing this description of the author of "Timon":

> Unmark'd at first! necessitous and scorn'd!
> No Patron own'd him, and no Bays adorn'd:
> One Critic's Pupil, with one Bard he vy'd;
> And knew not to be "sick with civil Pride."
> A hungry Scribbler, and without a Name,
> Till Fraud procur'd him Wealth, and Falshood Fame!
> That Wealth obtain'd, Faith, Friendship he disclaims;
> Sneers, where he fawn'd, and where he prais'd, defames—[5]

the same readers may have concluded that Pope's point had been taken. Taken, deflected, and turned back upon him. For the quoted words in line 4 could refer to nothing but his own lines in "Timon":

> Treated, caress'd, and tir'd, I take my leave,
> Sick of his civil Pride from Morn to Eve;
> I curse such lavish cost, and little skill,
> And swear no Day was ever pass'd so ill.   (165–68)

But to what did Welsted's other allusions, those about the poet's conduct after gaining fame and fortune, refer? Was it not remarkable that in verses so clearly inspired by the *Epistle to Burlington* and the portrait of "Timon," the alleged identity of the victim and even of the offense should remain so shadowy? Could

---

5/*Of False Fame*, 171–78. A note on verse 3 indicates that "one critic" is Henry Cromwell (with whom Pope had discussed critical problems in a correspondence published by Curll in 1726) and that "one Bard" is Charles Gildon.

The following lines give a fairer sample of Welsted's tone:

> No Virtue leaves unwrong'd, or Vice untry'd;
> No Fame not scarr'd, no Genius not decry'd:
> In Scandal curious, busy still to pry;
> Ill-natur'd, servile, scraping, weak, and sly!
> When most provok'd, a patient fearful Muse!
> When most oblig'd, most ardent to abuse!
> The Rage of Envy, and the Reek of Spite,
> Spleen swell'd with Grief, and Dulness wrap'd in Night,
> His Head to Jargon, Heart to Guilt, incline:
> And the next Libel, Pembroke, may be thine.

this perhaps be part of the intention?[6] Did Welsted design to imply, on behalf of the first minister, that there had been ingratitude but not to Chandos? Could the lines have been a way of showing the little hunchback who was master? For if Pope *had* meant Timon to remind his readers of Walpole, the tables had been turned on him no less dramatically than they were often turned in parliament on the Opposition, and he had been tarred with a charge that would not be removed from him for two centuries.[7]

IV

All such undercurrents, if they were real, and such skirmishes, if they actually occurred, were to be added, certainly on Pope's side and probably on Walpole's, to a wider history of distaste. By 1731 or thereabouts, whatever resentments Pope may have harbored toward Walpole for hounding Robert Harley to the Tower, preventing Bolingbroke's re-establishment in the Lords, immobilizing Swift in an Irish deanery, exploiting Atterbury's correspondence to raise the cry of treason against the Tories, insulting Gay, banning Gay's *Polly*, dismissing the Duchess of Queensbury from Court, appointing Cibber to the laureateship, and so on, were assimilable to a far more general anxiety about the moral effect of Walpole's rule. A situation had been reached that for more than a decade was to make it as hard for English poets *not* to satirize, or at least criticize, the regime, as we are assured it was for Juvenal in Rome.

One man—Pope's friends in the Opposition were never weary of pointing

---

6/Miss Mahaffey (p. 221) suggests that Chandos's instruction to Anthony Hammond (on 1 January 1732) to ask Welsted to "forbear printing any thing on my behalf, that may tend to ye prejudice of a Person [i.e., Pope], who from what he has wrote, I ought to beleive [*sic*] neither hath nor had any ill will towards me," may have taken effect in time to prompt Welsted to dissociate the attack in *Of Dulness and Scandal*, published two days later, from Chandos's name. This is possible, but in view of eighteenth-century printing house practices, not very likely. Certainly he did not abstain from anything that might "tend to ye prejudice" of Pope! The following lines are typical:

> A LITTLE Monk thou wert by Nature made!
> Wert fashion'd for the *Jesuit*'s Gossip Trade!
> A lean Church-Pander, to procure, or lie!
> A Pimp at Altars, or in Courts a Spy!

7/Whether Pope's mockery in the Timon portrait was general or particular in intent, it seems improbable that any of it was aimed at Chandos. The evidence is carefully weighed in George Sherburn's " 'Timon's Villa' and Cannons" (*Huntington Library Bulletin*, VIII, 1935); in C. H. Collins Baker and Muriel Baker's *The Life and Circumstances of James Brydges, First Duke of Chandos* (Clarendon Press, 1949), *passim*, but esp. pp. 432–33; and in TE, III ii.

out, and with some truth—now bestrode the nation like a Colossus. Walpole's sagacity and cunning, his solid statesmanship and his system of briberies, his real amiability but absolute ruthlessness when threatened, had combined with the growing wealth and world importance of the country he governed to make him custodian of a power greater than the favorite[1] of any earlier British monarch had ever dreamed of wielding. His "pensioners" filled both houses of parliament and all government posts. His spies abroad, some placed to thwart the Jacobites, sat in all the capitals of Europe and dozens of lesser cities; other spies, informants, gazetteers sat at home, and Nicholas Paxton, organizer and paymaster of Walpole's newspaper campaigns, and evidently of his briberies in some elections, is reliably reported to have disposed during his term of office of £90,000[2]—a staggering sum for this kind of service in a budget of those days. "Preaching a rationalized scoundrelism, systematically deriding political decencies,"[3] he exercised an iron control of every nook and cranny of Church and State. Despite his virtues, therefore, which were many, he constituted increasingly as the years passed a threat to the quality of English life that no writer who aspired to speak for the vital moral concerns of his time could permanently ignore.

For ten years he had dominated the political life of the country, defeating intrigue, grinding down opposition, surviving all crises, growing ever stronger in the regard in which he was held by the King and Queen. Everywhere he was treated with God-like respect. Dukes, bishops, millionaires crowded his levées as suppliants. At Court he met the same servility. (Plumb, ii 245)

He became so used to his own greatness that he no longer bothered to adjust himself to circumstances. His sensibilities hardened. His language, always coarse, became brutal; his attitude to friends and foes franker, more unguarded. Flattery, no matter how gross, sweetened a vanity grown monstrous with a decade's sycophancy. The bright, gay, ever-laughing Robin Walpole of the Kit Cat had vanished in the vast,

---

1/In "The Walpoles: Father and Son" (*Studies in Social History* [London, 1955], p. 206), J. H. Plumb notes that in many ways Walpole was the last of the British royal favorites rather than the first of the British prime ministers. This, inevitably, was the light in which the Opposition saw him.

2/TE, IV 377. Coxe gives the figure as £95,000 (William Coxe, *Memoirs of the Life and Administration of Sir Robert Walpole* [London, 1800], iii 272–73). Paxton was officially Solicitor to the Treasury. From 1736 he was charged with reading "all printed pamphlets and newspapers" and bringing their contents to the attention of the Secretaries of State "when the King or Government are traduced and slandered (TE, IV 377)."

3/Romney Sedgwick, in his introduction to Hervey, I lix. See also L. I. Bredvold, "The Gloom of the Tory Satirists," in Clifford-Landa, pp. 11–14.

square-jowled hulk of a man who talked and acted as if power were his to eternity. (*Ibid.*, 249–50)

He grew impatient of criticism, regarded with hostility men of strong will who would not accept his yoke, bullied weaker characters with a coarseness and brutality that shocked. ... And, of course, he found it difficult to brook rivals; his career is littered with the broken careers of gifted men who crossed his path—Pulteney, Carteret, Townshend, Chesterfield, Cobham—and apart from Hardwicke, a man of massive moral integrity and great intelligence, and one or two others, he surrounded himself with faint replicas of himself or fools and flatterers. At least, by 1734 he had come to that and it is a measure of how power had hardened his character. (*Ibid.*, 330)

Not only was his power resented; and his royal favour loathed; his whole manner of life bred detestation wherever he went. He paraded his wealth with ever greater ostentation. He bought pictures at reckless prices, wallowed in the extravagance of Houghton, deluged his myriad guests with rare food and costly wine; his huge ungainly figure sparkled with diamonds and flashed with satin. And he gloried in his power, spoke roughly if not ungenerously of others, and let the whole world know that he was master. (*Ibid.*, 331)

So the stage was set. Here was a man in high place who was widely believed to represent all that was vicious in government. He was backed by a court which seemed to uphold all that was hostile to true cultivation. No writer having classical views of the function of his art, certainly no satirist, could avoid coming to terms sooner or later with such a man. It was simply a matter of time.

V

Whatever its motives, Pope's career in political satire began at a period when a remarkable instrument of satirical communication lay ready to his hand. This was the extensive vocabulary of disaffection minted by the writers of the *Craftsman* and kept bright by continual rubbing in the Opposition press generally, as well as, in some cases, the parliamentary debates themselves.[1] It was not simply that, as in all political communities, certain policies and alleged policies of the party in power had become grievances: standing armies, briberies, the size of the Secret Service funds, excessive forbearance by the government toward French and Spanish depredations on British shipping, the land tax, the excise scheme, the neglect of artists, the King's long visits to Hanover, and the like.

1/Some account of this may be found in Percival, xiv–xxvii, but it deserves a full length study, in conjunction especially with the work of Pope and his literary friends.

Apart from these general issues, dozens, even hundreds, of specific names and phrases had become charged with political implication and were capable of setting off long trains of association. Certain acts, attitudes, and gestures had been so often publicly appropriated to one or other of the principal actors in what a mock playbill of 1735 called "Robin's great Theatrical Booth, in Palace Yard"[2] that no one could remain in doubt for whom the reference was meant. Allusions to a woman who ruled her husband, loathed her heir, entertained too much affection for a royal favorite,[3] or indulged herself in theological hetero-doxies were almost certain to intend the Queen.[4] Allusions to a man ruled by

2/Egmont II 145:
At the Ball or masquerade in the Haymarket Tuesday was sennit [sennight] there was an incident that has made a good deal of noise. After the King had been there some time (for whose pleasure these masquerades were first set up, and have been hitherto continued during the winter) there came in a Harlequin and Punchinello, followed by divers others in different dresses, with bundles of printed play bills in their hands, one of which Harlequin gave the King, and then all throwing down their papers disappeared. The King read the bill, which was as follows:
"By permission,
        This is to give notice to all gentlemen and ladies and others that at the Opera House in the Haymarket this present evening will be presented
                        The Comical and diverting humours of Punch,
And on Thursday next by the Norfolk Company of Artificial Comedians, at Robin's great Theatrical Booth, in Palace Yard, will be presented a comical diverting Play of Seven Acts, called
                                Court and Country,
        In which will be revived the Entertaining Scene of
                        The Blundering Brothers,
        with the Cheats of Rabbi Robin, Prime Minister to
                                King Solomon.
The whole concluding with a Grand Masque called the Downfall of Sejanus, or the Statesman's Overthrow, with Axes, Halters, Gibbets, and other decorations proper to the Play.
                        To begin exactly at 12 o'clock.
        N.B.—These are a new set of Poppets as big as the life, chief part of which have been brought up from all parts of the country at a very great expense."
Those who know the times know the satire of this.
3/Walpole was sometimes called Aegisthus, with of course the implication that Queen Caroline was misbehaving like Clytemnestra while George-Agamemnon was overseas in Hanover also misbehaving. Pope alludes to this as a cry of the times in the first dialogue of *One Thousand Seven Hundred and Thirty-Eight*, 137 (TE, IV 51, textual note). Thomson's *Agamemnon* (1738) allegorizes the close political partnership of the Queen and Walpole in much the same terms.
4/Pope touches on each of these at one time or other. See *Epistle to Burlington*, 78; *Imit. Donne*, IV 89, 132–33; *Epistle to Dr. Arbuthnot*, 72, 76; *Epistle to a Lady*, 181 ff.; *One Thousand Seven Hundred and Thirty-Eight*, Dialogue I, 80–82.

Tanta hæ Mulier *potuit Suadere* Malorum

35 Aeneas in a Storm. Artist and engraver unknown.
January (?) 1737

his wife, or to a savage temper which could only be relieved by kicking somebody or something,[5] or to a strutting love of military show, or to a hereditary "glare" of stupidity, or to royal avarice, or to a "rump" or back firmly turned on persons disapproved,[6] or to a halting command of English and a detestation for every form of learning,[7] were certain to intend the King, especially if accompanied by

5/See below, pp. 138 and 199. Also, the satirical engraving of 1737 (Plate 35) entitled *Aeneas in a Storm*, where cherubs engage in actions imitative of the King, one of them kicking at a hat. (Stephens, no. 2326. See also Stephens, no. 2451, where the king's right foot is labeled "The k[ic]k[in]g Foot".)

6/There was a Rump Steak Club, whose membership consisted of twenty-seven Whig peers on whom the King had at one time or other vehemently turned his backside. (A. S. Foord, *His Majesty's Opposition, 1714–1830*, Oxford University Press, 1964, p. 127.) See also *The Festival of the Golden Rump*, below, pp. 138–47.

7/"The King used often to brag of the contempt he had for books and letters; to say how much he hated all that stuff from his infancy; and that he remembered when he was a child

allusions to King Solomon.[8] But by far the longest list of paraphrases applied to Walpole. His success in buying supporters and keeping himself in power caused him to be variously denominated magician, gamester, quack doctor, puppeteer, and stage-manager.[9] His long record of screening peculators and embezzlers from parliamentary enquiries had early won him the title of "Screen" or "Skreen-master general."[10] His broad florid countenance, said to be incapable of a blush,

---

he did not hate reading and learning merely as other children do upon account of the confinement, but because he despised it and felt as if he was doing something mean and below him" (Hervey, p. 261).

8/Pope glances rather frequently at most of these alleged attributes of the King: at Queen Caroline's management of him, in *Imit. Donne*, IV 132–33, and elsewhere; possibly at his temper, in *Imit. Donne*, II 62, and *Imit. Hor., Ep.* I i 61–64; at his love of military show, *ibid., Sat.* II i 23–6; possibly at his "glare," in *Imit. Donne*, IV 210–11; at his avarice, in *One Thousand Seven Hundred and Thirty-Eight, Dialogue* i 110, and elsewhere; at his English, in *Imit. Donne*, IV 68 and *Imit. Hor., Ep.* II i 206 ff.; at his lack of interest in learning, in the latter, *passim*. Also in the latter (29–30), Pope's allusion to I Kings, III 12, compares George mockingly with Solomon.

9/Walpole is gamester in *Robin's Game; or Sevens the Main* (1731), whose printer was taken into custody; puppeteer—"the Master behind the Scenes"—in *Craftsman*, IV 184 (29 March 1729), and see Egmont, above, p. 129, n. 2; magician in *Craftsman*, II 219 ff. (2 December 1727) and see below, p. 144; stage-manager in a variety of documents cited below, pp. 158–62; quack doctor in Stephens, no. 1931, which is possibly the print advertised in the *Gentleman's Magazine* (August, 1737) as "The Quack Triumphant: Or, the N[o]r[wi]ch Cavalcade"; Punchinello and puppeteer in the verses accompanying Stephens, no. 2540:

> Behind the SCREEN there stands a Wight,
> Safely conceal'd from publick Sight:
> He was the *Punch* at first you saw;
> He gives the other Puppets Law.
> And by his secret Strings he still
> Governs the others as he will.

See Index under "Walpole" for list of pseudonyms applied to him.

10/On the name, see Plumb, I 342. Hervey notes with reference to the South Sea affair (I 186–87) that Walpole opposed on principle all parliamentary inquiries:

He pursued this maxim from a fear of making this retrospective manner of inquiry, by the frequency of it, so familiar to Parliament, that one time or other it might, in any reverse of fortune and by the rage of party, affect himself, his family, and posterity; but by too strict an adherence to this principle he was often smeared with the filth of other people, and gave his enemies occasion to say that whoever had a mind to plunder the public or defraud particulars, they had but to keep out of the reach of the slow, uncertain hands of Westminster Hall, and let the notoriety of their crimes be never so manifest or the nature of them never so enormous, they would be secure of protection in Parliament whilst Sir Robert Walpole had any power there. His conduct in the affair of the Charitable Corporation, his opposition to a Bill for vacating the fraudulent sale of Lord Derwentwater's estate (by which the trustees for the sale of forfeited estates had cheated the public of an immense sum and by acting in flat contradiction to an Act of Parliament), his doing all he could to prevent the Parliament taking cognizance of the

invited allusions to brass and brazen.[11] His tendency to raucous laughter at appeals to honesty or religious scruple;[12] his appetite for perquisites and his childlike vanity in his Garter star and ribbon, so extreme that he had these decorations painted into portraits he had sat for before receiving them (Plumb,

---

frauds committed by the Directors of the York Buildings Company; and his having actually put a stop to this inquiry into the South Sea affairs in the House of Commons, had given but too just grounds for these reflections to be thrown out against him, and left his friends too little room to justify him when his adversaries represented him as the universal encourager of corruption and the sanctuary of the corrupt.   See also II 364–65:

He knew, whatever happened, he could be nothing greater than what he was; and, in order to remain in that situation, his great maxim in policy was to keep everything else as undisturbed as he could, to bear with some abuses rather than risk reformations, and submit to old inconveniences rather than encourage innovations. From these maxims, which in my opinion he sometimes carried too far, he would never lend his assistance nor give the least encouragement to any emendation either of the law or the church, though the expenses and hardships of the first, and the tyranny and injustice of the last in the ecclesiastical courts, were got to an excess wholly unjustifiable and almost insupportable. From this way of reasoning he opposed the inquiry into the South Sea affair, the bill to vacate the infamous sale of Lord Derwentwater's estate, the examination of the House of Commons into the affairs of the charitable corporations and the abuses in the gaols, besides many other crying instances of flagrant injustice and oppression, which he could not defend, and yet declined to correct by any extraordinary method, though, in the ordinary courts of justice, he and all the world knew it was impossible to come at the offenders, put any stop to the offences, or give any redress to the injured.

Screens became a common emblem of Walpole's career in contemporary satirical engravings (e.g. Stephens, nos. 2539, 2540, 2559) and pamphlet poems and plays: e.g. *The Honest Electors* (1733), where Walpole is "Sir Positive Screenall," and *The City Triumphant: Or, the Burning of the Excise Monster* (1733), p. 4.

11/Egmont, 19: "Pulteney replied he knew nothing was the brighter for rubbing but pewter and brass, alluding to Sir Robert's nickname of 'Brazen Face,'—ribaldry unfit for the House." See also II 165: "As he came out of his Majesty's closet he met Sir Robert going in, who, stopping him, expressed his surprise that he had not carried his election, asked him how it was possible, and declared nothing had surprised and vexed him more. Mr. Freeman replied, 'Don't ask me how I lost it, you know that better than I,' at which Sir Robert blushed up to his eyes, which, said Mr. Freeman, is the only time I ever saw him blush."
For other typical allusions, see *The N[o]r[fol]k Game of Cribbidge* (Percival, no. 33): "For he was to *Blushing* a Stranger, 'tis known"; *Craftsman*, 17 February 1728 (speaking of the *Beggar's Opera*): "Captain *Macheath*, who hath also a *goodly Presence* and hath a tolerable *Bronze* upon his Face, is designed for the *principal Character* and drawn to asperse *Somebody in Authority*"; and *Sir Robert Brass: or, the Intriegues, Serious and Amorous, of the Knight of the Blazing Star* (1731); 38–39.

> His *Skin* of yellow Damask Hue,
> Looks much the worst, when drest in Blue.

12/Pope refers to this in *One Thousand Seven Hundred and Thirty-Eight*, Dial. II 38: "A Horse-laugh, if you please, at *Honesty*." See also *The History of the Norfolk Steward* (1728), reprinted in *Craftsman*, III 316: "... he broke into a loud Laugh, and told the Tenants they knew nothing of Accounts. ..."

Come let us take our Fill of Love untill the Morning let us Solace our selves
with Love; For the Good Man is not at Home. He is gone a Long Journey,
He hath taken a Bag of Money with him & will come home at the Day appointed.
Queen Caroline died, Dec. 1737 Proverbs 7. 18. 19. 20. 19 Jul. 1738
Published according to Act of Parliment Dec. 19 1738

36 Solomon in his Glory. Artist and engraver
unknown. Dated 19 December 1738

II 101); his immense sensitivity to criticism[13]—all these attributes too, along
with the name of every corrupt favorite and vicegerent in English and Roman
history: Gaveston, Dudley, Wolsey, Villiers, Sejanus, Clodius, Verres[14] (not
to mention an assortment of tyrants and would-be tyrants, including especially
the man who according to Livy was prevented from becoming a tyrant only by
Cassius and Brutus, last of the patriots, *ultimi Romanorum*),[15] attached them-

13/Cf. J. H. Plumb, *The First Four Georges* (London, 1956), p. 27; *The Norfolk Sting:
or, The History and Fall of Evil Ministers* (1732), pp. 34–35.

14/For examples, see *Craftsman*, IX 132 ff. (Gaveston), III 6 ff. (Dudley), III 4, 49–50, 54,
97–99 (Wolsey), IV 191–194 (Villiers), III 137–39, 200 (Sejanus), VIII 23 ff. (Verres). Even
Pericles, who is reproached for having subverted Athenian liberties and screened corruption,
is brought into the picture as surrogate for Walpole (IX 240–52).

15/See Addison Ward, "The Tory View of Roman History," *Studies in English Literature*,
IV (1964), 425; *Craftsman*, VIII 97.

selves to Walpole's public image and made up increasingly, after the founding of the *Craftsman* in 1726–27, the daily fare of the Opposition press.

The consequence for satire was the formation of an argot whose variations were inexhaustible. Quite opposite in purpose to the "unison" that Pope imagined flowing in the ideal State from "Order, Union, full Consent of things,"[16] it had like that an interior coherence which made it possible in touching one string to strike another too, or even to set them all vibrating without, apparently, touching any. This effect could be managed by means of the extraordinary range of equivalences which the argot made possible, on one small group of which, for example (Walpole as highwayman and thief, borrowed partly from Shakespeare's Henry IV plays) Gay founded his *Beggar's Opera*. Or it could be managed by allusions whose range of implication was more or less indefinitely expansible according as the reader's knowledge and inclination allowed him to understand it, or, possibly in some instances, invent it. When Pope, using Bolingbroke in the *Essay on Man* as a representative of "Parts superior," rounds off his assessment of their value—

> Painful preheminence! yourself to view
> Above life's weakness, and its comforts too—   (IV 267–68)

the lines touch shrewdly (in their association of eminence with pain instead of gratification and of weakness with comfort instead of shame) on a loneliness in genius which we can all at least imagine and on a comfort in mediocrity with which most of us are personally acquainted: they need, in short, no dimension of meaning beyond the one they clearly have, especially at this point in the development of a poem whose patterns are abstract. Yet by contemporary readers who came to them suitably informed, the identity of "Painful preheminence" with an exclamation by Cato (in the tragedy by Addison) at a critical moment in his defense of Roman liberties against tyranny[17] could be interpreted as according Bolingbroke a similar role in the defence of English liberties. The ever-present equivalence of Roman history and British would allow these same readers to see Bolingbroke in the "Marcellus exil'd" of a few lines earlier, and Walpole in the accompanying "Caesar":

16/*Essay on Man*, III 296.
17/III v 21–23: "Am I distinguished from you but by toils,
              Superior toils, and heavier weight of cares!
              Painful pre-eminence!"

> And more true joy Marcellus exil'd feels,
> Than Caesar with a Senate at his heels.   (IV 257–58)[18]

Would such readers have also seen a reference to Walpole in an earlier couplet about titles and decorations?

> Stuck o'er with titles, and hung round with strings,
> That thou may'st be by kings, or whores of kings?   (IV 205–6)[19]

If they did so, would they have decided that its phrasing was calculated to remind them of the popular jest about Walpole's own decorations: that to those of the Bath and the Garter should be speedily added a hempen third?

> Sir Robert, his Interest and Merit to shew,
> Laid down the Red Ribbon, and put on the Blue;
> To Two Strings already this Knight is preferr'd,
> Odd Numbers are lucky, we wait for a Third.   (Percival, p. 1)

Questions like these raise, of course, the problem of innuendo, which feeds like jealousy upon itself. Walpole had made it clear that criticism of himself or his administration, if sufficiently explicit (such as *The Vision of Camilick* or Gay's *Polly*), would be suppressed and if possible punished. The Opposition answer was to refine yet further the elaborate system of equivalences and apparent insinuations whose intended character in any given context was, as we have just seen, highly problematical.[20] When the government writers retaliated by searching out insidious applications from under every plausible surface and shaping them to look like disloyalties to the throne rather than criticisms of the ministry, innuendo for both readers and writers throve. As almost any political referent

---

18/In the Morgan MS., a version of this line reads "W- - - -" for "Caesar." See *Alexander Pope: An Essay on Man. Reproductions of the Manuscripts in the Pierpont Morgan Library and the Houghton Library with the Printed Text of the Original Edition* (Oxford: Printed for Presentation to the Members of the Roxburghe Club, 1962), p. xxxiii.

19/In view of Walpole's love of decorations, especially his Garter ribbon, and the fact that in Opposition literature "Sir Blue-String" was his commonest nickname, the question could easily arise.

20/Cf. Shaftesbury, *Sensus Communis: An Essay on the Freedom of Wit and Humor* (1709), p. 18: "And thus the natural free Spirits of ingenious Men, if imprison'd and controul'd, will find out other ways of Motion to relieve themselves in their *Constraint*: and whether it be in Burlesque, Mimicry or Buffonery, they will be glad at any rate to vent themselves, and be reveng'd on their *Constrainers*. ... 'Tis the persecuting Spirit has raised the bantering one."

might stand for almost any other, there was no limit to what a clever writer could insinuate, nor was there any limit to what a clever interpreter could decide must be insinuation. The resulting darkness visible is described with mock alarm by a writer in the *Craftsman* in 1730, who manages, like all the contributors to that journal, to establish his innuendo in the very act of disclaiming it.

It hath lately been asserted very roundly [i.e. by the government writers, in speaking of the *Craftsman*] *that there is not a* Virtue *mention'd in one of our antient Kings with any other View than to insinuate that it hath* no Parallel at present; *nor any* Vice *mention'd, but to hint that there is* a Parallel at present.

... If you endeavour to recommend the *Virtues* of a *good Prince*, such as *Edward the third*, it may be represented that your Design was to shew that it hath *no Parallel at present.* If you think proper to expose the *Vices* of a *bad Prince*, such as *Richard the second*, by shewing the Consequences of them, it may be said that you do it with an Intention of hinting that there *is a Parallel at present*; so that whether there is a *Parallel*, or there is *no Parallel*, you may be prosecuted for a *Libeller.* (31 October: VII 93)

VI

Shaped under these conditions, Pope's satires and epistles became to an inevitably large extent exercises in innuendo. Political references flash casually on the unruffled surface of the verse, then disappear so swiftly that it often remains uncertain whether the satirical lens has in fact been opened, and if so, on what. To illustrate this problem, let us examine first of all six short passages from the Horatian poems. These I range in what I take to be an order of increasing openness and obviousness with respect to their potentialities as innuendo.

1
> It anger'd TURENNE, once upon a day
> To see a Footman kick'd that took his pay:
> But when he heard th' Affront the Fellow gave,
> Knew one a Man of Honour, one a Knave,
> The prudent Gen'ral turn'd it to a jest,
> And begg'd, he'd take the pains to kick the rest,
> (*One Thousand Seven Hundred and Thirty-Eight, Dial.* ii 150–55)

2
> Does not one Table *Bavius* still admit?
> Still to one Bishop *Philips* seem a Wit:
> Still *Sapho*—"Hold! for God-sake—you'll offend:
> No Names—be calm—learn Prudence of a Friend."
> (*Epistle to Dr. Arbuthnot*, 99–102)

3   But Britain, changeful as a Child at play,
    Now calls in Princes, and now turns away.
    Now Whig, now Tory, what we lov'd we hate.
           (*Imit. Hor., Ep.* ɪɪ i, 155–57)

4   Swears every *Place entail'd* for Years to come,
    In *sure Succession* to the Day of Doom.
           (*Imit. Donne,* ɪᴠ 160–61)

5   Be furious, envious, slothful, mad or drunk,
    Slave to a Wife or Vassal to a Punk,
    A Switz, a High-dutch, or a Low-dutch Bear—
    All that we ask is but a patient Ear.
           (*Imit. Hor., Ep.* ɪ i, 61–64)

6   And lyes to every Lord in every thing,
    Like a King's Favourite—or like a King.
           (*Imit. Donne,* ɪɪ 77–78)

For passages 5 and 6 here, a contemporary reader needed only an inclination to fill in, behind the lying "Favourite" and "King," the figures of Walpole and George Augustus (a transformation in which he had been trained by the Opposition press for years), and to see in the collocation of ideas presented by "Slave to a wife," "Vassal to a Punk" (i.e. Mme. Walmoden), and "a High-dutch, or a Low-dutch Bear," an image of the foreign King;[1] yet no one could prove before a jury that any of these references was in fact specific. The contemporary reader's interpretation of passage 4 would likewise depend on his political inclination, plus his alertness to the possibility that "the Day of Doom" might be a cryptic way of referring to Walpole's fall and punishment—a favorite topic on all sides during the aftermath of his first great political defeat in 1733, when these lines were published. Passage 3 *could* be read, like 4, as a reminder: that a certain present incumbent of the throne might do well not to take his position for granted, Britain having "called in" Charles ɪɪ, William ɪɪɪ, and George ɪ, "turned away"

1/Cf. the comment on the boorishness of reigning monarchs attributed to Jonson and Dennis in *Imit. Hor., Ep.* ɪɪ i 389: "No Lord's anointed, but a Russian Bear"; and Pope's own comment on the Hanoverians in *Imit. Donne,* ɪɪ 61–62:

   Language, which Boreas might to Auster hold,
   More rough than forty Germans when they scold.

George ɪɪ is referred to as riding on the back of the *"Great Bear"* in *Common Sense* (19 March 1737). See below, p. 146.

James ii, and executed Charles i. Two, I suspect, is genuinely esoteric. Those who read it in the folio and quarto *Works* of 1735, where, for two editions only, "Arnall" (one of the government's chief journalists) replaces "Bavius," could possibly be relied on to consider the "one Table" Walpole's; but only Pope, or one of his intimates, or one of Walpole's intimates, would have occasion to ask whether the unspoken name which causes the poet's interlocutor to interrupt and urge prudence, and which evidently belongs to a person standing in the same "patronal" relationship to Lady Mary as the Bishop to Philips, as the "one Table" to Arnall, as the "Butchers" to Henley, and as the Free-Masons to Moore, was going to be, once again, that of the Great Man.

The remaining passage in the first group shows clearly how difficult it is to set any precise bounds to innuendo. Pope is essentially saying here that Walpole, whose "Tools" he feels at liberty to maul if he spares the Minister himself, ought to behave like Turenne and urge Pope to maul them all for their offensiveness. But the act of "kicking" being especially highly charged during 1737–38 by representations in both press and popular engravings of George ii so engaged, and his capacities in this department being well known, Walpole's censor Paxton, employed to keep track of reflections on the King and government, might well have wondered if the word in this context, used twice, was innocent. Especially he might have wondered if he recalled that about a year earlier a writer for *Common Sense*, one of the Opposition journals, had proposed in "An Essay on Kicking" that this exercise should be established for everyone at Court: "I should think it would be too great a Fatigue for the Prince himself to kick the whole Court, especially in Countries where the Court is numerous; I should therefore be of Opinion, that nobody should have the Honour of being kicked by the Sovereign, except the first Minister, the principal Secretaries of State, the President of his Council, and some few others [of] the great Officers of the Crown. ..."[2]

2/Eleven June 1737. *Fog's Weekly Journal*, 16 July 1737, in an article expatiating ironically on the pleasures of being able to call up, through memory, the great of the past, recurs to this subject:

I called in, the Day I read the Paper of *Common Sense* upon *kicking* [,] *Augustus*, and set him to kicking a Football, his former usual Imperial Diversion, and was not a little pleased to see the Emperor at this Sport, in his high Shoes, and Roman Tryumphal Robe, as my Fancy had dress'd him; on a sudden my Fancy surrounded him with a Crowd of Courtiers, who were extravagant in their Praises, and by that heighten'd my Satisfaction: One, extolled his Air in kicking; another, his Strength; a third, his Agility, and all allowed it to be the most healthful, Majestick, and innocent Exercise that ever was used by a Prince; advising that by a Decree of the Senate the Practice of *kicking* might be restrained to the peculiar Family of the *Caesars*. I asked *Augustus* why he had made Choice of this Diversion? He told me, that he had been grievously troubled with the Gravel, and he found this Exercise eased him. Then said I, you

The notion that Pope's comment about "kicking the rest" was in any way calculated to bring these contemporary jokes to mind, is of course preposterous. Or is it? How could Paxton be sure? How can we?

A different aspect of the problem may be seen in the four passages which I now present. Here innuendo leans heavily toward allusion without, however, quite certainly maintaining a foothold there.

I

    I fain wou'd please you, if I knew with what:
    Tell me, which Knave is lawful Game, which not?
    Must great Offenders, once escap'd the Crown,
    Like Royal Harts, be never more run down?
    Admit your Law to spare the Knight requires;
    As Beasts of Nature may we hunt the Squires?
    (*One Thousand Seven Hundred and Thirty-Eight, Dial. ii* 26–31)

II

    Your Plea is good. But still I say, beware!
    Laws are explain'd by Men—so have a care.
    It stands on record, that in *Richard*'s Times
    A man was hang'd for very honest Rhymes.
                (*Imit. Hor., Sat.* ii i 143–46)

III

    Edward and Henry, now the Boast of Fame,
    And virtuous Alfred, a more sacred Name.
                (*Imit. Hor., Ep.* ii i 7–8)

IV

    True, conscious Honour is to feel no sin,
    He's arm'd without that's innocent within;
    Be this thy Screen, and this thy Wall of Brass;
    Compar'd to this, a Minister's an Ass.
              (*Imit. Hor., Ep.* i i 93–96)

In the lines from the second dialogue of *One Thousand Seven Hundred and Thirty-Eight* Pope has kept his references general in the manner of the *Craftsman*: his "Knave" is one of many, his "great Offenders" is a generic phrase, his

---

will reap a double Benefit if instead of a Football, you would kick these Adulators. *Augustus* who was, you know, a wise Prince, took the Hint, and replying that such *Rascals* were indeed fit for nothing but *Footballs*, kick'd 'em all out of the Apartment, which gave me an inexpressible Pleasure, and taking Leave of the Emperor, we retired to our different and usual Retreats.

There is a further reference to George ii's habit in *Common Sense* (17 September 1737), below, p. 147, n. 4.

"the Knight" is simply one term of an antithesis between knight and squire. But the well-established habit of applying all three of these terms to Walpole could be counted on to make its point and no doubt did.[3] The same principle operates in II and III. All that Fortescue seems to be saying to the poet in II is that poets have on occasion been punished for reflecting on the government—even hanged: for example, "in *Richard*'s Times." But the bridge of likeness between either Richard II or Richard III (wicked, arbitrary, favorite-ridden) and George II was so easily crossed by contemporary readers[4] that Pope did not in fact risk the phrase "*Richard*'s Times" in the first edition, but only "ancient Times," reserving the name Richard, as he so often did with something particularly dangerous, for the next edition.[5] To his auditor George II, in the third passage, Pope innocently cites a number of great rulers who have enjoyed less recognition of their labors in their own lifetimes than he; but the insinuation that strong kings like Henry and Edward have "no Parallel at present" (as the *Craftsman* writer put it) is available to any reader who cares to find it, as is also the connection between Alfred and the doctrine that essential English liberties began in Saxon times—not, as the government writers were contending, with the Revolution of 1688.[6] The connection had been well publicized when, in 1735, to stress his own adoption of this Opposition view, the Prince of Wales had ordered "a fine Statue of King ALFRED to be made for his Gardens in *Pall-Mall*," with a Latin inscription stating that Alfred was "*the Founder of the LIBERTIES and COMMON-WEALTH of England*."[7] For most readers in 1737 this innuendo cannot have been other than transparent.

3/"Knave" may be an especially charged term here. See below, p. 180, n. 4 and Plate 42n; also Egmont, II 461 (20 January 1738): "A joke runs about the town that in the late new vault made for the Queen the third place therein is designed by her Majesty for Sir Robert Walpole; so that when both the latter die there will lie together King, Queen and Knave."

4/See the quotation from the *Craftsman*, above, p. 136. This gives the usual comparison, which is of George II and Richard II. For a more extensive example, see the *Craftsman*, VII, 16 October 1730, 70 ff.

5/"Mr. Pope used to tell me, that when he had any thing better than ordinary to say, and yet too bold, he always reserved it for a second or third edition, and then nobody took any notice of it" (William Warburton to Richard Hurd, 22 September 1751, *Letters from a Late Eminent Prelate* [London, 1809], p. 86). See TE, III ii 43–44.

6/See Mallet and Thomson's *Alfred*, and A. D. McKillop, "Ethics and Political History in Thomson's Liberty," in Clifford-Landa, pp. 222 ff. Also, his *The Background of Thomson's Liberty, Rice Institute Pamphlets*, XXXVIII (1951), ch. vi.

7/*Craftsman* XIV, 6 September 1735, 103–4. This view of the origins of English liberties had been put forward eloquently in Bolingbroke's *A Dissertation upon Parties*, which appeared in successive issues of the *Craftsman* between 27 October 1737 and 2 February 1734.

Number IV is another clear case of the use of the contemporary argot, possibly enhanced by a further allusion. The "screen" points always at Walpole, the "brass" always at his brazenness of appearance or of manner, and the addition of "Minister" to this already explosive group could only have clinched the point for Pope's contemporaries. But perhaps there was an additional reverberation for those with long memories. The third verse of the passage is Pope's paraphrase of Horace's *Hic murus aheneus esto:* "Let this (i.e. virtue) be your wall of brass." Was he recalling, as he wrote this and the following verse, and expecting an inner circle of informed readers to recall, certain sentences published by William Pulteney in 1731 applying this same Horatian phrase to Walpole? In a pamphlet against Hervey, from which Pope had already borrowed several details for his portrait of Sporus, Pulteney had written: "The greatest Security to your *Patron* [i.e. Walpole, to whom Hervey had then recently gone over] ... consists in the Hardness of his Metal. A *Squib*, or a *Fire-ball* cannot melt down *Brass*; and He hath that *murus aheneus*, that *Brazen-Wall*, not of *Innocence* indeed, but of *Assurance*, to protect Him."[8] In this case the instrument of disaffection, like an Aeolian harp, tends to respond to whatever a reader breathes on it.

VII

For a final problematic exhibit, here are two passages that lock insinuation and allusion in a close embrace, the insoluble difficulty being to decide how far the allusions reach.

A   See thronging Millions to the Pagod run
     And offer Country, Parent, Wife, or Son!
    (*One Thousand Seven Hundred and Thirty-Eight, Dial.* i, 157–58)

B   Nor absent they, no members of her state,
     Who pay her homage in her sons, the Great;
     Who false to Phœbus, bow the knee to Baal.
    (*Dunciad,* IV 91–93)

That "Pagod" in A and "Baal" in B *can* be interpreted to mean Walpole and/or George II will appear plausible to any reader who reflects on the contexts in which the words occur. Contemporary readers had grounds more relative than this—certainly general grounds and possibly specific ones. The sycophancy en-

---

8/*A Proper Reply to a Late Scurrilous Libel*, p. 34.

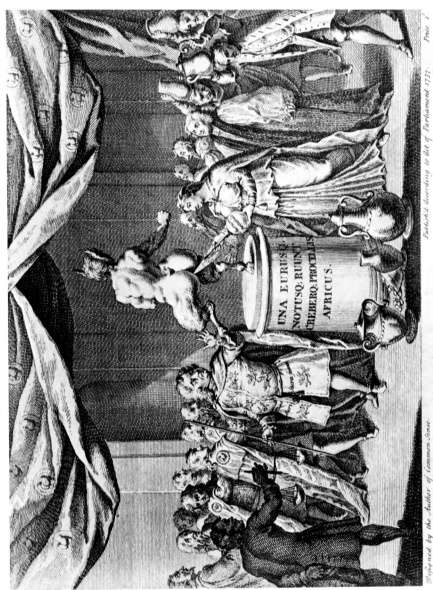

37 The Festival of the Golden Rump. *"Design'd by the Author of Common Sense."*
Artist and engraver unknown. March (?) 1737

gendered by Walpole's iron hold on all positions of privilege had inevitably invited comparisons of his rule to Oriental despotisms and idolatries, such as were already implied in the early *Vision of Camilick*, and two notorious engravings of the time had made the point unforgettable. One, published in March 1737, exactly a twelve-month before Pope published the lines quoted in A, was entitled *The Festival of the Golden Rump* and is described as follows in F. G. Stephens's great catalogue of satirical prints:

On an altar is George II. in the form of a satyr, one leg lifted up to kick; near him, Queen Caroline, as a priestess, with a bell on her wrist, preparing to administer an injection of "*Aurum potabile*" [into the image's posterior]: behind her a bishop, Hoadly, who was lame and required a stick; and several persons bringing vessels to offer at the altar: on the other side is Sir Robert Walpole as chief magician, his coat embroidered with dragons and inscribed "*Auri Sacra fames;*" near him, his brother Horace balancing a pair of scales, as he was called the "Balance-Master of Europe;" likewise near a group of peers wearing the badge of the "Golden Rump." A splendid curtain, embroidered with golden rumps, is suspended over the idol. On the altar is inscribed, "UNA EURUSQ. NOTUSQ; RUUNT CREBERQ; PROCELLIS AFRICUS."[1]

To explain this design, a "vision" appeared in the March 19th issue of *Common Sense*:[2]

Methought I was upon a large River, in a small *Indian* Canoe, without either Oars or Sails. My Canoe was for some time carried down the Stream with great Rapidity, and at length, by good Fortune, was driven into a little Creek. By this Means I landed, without any Difficulty, in a pleasant Meadow, in which were several Walks of tall Elms, like those in *Greenwich* Park. The broadest of these Walks, which was full of Cavaliers all magnificently dressed, was an Avenue that led, at about half a Mile's Distance, to a Temple whose gilded Spires reached the Clouds. Resolving to gratify my Curiosity, I joined the Company, which I perceived were hastening to the Temple, when an elderly Gentleman, habited in a Suit of black Velvet, observing I was a Stranger, made me a handsome Compliment, and offered me his Service.

1/No. 2327. See Plate 37. The Latin inscription is from *Aeneid*, 1 85.

2/I quote the *Common Sense* article from the original separate issue, which differs in many textual points from the version more easily accessible in the collected edition of 1738. Though very long, it expresses the contemporary political scene so vividly (however crudely) that it has seemed best to give it entire. The episode soon became a *cause célèbre*, and a lost (or alleged?) play on the subject proved to be one of Walpole's most effective justifications in asking for passage of the Licensing Act. See John Loftis, *The Politics of Drama in Augustan England* (Clarendon Press, 1963), pp. 139 ff.

I thanked him for his Civility, and took the Liberty to ask him the Meaning of what I saw. He informed me, that the Persons I observed so richly habited were the *Noblesse* of the Kingdom, who were going to the Temple to celebrate the annual Festival of the GOLDEN RUMP; for so, it seems, the PAGOD was called: That he was an Officer belonging to the CHIEF MAGICIAN, or VICAR GENERAL of the HIGH-PRIESTESS; and would place me where I might see the whole Ceremony, without being incommoded. Saying this, he led me into the Temple, and directed me to stand in a Niche near the Altar, himself standing close by me during the whole Time the Celebration of the Festival lasted. The Temple was a plain, large Room, with a flat Roof, but without any Pillars, like the Theatre at *Oxford*. At the West End was an Altar raised about five Foot from the Floor, on which the Image of the PAGOD was placed. This IDOL was an human Figure [George II], excepting only that he had Goats Legs and Feet, like those which are given by Poets and Statuaries to the old *Satyrs*. His Head was made of Wood, his Body down to the Waist of Silver; and his Posteriors, which were large and prominent, and from whence he derived his Title, were of solid Gold. By this Description the Reader will easily conceive that the Back of the IDOL was turned to the Congregation; an Attitude which I do not remember to have observed among the *Chinese* and *Indian Pagods*. But my friendly Conductor informed me, that he had placed himself in this Posture upon his first Entrance into the Temple, as well to shew his Politeness, as to testify his Respect and Gratitude to a Nation which had elected him into the Number of the *Dii majores*, or *Greater Gods*. Here I could not help smiling, to think how widely the Custom of this Country differed from mine, where the same Thing, which passed here for Civility, and good Manners, would be reckoned a Mark of Insolence and Brutality.

But to proceed in my Vision—On the Right Hand of the PAGOD stood the TAPANTA (for so the HIGH-PRIESTESS was styled) dressed in the Habit of a *Roman* Matron [Queen Caroline]. Her *Stola*, or upper Garment, was of Gold Brocade, adorned with Diamonds and other Jewels. She had a Silver Bell in one Hand, and a small Golden Pipe or Tube in the other, with a large Bag or Bladder at the end of it. It exactly resembled a common Clyster-pipe, and was used, as my Friend explained it to me, in the same manner. For the Bladder was full of *Aurum potabile*, compounded with Pearl Powders, and other choice Ingredients. This Medicine, at proper Seasons, was injected by the TAPANTA into the F——d——t of the PAGOD, to comfort his Bowels, and preserve his Complexion. It was likewise applied, upon extraordinary Occasions, to appease the IDOL, when he lifted up his cloven Foot to correct his Domesticks who officiated at the Altar. However, as he was naturally very cholerick, so his Fury was sometimes so very sudden and unexpected, that he imprinted visible Marks of it on all who stood near him, ere the HIGH-PRIESTESS had time to apply the golden Clyster. And sometimes the Storm was so loud and violent, and the PRIESTESS met with such Opposition in those Parts to which she directed her Tube,

(*Una Eurusq; Notusq; ruunt, creberq; procellis Africus)

that she was unable to apply it at all, at least with any Success. But these unnatural Sallies or Hurricanes had not happened, as my Conductor assured me, above two or three times since the Deification of the PAGOD; and only then, when his Godship was deeply smitten with the Charms of a mortal Dame.

On the Left Hand of the IDOL, opposite to the TAPANTA, stood the CHIEF MAGICIAN, or VICAR-GENERAL [Walpole]. His Habit was a Robe or Mantle of blue Velvet, and underneath a Cassock of white Sattin, embroider'd all over with flying Dragons. He was called GASTER ARGOS, being thus denominated from his Belly, which was as large and prominent as the PAGOD's Rump. On that Part of the Cassock which covered his Belly, and just beneath his Surcingle, were embroidered these Words in Gold Characters: AURI SACRA FAMES. He had a Rod or Wand in his Hand, which he waved continually to and fro, like *Harlequin Faustus* in a modern Pantomime. This Rod, my Conductor told me, belonged heretofore to *Pharaoh*'s chief Magician, and still retained its marvelous Virtue; that is, it would change itself into Serpent or Dragon, whenever GASTER ARGOS cast it upon the Ground. There was moreover an ancient Prophecy or Tradition which prevailed throughout the Land, that the GOLDEN RUMP should continue in the Fullness of his Glory, and the HIGH-PRIESTESS and GASTER maintain their Authority, as long as the latter possess'd that Rod; which could never be destroyed or eaten up, but by the Rod of *Aaron*.

My good Friend was proceeding to explain the excellent and miraculous Properties of the magic Rod, and to give me a Detail of the rare Exploits of GASTER ARGOS, when the HIGH-PRIESTESS made the Signal of Adoration by ringing her Silver Bell.

When the People who were gathered together in the Temple, heard the Sound of the Silver Bell, they prostrated themselves before the PAGOD. I was likewise obliged to fall down flat on my Face, lest I should have been marked for an Unbeliever, and consequently expelled the Temple, or, perhaps, have been sacrificed to the IDOL by the superstitious Multitude. After we had continued in that humble Posture two or three Minutes, an hollow, hoarse Voice which proceeded from the GOLDEN RUMP

Cotton's Translation of this Verse in *Virgil* will best explain my Meaning.[3]

3/*Aeneid*, 185. Charles Cotton's translation in *Scarronides: Or, Virgile Travestie* (London, 1664), p. 14, has Virgil's Aeolus respond to Juno's plea for "winds" with a gross resourcefulness:

> He let at once his General Muster
> Of all that ere could blow, or bluster. ...

uttered the following Words. 'Hearken to my Voice, all ye People, and receive with Reverence the Oracle of Truth. I am the Mightiest among the Mighty, even he that rideth through the Firmament on the Back of the *Great Bear*. In my Presence the Sun is Darkness, and the Moon and Stars are my Footballs. Hearken unto my Voice, all ye Nations, and offer up unto me yourselves, your Sons, and your Sons Sons; your Wives and your Daughters, your Man-servants and your Maid-servants! Hearken unto my Voice, all ye People, and offer up unto me Vessels of Silver, and Vessels of Gold. I say unto you, Vessels of pure Gold, your own and your Neighbours Vessels! so shall ye find Favour in my sight, and the Man who changeth his Rod into a Serpent, shall fill you with good Things.' When the Oracle of the GOLDEN RUMP had thus delivered himself, all the People rose from the Ground. Immediately the HIGH-PRIESTESS rung the Silver Bell a second time; and the CHIEF MAGICIAN making a profound Obeisance to the IDOL, kneeled before the Altar, and made the following Address, in the Name of the Congregation.

"Most illustrious RUMP! Thou who art Mightiest among the Mighty, who ridest on the Back of the *Great Bear*, and whose Brightness exceedeth the Brightness of the Sun! With Hearts full of Gratitude we acknowledge thy gracious Favour, and we obey thy Voice. Lo, we offer up ourselves, our Wives, and our Daughters, our Sons, and our Sons Sons, and their Sons which are yet unborn. Lo! we offer up unto Thee our Vessels of Silver, and Vessels of Gold; our own and our Neighbours Vessels, and our Neighbours Neighbours, and their Neighbours, even the Vessels of those who inhabit the remotest Corner of the Land."

Then the CHIEF MAGICIAN rising up, turned his Face to the Congregation, and making a Sign with his Hand, there advanced from the middle of the Temple twelve Men clad in blue Velvet, and about twenty-four in Red, each having a Basket Hilt Sword by his Side, and a large *Rump* embroidered in Gold on his Vest, with this *Motto* round it;

RUMPATUR, *quisquis* RUMPITUR *invidia.*

I considered this *Motto* as a mere Pun or Quibble, explaining it to myself in this manner; *Whoever envies me, or whoever is not on my Side, let him be* RUMPED. And I was afterwards much pleas'd to find, that my Friend's Construction of those Words differ'd but little from mine; only he translated the *Latin* Verse into French. It will be necessary to inform my Reader, that those goodly Personages, *who bore Semblance of Worth, not Substance*, were called *Knights* of the GOLDEN RUMP [above, p. 130, n. 6], which was the Badge of their Order; that they were the most considerable Inhabitants of the Country, and were the principal Domesticks of the PAGOD.

Next after the *Knights* of the GOLDEN RUMP, came twenty-two Knights in Party-coloured Robes of Black and White. These were all *Castellans* [i.e. bishops]; and because they received their Commissions from the HIGH-PRIESTESS, they were commonly called TAPANTA's *Knights*. They approached the Altar with great Reverence, their Eyes being steadily fixed on the IDOL. But my Friend assured me, they were generally Hypocrites; and were attracted by the Brightness of the Metal of which the PAGOD's Body was made, and not by the Divinity of his Person; that their whole Study was to get a better *Castellany*, and so enrich their Families by the Revenues and Perquisites of their Imployments. These *Castellans*, who were likewise Domesticks of the PAGOD, ranged themselves together with the *Knights* of the GOLDEN RUMP, on each Side of the Altar. The third Procession was composed of about two hundred and fifty Men of different Ages, and dressed in different Habits. They were called the *Ecuyers* of the CHIEF MAGICIAN, but were in Truth his Slaves and Vassals. Every one of these *Ecuyers* carried a large Vessel of Gold on his Head, full of square Pieces of the same Metal, each about the size of a Dye. They set down their Vessels at the Foot of the Altar, and then making three Genuflexions, they filed off to the Right and Left, and ranged themselves behind the *Castellans*. Their Vessels, it seems, contained the annual Offerings, to which the whole Body of the People were obliged, and which had been collected some Days before under the Direction of the CHIEF MAGICIAN, who superintended that Work *ex Officio*. The Offerings (or more properly I may call it a Tribute) were presented in this manner, to prevent Confusion, and shorten the Time of the Solemnity; which must have lasted many days, if every Native of the Country had been permitted to make his Offering in Person. When all the Vessels were placed on the Altar, and the HIGH-PRIESTESS had consecrated them in Form to the Service of the PAGOD; GASTER ARGOS cast his Rod upon the Pavement, which immediately changed into a Serpent, or rather, a monstrous Dragon. The Jaws of the Beast were so wide, that he could easily have swallow'd a whole Ox. But other Prey was designed for him. For no sooner had he beheld the Vessels of Gold, but, seizing them one after another, he gulp'd them down with all their Contents and Appurtenances, in less time than a Dunghill Cock would have pick'd up a dozen Barley-Corns from a Threshing Floor; and yet he did not seem to be half filled or satisfied with his Meal, but looked about for more Food of the same Kind. I once thought he would have snapt at those Parts of the PAGOD which were formed of Gold, when the CHIEF MAGICIAN taking him by the Tail, he became a small Rod or Wand, as before.[4]

4/Pretending to be talking about a cult of the Callipygian Venus, *Common Sense* returned to the subject of rumps on 17 September. A correspondent found fault with the former piece on the ground that it was presented as a dream—which "gives the whole an Air of Fable." The truth is that Atheneus gives us plainly "the very Name of the Island where, the Situation of the Temple in which, and a Description of the Figure under which the *Rump* was worship'd. He

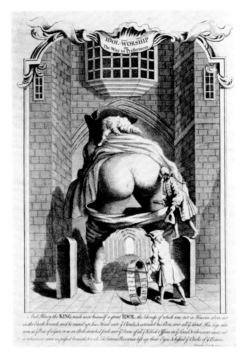

38 Idol-Worship or The Way to Preferment.
Artist and engraver unknown. February (?) 1740

Pope had used the word "Pa-god" in his paraphrase of the *Fourth Satire of Dr. John Donne* in 1733. It is not difficult to believe that the graphic representation of such an idol in the *Festival of the Golden Rump* and the insistent appearance of the term itself in the explanatory vision published by *Common Sense* refreshed his memory of the term and kept it in his consciousness (along with the image of offering up sons, sons' sons, wives, and daughters) as he shaped his picture of

indeed does not inform us whether all the People in that Island paid the same Deference to the *Rump*, but we have Reason to believe, that it was of most Advantage to them who most reverenc'd it; and that there was no Person to whom the *Rump* had been favourable, but had a Statue of it in his House." The writer also asserts that King James I had begun a treatise against rump-worship in connection with his *Demonology*, and (with a glance at George II's kicking—above, p. 138) that "the frequent Changes he made of his Ministers, were owing to the unmeasurable Protuberance of that Part of their Bodies after they were in Power, which was so disgustful to that Monarch, that he *kick'd* every one of them out of Office by Turns. ..."

the apotheosis of Vice from which the lines of passage A (p. 141) are taken—and in the consciousness of his readers too.

The other engraving, published in 1740, relates primarily to the theme of idolatry as presented in passage B. Entitled *Idol Worship or the Way to Preferment*, it portrays a broad bared Walpolian posterior straddling a road that leads under a great gate to various government employments and requiring to be paid suitable homage by all who wish to pass beneath it (Stephens, no. 2447; Plate 38). Its legend reads:

And Henry the KING made unto himself a great IDOL, the likeness of which was not in Heaven above, nor in the Earth beneath; and he reared up his Head into yᵉ Clouds, and extended his Arm over all yᵉ Land; His legs also were as yᵉ Posts of a Gate, or as an Arch stretched over yᵉ Doors of all yᵉ Publick Offices in yᵉ Land, and whosoever went out, or whosoever came in, passed beneath, and with Idolatrous Reverence lift up their Eyes, and kiss'd yᵉ Cheeks of yᵉ Postern.

For contemporaries, Pope's lines about the Great "who bow the knee to *Baal*" must have looked out, at least in a general way, toward representations of servility and idolatry of this kind, which had been multiplying throughout the 30's. For the poet himself, and possibly a few of his inner audience, they may have looked out also to a passage in a famous Opposition manifesto by Bolingbroke, published in the *Craftsman* many years before, but widely circulated and long remembered. In a stirring appeal to his countrymen to unite against the common enemy, Bolingbroke had written:

If this Nation was as *corrupt* and *depraved* as it is said to be by *Those*, who do their utmost to *corrupt* and *deprave* it; if our Country was in that *declining State*, and the *Freedom of our Government* as near its Period as They affirm, there would remain no Part for any honest Man to take, except That of sitting silently down and perishing in the common Shipwreck; but surely This is not yet our Case, nor will it become our Case, unless We are induced to believe it so; unless We make our Ruin irretrievable by struggling no longer against it. There are Men, many We think, who have not bowed the Knee to *Baal*, nor worshiped the *brazen Image*. We may therefore hope that there is still a Blessing in store for us.[5]

5/22 May 1731 (VII 401). See also *Yes, They Are: Being an Answer to Are these Things So?* (1740), p. 10, where the author professes to address Pope:

> You ask if *Things are so?* or fiction all?
> *You*, Sir, are one on whom the weight may fall;
> The weight of taxes, and *Convenio*'s [Walpole's] rod,
> Unless you bow to *Baal*, or wait his nod.

When, in the spring of 1742, Pope published the lines of passage B with their echo, intentional or unintentional, of this letter, the "Blessing" had come about for all to see: Walpole had fallen.[6]

VIII

Walpole's fall made possible the publication of two works in which the entire repertory of innuendo is effectively acted out, from the stare of simulated innocence to the knowing wink, from the factitious cough to the muttered not quite audible aside. These were the *New Dunciad* and the revised *Dunciad* in four books. Small changes in successive texts of the three-book *Dunciad* had already for some years been deepening its political complexion. Names like Arnall[1] (government journalist whom we have already encountered in one of the variant readings of the *Epistle to Dr. Arbuthnot*), "Mother Osborne"[2] (i.e. James Pitt, another writer for the ministry under the pseudonym of "Frances Osborne"), and "Kelsey"[3] (in the MS. "Kelsall," evidently Henry Kelsall, Clerk of the Treasury, one of those whom Pope charges explicitly in his *Master Key to Popery* with fostering the application of "Timon" to the Duke of Chandos) begin increasingly to show up in the poem's verse or notes. "God save King Tibbald!"—the roar of Grubstreet alleys in 1729—becomes in and after 1735 (*1735–42*, TE V 94) "God save the king," acknowledgement of a less specific but therefore actually much more libelous allusion. A vision of triumph, in which the Dulness of 1729 sees her "chosen sons" led by their "King" (i.e. Tibbald) "To lands, that flow with clenches and with puns" and then to speedy conquest over "each fam'd Theatre," takes on, through revisions of this same period (*ibid.*, p. 93), a wider range of satirical objectives:

6/Walpole retired in early February, 1742; the *New Dunciad* (the early and separate version of Book IV in which the couplet cited in the text first appears) was published on 20 March. The revised *Dunciad* in four books, with Cibber as hero, was published a year and a half later, on 29 October 1743, the day before the birthday of George II. The poem was, in George Sherburn's words, "almost a birthday present for the King" (TE V xxxiin).

1/William Arnall, who appears at II 385 in *1735 ab* (TE V 148) and at II 293 in *1735a–42* (*ibid.*, 138), had also appeared at line 99 in the *1735 ab* editions of the *Epistle to Dr. Arbuthnot* (*ibid.*, IV 102, and above, p. 138).

2/"Mother Osborne" appears in the three-book *Dunciad* for the first time in *1741–42* (at II, 159, 163, 181: TE V 121, 124).

3/Kelsey takes the place of Motteux at II 382 in *1735a–42* (TE V 147). In the *Master Key to Popery* he is "Henry K———y Esq."

> I see a chief, who leads my chosen sons,
> All arm'd with points, antitheses, and puns!
> I see a Monarch proud my race to own!
> A Nursing-mother, born to rock the throne!
> Schools, courts, and senates shall my laws obey.

In view of what had been stressed publicly about his style by the time these lines were published,[4] the "chief" here could more readily be supposed Lord Hervey than Lewis Theobald.[5] The "sons" he leads could be identified with the ministerial writers, the Monarch with George II. The "Nursing-mother," whom Pope riddlingly associates in his note (TE V 93) with either "*Alma Mater*" or "*Mother Osborne*," could be taken as a hit at Queen Caroline, who is born to "rock the throne" both in the sense of keeping the king pacified and his power somnolent (Pope so describes him in memorable lines at the close of the *Epistle to Augustus*), and also in the sense of shaking the throne by wielding that royal power herself. A little later, in a letter to Swift of 19 May 1739 (IV 178–79), Pope set down some verses "for the next new Edition" of the *Dunciad* which show a still stronger political preoccupation. "In the second Canto," he tells Swift, "among the Authors who dive in Fleet ditch, immediately after *Arnall*. Vers. 300. add these

> Next plung'd a feeble, but a desp'rate pack,
> With each a sickly Brother at his back:
> Sons of a *Day*! Just buoyant on the flood,
> Then number'd with the Puppies in the Mud.
> Ask ye their *Names*? I could as soon disclose
> The names of these blind Puppies as of those.
> Fast by, like Niobe, her children gone,
> Sits Mother Osborne, stupefy'd to Stone!
> And rueful Paxton tells the world with tears,
> 'These are—ah no! these were, My *Gazetteers*!' "

When these lines first appeared in print, after the fall of Walpole and Paxton, in the *Dunciad* of 1743, the next-to-last line had been altered to read: "And

---

4/In, for example, the portrait of Sporus (1735) and, earlier (1731), in William Pulteney's *Proper Reply to a Late Scurrilous Libel*. See TE V 119 and nn.

5/Revisions of this passage in the 1743 edition (I 305 ff.) indicate clearly that the second line points at Hervey, though in that redaction he has been demoted to "Aid-de-camp."

Monumental Brass this record bears." Paxton was thus removed, as he had been in fact removed from his position of literary whip and censor, and into his place was slipped an allusion that could be counted on to remind contemporaries, not simply of some vast sepulchral ornament commemorating the demise of Walpole's system of ministerial hacks, but of a certain huge "brazen" figure—"Sir Robert Brass," as he was sometimes called[6]—whose creatures they had been. In a curious surreal way, he has become their monument and they his.[7]

All these, however, were simply straws in the wind. Once the *New Dunciad* had actually appeared, it was evident to all of Pope's informed readers that the fall of Walpole had brought forth a satire of 600-odd lines of unparalleled specificity and boldness, attributing to the Hanoverian court and its former first minister primary responsibility for a general moral and cultural decay which since the middle 30's even Whig observers had been deploring.[8] In the new poem of 1742, the Goddess Dulness of the 1729 Variorum unmistakably "mounts" a

6/Above, p. 132, n. 11. Pope presumably plays too with Dryden's memorable phrase for Titus Oates ("Erect thy self, thou Monumental Brass," *Absalom and Achitophel* 633), behind which finally lies, one supposes, Horace's *monumentum aere perennius*. Considering Oates's talent for discovering plots (*ibid.*, 650 ff.), Pope may have wished to imply a kinship between him and Walpole, who was believed to have manufactured a plot in 1720–23 to trap Atterbury. (Though Atterbury was in fact guilty of correspondence with the Pretender, the government's legal case against him at this time left something to be desired.)

7/Pope's 1743 note on the word "*Gazetteers* (TE v 311–12) shows plainly what is in his mind. After citing the figure of £50,077–17–0 as the amount paid out by the regime for political journalism between 1731 and 1741, he adds: "Which shews the Benevolence of One Minister to have expended, for the current dulness of ten years in Britain, double the sum which gained Louis XIV. so much honour, in annual Pensions to Learned men all over Europe. In which, and in a much longer time, not a Pension at Court, nor Preferment in the Church or Universities, of any Consideration, was bestowed on any man distinguished for his Learning separately from Party-merit, or Pamphlet-writing."

8/Thomson, for example, by this time no less disenchanted than the Tories, writes to Aaron Hill despondently of "that vast Temple of *Corruption*, under which this Generation ... worships the dirty, low-minded, insatiable Idol of Self-interest" (23 August 1735: *A Collection of Letters ... Written ... To the Late Aaron Hill, Esq.* [1751], p. 72), and of the nation's "sordid Turn" to "private Jobs, instead of public works," to "profitable, instead of fine Arts," to "Gain, instead of Glory," to "the whole venal System of modern Administration" (11 May 1736: *ibid.*, p. 74). In a letter to Solomon Mendez, he observes sarcastically of Richard Savage's celebratory poem *Public Works*: "When he sees a senate uncorrupted, he will see a magnificent senate-house; and when a court becomes the patron of arts, another Whitehall. He will see a play-house such as he recommends, when a chamberlain shall be the proper judge of plays, and when slavery more exalts the genius than liberty" (21 July 1737: *British Magazine and Review*, 1 [1782] 175. I am indebted for these passages to A. D. McKillop's "The Background of Thomson's *Liberty*," *Rice Institute Pamphlets*, XXXVIII (1951), p. 99, and to his "Ethics and Political History in Thomson's *Liberty*," in Clifford-Landa, pp. 217–18.

political throne.[9] Her distribution of Orders and Degrees, as has been often noticed,[10] bears resemblance to the award of honors on the occasion of a royal birthday. On her lap during the ceremonies, her "Laureate Son" reclines; this is Cibber, of course, but it is also a greater. "Nor ought this, well-considered," says Pope's note, referring to the circumstance that his hero does nothing ("he has done little or nothing from the day of his anointing"), "to seem strange in our days, when so many King-Consorts have done the like" (*New Dunciad*, 20n).

Dulness's triumph, too, takes place in the new poem under suggestive meteorological and psychological conditions:

> 'Twas when the Dog-star's unpropitious ray
> Smote ev'ry Brain and wither'd ev'ry Bay;
> Sick was the Sun, the Owl forsook his bow'r,
> The Moon-struck Prophet felt the madding hour:
> Then rose the Seed of Chaos, and of Night,
> To block out Order, and extinguish Light,
> Of dull and venal a new World to mold,
> And bring Saturnian days of Lead and Gold.

We are here to some extent, obviously, in the territories of epic convention: these are circumstances appropriated by a long poetical tradition to the fall and change of dynasties:

> As when the Sun new ris'n
> Looks through the Horizontal misty Air
> Shorn of his Beams, or from behind the Moon
> In dim Eclipse disastrous Twilight sheds
> On half the Nations and with fear of change
> Perplexes Monarchs.

Could they refer also to territories closer home? Could the Dog-star, always an

---

9/In Book 1 of both the 1729 and 1743 versions, Dulness is disclosed presumably sitting on a throne supported by "Fortitude," "Temperance," "Prudence," and "Poetic Justice," each defined in ways suited to a purely literary monarch (1 45–54). In the *New Dunciad* (1742) and Book IV of the 1743 version, the throne she mounts is the throne of a monarchy that has displaced (I use the orthography of 1742) "Science," "Wit," "Logic," and "Rhet'ric" with "Sophistry" and "Billingsgate," made "Morality" the ward of "Chicane" and "Casuistry," and all but dispossessed "Tragedy," tragedy's "gay Sister" (i.e. Comedy), "History" and "Satire." The gain in significance is notable.

10/E.g. in George Sherburn's "The Dunciad, Book IV," *Texas Studies in Language and Literature*, XXIV (1944).

agent of midsummer madness and hysteria, have anything to do with the fact that Queen Anne died on August 1st, to be succeeded in September by a dour-faced foreigner who was ignorant of his adopted country's language and culture and intended to remain so?[11] How, precisely, was the phrase "Seed of Chaos, and of Night" to be understood? Was the note appended to the opening of the book offered as a clue: "The Poet willing to approve himself a genuine Son, beginneth by shewing (what is ever agreeable to *Dulness*) his high respect for *Antiquity* and a *Great Family,* how dull, or dark soever"? (*New Dunciad* 1n) What did this italicized *Antiquity* and *Great Family* refer to if not to the fact that George 1 was a descendant of the Guelphs, one of the most ancient families of Europe? What were these "Saturnian days" if not the golden Hanoverian era, predicted and tirelessly celebrated by the Whig panegyrists, which had in fact turned out to be an age of "gold" in a less attractive sense, and to be presided over by the alchemical Saturn rather than by the god?[12] And why was the author insisting from the start that there were "Mysteries" in his poem "which he durst not fully reveal"? (*New Dunciad,* 4n)

Though Walpole was no longer in power, the end of the poem was similarly daring and was speedily to be made more so. As a "WIZARD OLD," one of the disguises in which the Opposition writers most like to represent him (above, pp. 144 ff.), Walpole extends his transforming "*Cup*"—"The *Cup* of *Self-love,*" says the poet's note, "which causes a total oblivion of all the obligations of Friendship, Honour, and Service of God or our Country: all sacrificed to Vain glory, Court-worship, or to yet meaner Considerations, of Lucre and brutal Pleasures"

11/The allusions in this passage to eclipses, portents, and prophecies are presumably literary and therefore historically unspecific. "Prodigies" seem to have been entirely lacking at the death of Anne, if we may believe a poem by Lewis Theobald (*The Mausoleum, A Poem Sacred to the Memory of Her late Majesty Queen Anne* [London, 1714], p. 19), where he laments the fact there were none; though on 2 May 1715, a few months before the Jacobite uprisings, there was an eclipse of the sun. More likely to have been on Pope's mind, if any topicality was intended at all, are such later satirical hints as are represented in a 1740 print described by Stephens (no. 2452). This print has inscriptions prophesying eclipses of the sun and moon. "Below the former ... is the head of Cardinal Fleury, enclosed by a crescent moon, passing over that of Sir Robert Walpole, which is on the face of the sun, and, over the latter inscription, the head of Admiral Vernon, on a map of "Porto Bello," passing over that of a Spanish commander, enclosed by a crescent moon." As Stephens acknowledges, "The prophecies involved in these representations of eclipses are very obscure." Even more obscure is the specific (though not the general) intent of Pope's references in the passage quoted above.

12/The combination of "Gold" with "Lead" (the alchemical Saturn) in the pasage quoted, hinting at ministerial bribery, avarice, and materialism as one cause of the current dulness and decay of the arts, shows again how far the political implications of the poem have widened since 1729, when the new age a-borning was simply designated "a new Saturnian age of Lead" (1 26 and n.).

—to the followers of Dulness, and they respond by becoming knaves, fools, and triflers of various kinds.[13] In the note that the revised *Dunciad* of 1743 affixed, this passage about Walpole is revealed as the goal to which the 1742 poem has been gravitating from the start:

Here beginneth the celebration of the *greater Mysteries* of the Goddess, which the Poet in his Invocation ver. 5. promised to sing. For when now each Aspirant, as was the custom, had proved his qualification and claim to a participation, the High-Priest of Dulness [i.e. Walpole] first initiated the Assembly by the usual way of *Libation*. And then each of the initiated, as was always required, putteth on a *new Nature*. ...

... *Initiation* into the Mysteries was anciently, as well as in these our times, esteemed a necessary qualification for every high office and employment, whether in Church or State. (IV 517n, TE V 393)

The portentous obliquity of these passages may show the influence of such works as *The Vision of Camilick* and the description in *Common Sense* of *The Festival of the Golden Rump*. It may also be supposed to bring that tradition, grown considerable by 1743, to our minds.

IX

In general, then, both by added notes and added or revised lines, Pope made the political intent of the *New Dunciad* of 1742 yet more explicit in Book IV of 1743, which it became. At the same time, to the Variorum *Dunciad* of 1729, which provided Books I–III, he added a vein of political innuendo that was not originally present. Two examples must suffice. The famous passage that opens Book II, based on the opening of the second book of *Paradise Lost*, where Satan is discovered on his throne of state, reads as follows in 1729:

> High on a gorgeous seat, that far outshone
> Henley's gilt Tub, or Fleckno's Irish Throne,
> Or that, where on her Curlls the Public pours
> All-bounteous, fragrant grains and golden show'rs;

13/*New Dunciad*, 507n.) Pope possibly owes something in this passage to Fielding's reference to Walpole (in *The Vernoniad*, 1741, n. 24) as a "Magician" who had "invented a certain *Aurum potabile*, by which he could turn Men into Swine or Asses. ..." See Martin Battestin, "Pope's *Magus* in Fielding's *Vernoniad*: The Satire of Walpole," *Philological Quarterly*, XLVI (1962), 137–41.

> Great Tibbald sate: The proud Parnassian sneer,
> The conscious simper, and the jealous leer,
> Mix on his look. All eyes direct their rays
> On him, and crowds grow foolish as they gaze.
> Not with more glee, by hands Pontific crown'd,
> With scarlet hats, wide waving, circled round,
> Rome in her Capitol saw Querno sit,
> Thron'd on sev'n hills, the Antichrist of Wit.   (1–12)

Except for the revised spelling "Curls," the substitution of "Cibber" for "Tibbald" and of "turn Coxcombs" for "grow foolish", 1743 follows 1729. But between ll. 8 and 9 in 1743 four new verses have been inserted, which alter the possible implications of the passage significantly:

> His Peers shine round him with reflected grace,
> New edge their dulness, and new bronze their face.
> So from the Sun's broad beam, in shallow urns
> Heav'n's twinkling Sparks draw light, and point their horns.
>
>   (9–12)

Cibber's "Peers" here, as James Sutherland points out, "are his brother dunces of the pen, but also those among the English nobility who delighted in his society at White's and elsewhere" (TE v 296). But for some of Pope's readers in 1743, we may imagine that a further question arose. What it was becomes easier to guess if we turn to our second example, I 27–32 in the poem of 1729:

> Where wave the tatter'd ensigns of Rag-Fair,
> A yawning ruin hangs and nods in air;
> Keen, hollow winds howl thro' the bleak recess,
> Emblem of Music caus'd by Emptiness:
> Here in one bed two shiv'ring sisters lye,
> The cave of Poverty and Poetry.

These lines became 29–34 in 1743:

> Close to those walls where Folly holds her throne,
> And laughs to think Monroe would take her down,
> Where o'er the gates, by his fam'd father's hand
> Great Cibber's brazen, brainless brothers stand;
> One Cell there is, conceal'd from vulgar eye,
> The Cave of Poverty and Poetry.

Here the scene has been changed to Bethlehem Hospital, partly at least to make a joke about the two "Statues of the Lunatics"[1] by Cibber's father, Caius-Gabriel Cibber, which formerly adorned the Bedlam gates. In his second public *Letter* to Pope, dated 13 February 1743, Cibber protests the above lines, of which he has seen a copy and which he has been told are to appear "in the next Edition of your *Dunciad*,"[2] observing that the statues are not bronze but stone. Or, as Pope put it in his notes to *Dunciad*, II 3, in 1743: "Mr. Cibber remonstrated that his Brothers at Bedlam ... were not *Brazen*, but *Blocks*; yet our author let it pass, unaltered, as a trifle, that no way lessened the Relationship" (TE V 296). "Rather than sacrifice the admirable epithet 'brazen,'" comments the editor of the Twickenham *Dunciad*, "Pope wrote a facetious note acknowledging the inaccuracy" (*ibid.*, 271). I believe this to be true—but why was the epithet so admirable? Because it alliterated with "brainless" and "brothers"? Or because, in addition, it suggested a possible other identity for the brothers—one brother for whom *brass* and *brazen* had become the standard nicknames, and one brother who in all Opposition quarters was unfailingly known as *brainless*?[3] That the second possibility must at least be entertained is shown by further evidence. For a few months before Cibber's letter, another reader of these same lines had also protested. This was William Bowyer, Pope's printer. We do not have his letter, but the postscript of the poet's reply reads: "Just now I receive yours about the *Brazen* Image. I would have it stand as it is, & no matter if the Criticks dispute about it."[4] There was more at stake in the term "brazen," it would seem, than a happy but mistaken epithet; and if I am right in supposing that what was at stake was an allusion to Robert Walpole, triggering a further allusion to Horatio

---

1/Representations of "Raving Madness" and "Melancholy Madness." They were preserved and may now be seen at the Royal Exchange, London (TE V 271).

2/*A Second Letter from Mr. Cibber to Mr. Pope*, p. 3.

3/Horace Walpole calls his uncle Horatio "a dead weight on his brother's ministry" in his *Memoirs of the Last Ten Years of the Reign of George the Second* (London 1822), I 122. The Opposition writers wholeheartedly agreed. In Whitehead's *The State Dunces* (1733), p. 13, he is "firm Foe to Cleanliness and Sense." *Fog's Weekly Journal* (3 October 1730), speaking of the brothers as "Noodle" and "Doodle," finds Doodle "Fool enough by Nature" though always endeavoring to appear yet more so. In the same paper, 28 July 1733, he is represented first as the stupid Whachum (Sir Sidrophel's zany) of *Hudibras* and second as Sancho's ass (see Appendix F). A ballad of 1733 (Percival, pp. 83–85), referring again to the brothers as Sir Sidrophel and Whachum, calls both of them "brainless":

> Thus did these *silly, brainless Elves,*
> Over their Cups, *betray Themselves.*

See also "The Blundering Brothers," above, p. 129, n. 2.

4/13 November [1742] (*Correspondence*, IV 426).

Walpole in "brainless," this would account for the fact that in the surviving
letter Bowyer, or someone, has cut at least one line of Pope's postscript away.

When we turn back to our first example with this second one in mind, the
conclusion is obvious. It is not that there unmistakably *is*, in *Dunciad*, II 9–12, a
Walpole image that suddenly floats in and merges with Cibber's. It is rather—as
always in the operation of innuendo—that a troubling question is raised. Whose
"Peers" are these who "new bronze their face" evidently from the fountain of all
brazenness? They are Cibber's, without doubt. In the light of the passage we
have looked at in Book I could they be supposed to belong, also, to someone else?
Even for contemporary readers this cannot have been an easy question to decide.[5]

For contemporaries, the difficulty was compounded further by an analogy that
was certain to affect their interpretation both of individual passages in the
Dunciad and of the drift of the poem as a whole. This was the analogy, well
rooted by 1742–43, between the actor, gambler, and stage-manager who was
patentee of Drury Lane and the "actor"-"gambler"-"stage-manager" who for
two decades seemed to have a permanent hold on St. James's and St. Stephen's.[6]
As early as 1729 (7 June) the *Craftsman* had seized on this analogy and elaborated it at length. Caleb d'Anvers, the supposed author of the paper, recounts
an interview with his nephew in which he is shown a play that his nephew has
adapted from Ben Jonson called *"The Fall of SEJANUS,"* whose leading role
he would like to have performed by Colley Cibber. Discussion of the play thus
obliges the uncle to make use of the names Sejanus and Cibber, in neither of
which uses does he wish to be misinterpreted:

> The Regard I have for a *certain Person*, to whose Use and Service many of my
> Lucubrations have been principally dedicated, had almost prevailed upon me never

---

5/Paul Whitehead had perhaps made the question easier to *raise* by equating Walpole with
the *Dunciad*'s Tibbald ("the *Tibbald* of the State," p. 4; "Dulness' fav'rite Son," p. 8) in
his *The State Dunces* (1733), and by describing him in terms borrowed from Pope's lines on
Tibbald:

> Pensive he sat, and sigh'd, while round him lay
> Loads of dull Lumber, all inspired by *Pay*:
> Here, puny Pamphlets, spun from *Prelates* Brains;
> There, the smooth Jingle of *Cook*'s lighter Strains;
> Here *Walsingham*'s soft lulling Opiates spread;
> There gloomy *Osborne*'s Quintessence of Lead.   (p. 5)

The burden of the poem is that Pope should extend his satire to include "The *big, rich, mighty,
Dunces* of the *State*—" as he had in fact begun to do.

6/See John Loftis, *The Politics of Drama in Augustan England* (Clarendon Press, 1963),
p. 135. Cibber notes in his *Apology* (ch. xv) that the Opposition press often "drolled upon"
the "State" and the "Stage" and on "the Minister" and "Minheer Keiber the Manager."

to have mentioned again the words, *Wolsey, Menzikoff, Mackheath, Catiline, Sejanus,* &c. *He* having taken a particular Fancy, from time to time, to declare that *He* was allegorically meant under all these Titles: but as the Favour I am to ask of the Publick this Day, in behalf of my *Nephew,* will oblige me often to use the word *Sejanus,* I desire *He* will be so good, this Time, as not to apply it to *Himself,* or imagine, when I talk of Mr. *Cibber* and his *Acting,* that I intend *Him* and *his Transactions.* (v 14)

In the discussion with his nephew, d'Anvers feels obliged also to caution him as to the degree of Cibber-Walpole's competence for the leading role:

I have, said I, young Kinsman, a great Regard for Mr. *Cibber*'s Performances as an *Actor.* In some Parts he does mighty well; as in the *Buffoon,* the *Coxcomb,* the *Pert,* the *Impudent,* the *Bamster.*[7] He tops the Part of the Sharper. He is *felonious* within, or out of the reach of the *Law,* with a becoming and a natural Grace; and accordingly, he has generally the Applause of the House. I have heard, indeed, that he has sometimes *hired* Voices to applaud Him, and not improperly; since in that very Character he has put the *Doctors* [loaded dice] upon his Audience. The part of *Brazen* seems likewise to be naturally design'd for Him; but in *Gibbet* he is all Perfection. He plunders with an Air adroit, genteel, and intrepid. There is a Gallantry and a Frankness in his Behavior, even to the People, whom he injures. He persuades them that he hath a Right to rob them; and he takes upon him very pleasantly an *authoritative* and *decisive* Behaviour, as if what he did was perfectly agreeable to, and justifiable by the Laws of his Country; and tho' his *Gang* second him pretty well, he sustains manifestly the Character of their Chief; *supereminet omnes.* But give me leave to say, that he very seldom fills the Scene in the *serious Character.* We know his Purposes, before He speaks, by his Gesture, and his Voice. He is no *Politician*; not even in his *Looks.* He cannot disguise them. For example, in *Syphax,* when he is tempting his Prince to Dishonour, he does it with *open* and *risible* Muscles, tho' his Master himself tells him that he observed his looks are *fallen* and *over-cast with Care and Discontent.* There is something in the Dignity of *Wolsey,* that he does not support. He submits indeed to the passions of the *King* with becoming Servility; but he very faintly maintains his Character against the *great* and *honest Men,* who oppose him. In *Cardinal Beaufort,* he still wants Dignity; and we cannot believe so *profest a knave,* even in outward Appearance, can have any weight with the *King* or his *Royal Consort,* or even the *lowest* of the *People,* against the Counsels of the most wise and upright Statesman, perhaps, that ever was; I mean the *good Duke of*

7/I.e. hoaxer. (Curiously enough, the word is not in *OED.*)

Gloucester. I grant you, *Nephew*, said I, that in this Character of *Sejanus*, Mr. *Cibber* will do better than in the rest; but you must take particular care that he does not play his *Index expurgatorius* upon you, or your Author. He has, I must tell you, a very laudable hatred to the Writings of the *Antients*; and perhaps, as *old Ben* is by Time removed a little from us, he may look on him with an evil Eye. (*Ibid.*, 15–16)

This was in 1729. During the first years of the 1740's, when the *New Dunciad* was meditating, the Opposition paper *Common Sense*[8] re-emphasized these themes. Keeping always to the fore the original *Dunciad* idea of the invasion of Britain by Dulness (this, thanks to the political writings of Fielding and others, had never been allowed to lapse[9]) and the comparison of Walpole to Cibber, the paper reviews on 13 December 1740, for example, two attacks on Cibber's *Apology*, one entitled *The Laureat: Or, the Right Side of Colley Cibber*, and a second entitled *A Life of Aesopus the Tragedian*. The reviewer affects to discover with surprise that the intent of these pamphlets is not simply "to make the Publick merry at the Expense of an absurd, wrong-headed Character, who contrived to become as odious in his Mock-Ministry as it was possible for a Man in his low Station of Life to make himself." On the contrary: "by Degrees the Lineaments of another Person began to appear, at last his whole Figure, so plain, that I forgot *Cibber* and *Aesopus.*" The "Figure" is of course Walpole—

another Actor, (I am afraid a much worse Actor than *Cibber*) one who has play'd his Part upon a very large Stage, and had the greatest part of *Europe* for Spectators; his Fate has indeed been different from that of *Cibber, Cibber* has met with various Success, sometimes applauded, tho' oftner rebuked; but this other Actor has been hiss'd from his first Appearance upon the Stage, to this very Day. ...

A year later, in the same paper (26 December 1741), the relation of Walpole to the mythology established in the 1729 *Dunciad* was stated in unmistakable terms:

That Legion of Dunces which our Great Man, to show his excellent Judgment and

---

8/Named for "Queen Common Sense," who contends in Fielding's *Pasquin* (1736) with "Queen Ignorance," implied mentor of Walpole's administration, and is defeated—like her representatives in the *New Dunciad* and the *Dunciad* of 1743.

9/John Loftis, *The Politics of Drama in Augustan England* (cited above, n. 6), chs. v–vi. Anticipating the Great Sleep that envelops all in *Dunciad* iv, Samuel Johnson had ironically advocated in his *Compleat Vindication of the Licensers of the Stage* (1739) that schools be abandoned and reading made a felony, so that the licenser in due time will "enjoy the Title and the Salary without the Trouble of exercising his Power, and the Nation will rest at length in Ignorance and Peace" (p. 31).

39 The late P[re]m[ie]r M[i]n[iste]r.
3 December 1743

fine Taste, hath listed into his Service, have tired all the Excisemen and Custom-House Officers, from the Orchades to the Land's End of the County of *Cornwall*, with stupid Encomiums on the Advantages of Bribery, Corruption, and all the Tricks and Rogueries necessary for supporting an arbitrary and blundering Minister; but they have not (that I can recollect) made their Addresses in Form to that Goddess under whose auspicious Influence they live and write. ...[10]

Repeated allusions of this sort in the Opposition press must have made it clear to almost everybody whose figure the laureate was surrogate for, or rather, whose figures—since sometimes the image of Cibber blurs into the image of George II as well, just as Queen Dulness blurs into Queen Caroline. This effect is gained

---

10/A fuller account of the Cibber-Walpole-Dulness analogy as it appears in *Common Sense* will be found in the introduction of John M. Evan's valuable new edition of Cibber's *Apology*, now in preparation.

not primarily in the passages that the poem devotes directly to Cibber (though sometimes in these too Pope's notes hint at a fruitful ambiguity), but through a sense that must grow on all readers of the 1743 text as they move from the first lines of Book I to the famous close of Book IV that the poem's professed hero is a symptom not a cause. As Pope puts it himself in the note that in 1743 opens Book I:

the very Hero of the Poem hath been mistaken to this hour, so that we are obliged to open our Notes with a discovery who he really was. We learn from the former Editor, that this Piece was presented by the Hands of Sir Robert Walpole to King George II. Now the author directly tells us, his Hero is the Man

> who brings
> The Smithfield Muses to the ear of Kings.   (TE v 26)

The true hero of the poem, in other words, is Walpole, who, with the aid of a do-nothing foreign king and a queen whose name is Dulness but who is occasionally to be identified with Queen Caroline, has created the conditions that make it possible for Dulness to mount in Book IV a much solider and more influential throne than the one she was seen on or near in Book I.

But at this point, having spoken so much so boldly, the poet immediately converts everything he has just said to innuendo by insisting that no one but Cibber has been in his mind all along: "And it is notorious who was the person on whom this Prince conferred the honour of the *Laurel*."

Chapter 5

Then is the Poet's Time

If Satyres here you find, think it not strange:
'Tis proper Satyres in the Woods should range.
　　　　　　　　—James Howell, *Dedicatory Poem to Dendrologia*

I

Thanks to the long reach of innuendo, of which we have just taken some preliminary measurements, Pope's poems of the 30's could be read by his contemporaries in two quite different lights. Read thematically as poems, they raised issues of a sort that poets have often raised against the governing values and pursuits of their times, conveyed and dramatized in ways that will concern us later. Read topically and politically (and this is no doubt how they were read by a great many of Pope's contemporaries), they looked almost like stages in a personal war with the ministry and court. Clearly, they did continually tease up into the foreground Opposition catchwords and favorite themes, no matter how difficult the Latin original (where there was one) made it to do so. Walpole's peace policy; standing armies; George II's inadequacies as man and monarch and his domination by his queen; royal favorites and ministerial influence; parliamentary corruption; encroachment on individual liberties and especially on freedom of the press by governmental statutes, spies, and hacks; luxury and self-indulgence eroding national character and threatening inglorious servitudes at home as well as abroad—all these familiar Opposition points, and more, were glanced at repeatedly.

Furthermore, the poet seemed to go out of his way to commend leaders of the Opposition, government supporters who came over to the Opposition, and young men gathering about the Prince of Wales in hostility to the King and Walpole. He also seemed bent on allowing any names or episodes that could bring discredit on the regime to slide (as he himself put it) into verse and hitch in a rhyme.[1] The *Epistle to Bathurst* (January 1733), the poet's next publication after the *Epistle to Burlington* with its portrait of "Timon," swarmed with hints of evil-doing connived at by the government and allowed to go unpunished or insufficiently punished, in Walter, Chartres, Japhet Crook, Denis Bond, Sir John Blunt, Sir Robert Sutton, and numerous others, including, by insinuation, Walpole. The first imitation of Horace (February 1733) turned its attention to the king and royal family, and, to adopt Lord Hervey's terms, sneered "rather more than obliquely" (Hervey, 1 383) at both:

> P.   What? like Sir *Richard*, rumbling, rough and fierce,
> With ARMS, and GEORGE, and BRUNSWICK crowd the Verse?
> Or nobly wild, with *Budgell*'s Fire and Force,
> Paint Angels trembling round his *falling Horse*?
>   L.   Then all your Muse's softer Art display,
> Let *Carolina* smooth the tuneful Lay,
> Lull with *Amelia*'s liquid Name the Nine,
> And sweetly flow through all the Royal line.   (23–24, 27–32)[2]

The adaptation of Dr. Donne's fourth satire, also published that year (November), became in the poet's modernization a stalking horse from behind which, through the mouth of a yet more contemptible courtier than Donne's, alleged knaveries of the ministry and court could be leveled at in gross:

> When the *Queen* frown'd, or smil'd, he knows; and what
> A subtle Minister may make of that?
> Who sins with whom? who got his Pension *Rug* [i.e. safe],
> Or quicken'd a Reversion by a *Drug*?

1/*Imit. Hor., Sat.* II i 78.

2/I quote the passage as in the first edition before ll. 25–26 were added. In this edition the initial given the interlocutor is "L" (for Lawyer?).

Whose Place is *quarter'd out*, three Parts in four,
And whether to a Bishop, or a Whore?
Who, having lost his Credit, pawn'd his Rent,
Is therefore fit to have a *Government*?
Who in the *Secret*, deals in Stocks secure,
And cheats th' unknowing Widow, and the Poor?
Who makes a *Trust*, or *Charity*, a Job,
And gets an Act of Parliament to rob?   (132–43)

He tells what Strumpet Places sells for Life,
What 'Squire his Lands, what Citizen his Wife?
And last (which proves him wiser still than all)
What Lady's Face is not a whited Wall?   (148–51)

Then as a licens'd Spy, whom nothing can
Silence, or hurt, he libels the *Great Man*;
Swears every *Place entail'd* for Years to come,
In *sure Succession* to the Day of Doom:
He names the *Price* for ev'ry *Office* paid,
And says our *Wars thrive ill*, because delay'd;
Nay hints, 'tis by Connivance of the Court,
That *Spain* robs on, and *Dunkirk*'s still a Port.[3]   (158–65)

II

So it went, more or less continuously, from 1731 through 1738. Every year the poet managed new insults or revived the old.[1] The *Epistle to Cobham* (January 1734), though largely an essay on the ruling passion, addressed itself to a former Walpole supporter who had broken with the Government over the Excise Bill and in retaliation had been relieved of his colonelcy. Its last lines, besides being a compliment to the dedicatee, contained a prayer (often repeated in the writings and private letters of the literary Opposition) that could comfortably be read as a slur on those in power:

3/In his imitations of Donne and Horace, Pope follows the method of the *Craftsman* and other Opposition literature in using and adapting an earlier author to speak to the present times.

1/I make no attempt in what follows to be exhaustive, but merely give a range of examples. To untangle all the innuendo in these poems would require a book or a new edition.

> And you! brave COBHAM, to the latest breath
> Shall feel your ruling passion strong in death:
> Such in those moments as in all the past,
> "Oh, save my Country, Heav'n!" shall be your last.   (262–65)

The fourth epistle of the *Essay on Man* (published the same month) closed with the personal tribute to Bolingbroke that everyone remembers; it also contained those cryptic references to "Painful preheminence!" and to "Marcellus exil'd" and "Caesar with a Senate at his heels" already touched on (above, p. 134). In December, under the mask of an anonymity perhaps not meant to be wholly impenetrable, *Sober Advice from Horace* went a great deal further. It used Walpole's name overtly, and by means of what appears to be an unstated pun on member of parliament and privy member drew an exquisitely comic analogy between an imaginary interior dialogue and the question period in the House— climaxing at the middle in references to courtly dissoluteness and perversion that were all the more damning for being offered so casually.

> Suppose that honest Part that rules us all,
> Should rise, and say—"Sir *Robert*! or Sir *Paul!*
> "Did I demand, in my most vig'rous hour,
> "A Thing descended from the Conqueror?
> "Or when my pulse beat highest, ask for any
> "Such Nicety, as Lady or Lord *Fanny?*—
> What would you answer? Could you have the Face,
> When the poor Suff'rer humbly mourn'd his Case,
> To cry "You weep the Favours of her GRACE?"
>
> (*Sat.* 1 ii 87–95)

A year later, in the poet's collected works in quarto, volume II (April 1735), a new and challenging couplet was added to the *Essay on Man*'s praise of Bolingbroke, on the eve of the latter's retirement to France:

> When statesmen, heroes, kings, in dust repose,
> Whose sons shall blush their fathers were thy foes.   (IV 387–88)

In this same edition, in the *Epistle to Dr. Arbuthnot*, which had carried from the beginning (January 1735) several slurs such as the "ass's ears of Midas" (69 ff.), the portrait of "Paris" was renamed "Sporus" (305 ff.). This was a bold change indeed. Contemporaries could hardly fail to notice that the new name (packing implications of the abdication of manhood into the gross physical analogy of sodomist and catamite), reflected as much contempt on a minister and monarch who required this sort of total political possession as on those who were willing to suffer it.[2] At the very least, the passage invited subversive comparisons between the courts of Nero and George II.

Two years later (May 1737)—Pope published no new work of consequence in 1736—the *Epistle to Augustus* blew the king sky high ("with a puff," as a witty acquaintance of mine once said), and in the following year, on the ground that "Ridicule was become as unsafe as it was ineffectual,"[3] Pope put an end to the series. It died proudly, nevertheless. An epistle imitating Horace's sixth of the First Book was addressed in January 1738, to young William Murray, the future Lord Mansfield, who at this time moved in Opposition circles and was to support the petition of English merchantmen against Spanish depredations before the House of Commons that very spring.[4] A baker's dozen of its lines, though without mentioning Walpole's name, glanced sidelong at him through allusions to power, place, slaves, levees, election management, and cynical laughter:

> But if to Pow'r and Place your Passion lye,
> If in the Pomp of Life consist the Joy;
> Then hire a Slave, (or if you will, a Lord)
> To do the Honours, and to give the Word;
> Tell at your Levee, as the Crouds approach,
> To whom to nod, whom take into your Coach,
> Whom honour with your hand: to make remarks,
> Who rules in Cornwall, or who rules in Berks;

2/The wider political implications of the metaphor are suggested in William Pulteney's *A Proper Reply to a Late Scurrilous Libel* (1731), written in answer to *Sedition and Defamation Display'd* (1731), which was at the time widely credited to Hervey. *Sedition and Defamation Display'd* had challenged the Opposition to prove their charges of corruption. Pulteney acknowledges that this is difficult, and then goes on to add (pp. 27–28): "Give me Leave to illustrate This by a parallel Case—There is a certain, unnatural, reigning Vice ... which hath, of late, been severely punish'd in a neighbouring Nation. It is well known that there must be *two Parties* in this Crime; the *Pathick* and the *Agent*; both equally guilty. ... The Proof of the Crime hath been generally made by the *Pathick*; but I believe that Evidence will not be obtained quite so easily in the Case of *Corruption* when a Man enjoys every Moment the Fruits of his Guilt." Pope makes a similar point in "Sporus" (though by a different image), when he relates Hervey to Walpole (318): "And, as the Prompter breathes, the Puppet squeaks."

3/*One Thousand Seven Hundred and Thirty-Eight, Dial.* ii, 254n.

4/In John, Lord Campbell's *Lives of the Chief Justices of England* (1849), II 330, Pope is said to have been Murray's preceptor in the art of oratory.

> "This may be troublesome, is near the Chair;
> "That makes three Members, this can chuse a May'r."
> Instructed thus, you bow, embrace, protest,
> Adopt him Son, or Cozen at the least,
> Then turn about, and laugh at your own Jest.   (97–109)

In February (it had first been published in 1727), Pope republished Swift's fragment in imitation of Horace's sixth satire of the Second Book to introduce a version of the rest of the poem in which Horace's Country Mouse visits a Court Mouse rather than the City Mouse of the Latin original and discovers, in the words of the *Craftsman*, that "Independency" and a "private Fortune" are preferable to "publick Plunder."[5] The last line in the English rendering reiterated again a favorite Opposition theme and closed upon a term that by 1738 the Opposition press had almost pre-empted:

> Give me again my hollow Tree!
> A Crust of Bread, and Liberty![6]   (222–23)

This poem was succeeded in March by an imitation of Horace's epistle to Maecenas (1 i), addressed to Bolingbroke, who was now (in view of the death of Walpole's staunchest supporter, Queen Caroline, and the ever-mounting unpopularity of his peace policy) on the verge of returning to England. A compliment at this time to the ministry's arch-enemy was itself a calculated affront. Did it also insinuate that if ever England had a true Augustus on the throne, it might aspire to a true Maecenas and, correspondingly, a true laureate? Whether it did or not, there were some strong lines in it about a "Screen" and "Wall of Brass";[7] about "The modern language of corrupted Peers"; about getting wealth and place—

> For what? to have a Box where Eunuchs sing,
> And foremost in the Circle eye a King;   (105–6)

5/16 August 1735. (This passage is omitted from the collected edition.)

6/For typical Opposition rhetoric on the subject, see *Craftsman*, 11 August and 22 September 1733 (XI, 115ff, 157ff). Thomson's long poem *Liberty* (1735–36), though Whiggish, is anti-government and often indistinguishable in attitude from Old Whig positions taken up by Bolingbroke and his followers. See A. D. McKillop, *The Background of Thomson's Liberty*, *Rice Institute Pamphlets*, xxxviii, 1951, ch. vii.

7/Discussed more fully above, p. 141. See also Thomas E. Maresca, *Pope's Horatian Poems* (Ohio State University Press, 1966), p. 160.

and about the "Royal Cave" of the Hanoverian lion, where

> "Full many a Beast goes in, but none comes out."
> Adieu to Virtue if you're once a Slave.
> Send her to Court, you send her to her Grave.   (117–19)

In May of that same year, Pope closed his first dialogue of *One Thousand Seven Hundred and Thirty-Eight* with the picture of a whole nation rushing to pay tribute to its "Pagod" that we have noticed on an earlier page. For those who could read between the lines, this passage glanced also at an analogy between the marriage of Justinian with the prostitute Theodora and Walpole's recent marriage with his mistress Molly Skerrett:[8]

> *Vice* is undone, if she forgets her Birth,
> And stoops from Angels to the Dregs of Earth:
> But 'tis the *Fall* degrades her to a Whore;
> Let *Greatness* own her, and she's mean no more:
> Her Birth, her Beauty, Crowds and Courts confess,
> Chaste Matrons praise her, and grave Bishops bless.   (141–46)

In its last verses, following the Pagod reference, the poem placed satirist and establishment on a direct collision course:

> The Wit of Cheats, the Courage of a Whore,
> Are what ten thousand envy and adore.
> All, all look up, with reverential Awe,
> On Crimes that scape, or triumph o'er the Law:
> While Truth, Worth, Wisdom, daily they decry—
> "Nothing is Sacred now but Villany."
> Yet may this Verse (if such a Verse remain)
> Show there was one who held it in disdain.   (165–72)

July brought a sequel, Dialogue ii. Singing a swan-song for "proud satire," the poet here rose to some ringing sentences on the power of poetry in which the reference to Walpole could hardly have been clearer:

> Yes, I am proud; I must be proud to see
> Men not afraid of God, afraid of me:

8/See J. M. Osborn, "Pope, the Byzantine Empress, and Walpole's Whore," *Review of English Studies* (New Series), VI (1955), 372–82.

40 A Cheap and Easy Method of Improving English Swine's Flesh by a Generous
Method of Feeding. Artist and engraver unknown. 1743(?)

Safe from the Bar, the Pulpit, and the Throne,
Yet touch'd and sham'd by *Ridicule* alone—   (208–11)

and to some further ringing sentences on the integrity of the poet in which the
challenge to Walpole to open a proceeding could hardly have been made more
forthright:

Yes, the last Pen for Freedom let me draw,
When Truth stands trembling on the edge of Law:
Are none, none living? let me praise the Dead,
And for that Cause which made your Fathers shine,
Fall, by the Votes of their degen'rate Line!   (248–53)

How far Pope would have shown the courage here claimed in the real world,
we can only guess. Probably no farther than has been the custom of poets, which

41 The State Pack-Horse. Artist unknown, engraved by
C. Mosley. Dated 15 November 1739

is generally not far. But within the fiction of the poem and its genre, the role of
the fearless satirist supports the lines and gives them thrust. We may even say
that one idea and ideal of poetry—the same Renaissance ideal to which Marvell
or another had given expression three-quarters of a century earlier:

> When the Sword glitters ore the Judges head,
> And fear has Coward Churchmen silenced,
> Then is the Poets Time, 'tis then he drawes,
> And single fights forsaken Vertues cause—[9]

blooms fully for the last time in English in the two dialogues of *One Thousand
Seven Hundred and Thirty-Eight.*

9/*Tom May's Death*, 63–66. (Marvell's authorship of this poem is today in question.)

III

Possibly there is yet more to the story of Pope's private satirist's war with Walpole than this. My own suspicion is that his most formidable and problematical exercise in the vocabulary of innuendo occurs in his first Horatian imitation (*Sat.* II i), of which so far in this discussion little has been said. This poem, he told Spence, was suggested to him by Bolingbroke, who "observed how well that would hit my case, if I were to imitate it in English" (no. 321*a*). It was addressed, most appropriately, to Fortescue, Walpole's friend as well as Pope's, who had made some efforts in the late 20's, as we have seen, to keep the two men on polite terms. By now, however (February 1733), if my reading of the relationship is correct, Pope had declared war—for reasons that will probably never be clear to us and may not have been so to him—with the portrait of Timon in the *Epistle to Burlington* and with the network of allusions to governmental fraud in the *Epistle to Bathurst*. Were there personal resentments at work, perhaps corollary to the quarrel with Lady Mary, whose alleged libeling Pope had protested to Walpole in 1729 and whose "Encouragement" by Walpole he deplored in a letter to Fortescue in March 1733?[1] Was the influence of Bolingbroke and other Opposition friends, whose *Craftsman* never missed a gibe at the gargantuan character of Houghton and the greed and corruption of its owner, at this time decisive? Was the temptation to link the vulgarities of display attacked in the *Epistle to Burlington* to the vulgarities of display indulged by the king's chief minister (gross parody in Pope's view of Horace's Maecenas, Boileau's Colbert)[2] simply too great to be resisted?

Whatever the motives, it seems to me likely, as I have indicated earlier, that Pope published the *Epistle to Burlington* with the intention that Timon and his villa should be recognized. That some of its details did not apply provided the needful escape clause in the event of prosecution or other embarrassment, while at the same time the character's general orientation toward Walpole, insinuated repeatedly in the *Post Boy* letter and the unpublished *Master Key to Popery* (TE III ii 186), conveyed both the Opposition's censure of the ostentatious ex-

---

1/To Fortescue, 13 September [1729?] and [18] March [1733] (*Correspondence*, III 53 and 357). See also the possible implication in the *Epistle to Dr. Arbuthnot* (99–103) that the unnamed "patron" of Lady Mary is Walpole (above, p. 138). On the poet's quarrel with Lady Mary, see Robert Halsband's *Life of Lady Mary Wortley Montagu* (Clarendon Press, 1956), esp. chs. viii–ix.

2/In the MS. of Pope's imitation of the first satire of the second book, the scribblings that eventually became 123 ff. cite both "Maecenas" and "Colbert" as men of power who associated with and protected poets.

penditures at Houghton and the poet's own characteristic concern (eventually to find its best vehicle in the revised *Dunciad*) at materialism and philistinism in high places. But the government party (to continue what is admittedly speculation) proved to be expert sappers, and the little engineer was hoist with his own petard. The generic character of "Timon," together with the *in potentia* nature of innuendo, permitted the portrait to be deflected to the Duke of Chandos, and this was done—either in error, or, as Pope seems to have thought, disingenuously by members of the chief minister's claque.

The *Epistle to Bathurst* followed the *Epistle to Burlington* by approximately a year, as we have seen. That it contains any passage aimed quite as high politically as "Timon" cannot in the present state of our information be confidently affirmed, though there is much in the fable of "Balaam" and his Tempter that might have been taken by a partisan contemporary as a type-case of Walpole's mischievous moral influence.[3] In any event, the shadowy figure of Sir Robert Walpole, it has been well said, hovers "in the background of the entire poem, just as it hovered over the politico-economic morality of the age":

Indeed, it may be said that by indirection the entire poem is really an attack on Walpole, leader of the Whigs, friend of Chartres and other villains in the poem, patron of Phryne, screener of the directors of the South Sea Company, proponent of the Excise Bill. When Sir Balaam becomes a Member of Parliament [393 ff.], "one more Pensioner St. Stephen gains" because Walpole ... used ... his access to the nation's funds to make hirelings (or "pensioners") of the House of Commons, whose meeting place was St. Stephen's Chapel in Westminster. It was at this very moment that the word "pension" was gaining its Johnsonian definition as "pay given to a state hireling for treason to his country"; for Parliament had recently been debating the Pension Bill, designed to prevent its members from holding government grants, which, said the *Craftsman*, are intended not to reward a man for "his Service, but to corrupt his Conduct." To be of the group meeting in the Chapel once dedicated to St. Stephen is, therefore, to be a hireling of that other

---

3/Lady Ann Irwin sent a now lost copy of this poem to her father Lord Carlisle on 18 January 1732, with the characters "marked" as she interpreted them, adding in a letter: "The last character does not hit in every particular, but I think where 'tis disguised, 'tis with a design it mayn't be fixed" (TE, III ii 342n). Thus at least one contemporary reader believed that "Balaam" had an identifiable original. Perhaps a persuasive candidate will yet turn up.

Walpole was frequently represented in association with Satan—sometimes as his victim, who had sold his soul for power; sometimes as his surrogate to tempt others. (See e.g. Stephens, nos. 2418, 2439, 2516.) Thus in the "Dedication to the Publick" which Fielding wrote for his farce *The Historical Register for the Year 1736*, a character named Quidam (obviously

patron saint to whom the House of Commons is now dedicated and who is its pre-
siding spirit, the Lord Treasurer.[4]

A month after *Bathurst* came the poem we are now considering, *The First
Satire of the Second Book*. As the Twickenham editor points out (TE IV xiv), it
was clearly intended to be a codicil to *Bathurst* and *Burlington*, and to be read,
as the Horatian analogue suggests, in the light of the archetypal situation of the
publishing satirist, who cannot bring himself to glorify the status quo and the
great men supporting it, but finds himself driven instead to make criticisms that
creatures of the status quo call libels (*mala carmina*: *Sat.* II i 83). The imitation
should also be read, however, as it must have been by some of Pope's contemporaries, in the light of the debate about "Liberty of the Press" which was carried
on continuously during these years between the *Craftsman* and the government
writers; and in the light too of Pope's personal situation, now that he had crossed
swords with a man who could wield the whole power of the state against him
if he chose.

IV

The pages of the *Craftsman* have recourse frequently to positions identical with
those taken up by Horace in this satire and sometimes borrowed from them. In a
paper of 28 September 1728, for example, the *Craftsman* writer takes to task a
spokesman of the *London Journal* for proposing restraints on political satires and
libels (III 228 ff.). The argument of the government writer is that there is no
evidence such writings have ever prevented any vice; that they place the power
of infamy, which ought to be an instrument of the state, in private and indiscrimi-
nate hands; that, carrying no proofs, they disseminate only "*Suspicions, Hear-*

Walpole) who bribes a group of "Patriots" into a happier view of the state of England than
they had meant to take, is identified as follows: "But I am aware I shall be asked, who is
this Quidam ... ? Who but the devil could act such a part? ... Gold hath been always his
favorite bait, wherewith he fisheth for sinners; and his laughing at the poor wretches he
seduceth, is as diabolical an attribute as any. Indeed it is so plain who is meant by this Quidam,
that he who maketh any wrong application thereof might as well mistake the name of ... old
Nick for old Bob."

4/E. R. Wasserman, *Pope's Epistle to Bathurst* (Johns Hopkins Press, 1960), p. 54. It is
worth adding that Pope's concern in the poem with money-lenders like Peter Walter, with
speculators and stock-jobbers and (often corrupt) directors of great companies, with paper
credit and the land tax, reflects standard Opposition disapproval of the financial revolution that
was going forward in Walpole's time. See, for example, the *Craftsman*, 25 January and 6
September 1729; 29 April 1732; also, above, p. 119, n. 5, and below, p. 183, n. 2.

says, Coffee-house Tales, Tittle-Tattle, and idle Stories" (*ibid.*, 233); that they are motivated mainly by "*the Malignity of some Men's Tempers*," which "*represents it as an Offence in* others *to be great*" (*ibid.*, 234); and that if the victim is really wicked he should be accused in law, not libelled with innuendo. In other words, "*If a great Man be* lawful *Game, He ought to be* fairly chased, *not* shot *from a* Covert": "*... Men, who have Recourse to* obscure Invective, *are such as want Courage to bring an* open Charge; *as among Beasts, none ever bite or pinch their Adversaries with their* Teeth, *but such as are destitute of* Horns, *fairly to attack and annoy them*" (*ibid.*, 235–36).

The *Craftsman* writer's replies to all this are predictable. He makes much of the distinction between satire and libel that Horace also makes:

... the only Design of it [a libel], is to calumniate the Persons and misrepresent the Actions of Men, either in a publick or private Station, for vile, wicked and unjust Purposes. Whatever therefore is written without any *such Design* and for no *such Purpose*, is not a *Libel*. But Men, whose Characters are open to *Censure*, call every thing, of a *satirical* Nature, a *Libel*. ... (*Ibid.*, 231)

He also appeals to the traditional masking devices of satire, which have in all times enabled the satirist to speak of guilt by indirection:

If general Reflections upon *Vice, Ambition* and *Corruption*, under *fictitious* or *real Characters* of dead Men, universally allowed to be guilty of those Crimes; or under *Allegories, Parallels, Fables* and *Dreams*, ought to be accounted *Libels*; I will undertake to prove the same Charge, not only against the finest *Satirists*, the *wisest Mythologists*, the *chastest Poets*, the *most celebrated Moralists*, and the *gravest Divines*; but even against the *inspired Writers* Themselves. (*Ibid.*, 233–34)

Let the government writers call such devices shooting from a covert if they choose —what else is possible when the civil power is in hostile hands?

... supposing a *great Man*, which hath been the Case of many Nations, to be a *terrible, wild Beast of Prey*; who, besides his own *Strength* and *Fierceness*, hath got the Advantage of such an *Eminence* that we cannot dislodge or *chase him fairly*; what is to be done? Must we stand still and see Him continue his Depredations, though we have it in our Power to gall Him from a *Covert*? (*Ibid.*, 235)

As for the government writer's point about teeth and horns:

... I am afraid it will not, upon Examination, redound so much to his Honour as He may apprehend; for Providence hath given to every Creature some particular

Weapons of Offence and Defence against its Adversaries; to some *Claws or Talons*; to some *Teeth, Wings* and *Legs*; and *Horns* to others; so that I cannot conceive how *one Method of Attack* or *one Kind of Weapons* can be more honourable than *another equally natural*. (*Ibid.*, 236)

The real purpose of the government is to silence criticism of every kind: "the only *Liberty of the Press*, which this Author seems to allow, is a Liberty to write *Praise, Flattery* and *Panegyrick*, with a *Restraint* on every thing, which happens to be offensive and disagreeable to Those who are, at any Time, in Power" (*ibid.*, 239). All this is clearly reminiscent of the argument of Horace's poem.

Five weeks later (2 November 1728), having devoted two of the four intervening issues to the same general subject, the *Craftsman* (*ibid.*, 283 ff.) renewed its attack on the spokesman of the *London Journal*, who in the meantime had ventured to cite Horace's passage about *mala carmina* as evidence that reflections on the government were punishable even under Augustus in Rome. To this the *Craftsman* retorts:

If the *Journalist* quoted *Horace* with any other intent than to prove that there were Laws in *Rome* against Libels, He is as unfortunate in his Authority as ever; since the very Satire, from whence he takes one of his Quotations, is a direct Justification of *satirical Writings*. Nay, it appears from it that He not only attacked the *Vices*, but even the *Persons* of *wicked, great Men*; for otherwise why should He introduce his Friend *Trebatius* as apprehensive *that He would* not *be long-lived, but that the Creatures of some Men in Power would dispatch Him*? (*Ibid.*, 285)

The Craftsman writer then quotes lines 60–62 of the Latin and continues: "But *Horace* tells Him, like an honest brave Man, that whatever should be the Consequence, he would continue to write *Satire*, as *Lucilius* and others had done, and that only *wicked* Men would be offended at Him" (*ibid.*, 286).

In support of this he quotes further lines 62–70 of the Latin—the famous passage about the immunity granted to Lucilius when he satirized the great men of his day (*primores populi*) and consented to be a friend only to virtue and the friends of virtue. He then acknowledges that Trebatius does give Horace a "friendly Caution, to take Care of the *Laws*," since there was in fact a penalty in Rome for writing libels:

> Si mala condiderit in quem quis Carmina,
> Jus est Judiciumque;

("If anyone writes ill verses against another, there exists a right of redress by judgment.")

but adds that Horace "very justly" replied to this:

> Esto, si quis mala; sed bona si quis
> Judice condiderit, laudatur[1] Caesare.
>   Si quis
> OPPROBRIIS DIGNUM[2] latraverit, integer
>   ipse,
> Solventur Risu Tabulae; tu missus abibis.

("Of course—if a man writes ill verses. But if a man writes good verses and is praised by Caesar as judge? if, himself blameless, he barks at one who deserves abuse?— The proceedings will break up in laughter; you will get off free.")

It seems somewhat unlikely that as an associate of contributors to the *Craftsman* and possibly an occasional contributor himself,[3] Pope wrote his first imitation with no consciousness of the general debate about political satire against which it was certain to be seen by a number of his readers. It seems even more unlikely that in suggesting that Pope imitate this particular satire, Bolingbroke— the leading spirit behind the *Craftsman*—spoke without an *arrière-pensée* of which the poet likewise was conscious.

V

This brings us to Pope's personal situation vis-à-vis a minister on whose vulgarity of taste he had reflected (however ineffectually, as it turned out) in the *Epistle to Burlington* and on whose creatures he had poured scorn in the *Epistle to Bathurst*. Are we to infer that Horace's satire particularly "hit his case" because it allowed him to make his present position and future intentions clear with the help of a friendly interlocutor—his own and Walpole's long-time intermediary— who would speak with the grave accents of Horace's Trebatius but at the same time with the arguments of the government gazetteers? By following Horace in choosing a lawyer who was part of the political establishment to hear a defence of satire that was in his own case (if not in Horace's) aimed directly at the

---

1/Most modern editors read *laudatus*.

2/The capitals seem intended to alert the reader to the allusion to Walpole.

3/Pope is named as a contributor by Walter Sichel (*Bolingbroke and His Times* [London, 1901–2], 236 ff.). The possibility cannot be entirely ruled out, since some of the papers, passages, and advertisements could easily have been composed by the hand that wrote *The Art of Sinking in Poetry* and rewrote the *Memoirs of Scriblerus*. But there is no firm evidence of any kind.

establishment, was he intimating his awareness of potential danger? By rejecting, like Horace, the lawyer's suggestion that he glorify the regime, was he taking public account of what may in fact on occasion have been proposed to him, either by Fortescue or others, and what even if not actually proposed, must sometimes have been desired or expected of him, by at least a part of his audience, as chief poet of the age? Perhaps. Or perhaps not. Suffice it to say that with just a slight adjustment of Horace's demurrer, he could, as we have earlier seen, convey the incongruity of writing seriously about the house of Brunswick—either epic:

> What? like Sir *Richard*, rumbling rough and fierce,
> With ARMS, and GEORGE, and BRUNSWICK crowd the Verse?—

$$(23-24)$$

or lyric:

> Lull with *Amelia*'s liquid Name the Nine,
> And sweetly flow through all the Royal Line—   (31-32)

so that by implication only satire remained.

With an even slighter adjustment, he could convert Horace's statement about using his satiric weapon only when attacked into a comparison between himself and the minister, whose hypersensitivity to criticism he affects to share in the very moment that he abrades it further with pointed allusions to standing armies, Cardinal Fleury's alleged domination of English foreign policy, and what *looks* like a warning:

> Satire's my Weapon, but I'm too discreet
> To run a Muck, and tilt at all I meet;
> I only wear it in a Land of Hectors,
> Thieves, Supercargoes, Sharpers, and Directors.
> Save but our *Army*! and let *Jove* encrust
> Swords, Pikes, and Guns, with everlasting Rust!
> Peace is my dear Delight—not *Fleury's* more:
> But touch me, and no Minister so sore.
> Who-e'er offends, at some unlucky Time
> Slides into Verse, and hitches in a Rhyme,
> Sacred to Ridicule! his whole Life long. ...   (69-79)

If it occurred to contemporary readers to ask themselves who was being addressed in these lines, one imagines the answer cannot have eluded them indefinitely.

So much for ridicule as self-defense in case it should come to that: Pope promises to give as good as he receives, and in the next three verses allows three names of persons close to Walpole ("Delia," Sir Francis Page,[1] and "Sappho") to "slide" and "hitch," evidently to show his skill. What remains yet unresolved, however, is the question of the satirist's immunity as licensed censor of vice and folly, which was the purpose of the original application to Trebatius-Fortescue:

> There are (I scarce can think it, but am told)[2]
> There are to whom my Satire seems too bold. ...   (1–2)

To this question Pope now returns eloquently in his rendering of Horace's *quid? cum est Lucilius ausus* (62 ff.). This is the passage, to refer again to the words of the *Craftsman* writer, where "like an honest brave Man" the Roman poet tells Trebatius he will continue to write satire. It is also the passage that Pope cites in a letter to Swift as "my own single motive"[3] for writing and publishing the imitation. In reworking the lines, Pope replaces Horace's precedent of Lucilius with his own precedents of Boileau and Dryden (without however losing the force of the additional Roman antecedents, whose names are visible on the left-hand page), then asks of Fortescue essentially the question that Horace places before his own lawyer friend: is the privilege of satire that was conceded to Lucilius when he stripped off the skin of moral offenders without forfeiting the favor of those in power, such as Laelius and Scipio; and to Horace, who won the approval and protection of Augustus; and to Boileau, who even had a pension from the French establishment, and under an absolutist king at that;

1/On Page, see Paul Whitehead's *The State Dunces. Part II.* (1733), pp. 8–9, which charges him with being Walpole's tool:

> In the next Place comes equitable—,
> That *uncorrupted* and *Law-learned* Sage,
> At once the *Shame* and *Glory* of the Age.
> He ne'er, by arbitrary Statesmen *gain'd*,
> The *Laws t'oppress* unhappy *Culprits strain'd*;
> Nor did the Cause of LIBERTY *betray*,
> By *fining* Pris'ners *more* than they can pay,
> Witness poor—but the other Day.

(The allusion in this last line is probably to Richard Savage). Page seems also to be meant by "Old *Gruff*," with "*unclean Hands*," mentioned among Walpole's creatures in *The State Weather-Cocks*. See Stephens, no. 2021. The Suffolk papers (Brit. Mus. MS. Add. 22628) contain a mock love-song which says of him: "When Page one uncorrupted finger shows, ... Then shall I cease my Charmer to adore."

2/The problem posed by innuendo is again illustrated in "told." How literally are we to take this? *Was* Pope "told"? by "Fortescue"? at Walpole's behest following the *Epistle to Bathurst*? Or is this (like a mad Hamlet) to consider too curiously?

3/16 February 1733 (III 348).

and to Dryden, who was never harried by either of the Stuart kings he wrote under and had money from—is this privilege not still available today, especially to a poet who has no obligations whatever to the political status quo? The answer of course is yes—provided the writer can muster the necessary courage, which, as the drift of the whole poem to this point has shown, is required to be somewhat greater under George Augustus and Walpole than was called for under the Roman Augustus, the Sun King, or Charles and James, who were all supporters of poets:

> Could pension'd *Boileau* lash in honest Strain
> Flatt'rers and Bigots ev'n in *Louis'* Reign?
> Could Laureate *Dryden* Pimp and Fry'r engage,
> Yet neither *Charles* nor *James* be in a Rage?
> And I not strip the Gilding off a Knave,
> Un-plac'd, un-pension'd, no Man's Heir, or Slave?
> I will, or perish in the gen'rous Cause.
> Hear this, and tremble! you, who 'scape the Laws.
> Yes, while I live, no rich or noble knave
> Shall walk the World, in credit, to his grave.   (111–20)

These are the traditional accents of satire, standing its ground "whatever should be the Consequence," as the *Craftsman* writer has it. Did they have for Pope personal urgency as well, in view of what I have argued to be his under-cover war with Walpole, giving them that special dignity which seems always to characterize his verse when individual passion coalesces ideally with poetic role? One wonders.[4] One wonders further why the final two lines in the passage

---

4/"Knave" in l. 115 *could* be read by contemporary readers as an allusion, since this was a term frequently applied to Walpole (above, p. 140 and n. 3). The term could even be expanded to include allusions to Walpole as both knave and gamester, as in the following couplet from *The N[O]R[FOL]K Game of* CRIBBIDGE (Percival, no. XXXIII).

> Be that as it will, he did oft' *play the* KNAVE,
> By which many Games at a Pinch he did save—

and as gamester playing his knaves, as in Paul Whitehead's *The State Dunces. Part II* (1733), p. 14:

> For if his *Game* you rightly understand,
> The KNAVES are still the *best Cards* in his Hand;

and in *The State of Rome, under Nero and Domitian: A Satire* (1739), p. 5:

> Fierce Indignation boils within my Veins,
> To see big sharpers proud with impious gains,
> Roll in their Cars, and boast their *knavish* Mains.

42 The Champion; or, Evening Advertiser. Artist and engraver
unknown. Dated 5 July 1740

just quoted were not published till the second edition of the poem in 1734. Were
they inserted simply as an improvement, as apparently was the case with the
couplet added to the description of Blackmore and George II, conjugating in the
epic mood:

> Rend with tremendous Sound your ears asunder,
> With Gun, Drum, Trumpet, Blunderbuss, & Thunder;   (25–26)

or was it, as with the allusion to the hanging of a poet for satire "in Richard's
Times" (as we have seen, a favorite analogy for George II in Opposition
innuendo), felt to be in this context a challenge too precisely aimed, too
dangerous?[5]

5/The couplet is not contained in the MS. Possibly it was added to increase the pointedness
of "knave" by repeating it.

VI

I suspect an answer to these questions lurks in the opening lines of the passage, where Pope extends Horace's *primores populi* into a rather odd collection of specifics:

> What? arm'd for *Virtue* when I point the Pen,
> Brand the bold Front of shameless guilty Men,
> Dash the proud Gamester in his gilded Car,
> Bare the mean Heart that lurks beneath a Star;
> Can there be wanting to defend Her Cause,
> Lights of the Church, or Guardians of the Laws?   (105–10)

Contemporaries attuned to the argot of the day cannot have missed these allusions, however glancing, to a "bold Front," a "proud Gamester" (in fact, "the" proud Gamester), and a Garter "Star": attributes appropriated to Walpole by the Opposition for many years.[1] Yet there was nothing anyone could pin down, nothing he could even resent unless he first were willing to accept the charge that Walpole's singularity and eminence in vice was such that these terms could apply to no one else; whereas in fact the impudence of villains' faces was a stereotype, London was notorious for successful gamesters in luxurious circumstances, not least among them the Colonel Chartres who had figured so prominently in the poet's *Epistle to Bathurst*, and "mean" Garter-wearers could be cited all the way back to the founding of the order by Edward III. An equal ambiguity lay in wait further along in the passage. What were "you, who 'scape the Laws" if not the usual great villains of satiric theory, so eminent that no power but that of publicity and ridicule can touch them? Yet there was one particular "great villain" who, according to Opposition literature, had again and again escaped the laws

---

1/"Gamester" was a term particularly loaded. See for example, *The Norfolk Gamester: or, The Art of Managing the Whole Pack, Even King, Queen, and Jack* (1734), which contains (1) "The N[O]R[FOL]K Game of CRIBBIDGE: Or, the ART of *Winning All Ways*" (Percival, no. XXXIII); (2) "B[O]B, take Care least your CRIB be BILK'D"; (3) "The GAME of *CHESS* Versify'd, from the *CRAFTSMAN*"; and (4) "*APPIUS* Unmasqu'd." See also the quotation immediately above from *The State of Rome, under Nero and Domitian*. A couplet in Paul Whitehead's *Manners: A Satire* (1739), p. 14, may (or may not) suggest that he recognized the object of Pope's "dash" (107) to be a specific person:

> Safe may he dash the Statesman in each Line,
> Those dread his Satire, who dare punish mine.

Whitehead's "he" is Pope, his "Statesman" Walpole. Compare Pope's "I must be proud to see Men not afraid of God, afraid of me."

—though it was hoped his luck would not hold forever. Were *all* great villains to
"hear this, and tremble"—or was it primarily one? And was it to hint this more
effectively that the couplet we have been considering (119–20) was added in all
editions after the first?

Whatever the right answers to these questions may be, once they cross the
mind, Pope's first imitation of Horace appears in a somewhat changed light.
Perhaps it is a "rearguard" for his epistles to Burlington and Bathrust not only,
as the Twickenham editor reminds us, in pleading the general cause of satire
before the court of public opinion, but even in seeking to communicate to
Walpole and his associates a measure of the particular kind of defensive power
that this particular satirist has, together with a warning (*ut quo quisque valet
suspectos terreat*: *Sat.*, ii i 50) visibly enacted. Perhaps it is for this reason that
the poem begins with three names of persons well known to be of Walpole's train
and representative of his influence: Peter Walter, the grasping New Man of
aristocratic household finance, who was steward to Newcastle, Walpole's Secretary of State;[2] Francis Chartres, Walpole's runner, known as "Rape-Master
General" of Great Britain as his master was "Skreenmaster General," a multiple

---

2/Walter is explicitly likened to Walpole in Swift's *To Mr. Gay on his being Steward
to the Duke of Queensberry* (1731), 101–4, 115–16.

> Have *Peter Waters* always in your Mind
> That Rogue of *genuine ministerial* Kind:
> Can half the Peerage by his Arts bewitch;
> Starve twenty Lords to make one Scoundrel rich: ...
> Thus Families, like R[eal]ms, with equal Fate,
> May sink by *premier Ministers of State.*

Swift's and Pope's animus against Walter was probably impersonal. Walter represented a
class of men who had long been regarded by the landed class as their natural enemies (the
scrivener-lenders), and who, as pioneers of the money market, fitted easily into the new eco-
nomic order of national banks, funded national debts, and proliferating joint stock companies
that Walpole was held to have fostered for his own nefarious ends. This was Defoe's "age of
projects," or, as it has been more recently called, an age of financial revolution (P. G. Dickson,
The Financial Revolution in England: A Study in the Development of Public Credit 1688–1756
[London, 1967]), when the modern commercial establishment was forming, and Pope was
obviously troubled both by its representatives and its operations, harking back constantly, as we
have seen above in Ch. iii, to older times and ways.

Walpole, though a country squire, was rightly felt by the opposition to be in sympathy with
and in command of the moneyed interests represented by Walter and his kind. Hervey (i 38)
shrewdly remarks that while Walpole was "hated by the city of London, because he never did
anything for the trading part of it," he nevertheless "aimed at ... a corrupt influence over the
directors and governors of the great moneyed companies." He had of course given the financiers
reason to be grateful to him by his "screening" activities.

villain but "protected";[3] and Lord Fanny, effete courtier and literary dabbler,
Walpole's chief palace agent.[4] Perhaps it is for this purpose that Pope goes out of
his way to sneer at the king and his family, and at Cibber, their and Walpole's
laureate; at Stephen Fox, Hervey's friend and Walpole's follower; at Denis
Bond, lately incriminated in both the Derwentwater Estates and the Charitable
Corporation swindles, where Walpole had notoriously served to screen villainy;
at standing armies, Cardinal Fleury's influence, and England's alleged defeats at
the European political card-game called in contemporary slang "Quadrille";[5]
at misconduct by courtiers and government functionaries; at (very close home
now) bold Fronts, Gamesters, and Garter Stars; and, finally, in the very last
lines of the satire, at the great name itself:

> P. *Libels* and *Satires*! lawless Things indeed!
> But grave *Epistles*, bringing Vice to light,
> Such as a *King* might read, a *Bishop* write,
> Such as Sir *Robert* would approve—
>   *F.* Indeed?
> The case is alter'd—you may then proceed.
> In such a Cause the Plaintiff will be hiss'd,
> My Lords the Judges laugh, and you're dismiss'd.   (150–56)

There is of course in these lines a flick of irony at the entire establishment—
king, church, and ministry. In Augustan England, a "King" did *not* read, the

---

3/See William Pulteney's *An Answer to One Part of a late Infamous Libel* (1731), p. 43–44.
Addressing Walpole, Pulteney says of Chartres: "I know but *one other Estate in England*,
which hath been *scraped* together by such Means; and I make it a question whether all Mankind will not allow the Proprietor of it to be the honester Man; *Him* I mean, whom you lately
saved from the Gallows; and it is the only Thing you ever did in your Life for nothing, when
you had an opportunity of making a Penny; but perhaps, you might think the Similitude of
your Characters and Circumstances made it impolitick to let Him suffer the Punishment,
which He deserved." On Chartres's career, see Pope's *Epistle to Bathurst*, 20n, and Percival,
no. xiv: "On Colonel Francisco, Rape-Master General of Great Britain."

4/See Hervey's Memoirs, *passim*, and Romney Sedgwick's statement (1 50) that "so long as
the Queen lived he was, so to speak, chief eunuch of the Palace with a reasonable possibility
of becoming grand vizier."

5/Pope's reference to "Quadrille" here is in part a reminder of his earlier reference to it in
the *Epistle to Bathurst*, 63–64, which is sharply political. Imagining that the ancient fiscal
scheme of payments in kind has supplanted more modern forms of exchange, the poet sketches
the damping effect this might have on all sorts of (mostly disreputable) modern transactions,
including "Quadrille":

> Oh filthy check on all industrious skill,
> To spoil the nation's last great trade, Quadrille!

kind of "Bishop" Pope had in mind did *not* attack vice;[6] and Sir Robert—that strong-minded ruler who opposed all inquiries into fraud on the ground, Hervey tells us, that these might become so habitual with parliament as someday to "affect himself, his family, and posterity" (above, p. 131)—could hardly be supposed to approve the bringing of any vice whatever to light. Does the passage also have in reserve, besides this, a delicate thrust for the minister alone? It may be. The prompt capitulation of the legal interlocutor when the approval of Sir Robert is mentioned, followed by the capitulation of "the Judges," seems calculated to underscore the Opposition point that England was ruled by a man and not by her laws.[7] Moreover, the hissing of "the Plaintiff," who in the circumstances described could be no other than a government agent representing the ministry or the minister himself, might be expected to remind readers of several unavailing efforts by Walpole to silence the Opposition press in a court of law; or even of some occasion, not now identifiable, when the minister actually was hissed.[8]

The name refers not only to a fashionable contemporary card game, but—as its being "the nation's last great trade" hints—to the maneuvering for political and trade advantage which went on more or less continuously during the 1720's and 1730's between Austria, Spain, France, and Britain, especially during the Congress of Soissons in 1728. This was sometimes represented in Opposition propaganda as a card game wherein Britain under the two Walpoles always lost. See, for example, the title of the following: "*The Norfolk Congress. Or, A Full and True Account of their Hunting, Feasting, and Merry-making; ... To which is added,* QUADRILLE, *as now play'd at* Soissons"; also *A Supplement to the Norfolk Congress,* &c., p. 4, where "a Sycophant" (possibly his brother Horatio) says to Walpole:

> Since then our Fortune on your Rise depends
> And that our PRIVATE, not the PUBLICK-ENDS,
> Are the grand Articles we have in View,
> Those Steps you take, for my Part I'll pursue;
> The Quadrile Game, I cunningly will play,
> And what you leave unfleec'd, I'll sweep away.

Hence, when the present poem represents Pope as one who has ventured "to ridicule all Taste, blaspheme Quadrille," the line could be read as carrying a double jibe at Walpole—both for vulgar display at home, ridiculed earlier in "Timon," and for neglect of British interests abroad, ridiculed in the *Epistle to Bathurst.*

There is a ballad on Quadrille in both its senses, probably by Arbuthnot, in the Pope-Swift *Miscellanies*: "The Last Volume" (1727), pp. 197–201.

6/The MS. shows that Pope at one time considered putting "Gibson" in place of "Bishop"— i.e. Edmund Gibson, Bishop of London, Walpole's manager of the clerical vote. See Hervey, 190-91.

7/For those following Horace's Latin on the left-hand page, it would be obvious that where the Roman poet had invoked Caesar as the one who would "approve," the English poet had invoked Walpole—not the King.

8/Possibly there is a connection between Pope's "hissed" and the episode or attitude

In no other poem before 1738 does Pope engage the activities and personalities of the regime with such peculiarly personal intensity and (possibly reflecting the confidence of early 1733, when it seemed that Walpole's removal might be imminent) a tone that so clearly blends ridicule with threat and both with a parade of strength. To Horace's register of weapons, Pope rather strikingly adds the disquieting proposition (though it would have drawn no more than a horse-laugh from Walpole, who felt about fame much as Falstaff feels about honor) that he will reserve his censure of vice in the highest places for posterity:

> Publish the present Age, but where my Text
> Is Vice too high, reserve it for the next:
> My Foes shall wish my Life a longer date. ...   (59–61)

To Horace's simple resolve to continue writing satires, Pope adds the oddly self-conscious claim that he will "perish" if need be, and follows this with what appears to be a combination of threat and defiance, quite foreign to the Latin original: "Hear this, and tremble! you, who 'scape the Laws." Similarly, for Horace's vague *magnis*, who will protect Horace as Scipio and Laelius protected Lucilius, Pope substitutes two clearly identified "champions": the one a successful general in the Spanish wars of Marlborough's time, a gentleman of the old

---

obviously glanced at in an advertisement in the *Craftsman*, 22 July 1727 (II 71), which carries the words of Horace (*Sat.* I i 66) "Populus *me sibilat*, at mihi *plaudo*."

In Fielding's *Historical Register for the Year 1736*, II, ii, "Pistol" (representing Theophilus Cibber, well known in this role, and speaking—he calls himself "prime minister theatrical"—in terms calculated to remind the audience of Walpole), is hissed by the "Mob" that follows him. Still using a species of double-talk that *could* apply to Walpole, he welcomes

> Those glorious hisses, which from age to age
> Our family has borne triumphant from the stage.

Later (III i) a character named Quidam representing Walpole (above, p. 173, n. 3), stands in the wings and laughs at a meeting of "Patriots" (whom he will eventually join and successfully bribe into adopting a more favorable opinion of the state of the realm). At this point the following dialogue ensues.

Sourwit. Why do you suffer that actor to stand laughing behind the scenes ...?
Medley. O, Sir, he ought to be there, he's a laughing in his sleeve at the patriots; he's a very considerable character. ...
Sourwit. Methinks the audience shou'd know that, or perhaps they may mistake him as I did, and hiss him.
Medley. If they should, he is a pure impudent fellow, and can stand the hisses of them all; I chose him particularly for the part.

The Fielding reference is of course later than Pope's, but all of them may look back to an unidentified specific episode, or episodes. See also Fielding's *Eurydice Hissed* (1737), which treats Walpole's failure with the Excise Bill allegorically in terms of the playwright's own failure with his earlier farce *Eurydice*, and above, p. 160.

school whose contempt for the Hanoverian court seems never to have been disguised; the other Walpole's most implacable enemy and, in Pope's view presumably, best successor if the government should fall. If Pope, in adapting this satire, did have in view not simply the usual apologia of the satirist but the intimately personal intentions that Bolingbroke's participation at the genesis of the poem probably implies, his performance is more versatile than we had supposed.

VII

Let this be as it may. It was, at any rate, through an intense engagement of his own personality and situation with the traditional topics and situations of satire that Pope always found his distinctive rhetorical voice; and just here, I take it, innuendo proved to have a usefulness of which possibly he was not aware. The more "dangerous" allusions to Walpole and his regime throughout the satires and epistles must have fed his sense of participation in the great concerns of his time, a sense that was always dear to him, all the more fiercely perhaps because of his disabilities; and the sense of participation enabled his feelings to kindle, whether they sprang from provocation, as obviously in some instances, or from a genuine moral concern which (as with the rest of us) was no less genuine for his own lapses:

> When Truth or Virtue an Affront endures,
> Th' Affront is mine, my Friend, and should be yours.
> (*One Thousand Seven Hundred and Thirty-Eight, Dial.* ii, 199–200)

In the world of conduct, as elsewhere, never ask for whom the bell tolls: it tolls for thee. Pope saw this, and when he speaks both for his own island and the continent of mankind, his lines sing.

To make the same point from another direction, the advantage of innuendo was that it left the apparent detachment of the satirist unruffled, while allowing for the emotional commitment that makes poetry possible. Bold front, gamester, and mean heart beneath a Garter Star could serve as lineaments of Walpole without ceasing to serve as traditional and generic objects of satire. Similarly, a poet could speak, as I think Pope does in this first Horatian imitation, from a certain highly personal situation in his own career as a writer without giving up any of the advantage that accrues to a satirist as spokesman in a more general cause: "TO VIRTUE ONLY, and HER FRIENDS A FRIEND." Hence in the last analysis, though their immediate political vein runs deep, the poems of the 30's are enabled to be political in a larger sense of that term, to which we must now turn.

Chapter 6

Mighty Opposites

Multa quoque et bello passus, dum conderet urbem.
—Virgil, *Aeneid*, I   5

I

Whatever political intentions Pope may or may not have incorporated into his first Horatian imitation, the example of Horace had encouraged him to assume for the first time publicly—though, as his letters show, by no means for the first time in his own imagination—the role with which he would thereafter be oftenest identified during his life. This, as we have seen, was the role of poet-sage, cultivator of a Muse, a garden, and himself, whose daily life of old-fashioned friendships and simplicity, with a grotto at its center, could be felt to differ pointedly from the sick hurry and divided aims of the madding world—

> Know, all the distant Din that world can keep
> Rolls o'er my *Grotto*, and but sooths my Sleep—

and whose independence of mind and manners—

> Un-plac'd, un-pension'd, no Man's Heir, or Slave—

could be regarded as supplying both a tonic contrast and a visible alternative to the general scheme of things under a minister who sold political security and advancement only at the price of sycophancy.

We have already seen how this Twickenham role appeared to an enemy in James Ralph's verses of 1728 (above, p. 65). It appeared of course quite otherwise to Swift, who paid it a handsome tribute in his *Libel on Dr. Delany* (1730), emphasizing like Ralph, however, though now from a friendly point of view, its isolation and independence of the world, and its relation to a long tradition of such isolation and independence:

> Hail! happy *Pope*, whose gen'rous Mind,
> Detesting all the Statesmen kind,
> Contemning *Courts*, at *Courts* unseen,
> Refus'd the Visits of a Queen;
> A Soul with ev'ry Virtue fraught
> By *Sages, Priests,* or *Poets* taught;
> Whose filial Piety excels
> Whatever *Grecian* Story tells:
> A Genius for all Stations fit,
> Whose *meanest Talent* is his *Wit*:
> His Heart too Great, though Fortune little,
> To lick a *Rascal Statesman*'s Spittle,
> Appealing to the Nation's Taste,
> Above the Reach of Want is plac't:
> By *Homer* dead was taught to thrive,
> Which *Homer* never cou'd alive.
> And, sits aloft on *Pindus* Head,
> Despising *Slaves* that *cringe* for Bread.   (71–88)

Expressing similar attitudes, Paul Whitehead, in an address to Pope in his *State Dunces* of 1733 (p. 1), sets the self-sufficient garden world of Twickenham over against Walpole's "faithless Levees," in phrases calculated to remind his readers of Virgil's contrast between the happy retirement figures of his second *Georgic* and those who throng to the portals of kings or plough unknown seas for gold:

> While cringing Crowds at faithless Levees wait,
> Fond to be Fools of Fame, or Slaves of State,
> And others, studious to encrease their Store,
> Plough the rough Ocean for *Peruvian* Ore;

How blest thy Fate, whom calmer Hours attend,
Peace thy Companion, Fame thy faithful Friend;
While in thy Twick'nham Bowers devoid of Care,
You feast the Fancy and enchant the Ear.

The rest of Whitehead's poem, however, as may be inferred from its title, is a cutting satire on the entire Walpole regime, and the fact that it carries "Inscrib'd to Mr. Pope" on its title-page suggests that the message of the first Horatian imitation has been correctly read: the little squire of Twickenham, having shown his hand, is from now on to be regarded as spiritual patron of the poetical Opposition to Walpole—not only in being an eloquent spokesman for the life of disinterested virtue that Opposition writers claimed to wish to restore to their native land, but in being at the same time its emblem.[1] A poem of 1735, for example, calling itself *Seasonable Reproof: A Satire in the Manner of Horace ... To be continued occasionally as a poetical Pillory, to execute Justice upon such Vices and Follies as are either above the Reach, or without the Verge of the Laws*, has a speaker who by his careful echoings of the *Epistle to Dr. Arbuthnot* seems to labor to be mistaken for Pope.[2] If so, the implication of his subtitle is presumably

---

1/The view of Pope taken during the 30's by those friendly to him may be further sampled in the anonymous *Epistle from a Gentleman at Twickenham* [i.e. Pope] *to a Nobleman at St. James's* [i.e. Hervey]. *Occasion'd by an Epistle from a Nobleman to a Doctor of Divinity* [1733], p. 4:

As for my Part, I chuse to live remote,
Nor will I be induc'd to turn my Coat;
I hear, but yield not to the *Syren*'s Note.
Let others in Brocaded Silks and Sattins
Appear abroad, while I attend my *Mattins*.
My Home-spun Lindsy-Wolsy pleases me,
Nature's Intent it answers, and I see
With Unconcern, each dapper, spruce *Toupee*.
Your pretty Face and Shape I envy not,
But rest content with what has been my Lot:
My rural Mansion is to me a Court,
Tired with the Town I thither do resort;
Divide my Hours between my Friends and Study,
And sometimes sit and chat with honest Cuddy.

(Cuddy is John Gay.)

2/Having laid claim to "Candor" in the eighteenth-century sense of benignity, the speaker is interrupted by an interlocutor, whereupon the following dialogue takes place:

But, Sir, your *Writings*—Well, Sir, what of them?
They're *guilty* of the *Crime*, which you condemn.

that the Twickenham poet has now engaged himself in a further phase of the campaign he promised in his first Horatian imitation: "Hear then, and tremble! you, who 'scape the Laws." In an anonymous poem of 1737, Pope is celebrated by name as one whose versatile poetic powers support, or even in fact perform, all the functions of church and civil state—a marked escalation of his own moderate hope in the first imitation that defence of virtue will find judges and ecclesiastics rushing to his aid:

> Whether the nobler Monument he frame,
> To those whom Virtue, Arts, or Arms adorn;
> Or snatch from Envy, or the Grave, Their Fame,
> Whom Pride oppresses, or the Virtues mourn.
>
> Till (as of old, some Heav'n instructed Bard)
> To Man he pleads in Truth and Wisdom's Cause;
> Chastises Vice, deals Virtue her Reward,
> Supports the Pulpit, and supplies the Laws.[3]

> Each Page is blotted with some injur'd Name;
> Each Line's destructive of some Neighbour's Fame[—]
> Whence this black Charge on me? Who know me best,
> Know 'tis a Crime, I from my Soul detest.
> The Man, who loves to *wound* an absent Friend,
> Or, *wounded*, cares not, dares not to defend:
> Who ne'er would stifle an injurious Joke,
> To gain a Laugh regardless what he spoke:
> Who sweats to spread forg'd Scandal thro' the Town,
> And basely whispers Reputations down:
> Who, what he never saw, proclaims for true;
> And vends for Secrets what he never knew;
> That, that's the Wretch, to whom the Censure's due.
> But, have I acted such a brutish Part?
> No; 'tis not in my *Writings*, or my *Heart*:
> Here, Sir, you'll find, if you'll be pleas'd to read,
> None, but the *Vicious*, in my Verses *bleed*. (261–79)

It is always possible that the apparent reminiscences of the *Epistle to Dr. Arbuthnot* result from the common origin in Horace (*Sat.* 1 iv 78–85) and the fact that, once the lines had been Englished in Pope's way, it was difficult to avoid echoing them. On the other hand, the title and subtitle with their suggestion of vice and folly challenged in high places, seem calculated to remind contemporary readers of Pope's earlier pieces "In the Manner of Horace," especially his imitation of the first satire of the second book. *Seasonable Reproof* has been attributed to the Rev. James Miller.

3/*An Ode to the Earl of Chesterfield, Imploring His Majesty's Return* (pp. 7–8). Footnotes tell us that "nobler Monument" refers to Pope's "Epitaphs," "snatch from Envy, or the Grave"

Three years later, an anonymous writer acknowledges Pope's long-standing leadership in "Virtue's Cause,"[4] but, with a curious anticipation of the poet's own note (first published in 1751) at the end of his second dialogue of *One Thousand Seven Hundred and Thirty-Eight*,[5] urges him to desist now, for the task is hopeless:

> Long have you been to Virtue a Defence,
> A Dread to Folly, Vice, and Insolence! ...
> And Men who were ev'n not afraid of God,
> Yet trembling dreaded thy chastising Rod.

---

to his "Epistles," and "To Man he pleads" to the *Essay on Man*, and so on. It is worth remarking that the functions attributed to Pope in the last two lines are those ordinarily attributed to the throne.

4/By those friendly to Pope this leadership was hailed from 1733 on. See above on Whitehead. See also *The Wrongheads. A Poem* (1733), p. 3:

> Shall knaves and fools command the world's applause,
> And censure 'scape, because they 'scape the laws?
> No—*Pope* forbids, and, fir'd with honest rage,
> Resolves to mend, as well as charm, the age;
> Nor fears the cause of virtue to defend,
> Nor blushes to confess himself her friend.
> Hail, gen'rous bard! fair virtue smiles to see
> Thy toil, design'd by her and heav'n for thee.
> Bravely proceed;—chastise the vain, the proud,
> Nor heed the murmurs of the guilty crowd;
> Point out the follies of the rich and great;
> Mark the Plebean soul disguis'd in state;
> Disclose the meanness of the P[ension]'d train;
> Thy theme will last while fools and knaves remain.

See also *The Parsoniad; A Satyr. Inscribed to Mr. Pope* (1733), p. 4:

> Oh thou distinguish'd Bard whom I revere,
> In Life unblemish'd, and in Verse sincere;
> Oh most obliging, where the le[a]st oblig'd,
> In Crowds, surrounded, and in Courts, besieg'd;
> Thou School of Virtue, and thou Scourge of Vice. ...

5/L. 255n: "This was the last poem of the kind printed by our author, with a resolution to publish no more; but to enter thus, in the most plain and solemn manner he could, a sort of PROTEST against that insuperable corruption and depravity of manners, which he had been so unhappy as to live to see. Could he have hoped to have amended any, he had continued those attacks; but bad men were grown so shameless and so powerful, that Ridicule was become as unsafe as it was ineffectual. The Poem raised him, as he knew it would, some enemies; but he had reason to be satisfied with the approbation of good men, and the testimony of his own conscience." (TE IV 327)

But now not so—Vice is grown strong and bold,
Takes deeper Root, and spreads as it grows old.
Wherefore accept th' Advice of me your Friend,
And cease to strive this vicious Age to mend.[6]

II

The above quotations are samples merely. They may be duplicated many times over during the years 1733–40 as the literary opposition to Walpole grew, and Pope, first in poems and then in published letters as well as poems, drew about him publicly (as we saw) the now almost seamless garment formed of ancient Rome and Twickenham and seventeenth-century retirement precedents, which signalized the posture of the honest satirist protesting a corrupt society.[1]

6/*A Satirical Epistle to Mr. Pope* (1740), p. 3. See also *Epidemical Madness: A Poem in Imitation of Horace* (1739), where a speaker plainly meant to pass for Pope says (p. 3):

And since I can't reclaim the Sins of Men,
Who blaze above the Lashes of the Pen;
Far from the Crimes and Mischiefs of the Great,
Whose Factions scarce allow them Time to eat,
In rural Pleasures, free from Din and Strife,
I think I'm now resolv'd to end my Life.

1/By 1738, even the editor of the government's *Daily Gazetteer* felt it expedient to take notice of Pope's position as Opposition spokesman. On 27 March, the poet's compliments to Bolingbroke in the *Essay on Man* and also in the just-published imitation of Horace's epistle to Maecenas (1 i) are politely judged to be so false as to be actually "Satyr," not "Panegyrick." On 6 April, a piece in verse is inserted in which Bolingbroke, "always the Hero of his old Patriots," and Lyttelton, the hero "of his young ones" are both held up to scorn as incompetents; and this is introduced by the observation: "A Celebrated Poet having lately published several Imitations of the *Epistles* and *Satires* of *Horace*, ... I cannot but observe that in these Performances, the Friends to the present Government are continually the Subject of his Satire, as they who are the avowed Enemies to their Country are thought worthy of his Panegyricks." Some doggerel verses appearing in the issue of 11 April are less respectful. Purporting to be a further address from Pope to Bolingbroke, they conclude:

If Spight of Fears, of Mercy Spight,
My Genius still must rail, and write,
Haste to thy Twick'nham's safe Retreat,
And mingle with the grumbling Great.
There half devoured by Spleen, you'll find
The rhyming Bubbler of Mankind;
There (Objects of our mutual Hate)
We'll ridicule both Church and State.

Twickenham is plainly seen here as a center of disaffection.

43 The Roman poet and satirist, 1740.
By Louis François Roubiliac, 1695–1762

The symbolic status that he had gradually acquired is nowhere better illustrated than in two anonymous pamphlets which appeared in 1740.[2] The fiction of these pamphlets is that a confrontation is taking place between a certain poet and Walpole, and the poet is Pope—not quite, however, the historical Pope, but Pope the symbol, the incorruptible grotto figure. The earlier of the two is entitled *Are These Things So? The Previous Question, From an Englishman in his Grotto to a Great Man at Court*. Its epigraph consists of two lines taken from the close of Horace's second epistle of the Second Book, with application to Walpole's hoped-for fall:

Lusisti Satis, edisti Satis, atque bibisti,[3]
TEMPUS ABIRE TIBI.

Its substance is an address to the Great Man, in inferior verse but in Pope's

2/The two pamphlets described in the text have been attributed to James Miller, who was also, reputedly, the author of *Seasonable Reproof* (above, p. 190, n. 2). If this attribution is correct, Miller's relations with Pope should be looked into.

3/"The Second Edition Corrected" (also 1740) carries this note: "Some great and erudite

44 Bust of Sir Robert Walpole, *c.* 1730.
By John Michael Rysbrack, 1693(?)–1770

general manner, made by a virtuous withdrawal figure whose accents are often
drawn from or based on Pope's previous poems.

> My sole *Ambition* o'er myself to reign,
> My *Avarice* to make each Hour a Gain;
> My *Scorn*—the Threats or Favours of a Crown,
> A Prince's Whisper, or a Tyrant's Frown;
> My *Pride*—forgetting and to be forgot,
> My *Luxury*—lolling in my peaceful Grott.
> All Rancour, Party, Pique, expung'd my Mind,
> Free or to *laugh* at, or *lament* Mankind;
> Here my calm Hours I with the wise employ,
> And the great *Greek*, or *Roman* Sage enjoy;
> Or, gayly bent, the Mirth-fraught Page peruse,

Criticks, instead of *Bibisti*, read BRIBISTI in this Place. Which of the two is the most applicable,
our QUERIST does not pretend to determine."

> Or, pensive, keep a *Fast-day* with the Muse.
> Close shut my Cottage-Gate, where none pretends
> To lift the Latch but Virtue and her Friends;
> Tho' pardon me—a Word, Sir, in your Ear,
> Once, *long ago*, I think I saw YOU here.[4]   (pp. 1–2)

Despite his isolation, however—"all Hermit as I live"—this speaker loves his country deeply and has been troubled by reports reaching him of her degeneracy, of her famed dominion of the seas lost to "Gaul and Spain," her parliaments grown servile, her great men who dare speak out "Stripp'd of all Honour, Dignity, and Rule," her moral health "Polluted," her "Commerce" fled. "Are These Things So?" the "Englishman in his Grotto" asks the "Great Man at Court," or are they simply slanders of the out-party—"Of those who *want*, or who have *lost* a *Place*?" If the latter, why not defend yourself in detail, *viz.*:

> "In my dear Country's Service now *grown gray*,
> *Spotless* I've walk'd before you to this Day,
> My Thoughts laid out, my precious Time all spent
> In the hard *Slavery* of *Government*; ...
> You have my SONS too with you, who bow down
> Beneath the weighty Service of the Crown;
> My COUSINS and their COUSINS too—hard Fate!
> Are *loaded* with the Offices of State;
> And not *one Soul* of all my Kindred's free,
> From *sharing* in the Publick Drudgery."   (p. 8)

But if the charges, on the other hand, are true—if, just for instance,

> all your Kindred, BROTHER, SONS, and COUSINS,
> Have *Titles* and *Employments* by the *Dozens*;
> And for as many *Sidesmen* as are wanted,
> *New Places* are contriv'd, *new Pensions* granted—   (p. 10)

then you should reflect on what awaits you once your hour is out. It will not be the recognition that attends those who were "as Good as Great";

> No! with the *Curs'd* your Tomb shall foremost stand,
> The GAVESTON's and the WOLSEY's of the Land.

4/Walpole had visited Pope at Twickenham in 1725. Pope to Fortescue, 23 September 1725 (II 323).

Your EPITAPH.
In this foul Grave lies HE,
Who dug the Grave of British *Liberty.*   (p. 11)

Therefore: "Quit the Reins before we're quite undone."[5]

The second pamphlet is entitled *The Great Man's Answer to Are These Things So?* and shifts from address to direct dialogue, as its subtitle indicates: *A Dialogue Between His Honour and the Englishman in His Grotto.* This time

---

5/*Are These Things So?* was published 23 October (*London Daily Post and General Advertiser*). A second edition, "with the Addition of twenty Lines omitted in the former Impressions," the classical pseudonyms dropped (e.g. *Demosthenes* becomes "*Pultney*," *Atticus* "*Chesterfield*") and an author's preface, followed on 6 December (*Daily Post*). According to an advertisement in the *London Daily Post and General Advertiser* on 20 December, the omissions had been caused "thro the Timorousness of the Printer." There is evidence that the satire was felt. Paul Whitehead, whose *The State Dunces* (1733) and *Manners* (1739) had already won him the displeasure of the government, felt obliged on 15 November to advertise in the *London Daily Post and General Advertiser*: "Whereas it has been generally reported that I am the Author of a Poem, lately publish'd, entitled *Are These Things So?* I think it necessary to assure the Public, that the Said Report is without any Foundation. ..."

The pamphlet provoked a cluster of confirmatory pamphlets and replies: (1) *Yes, They are: Being an Answer to Are these Things So? The Previous Question, From An Englishman in his Grotto To A Great Man at Court.* "London: Printed for the Perusal of all Lovers of their Country. 1740." Published 8 November (*London Daily Post and General Advertiser*). (2) *The Weather-Menders: A Tale. A proper Answer to Are These Things So?* By Mr. Spiltimber [Split-timber?]. "*London*: Printed for J. Roberts ... MDCCXL." Published 18 November (*London Daily Post and General Advertiser*). (3) *What Things?* or, *An Impartial Enquiry What Things are so, and What Things are not so. Occasion'd by two late Poems. The one entitled Are these Things so? And the other entitled, Yes, they are.* "Printed for J. Roberts." This is advertised for 2 December (*London Daily Post and General Advertiser*), but I have not been able to see a copy of it. (4) *What of That! Occasion'd by a Pamphlet, intitled Are these Things So? and its Answer Yes, They are.* "London: Printed for J. Hooper in the Strand; and to be had of all true Hearts and sound Bottoms" [n.d.]. A "second Edition" of this is advertised for 6 December (*Daily Post*). (5) *A Supplement To a late Excellent Poem, Entitled, Are these Things so? Address'd to the * * * *.* "London, Printed for J. Roberts ... 1740." Published 20 December (*London Daily Post and General Advertiser*). (6) *They are Not.* "London [:] Printed for the Perusal of all Lovers of their Country. 1740." A "Third Edition" is advertised for 23 January 1741 (*Daily Post*). (7) *Have at you All: Being a Proper and Distinct Reply To Three Pamphlets Just publish'd, Intituled, What of That? The Weather Menders, and, They are Not.* "By the Author of Yes, They Are." "*London* [:] Printed for the Perusal of all Lovers of their Country. 1740." I have found no advertisement of this.

Nos. 1 and 7 support the arguments of *Are These Things So* that the nation is in dire straits thanks to Walpole; nos. 2–6 protest this. Nos. 1 and 7 profess to be written by a garret-poet, who is as much concerned for his country as the grotto-poet who has asked *Are These Things So?* References to a grotto recur here and there in the seven poems, but otherwise they show no effort to identify the speaker (or, in the pro-Walpole pamphlets, those spoken against) with Pope personally.

the epigraph "Qui capit" belongs to a proverb (*Qui capit ille facit*) freely translatable as "If the shoe fits, put it on."[6] Whether by typographical accident or design, the grotto poet has now become "*the* Englishman," representative of the whole nation, but he remains, for all that, the retired Twickenham spokesman deeply disquieted by his country's peril:

> HAIL blest *Elizium*! sweet, secure Retreat;
> Quiet and Contemplation's sacred Seat!
> Here may my Life's last Lamp in Freedom burn:
> Nor live to light my Country to her Urn.   (p. 1)

Hearing an enormous fracas at his grotto door, the speaker sends "John" (Pope's John Searle, who is asked to shut his door in *Arbuthnot*) to investigate:

> ... what Tempest shakes my Cell?
> Whence these big Drops that Ooze from ev'ry Shell?
> From this obdurate Rock whence flow those Tears?
> Sure some *Ill Power's* at hand.   (p. 1)

The "*Ill Power*" proves of course to be Walpole, come for a personal call:

> E.M. What's That approaches, *John*?
> J. Why Sir, 'tis He.
> E.M. What He?   J. Why He Himself,
> Sir; the *great* HE.
> E.M. Enough.   G.M. Your Slave, Sir.
> E.M. No, Sir, I'm *your Slave*,
> Or soon shall be.—How then must I
> behave?
> Must I fall prostrate at your Feet?
> or how—
> I've heard the *Dean*, but never saw
> him *Bow*.
> G.M. Hoh! Hoh! you make me laugh.
> E.M. So *Nero* play'd,
> Whilst *Rome* was by his Flames in
> Ashes laid.

6/This seems to have been a routine disclaimer with the Opposition: "... *I make no Application. If any Body has a Mind to take the Scandal to himself, much Good may it do him.*—Qui capit, ille facit." (*The Sly Subscription: or The Norfolk Monarch* [1733], p. x).

> *G.M.* Well, solemn Sir, I'm come, if
>   you think fit,
> To solve your Question. *E.M.* Bless
>   me! pray, Sir, sit.
> *G.M.* The Door!   *E.M.* No Matter, Sir,
>   my Door won't shut:
> Stay here, *John*; we've no *Secrets.*
>   *G.M.* Surly Put!
> How restiff still! but I have *what*
>   will win him
> Before we part, or else the Devil's
>   in him.   (p. 2)

The interesting feature of the debate that follows—on the usual subjects: the throttled fleet, standing armies, misuse of Secret Service funds, briberies, taxes, and so on, —is that Walpole is given some of the arguments that went farthest, in a period when nothing like modern party discipline was known, to excuse his system of placemen and pensioners:

> Free P[arliamen]ts! mere stuff—What would be done?
> Let loose, five hundred diff'rent Ways they'd run;
> They'd Cavil, Jarr, Dispute, O'return, Project,
> And the great Bus'ness of *Supply* Neglect;
> On *Grievances*, not *Ways* and *Means* would go.   (p. 5)

He is also given the arguments that in his time served those who did not suffer from any refined sense of *meum* and *tuum* (here it is important to remember that some did: Walpole's brother-in-law Townshend left office poorer than he entered it) to justify their spoils of office:

> Besides, who'd drudge the *Mill-Horse* of the State;
> Curst by the Vulgar, envy'd by the Great;
> In one fastidious Round of Hurry live,
> And join, in Toil, the *Matin* with the Eve. ...
> Who'd cringe at *Levees*, or in *Closets*—Oh!
> Stoop to the *rough* Remonstrance of the *Toe*?
> Did not some Genius whisper, "That's the Road
> To Opulence, and Honour's bless'd Abode;
> Thus you may aggrandize yourself, and Race."   (p. 11)

Moreover, he is finally allowed to set against the "Epitaph" of the preceding pamphlet a résumé of his achievements as he sees them, with an epitaph of his own:

> I want no *Grave-Stone* to promulge my *Fame*,
> Nor trust to *breathless Marble* for a *Name*,
> BRITANNIA's self a *Monument* shall stand
> Of the *bless'd Dowry* I bequeath my Land:
> Her Sons shall hourly my *dear Conduct* boast;
> They *best* can speak it, who will *feel* it most.
> But if some grateful Verse *must* grace my Urn,
> Attend ye *Gazeteers*—Be this the Turn—
> *Weep*, Britons, *weep—Beneath this Stone lies* He,
> *Who set your Isle from dire Divisions free*
> *And made your various Factions all agree.*   (p. 12)

It is very nearly the epitaph pronounced on Walpole by today's historians.

All this is irony, however, not prescience, as the ending of the poem makes clear. Finding he has nothing to say that will mollify the grotto-speaker's "starch'd unbending temper," the Great Man gets up to go, proposing to leave behind "his last *best* answer ... in *Writing*."

> *G.M.* Pray mark it—*E.M.* How! May I my Eyes Believe?
> *G.M.* You may—I thought I should convince you, *E.M.* Yes,
> That Fame for once spoke Truth—And as for *This*—
> *G.M.* Furies! My *thousand Bank*, Sir, *E.M.* Thus I Tear,
> Go, blend, *Corruption*, with *corrupting*
>   Air.
> *G.M.* Amazing Frenzie! Well, if this won't
>   do,
> What think you of a *Pension*?   *E.M.* As
>   of *You.*
> *G.M.* A *Place*—   *E.M.* Be gone, *G.M.* A
>   *Title*—   *E.M.* is a *Lie*
> When ill conferr'd   *G.M.* A *Ribband*—
>   *E.M.* I defie.
> [*G.M.*] Farewell then Fool—If you'll
>   accept of *Neither,*
> You and your *Country* may be *damn'd*
>   together.   (p. 13)

III

The acknowledgement of Pope and Walpole—overtly in this cluster of pamphlets but implicitly in a good deal of the ephemeral poetry of the 30's—as not simply feuding personalities but in some sense mighty opposites, representative of divided and distinguished worlds,[1] invites us to consider how far, each in his way, these two men dominated their time, and how oddly alike in some respects, despite wide differences of physique, temperament, inclination, and talent, they and their fortunes were. Both were commanding geniuses, and each ruled in his own world with an *imperium* all his own. Each attained unrivaled distinction in his own lifetime, and, in proportion to his opportunities, amazing affluence, Walpole accumulating possibly the greatest fortune of his day,[2] Pope becoming one of the very few writers of any day to gain financial security and even ease through poetry. Each wielded an influence that was publicly acknowledged; each was credited with an insatiable ambition summed up in various cant titles ("King Bob," "The Chelsea Monarch," "Pope Alexander"); each was dreaded and loved, beleaguered for favors, fawned on, frowned on, dedicated to, imitated. Pope may have "sought no homage from the Race that write,"[3] but he received it willy-nilly, and no evidence shows that he did not enjoy his literary eminence, and the publishing programs and intrigues required to maintain it, as thoroughly as Walpole enjoyed the plaudits of the moody, murmuring, headstrong race it fell to his lot to curb in parliament.

1/An anonymous undated satire (1740?), entitled *A Dialogue Which lately pass'd between The Knight and His Man John*, takes a view of Pope and Walpole similar to that in *The Great Man's Answer*, on which it may be based. Here the knight is Walpole, his man John possibly Lord Hervey. Some of the relevant lines are these:

> Shut, shut the Door, good *John*, I blame
> Myself for this—Pope us'd the same.
> I hate him for superior Sense;
> I want no Men of Excellence;
> He in his Grotto sits and sings,
> And sports with Ministers and Kings.
> Nor Greyhounds dreads, nor Writs uncouth,
> But laughs secure in Sense and Truth.
> His Pen's Venom galls my Heart,
> Bares the film'd Skin, and aids my Smart.

Greyhound was a term applied to Nicholas Paxton's emissaries and summoners. On Paxton, see above, p. 127, n. 2. A word is clearly missing from the next to last line: "black[?] Venom"?

2/Walpole's wealth is impossible to estimate because it came from so many sources and was spent so fast and lavishly. At the very least it was, as Plumb says, "enormous" ("The Walpoles: Father and Son," *Studies in Social History* [London, 1955], p. 195).

3/*Epistle to Dr. Arbuthnot*, 219.

Both men were artful managers—"under a seeming openness and negligence, devilish artful," says Hervey of Walpole;[4] and the same, as everyone knows, was true of Pope, of whom Johnson opined, rightly on the whole, though with exaggeration, that he could not drink his tea without a stratagem.[5] Both men were well thought of and much admired by those who knew them best. Walpole appears not to have had Pope's gift for friendships of all kinds and degrees of intimacy; perhaps in such a post as his this was impossible; but he knew how to command personal loyalties in addition to those based on interest, and what Spence, at the end of all his careful inquiries, said of the poet might to a large extent be said of the minister too: "All the people well acquainted with Mr. Pope, looked on him as a most friendly, open, charitable, and generous-hearted man; all the world almost, that did not know him, were got into a mode of having very different ideas of him" (Spence, I xx).

Yet both men were very good haters, made enemies in quantity, were envied the rewards their talents and hard work brought them, and spent much of their lives under savage attack, maligned in face, figure, family, friends, and (always) motives. Nor was all the obloquy that they suffered undeserved. Without much doubt—in Pope's case with no doubt whatever—both were capable of shady dealing. Everyone knows the story of Pope's lying claims about the extent of his assistants' contribution to the *Odyssey* translation, his equivocating "pretty genteelly" about the parody of the First Psalm, his "cooking" his correspondence, and so forth. Though no surviving evidence connects Walpole unmistakably with the transfer of national funds to his own account, no one has been able to show how a man in his position could so speedily have come by such immense wealth honestly, and no one denies that he supported his mistress Molly out of public money,[6] had his wines smuggled baldly up the Thames in an admiralty launch when Secretary of War,[7] and in certain elections used "such devious practices" as (had they been known) "would have startled even his colleagues."[8] Hostility to the Minister, whether on fair grounds or unfair, supported a whole journalistic industry, and he himself supported another to rebut it. Pope as a private man cannot claim quite so much, but one newspaper existed at least in part to defend him,[9] one publisher (Edmund Curll) found it profitable to make a business of

---

4/To Stephen Fox, 30 December 1731 (Ilchester, *Lord Hervey and His Friends* [London, 1950], p. 131).

5/Life of Pope (*Lives of the English Poets*, ed. G. B. Hill [Clarendon Press, 1905], III 200).

6/See Plumb, II 114n.   7/*Ibid.*, I 121, II 237.   8/*Ibid.*, II 176.

9/*The Grub-Street Journal.* For an account of it, see J. T. Hillhouse, *The Grub-Street Journal* (Duke University Press, 1928).

pillorying him, and the sordid ingenuities by which he seduced the same publisher into bringing out his letters compare favorably with those by which
Walpole manipulated places and pensions to get his votes in parliament, and the
postal service to interfere with the circulation of Opposition journals and to
expedite his own. If Walpole was threatened by angry mobs during the uproar
over the Excise Bill and hanged and burned in effigy, Pope was threatened with
whippings by angry Dunces, never went out at that period of his life without
pistols (Spence, no. 265), and later had his windows broken, presumably by
government sympathizers, while entertaining Bolingbroke.[10]

Both men, despite spectacular difference in bodily frame, were endowed with
intense nervous energy and drove themselves to the limit. Neither let ill health, of
which even Walpole had a far greater share than is commonly supposed, interfere with the dispatch of business a moment longer than required. Despite the
fact that Pope was rarely well "four days together,"[11] as he put it, he lived most
of the time in "a scene of continued hurry," amid "the scatterings of a mind
almost distracted by a thousand things," and more often than not in a "glut of
company,"[12] to say nothing of reading, writing, editing, and publishing—the
necessary activities of his trade. Bolingbroke describes him in 1728 "now hurry-
ing to London," whence "he will hurry back to Twickenham in two days more"
and "before the end of the week he will be, for aught I know, at Dublin."[13]
Bathurst pleads with him five years later not to wear out his body by letting his
soul ride it so hard: "therefore do not whip and spur perpetually, but give it some
rest."[14] When he felt well, he was "brisk as a wren,"[15] and was as likely as not to
hurry off to dinner with a friend, where he would over-eat (Kent called him "the
greatest glutton I know")[16] until he was sick again. When he felt ill, if he was not
totally prostrate, he seems to have sat down to write to a few friends. Letter after
letter ends with a statement we have every reason to believe: that his head aches
so he can hardly see the paper.[17] With the differences to be expected, this was also
Walpole's life: prodigious eating and drinking, weekly bouts of hunting, entertainments at his house in Chelsea, and twice a year at Houghton, on so huge a
scale that throughout 1733, for instance, his guests used some eleven dozen

10/Pope refers to this in *One Thousand Seven Hundred and Thirty-Eight, Dial.* II, 140–45.
11/To Bathurst, 7 November [1728] (II 525).
12/To Broome, 24 March 1720 (II 40–41).
13/To Swift [February 1728] (II 472).
14/9 September 1732 (III 313).
15/Fenton to Broome, 21 December 1725 (II 351).
16/To Burlington, 28 November 1738 (IV 150).
17/I have borrowed the preceding five sentences, slightly revised, from my review of
Sherburn's edition of the *Correspondence* in *Philological Quarterly*, XXXVI (1957), 395.

bottles of the best French wines a week plus an equal amount in casks.[18] But these frolics were paid for in long hours of labor on despatches from and to every corner of Europe, or with his henchmen concerting election strategies and plans to foil the Opposition in debate, or at those tricky details of Treasury business his consummate mastery of which made him the power he was—and of course in the regular meetings of parliament and commissions, his daily audiences with the king, his painstaking conferences with the queen, through whom his hold on the king was assured.

One other attribute Pope and Walpole shared. Under all the vanities and excesses, each had a residual moderation of temperament and outlook that was perhaps his single greatest strength. It involved not expecting too much of men or of the world or even of oneself ("Blessed are those who expect nothing," said Pope, "for they will never be disappointed").[19] It involved eschewing on the whole the *thèse* and the *système*,[20] cherishing the *ad hoc*, recognizing the flux, variety, and disorderliness of experience—outwardly:

> Shall only Man be taken in the gross?
> Grant but as many sorts of Mind as Moss—
>
> (*Epistle to Cobham*, 17–18)

as well as inwardly

> But when no Prelate's Lawn with Hair-shirt lin'd
> Is half so incoherent as my Mind,
> When (each Opinion with the next, at strife,
> One ebb and flow of follies all my Life)
> I plant, root up, I build, and then confound. ...
>
> (*Imit. Hor., Ep.* i i (165–69)

It involved allowing ample room and verge enough for chance, whim, prejudice, hunch, and also for the mole of nature, the growth of some complexion, the stamp of some defect that may be both our energizer and our destroyer:

> The young disease, that must subdue at length,
> Grows with his growth, and strengthens with his strength.
>
> (*Essay on Man*, ii 135–36)

18/J. H. Plumb, "The Walpoles: Father and Son," *Studies in Social History* (London, 1955), p. 201.

19/To Fortescue, 23 September 1725 (ii 323) ; to Gay 16 October 1727 (ii 453).

20/What Pope was willing to call a "system of Ethics" in the *Essay on Man* indicates the degree to which *l'esprit de système* was foreign to his temperament.

And it involved, at the same time, upholding the conviction that there *are* kinds, categories, precepts, maxims, schemes, and general truths, and that experience in the long run adds up to an order—or would, if one's perspectives were wide enough. All this, it strikes me, is eminently characteristic of the English temper in the Augustan age, and of the two representatives of that age and temper with whom we are concerned here. Pope was not simply idealizing himself when he wrote:

> But ask not, to what Doctors I apply?
> Sworn to no Master, of no Sect am I:
> As drives the storm, at any door I knock,
> And house with Montagne now, or now with Lock.
> Sometimes a Patriot, active in debate,
> Mix with the World, and battle for the State.
> Free as young Lyttelton, her cause pursue,
> Still true to Virtue, and as warm as true:
> Sometimes, with Aristippus, or St. Paul,
> Indulge my Candor, and grow all to all;
> Back to my native Moderation slide,
> And win my way by yielding to the tyde.
>
> (*Imit. Hor.*, *Ep.* 1 i 23–34)

The last line could hardly be bettered as a description of the methods by which Walpole often dominated his parliaments, and though Pope may have been more self-conscious about it than Walpole, a poised sanity is native to both, even, one guesses, in their personal relations. Pope, if my reading of his innuendos is right, made yet shrewder thrusts at king and minister than has been supposed, but he avoided the all-out direct attack that he made in retaliation for Hervey's part in the *Verses to the Imitator*—partly no doubt through discretion, but partly, it may be, through a sense of what is fitting to be said about a King and a King's chief minister.[21] To be convinced of Pope's restraint, one need only read through

---

21/Pope noted with reference to the names Sejanus and Wolsey (which were Aegysthus and Verres in the first edition) that "The writers against the Court usually bestowed these and other odious names on the Minister, without distinction, and in the most injurious manner" (*One Thousand Seven Hundred and Thirty-Eight*: *Dial.* i 51n). Since the remark appears in none of the editions of Pope's lifetime but only in 1751, it may not be disingenuous but intended simply as a gloss for later less well-informed readers. In *Dial.* II, 146–47, he seems also to confess a scruple:

> Sure, if I spare the Minister, no rules
> Of Honour bind me, not to maul his Tools.

the *Craftsman* and the other anti-Walpole literature of this decade—or Byron's satire on George III when old and blind. Even in the *Epistle to Augustus,* Pope carves the king rather "as a dish fit for the gods," to use the words of Shakespeare's Brutus, than "as a carcass fit for hounds," and in the poet's leave-taking—

> Not with such Majesty, such bold relief,
> The Forms august of King, or conqu'ring Chief,
> E'er swell'd on Marble; as in Verse have shin'd
> (In polish'd Verse) the Manners and the Mind.
> Oh! could I mount on the Maeonian wing,
> Your Arms, your Actions, your Repose to sing!—   (390–95)

one wonders whether, mixed into the mockery, there is not perhaps a note of genuine regret, not simply that he cannot rise to epic strains but that there is no occasion for a poet to do so in the England of 1737.

For his own part, though it might have made him a laughing-stock, Walpole could have crushed Pope like an egg-shell had he been so minded. Again, however, for all his sensitivity to criticism, which seems to have been fully as keen as Pope's, there was some kind of balance at work in him that inhibited the extreme response. As Harvey puts it, "Whether his negligence of his enemies, and never stretching his power to gratify his resentment of the sharpest injury, was policy or constitution, I shall not determine; but I do not believe anybody who knows these times will deny that no minister ever was more outraged, or less apparently revengeful" (1 18). Walpole broke his political opponents because they threatened his power; Pope of course had no such interest for him, was merely a gnat to be brushed aside.

IV

When all these comparisons have been made, however (and every reader will think of others), it remains true that the capacities and inclinations which separated Pope and Walpole are more important and more interesting to us by far than the qualities which give them a certain likeness. For they did represent, in fact, in some sort of ultimate sense, divided and distinguished worlds. Whatever either touched was immediately subdued and colored by the contact, not only of the individual personality but of the whole intellectual and social ambience in which each moved. Both, for example, were country boys in up-bringing, and both continued throughout their lives in a posture of rusticity that

was partly pose—if indeed in these matters pose, which implies calculated awareness, is ever separable from rooted habit, and the expression of deepest needs. Yet
how differently each selected, according to his nature (and no doubt his profes-
sion too) from the available repertory! We have examined Pope's retirement syndrome at length—"pastoral" in character, stemming from much reading as well
as from his boyhood at Binfield, rooted in the figure of the leisured singer and the
festal gathering in the garden, having the kind of exemplary ideality that we
recognize in Fielding's Squire Allworthy. Walpole's syndrome, altogether *un*-
literary, leaning away from ideality toward a Squire Western caricature of
reality, was perhaps less artificial but not less artful. As Professor J. H. Plumb,
who knows more about Walpole than any other man now alive, has pointed out,
Walpole "parodied the Norfolk squire" in order to enhance his resemblance to
and therefore his influence with the country gentlemen in parliament:

The gossip, much encouraged, ran that he always opened his game-keeper's letters
before his despatches. He had a trick of munching little red Norfolk apples to sustain
him during the debates. His language in private was as coarse as any squire's; in
debate so simple and direct that even the stupidest could follow him. His letters
possess the same plain, matter-of-fact quality. Like his oratory, they were free from
fine tropes, similes, metaphors. All this was a deliberate part of this public character.
Fortunately for Walpole—and, of course, he would never have convinced had it
not been so—this *persona* had its roots in his own temperament.[1]

This is the same man who built one of the outstanding collections of paintings
and sculpture in Europe, and who, according to Professor Plumb, "devoted as
much time to the embellishment of his house as to the pursuit of the fox" (II 83).

The house referred to is of course Houghton, for Walpole like Pope and almost
every other Augustan who had the price of moving one stone atop another or
planting out an arbor, was a builder and estate-maker. But again it is the differences that are instructive, reflecting as they do much more than income.
Walpole took his ancestral Norfolk acres, ignored the lack of water, tore down
the old village to make his park (building it again outside), had Bridgman
cover the windy Norfolk flats, where timber did not naturally grow, with plantations, scooped out basins that dried up in summer, and erected a Great House
in which he never lived more than about six weeks a year and never alone: it
was used only as a gallery for his collection, for his "Norfolk Congresses," and
to impress his guests and visitors. Pope improved a rented dwelling into one of
the earliest of English Palladian villas, consulted the genius of the place in making

---

1/*The First Four Georges* (London, 1956), p. 72. See also Plumb, II 91.

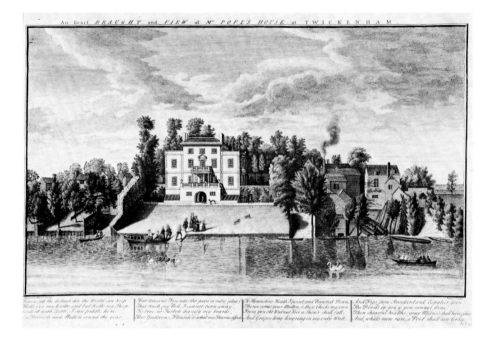

45 A view of Pope's house, 1735.
By Peter Andreas (?) Rysbrack, 1690–1748

his garden as Walpole spectacularly did not, let one aspect of his situation dic-
tate his grotto, another his "thick impenetrable woods," and made the place
his home for twenty-five years. As a villa, Pope's house belonged to a category
of building that, owing to its characteristic one-three-one window rhythm,
offered only modest accommodations and so was recognized to be, from the
beginning, "more in the nature of a retreat than an advertisement of its owner's
standing or ability to entertain."[2] Its necessary attributes were "Elegance, com-
pactness, and convenience ... in contradistinction to the magnificence and extensive range" (Summerson, 571) of the Great House, which was unavoidably a
status symbol (*ibid.*, 544), and in Walpole's case at Houghton, the status symbol
of a man who delighted in display. On the walls of Houghton hung Rubenses,

2/John Summerson, "The Classical Country House in 18th-Century England" *Journal of
the Royal Society of Arts*, cvii (1959), 551–52.

46 The front of Houghton Hall in the later eighteenth century.
"W. Watts del. et Sculpt.," 1782

Rembrandts, Vandycks, and Poussins, purchased, we are told, "at record prices."[3] On Pope's walls hung the portraits of his friends (above, pp. 31–32). "Our company at Houghton," says Hervey, describing a representative Norfolk Congress of 1731, "swelled at last into so numerous a body that we used to sit down to dinner a little snug party of about thirty odd, up to the chin in beef, venison, geese, turkeys, etc.; and generally over the chin in claret, strong beer and punch. We had Lords spiritual and temporal, besides commoners, parsons, and freeholders innumerable. In public we drank loyal healths, talked of the times and cultivated popularity: in private we drew plans and cultivated the country."[4] Pope's entertainments had an altogether different cachet, as we have

---

3/J. H. Plumb, *The First Four Georges* (London, 1956), p. 74.
4/To Frederick, Prince of Wales, 21 July 1731, in Ilchester, *Lord Hervey and His Friends* (London, 1950), pp. 73–74.

seen. If he over-ate and over-drank sometimes, as most men do, it was plain fare, nevertheless, that best expressed his constitution and his address to life,[5] and it is plain fare, serving as metaphor for physical and intellectual freedom from dependency, that he celebrates whenever his mantle of retirement is on:

> There *St. John* mingles with my friendly Bowl,
> The Feast of Reason and the Flow of Soul.
>
> (*Imit. Hor., Sat.* ii i 127–28)

> Content with little, I can piddle here
> On Broccoli and mutton, round the year;
> But ancient friends (tho' poor, or out of play)
> That touch my Bell, I cannot turn away.
>
> (*Ibid.*, ii 137–40)

> A frugal Mouse upon the whole,
> Yet lov'd his Friend, and had a Soul;
> Knew what was handsome, and wou'd do't,
> On just occasion, *coute qui coute.*
> He brought him Bacon (nothing lean)
> Pudding, that might have pleas'd a Dean;
> Cheese, such as men in Suffolk make,
> But wish'd it Stilton for his sake;
> Yet to his Guest tho' no way sparing,
> He eat himself the Rind and paring.
>
> (*Ibid.*, vi 161–70)

The comparison, it goes without saying, is unfair: Walpole had no poet to describe his congresses. Yet the essential distinction stands. What Jonson said of Penshurst, as we have already seen, in comparing it with the show places building in his time, Pope's friends might have said of his villa as compared with Timon's:

5/See, for example, his invitation to Atterbury to visit him at Twickenham, 19 March 1722 (ii 109–10): "The situation here is pleasant, and the view rural enough, to humour the most retir'd, and agree with the most contemplative. Good air, solitary groves, and sparing diet, sufficient to make you fancy your self ... one of the Fathers of the Desert. Here you may think ...
> That in Eliah's banquet you partake,
> Or sit a guest with Daniel, at his Pulse."

> Now, Penshurst, they that will proportion thee
> With other edifices when they see
> Those proud ambitious heaps, and nothing else,
> May say their lords have built, but thy lord dwells.   (99–102)

V

That Walpole was not and had not a poet (nor indeed any writer of the first or even second rank supporting him), points to a wider sort of gulf between these representative figures—who, when Walpole was weekending with Molly in Richmond, were physically divided only by a short stretch of the Thames. For one thing, though Walpole appealed to the hard sense of the majority of his contemporaries, like his two masters, George I and George II, he did not often kindle their imaginations: he had their votes but not (to any profound degree) their hearts. For another thing, the writer who lives, or deeply cares about, the life of imagination or—to use the old-fashioned ethical terms of Greece and Rome —

> What good, or better, we may call
> And what, the very best of all?—

must, when the chips are down, distinguish his own vision of the good life from that of rostrum and agora. This is owing in part, obviously, to the fact that the contemplative life and the active life have never been wholly congruous—As Marvell struggles to convey to us in *The Garden* and the *Horatian Ode* and *Upon Appleton House*. "From the perspective of the garden, ambitious men seem misguided and foolish; from the perspective of Cromwell's strenuous achievement, the 'Muses dear' and 'numbers languishing' "—to say nothing of a General Fairfax reviewing flowers "at Parade" instead of soldiers—"seem equally unseasonable and absurd."[1]

Moreover, from the retirement point of view, the problem complicates and the rift widens if the complexion of the existing city is so tyrannical or corrupt that to withdraw from it is the best, perhaps the only, protest available—as for Umbricius in Juvenal's satire retreating from Domitian's Rome; or if, as Plato seems to suggest in a famous passage (and as part of an entire generation seems to have concluded in the 1960's), the existing city has always to be viewed as

---

1/George Lord, "From Contemplation to Action: Marvell's Poetical Career," *Philological Quarterly*, XLVI (1967), 211.

tyrannical and corrupt by any man who is serious about preserving his integrity and independence. Speaking to Adeimantus in the sixth book of the *Republic*, Socrates first characterizes the "philosopher" as one who has come to know the sweetness of contemplation, who has come to understand "the frenzy of the multitude," who has come to see "that there is no soundness in the conduct of public life, nowhere an ally at whose side a champion of justice could hope to escape destruction. Like a man who has fallen among wild beasts, if he should refuse to take part in their misdeeds and could not hold out alone against the fury of all, he would be destined, before he could be of any service to his country or his friends, to perish, having done no good to himself or to anyone else." The consequence of this is that the philosopher "keeps quiet and goes his own way, like the traveller who takes shelter under a wall from a driving storm of dust and hail; and seeing lawlessness spreading on all sides, is content if he can keep his hands clean from iniquity while this life lasts, and when the end comes take his departure, with good hopes, in serenity and peace."[2]

Here again is the formula we have encountered so often in these pages, an image of withdrawn felicity inherited and elaborated by the Roman poets, restated often in the Renaissance and during and after the English Civil Wars, and still viable for Pope's time—perhaps with some necessary adjustments, for ours too. Pope saw his father partly in these terms, as we have noticed, and so far as possible himself (above, pp. 100–15). Addison saw his Cato in these same terms. In 1737, when feeling against Walpole was high and still higher against the king for his recent long stay in Madame Walmoden's arms in Hanover, the Prince of Wales, whose hostility to his parents and the Walpole regime was well known, was cheered at a performance of *Cato*, "and in that part ... where Cato says these words—'When vice prevails, and impious men bear sway, the post of honour is a private station'—there was another loud huzza" (Hervey III 839). The formula of withdrawal versus contamination is a durable one, experienced by every generation to some extent, and by those born at certain places and times in the extreme.

More than this formula, however, separates Pope's world from Walpole's, as these worlds are defined for us in the poems of the 30's: the ultimate divisive force is the calling of poet and Pope's high conception of that calling. That Vision should be united to Power, Wisdom—in the Socratic and Judaic sense—fruc-

---

2/VI 496 (tr. Cornford). I was put in mind of this passage by Michael J. K. O'Loughlin, whose brilliant dissertation, "The Garlands of Repose: Studies in the Literary Representation of Civic and Retired Leisure," is now being readied for press.

tified in the fiats of statesman and chief, has been the dream of poets and philosophers, and many who were not, apparently since civilization began. "The Minstrel should be at the King's side," says Schiller's Charles vii,[3] and the author of the *Odyssey* a long time ago said the same, placing a Demodocus in Phaeacia, a Phemius in Ithaca, and adding, in a wishful passage lovingly translated by Pope:

> But chief to Poets such respect belongs,
> By rival nations courted for their songs;
> These states invite, and mighty kings admire,
> Wide as the Sun displays his vital fire.[4]

In this vein, Plato dreamed of philosopher-kings (the passage just quoted is in fact the introduction he uses to that dream); and Virgil urged upon Augustus in the *Georgics* that peace has its victories no less renowned than those of war; and Spenser, remembering in his October eclogue Augustus and Maecenas and (in the last two lines below) the most cherished falsehood in all literature:

> But ah *Mecaenas* is yclad in claye,
> And great Augustus long ygoe is dead;
> And all the worthies liggen wrapt in leade,
> That matter made for Poets on to play:
> For[,]ever, who in derring doe were dreade,
> The loftie verse of hem was loved aye—

was moved to a touching apostrophe:

> O pierlesse Poesye, where is then thy place?
> If nor in Princes pallace thou doe sitt:
> (And yet is Princes pallace the most fitt)
> Ne brest of baser birth doth thee embrace. (61–68, 79–82)

Milton, likewise, forgetting what had happened to Homer and not yet knowing what would happen to himself, instructed the Lords and Commons of England:

Such honour was done in those days to men who professed the study of wisdom and eloquence, not only in their own country, but in other lands, that cities and

---

3/In his *Jungfrau von Orleans*, 484–85:
> "Drum soll der Sänger mit dem König gehen,
> Sie beide wohnen auf der Menschheit Höhen!"

4/xvii 382–86. See te, vii ccxxxi–ccxxxiii.

. F. Hayman inv. et del.   C. Grignion Sculp

47 The dying Pope, attended by Chaucer, Spenser, and Milton.
Title-page vignette appearing in 1747

seigniories heard them gladly, and with great respect, if they had aught in public
to admonish the state—[5]

and again, in our own time and idiom, though with some inevitable shrinkage,
Wallace Stevens has said:

I think then that the first thing a poet should do as he comes out of his cavern[6] is
to put on the strength of his particular calling as a poet, to address himself to what
Rilke called the mighty burden of poetry and to have the courage to say that, in
his sense of things, the significance of poetry is second to none. We can never have
great poetry unless we believe that poetry serves great ends.[7]

5/*Areopagitica, Prose Works*, ed J. A. St. John (London, 1914), II 52.
6/The persistence of the association between poet and cave is remarkable.
7/*Opus Posthumous* (New York, 1957), p. 245.

48 Pope gathered to Apollo and the Muses by Homer, 1751.
By Hubert François Gravelot, 1699–1773

This is the estimate of the poet's calling to which Pope also subscribed. Whether we take him in a paraphrase of perhaps the most famous lines in Horace, *Vixere fortes ante Agamemnona*:

> Sages and Chiefs long since had birth
> E're Caesar was, or Newton nam'd,
> These rais'd new Empires o'er the Earth,
> And Those new Heav'ns and Systems fram'd;
>
> Vain was the chief's and sage's pride
> They had no Poet and they dyd!
> In vain they schem'd, in vain they bled
> They had no Poet and are dead!
> (*Part of the Ninth Ode of the Fourth Book of Horace*, 9–16)

or in a confident passage from the last of his original epistles:

> Ye tinsel Insects! whom a Court maintains,
> That counts your Beauties only by your Stains,
> Spin all your Cobwebs o'er the Eye of Day!
> The Muse's wing shall brush you all away—
> (*One Thousand Seven Hundred and Thirty-Eight, Dial.* ii 220–23)

Pope never forgets that the king needs the minstrel—both in the narrow sense:

> Yet think great Sir! (so many Virtues shown)
> Ah think, what Poet best may make them known?—
> *Imit. Hor., Ep.* ii i 376-7)

and in the broad sense:

> Who counsels best? who whispers, "Be but Great,
> With Praise or Infamy, leave that to fate;
> Get Place and Wealth, if possible, with Grace;
> If not, by any means get Wealth and Place. ..."
> Or he, who bids thee face with steddy view
> Proud Fortune, and look shallow Greatness thro':
> And, while he bids thee, sets th' Example too?
> (*Ibid.*, i i 101–4, 107–9)

VI

"Who counsels best?" Taken collectively, Pope's satires and epistles are an extension of that question. Always they offer us in some form a dialogue, actual or implicit, between the poet and one or other representative of the existing city, who makes known to us its ordinances, expediencies, cautions, and evasions. This is Pascal's order of the flesh, and Hobbes's restless world of power, where " 'Honourable' is whatsoever possession, action, or quality, is an argument and sign of power" (*Leviathan*, ch. x), and where, in Martin Price's words, "It hardly matters who rules nor by what pretexts so long as the rule is stable"[1]—as Walpole well knew. Into this world a few years later Blake will look, and see and hear there the chartered Thames, the chimney-sweeper's cry, the soldier's sigh,

---

1/*To the Palace of Wisdom: Studies in Order and Energy from Dryden to Blake* (New York, 1964), p. 21.

the harlot's curse, and will show us what, for poetry, these things must always mean:

> How the Chimney-sweeper's cry
> Every black'ning Church appalls;
> And the hapless Soldier's sigh
> Runs in blood down Palace walls.

> But most thro' midnight streets I hear
> How the youthful Harlot's curse
> Blasts the new born Infant's tear,
> And blights with plagues the Marriage hearse.   (*London*, 9–16)

Closer to our own time, another poet will look in the same direction and bring back substantially the same report (as in fact all poets do) save that the soldier's name is now Stetson, the harlot is Belladonna the lady of situations, and the chimney-sweeper's cry has swelled into the voices of a boy's choir—being listened to by a pederast: *"Et O ces voix d'enfants, chantant dans la coupole."*

> Unreal City
> Under the brown fog of a winter dawn,
> A Crowd flowed over London Bridge, so many,
> I had not thought death had undone so many.

In the last book of the *Dunciad*, Pope will envelop his own actors in this murky setting. But in the poems of the 30's, following Horace, his landscape has a more familiar cast. The existing city is made to pass before us in its habitual scenes, episodes, gestures, liveries, languages, laws, and customs, to be decobwebbed by acts of imagination and so exposed to the eye of day. In Pope's case, the acts of imagination are usually oriented toward comedy, but the meanings uncovered can be sufficiently astringent for all that. There is the meaning, for instance, of the newly invented paper currency and credit of Pope's time—foundation (as his lines seem almost to anticipate) of finance capitalism and Gerontion's international "decayed house":

> Blest paper-credit! last and best supply!
> That lends Corruption lighter wings to fly!
> Gold imp'd by thee, can compass hardest things,
> Can pocket States, can fetch or carry Kings;
> A single leaf shall waft an Army o'er,
> Or ship off Senates to a distant Shore;

A leaf, like Sibyl's, scatter to and fro
Our fates and fortunes, as the winds shall blow:
Pregnant with thousands flits the Scrap unseen,
And silent sells a King, or buys a Queen.

(*Epistle to Bathurst*, 69–78)

There is the meaning of political sloganeering—the canned speech, the party-line, whether in Walpole's government or another:

Faith it imports not much from whom it came
Whoever borrow'd, could not be to blame,
Since the whole House did afterwards the same:
Let Courtly Wits to Wits afford supply,
As Hog to Hog in Huts of *Westphaly*;
If one, thro' Nature's Bounty or his Lord's,
Has what the frugal, dirty soil affords,
From him the next receives it, thick or thin,
As pure a Mess almost at it came in;
The blessed Benefit, not there confin'd,
Drops to the third who nuzzles close behind;
From tail to mouth, they feed, and they carouse;
The last, full fairly gives it to the *House*.

(*One Thousand Seven Hundred and Thirty-Eight, Dial.* ii 168–80)

There is the meaning of sycophancy—hell packaged to resemble heaven, as Pope presents it, long-run by-product of every power structure from royal courts to corporations:

There, where no Passion, Pride, or Shame transport,
Lull'd with the sweet *Nepenthe* of a Court;
There, where no Father's, Brother's, Friend's Disgrace
Once break their Rest, or stir them from their Place;
But past the Sense of human Miseries,
All Tears are wip'd for ever from all Eyes;
No Cheek is known to blush, no Heart to throb,
Save when they lose a Question, or a Job.

(*Ibid.*, 97–104)

And there is the meaning of the corruption of sex into conquest and commerce—

Blake's harlot, Eliot's Belladonna, the entertainment industry and the jet set winging into the valley of the dolls:

> Yet mark the Fate of a whole Sex of Queens!
> Pow'r all their end, but Beauty all the means.
> In Youth they conquer, with so wild a rage,
> As leaves them scarce a Subject in their Age:
> For foreign glory, foreign joy, they roam;
> No thought of Peace or Happiness at home.
> But Wisdom's Triumph is well-tim'd Retreat,
> As hard a science to the Fair as Great!
> Beauties, like Tyrants, old and friendless grown,
> Yet hate to rest, and dread to be alone,
> Worn out in public, weary ev'ry eye,
> Nor leave one sigh behind them when they die.
>
> See how the World its Veterans rewards!
> A Youth of frolicks, an old Age of Cards,
> Fair to no purpose, artful to no end,
> Young without Lovers, old without a Friend,
> A Fop their Passion, but their Prize a Sot,
> Alive, ridiculous, and dead, forgot!
>   (*Epistle to a Lady*, 219–30, 243–28)

VII

These are not of course the only "meanings" derivable from the evidence. They are certainly not the meanings that the existing city itself derives. Nor is it fair to say that the power-world yields the poet only sombre reflections. Most often in the satires and epistles (the case may be otherwise in the final *Dunciad*) Pope refrains from paying it the final tribute of dismay. His manner, with certain calculated exceptions, tends to be disengaged ("Divided between Carelessness and Care"),[1] moving within a spectrum whose poles are moderate scorn and half-sympathetic amusement:

> Did ever Proteus, Merlin, any Witch,
> Transform themselves so strangely as the Rich?
> "Well, but the Poor"—the Poor have the same itch:

1/*Imit. Hor., Ep.* II ii 291.

> They change their weekly Barber, weekly News,
> Prefer a new Japanner to their shoes,
> Discharge their Garrets, move their Beds, and run
> (They know not whither) in a Chaise and one;
> They hire their Sculler, and when once aboard,
> Grow sick, and damn the Climate—like a Lord.
>
> (*Imit. Hor., Ep.* i i 152–60)

He can be easy and self-deprecating too about the claims of poetry and poets. Doubtless poetry is an "idle trade,"[2] a "crying sin,"[3] a form of madness:

> Whether the darken'd Room to muse invite,
> Or whiten'd Wall provoke the Skew'r to write,
> In Durance, Exile, Bedlam, or the Mint,
> Like *Lee* or *Budgell*, I will Rhyme and Print.
>
> *Ibid., Sat.* ii i 97–100)

Doubtless it is produced by people who have the usual human supply of egoism:

> My Liege! why Writers little claim your thought,
> I guess; and, with their leave, will tell the fault:
> We Poets are (upon a Poet's word)
> Of all mankind, the creatures most absurd:
> The season, when to come, and when to go,
> To sing, or cease to sing, we never know;
> And if we will recite nine hours in ten,
> You lose your patience, just like other men.
> Then too we hurt our selves, when to defend
> A single verse, we quarrel with a friend;
> Repeat unask'd; lament, the Wit's too fine
> For vulgar eyes, and point out ev'ry line.
>
> (*Ibid., Ep.* ii i 356–67)

And doubtless there are studies more suited to men of ripe years:

> Wisdom (curse on it) will come soon or late.
> There is a time when Poets will grow dull:
> I'll e'en leave Verses to the Boys at school:

2/*Epistle to Arbuthnot*, 129.
3/*Imit. Donne,* ii 7.

> To Rules of Poetry no more confin'd,
> I learn to smooth and harmonize my Mind,
> Teach ev'ry Thought within its bounds to roll,
> And keep the equal Measure of the Soul.
>
> > (*Ibid.*, ii 199–205)

Even the self-deprecations, however, are subsumed finally into the general pattern of confrontation, as a world we recognize to be a tolerable facsimile of the existing city is brought before us by a sturdy, self-reliant, self-correcting grotto sage-and-poet, who is spokesman for another point of view. Some of the confrontations are direct in the manner of the following:

> Gold, Silver, Iv'ry, Vases sculptur'd high,
> Paint, Marble, Gems, and Robes of *Persian* Dye,
> There are who have not—and thank Heav'n there are
> Who, if they have not, think not worth their care.
>
> > (*Ibid.*, ii 263–67)

Some are more subtly effected through contrasting portraits, anecdotes, and tones. Some are managed by striking allusions in a way especially characteristic of Pope, like the evocation of Aeneas's interview with the Sybil in the passage on paper money. And some come about through the poet's stress on honesty of speech. Speech indeed takes a central position in any war between satirist and establishment, since it is always in the nature of the iron hand to seek its velvet glove.[4] Nobody, say the poet's various interlocutors, could object to his writing poetry, if it were poetry in praise of Caesar; or to his writing satires, if he did not name names; or to his naming names if they were not the names of persons currently represented in the power structure; or to their being persons represented in the power-structure if what was said about them were translated into Newspeak:

> But *Horace*, Sir, was delicate, was nice;
> *Bubo* observes, he lash'd no sort of *Vice*:
> *Horace* would say, *Sir* Billy *serv'd the Crown*,
> Blunt *could do Bus'ness*, H—ggins *knew the Town*,
> In *Sappho* touch the *Failing of the Sex*,
> In rev'rend Bishops note some *small Neglects*,

4/Like Thucydides in his history, Pope in his satires sees political and moral failure in terms of perversions and disintegrations of language.

> And own, the *Spaniard* did a *waggish thing*,
> Who cropt our Ears, and sent them to the King.
> His sly, polite, insinuating stile
> Could please at Court, and make AUGUSTUS smile.[5]
> (*One Thousand Seven Hundred and Thirty-Eight, Dial.* i 11–20)

The effort of power being thus to capture speech and so far as possible mollify and muddy it (till, as at the close of the *Dunciad*, nothing remains but an "uncreating" word), the poet's task must be to husband its purity and strength:

> Command old words that long have slept, to wake,
> Words, that wise *Bacon*, or brave *Raleigh* spake;
> Or bid the new be *English*, Ages hence,
> (For Use will father what's begot by Sense)
> Pour the full Tide of Eloquence along,
> Serenely pure, and yet divinely strong. ...
> (*Imit. Hor., Ep.* ii ii 167–72)

Therefore, from all the epidemic forms that complacency can take—Favonio's "Honey," Bubo's "Flowers," Yonge's "Flow," the preacher's "gracious Dew," the courtier's "well-whipt Cream";[6] from the orotundities and insipidities that have sprung up like fungi in the decaying language of epic and panegyric when misapplied to the house of Brunswick (above, p. 164); from the "hash of tongues" that serves a court made up of foreigners;[7] from the "new Court jargon"—"The modern language of corrupted Peers"[8]—wherein, as the Opposition paper *Common Sense* was saying in 1740,

When a Vice and Folly grows prevalent and fashionable, it changes its Name at its Confirmation, assumes a softer, if not a meritorious one, and under this Protection it becomes invidious, at least, if not dangerous to attack and expose it—[9]

from all these fakings and frivolities the poet must in his own self-interest cut free.

5/Pope may be remembering and turning the flank of Lady Mary and Lord Hervey's charge that, whereas Horace was "delicate," Pope could only "coarsely rail" (*Verses to the Imitator of the First Satire of the Second Book of Horace*, 1733, p. 4).

6/*One Thousand Seven Hundred and Thirty-Eight, Dial.* i, 67–70.

7/*Imit. Donne*, iv 52.

8/*Imit. Hor., Ep.* i i 99–100.

9/8 March 1740. The passage continues: "[One] would not at first imagine, that a man of nice and zealous Honour, only meant a deliberate Murtherer; a careful man, a Thief; an honest Fellow, meant nothing but a very drunken one; and a very Good Sort of Man, or a very Good-natur'd Man, meant either nothing at all, or meant a Fool."

He must frame a speech that will repossess the clarities of prose, even if to his audience this means he no longer seems a poet ("Verseman or proseman, term me which you will"),[10] a medium so unassuming that it can carry unabashedly "the Language of the Heart,"[11] "the Flow of Soul,"[12] the modulations of a living and highly personal voice. He must hammer out a style of irony that, like the argots of all undergrounds, will assert the moral victory of the weak over the strong—a style complete with "in" jokes, an "in" vocabulary, and such a cunning in maneuvering the permitted counters that a vote of no looks like a vote of yes:

> While You, great Patron of Mankind, sustain
> The balanc'd World, and open all the Main. ...
>
> > (*Imit. Hor., Ep.* ii i 1–2)

In short, to use his own words, he must "moralize his song."

The comparison with Spenser that Pope's phrase invites is suggestive. In coming to the *Faerie Queene*, Spenser has put away (he tells us) his "oaten reeds" and taken up "trumpets sterne" in order to

> sing of Knights and Ladies gentle deeds;
> Whose prayses having slept in silence long,
> Me, all too meane, the sacred Muse areeds
> To blazen broade emongst her learned throng;
> Fierce warres and faithful loves shall
> > moralize my song. (*Proemium*, st. 1)

So Pope, in coming to the poems of the 30's, puts behind him the "purling stream" and "painted mistress" of earlier achievements to celebrate "Fierce warres and faithful loves" of his own defining, and the instrument he uses—his own version of the "trumpets sterne"—is the new sinewy style of the satires and epistles. Spare, clear, unpretentious despite all its versatilities of sound and meaning, earned, as the manuscripts show, by infinite pains and a philosophy of composition in which "revision becomes an ethical imperative,"[13] Pope's mature style in the poems of the 30's was perhaps in the long run (whether he realized it or not) his most telling form of confrontation with the Newspeak of the existing city and the overstuffed verse and prose of Walpole's hacks and gazetteers. Like

---

10/*Imit. Hor., Sat.* ii i 64.

11/*Epistle to Dr. Arbuthnot*, 399.

12/*Imit. Hor., Sat.* ii i 128.

13/Paul Fussell, *The Rhetorical World of Augustan Humanism: Ethics and Imagery from Swift to Burke* (Oxford University Press, 1965), p. 79.

Thoreau's style in *Walden*, it was inexhaustibly civilized and allusive, yet at the same time it both preached and exemplified a doctrine of simplicity and disencumbrance—as if to say that genuine civility, in style as in life, comes best from traveling light:

I see young men, my townsmen, whose misfortune it is to have inherited farms, houses, barns, cattle, and farming tools; for these are more easily acquired than got rid of. Better if they had been born in the open pasture and suckled by a wolf, that they might have seen with clearer eyes what field they were called to labor in. Who made them serfs of the soil? Why should they eat their sixty acres, when man is condemned to eat only his peck of dirt? Why should they begin digging their graves as soon as they are born? They have got to live a man's life, pushing all these things before them, and get on as well as they can. How many a poor immortal soul have I met well-nigh crushed and smothered under its load, creeping down the road of life, pushing before it a barn seventy-five feet by forty, its Augean stables never cleansed, and one hundred acres of land, tillage, mowing, pasture, and wood-lot! The portionless, who struggle with no such unnecessary inherited encumbrances, find it labor enough to subdue and cultivate a few cubic feet of flesh.

It is hard to have a Southern overseer; it is worse to have a Northern one; but worst of all when you are the slave-driver of yourself. Talk of a divinity in man! Look at the teamster on the highway, wending to market by day or night; does any divinity stir within him? His highest duty to fodder and water his horses! What is his destiny to him compared with the shipping interests? Does not he drive for Squire Make-a-stir? How godlike, how immortal, is he? See how he cowers and sneaks, how vaguely all the day he fears, not being immortal nor divine, but the slave and prisoner of his own opinion of himself, a fame won by his own deeds. Public opinion is a weak tyrant compared with our own private opinion. What a man thinks of himself, that it is which determines, or rather indicates, his fate. Self-emancipation even in the West Indian provinces of the fancy and imagination,—what Wilberforce is there to bring that about? Think, also, of the ladies of the land weaving toilet cushions against the last day, not to betray too green an interest in their fates! As if you could kill time without injuring eternity.   (*Walden*, "Economy")

Simplicity, simplicity, simplicity! I say, let your affairs be as two or three, and not a hundred or a thousand; instead of a million count half a dozen, and keep your accounts on your thumb-nail. In the midst of this chopping sea of civilized life, such are the clouds and storms and quicksands and thousand-and-one items to be allowed for, that a man has to live, if he would not founder and go to the bottom and not make his port at all, by dead reckoning, and he must be a great calculator indeed who succeeds. Simplify, simplify. Instead of three meals a day, if it be necessary eat but one; instead of a hundred dishes, five; and reduce other things in proportion. Our life is like a German Confederacy, made up of petty states, with its boundary forever fluctuating, so that even a German cannot tell you how it is bounded at any moment. The nation itself, with all its so-called internal improvements, which, by the way, are all external and superficial, is just such an unwieldy and overgrown establishment, cluttered with furniture and tripped up by its own traps, ruined by luxury and heedless expense, by want of calculation and a worthy aim, as the million households in the land; and the only cure for it, as for them, is in a rigid economy, a stern and more than Spartan simplicity of life and elevation of purpose.

Hardly a man takes a half-hour's nap after dinner, but when he wakes he holds up his head and asks, "What's the news?" as if the rest of mankind had stood his sentinels. Some give directions to be waked every half-hour, doubtless for no other purpose; and then, to pay for it, they tell what they have dreamed. After a night's sleep the news is as indispensable as the breakfast. "Pray tell me anything new that has happened to a man anywhere on this globe,"—and he reads it over his coffee and rolls, that a man has had his eyes gouged out this morning on the Wachito River; never dreaming the while that he lives in the dark unfathomed mammoth cave of this world, and has but the rudiment of an eye himself. (*Ibid.*, "Where I Lived, and What I Lived For")

That the burden of Thoreau's counsel to his time should so closely match Pope's to his and Horace's to his is perhaps a tribute not only to the durability of vision but to the invincibility of power. "Though the word is common," said Heracleitus, "the many live as if they had a vision of their own." "When we consider," says Thoreau (in what may, or may not, be an echo), "what are the true necessaries and means of life, it appears as if men had deliberately chosen the common mode of living because they preferred it to any other." Perhaps for all times and places the best symbol of the human situation is the play within the play which is being watched and heard by a man who has seen a ghost, or listened to a Muse.

VIII

Fortunately, so far as Pope and Walpole are concerned, we can from this distance appreciate both sides. When we survey Hobbes's world of power with the optics it permits us, Walpole easily stands out as one of the great leaders and even benefactors of his people. Tough, cynical, self-serving, but also resilient, patient,

49 The Stone Hall at Houghton today

50 Pope in the line of Chaucer, *c.* 1736–41(?).
By Jonathan Richardson, 1665–1745

stubborn, and shrewd, actively responsive to the fears and hungers, the ghettos and bordellos of human nature as well as its more presentable civic monuments like loyalty and patriotism, he was, as Professor Plumb has said, an exceptionally skilled administrator and persuader who "made the cumbersome machinery of eighteenth-century government work more efficiently than it was ever to work again,"[1] and who held the nation together, by hook and sometimes by crook, for a crucial period of two decades while a change of dynasty was effected and England grew strong in peace. This was a tremendous feat of energy, strategy, and devotion, as he must have realized himself. From his point of view, therefore, as from that of many an historian who has written about him since, it was unimaginable that any of the Outs who opposed him could be activated by other motives than the desire to be In. About the politicians, no doubt he was right.

1/*The First Four Georges* (London, 1956), p. 75.

51 Pope in the line of Milton, 1738.
By Jonathan Richardson, 1665–1745

About some of the writers and poets, probably he was wrong. In any case, writers of the only kind he sought were for hire in quantity, and in the world of practical politics he was better off without the dewy-eyed idealists who talked in high terms of culture and corruption and the decay of national virtue; just as he was better off without any of his chief political rival's nonsense about Patriot Kings.[2]

With arguments like these, one supposes, Walpole would have defended himself, had it ever occurred to him that such a normal response to the existing city as his own required defense; for he was not much troubled by vision, political or otherwise (Plumb, I xiii–xiv), and among the qualities that make up the English temperament, he chiefly represented, as his biographer has rightly insisted, the

---

2/For Opposition use of Bolingbroke's ideas, see Mabel H. Cable, "The Idea of a Patriot King in the Propaganda of the Opposition to Walpole, 1735–39," *Philological Quarterly,* XVIII (1939), 119–30.

52 The translator of Homer, 1716.
By Sir Godfrey Kneller, 1646–1723

"Englishness," the self-confidence, even arrogance, that would in due course and for a considerable period assume the empire of the world.[3]

On the other hand, when we look at the power-world through the eyes of Blake and Eliot, or of Plato and Thoreau, or of poets generally (in the inclusive Greek sense of the word), we can understand why Pope and others regarded Walpole as they did. Poetry and history (history being defined as the chronicle of the existing city) step to different drummers—the image is again Thoreau's. There is always the actual Italy of Augustus and the Italy of the *Georgics* and *Aeneid*; the sixteenth-century England of Cecil and the New Men, and Faerie; any real pub and the Boar's Head; Lewis Theobald and "piddling Tibbalds." Poetry can never quite let history alone. As history sees it, there have always been and will always be the cries, sighs, and curses of chimney sweep, soldier, and

3/Plumb, *Men and Places* (London, 1963), p. 146.

53 The learned poet and critic, 1721.
By Sir Godfrey Kneller, 1646–1723

harlot; their causes are infinitely complex, a matter for case-workers and graphs of income distribution, and their significance in the individual instance is nil. As for the crowds reported to be flowing over London Bridge in the early decades of this century (above, p. 217), history has received no reliable information that they were actually dead or even mute. To eye-witnesses they appeared to be chattering about the things that it was timely and gratifying to chatter about on that particular morning, even as today, reader, you and I.

As much may be said of Pope. His intense and repeated references to a nation in decay had no historical foundation—so Johnson assures us,[4] looking back about forty years later from an historian's stance and therefore forgetting that

---

4/Life of Thomson, *Lives of the English Poets*, ed. G. B. Hill (Clarendon Press, 1905), III 289. Johnson also forgot his own Opposition pieces—*Marmor Norfolciense* (1739), and *A Compleat Vindication* (above, p. 160, n. 9).

the England of Pope's satires, like his own London in his poem *London,* is not wholly to be discovered on any of John Rocque's maps. For Pope did not, like Walpole, represent the self-confidence of the English which would one day rule the world. His part of the English temperament was that part which has so filled the national literature with commanding images of a City beyond the existing city that it is likely to remain the nation's glory long after the last vestiges of empire have disappeared. "But the City whose foundation we have been describing," protests Glaucon in the ninth book of the *Republic,* "has its being only in words; there is no spot on earth where it exists." To which Socrates replies: "No; but it is laid up in heaven as a pattern for him who wills to see, and seeing, to found that City in himself. Whether it exists any where, or ever will exist, is no matter."

Epilogue

What happens is a continual surrender of [the poet] as he is at the moment to something which is more valuable.
　　　　　　　　　　　—T. S. Eliot, *Tradition and the Individual Talent*

I

The outcome of these inquiries, is, I hope, now clear. To be a great satirist, a man must have, literally and figuratively, a place to stand, an angle of vision. For Pope—so my argument runs—the garden and the grotto supplied this. They supplied a rallying point for his personal values and a focus for his conception of himself—as master of a poet's "kingdom," a counter-order to a court and ministry that set no store by poets, a community bound by ties quite other than those uniting the "pensioners" of St. Stephen, as he sardonically calls the members of Walpole's parliament.[1] In a sense, they supplied him too with the materials of a *Selbstentwurf*, nourishing his feelings and imagination in the way that at a later time the tower and the swan would do for Yeats. Through them his retreat at Twickenham became, not only in his own eyes but in those of a number of his contemporaries, a true country of the mind. In a world where the

---

1/*Epistle to Bathurst*, 394. Above, p. 173.

many lived as usual, as if they had a wisdom of their own, his house, grotto, and garden with all that they implied could be grasped, at any rate in the poetry, as Henry James's "possible other case"—the case rich and edifying in the light of which the actuality of the other world seemed pretentious and vain.

In Pope's case as in Yeats's, the elements of the self-projection were such as required him, like Antaeus, to re-create his limited personal being by drawing on a large historical identity. This identity for Pope was that of the virtuous recluse, the Horatian *beatus ille* figure which he interpreted in the contemporary and very personal style that I have been exploring here. Thus the position of sophisticated rusticity, which he took up at Twickenham in 1720 in order to give scope to both the worldliness of his literary inclinations and his genuine love of gardening and privacy, became of value to him during the 1730's in more ways than he could possibly have foreseen. As a visible practitioner of the retired life, in manners "easy" but in life "severe,"[2] he had invested himself with the most honorific public image of the age, an image that by 1720, though it had earlier been appropriated to Cavaliers and Tories,[3] was sought by men of all persuasions and so could aid a writer to survive the currents of public faction, whose threat to artistic independence Pope must have sensed sufficiently when hawking subscriptions to his Homer. Moreover, as himself a species of country "squire," occupant and improver of a small "estate," living off annuities, investments, a small inheritance, and other revenues not gained by shopkeeping, he enjoyed at least fringe membership in the social group whose right to speak home about the condition of the nation was universally admitted and whose membership also comprehended the two parties in more or less equal shares—Walpole himself being no more than such a squire on a grander scale. Still further, through his interests as horticulturist and landscapist, experimenting with vegetables and fruits new to the English climate, studying Vitruvius and Palladio, building shell-temples, shaded walks, and grottoes in which to read Seneca and Plutarch, Cicero and Montaigne, he lived not only among the great, as he claimed, but like a number of them, and had access to a central vocabulary of assumptions about the practical means as well as ideal ends of living. And finally, as the rural singer recommending ancient ethical priorities, he had access, even without Horace, to some of the authority attendant upon withdrawal figures, from Diogenes to Piers the Plowman and Colin Clout.

Apart from the happy circumstance of his Twickenham villa, offering an

---

2/Dodsley, *The Cave of Pope*, 15.
3/Maren-Sofie Røstvig, *The Happy Man* (above, p. 21, n. 2), i, 60–62, 179–80.

54 The meditating poet, 1722.
By Sir Godfrey Kneller, 1646–1723

invitation to, and a suitable ambience for, a career that Reuben Brower rightly calls "progressively an *Imitatio Horati*,"[4] we may reasonably wonder whether Pope's work of the 30's might not have had a considerably different shape. The time was past when any serious writer could find his place to stand beside the throne. Dryden had managed this, and in his finest poems speaks as if the establishment, with the monarchy its center, spoke through him—the last principle of order in a disintegrating world. But for Pope, after the death of Anne, the throne as center of the dream of the civilized community has become absurd. What he gives us instead, in various versions, is intimations of a throne usurped,

---

4/*Alexander Pope: The Poetry of Allusion* (Oxford University Press, 1959), p. 165. In Pope's taking himself for a subject, as to an extent he does in the poems of the 30's, and in his favorite image of himself as a personality "moyen, divers et ondoyant," there is of course a transparent debt to Montaigne as well as Horace. This is a subject that has not so far been adequately explored.

55 Detail of Plate 54,
showing the "poetic" character of the pose

or a throne occupied by shadows. The throne of the *Epistle to Augustus* was
once genuinely filled by Horace's Augustus. The throne of the first dialogue of
the *Epilogue to the Satires* was formerly Virtue's, but is now seized by triumphant
Vice (141ff.). The Throne of the *Epistle to Burlington* awaits in vain a Brunswick who will fulfil in Britain the vision of law and government that Anchises
unfolds before his son in the sixth *Aeneid* and that Pope here echoes (191ff.).
And then there are the several thrones of the *Dunciad*, kept supplied (in an England where "Dunce the Second reigns like Dunce the First" [1 6]) with shadowy
incumbents by a shadowy queen mother.

    Dryden's angle of vision was no longer available to a serious poet, but there was
a possible alternative. The Roman poem that ran deepest in the blood stream of
Pope's age was Virgil's *Georgics*, a poem whose distinctive achievement, as Sir
Kenneth Clark has shrewdly reminded us, lies in combining an almost absolute
degree of realism in its account of farming, with an almost absolute degree of

myth in its identification of the life of husbandmen with the innocence and felicity, hardihood and piety of the lost Golden Age before Astraea left the earth.[5] Something of the same unlikely blend may be observed in Pope's satires of the 30's. They are all, in one dimension, entirely realistic, and this dimension has been authenticated sufficiently by the poet's editors, and I hope extended here. Yet in another dimension, which I should like to think has also been extended here, all play their part in an extended fiction (which is by no means all fiction) of the virtuous recluse who ventures in and out of London to remind his contemporaries of the City a little further up-river. Though the throne is empty, there remains an alternative center, and a power of a different kind: the poet-king-philosopher in his grotto, midway between the garden and the river. Under his magisterial wand, like the wrecked voyagers in *The Tempest*, lords and rich men, ministers and society-wenches, kings, courtiers, Quakers, clowns, and good Ralph Allens move through the paces of an intricate satirical ballet, which combines the features of reality and dream.

5/*Landscape into Art* (London, 1949), p. 54.

Appendix A

"*An* Epistolary Description *of the late Mr.* POPE's House and Gardens *at TWICKENHAM*"

THE FOLLOWING ACCOUNT is taken from the January 1748 issue of *The Newcastle General Magazine, or Monthly Intelligencer*, 1 25–28. I have not been able to identify the recipient or the sender.

An Epistolary Description *of the late Mr* POPE's House *and* Gardens *at* TWICKEN-HAM.

To Mr P - - - - - T - - - - -, *in* Newcastle.

Dear Sir,   *March* 18, 1746–7.

THO' now I have liv'd in *London* two Months, I have not been able to steal more than one Day from constant Attendance to the Business which brought me up; but that however, was made a most pleasant one, by an entertaining Ramble into the Country along with a few agreeable Companions. Nothing can excel the fine Views and Scenes about this great Town: Every Thing within the Compass of Art and Nature is carried to the highest Pitch: The Hills and Lawns, Wood and Fields, are cultivated and displayed to the utmost of Skill and Industry; and such a Multitude of elegant Seats and Villas rising on all Sides, amaze a new Spectator with their various Design and Grandeur. But it is not my present Purpose to entertain you with a general Description of this rich Country: I have a Particular in view, that I know will be infinitely more acceptable to your Taste and Curiosity. We set out early in the Morning, and made choice of the Road along the South Banks of the *Thames*, which leads to *Richmond*, where we proposed to bait; but arriving there before Noon, we found Time enough upon our Hands to ride up as far as *Twit'nam* and return to Dinner. You will instantly guess our Intention was to visit the Residence of the late Mr *Pope*: This indeed was our Design; and as we approach'd it, I could not help being agitated with a kind of glowing Ardour, flutt'ring at my Heart, often revolving these Lines,

> "Come let us trace the matchless Vale of *Thames*,
> "Fair winding, where the Muses us'd to haunt,
> "In *Twit'nam*'s Bowers, and for their POPE implore
> "The healing God."

They are a little alter'd, from *Thompson*'s Seasons; and you who know how infinitely fond I am of Mr *Pope*'s Poetry, will not wonder at my being seiz'd on this
Occasion, with a Gust of Enthusiasm; nor that I tell you I enter'd the Gardens with
a warm Offering of Respect and Reverence. And now, Sir, I will give you the best
Description of the Place that I can draw from the cursory View which our Time
allow'd us to take of it.

   Twickenham is a delightful Village, situated about a North Country Mile above
Richmond, on the opposite Side of the River. Mr *Pope*'s House stands in the Southwest End of the Village; the Area of the Ground is a gentle Declivity most agreeably
sloping to the *Thames*, which here exactly answers *Denham*'s inimitable Description
of it.

>   "Tho' deep yet clear, tho' gentle yet not dull;
>   "Strong without Rage, without o'erflowing full."

Between the River and the House ascends a Parterre or Piece of Grass, near Square;
on the uppermost Verge of which is the House, fronting the River, and backing
against the Wall of the high Road which leads thro' the Town of *Twit'nam*, and
passes behind the House: On the other Side of this Road, still easily ascending further
from the *Thames*, lie the Gardens, whose Bounds are of an irregular Form, not
encompassed with Walls, but Hedges, containing (I think) not much over or under
two Acres of Ground. This gives you a general Notion of the whole, and its Situation: and, to be more particular, I shall trace over as many of the Parts as occur to
me, beginning again at the Bottom of the Plan, where the lingring *Thames* glides
softly by, and washes the Margin of the green Parterre; at the Head of which, as it
were niched into a rising Mound, or Bank, stands the House; not of so large or magnificent a Structure, as a lightsome Elegance and neat Simplicity in its Contrivance. It
is at present neither inhabited nor furnished; but shut up and silent, as that great
Genius which lately resided in it. The Sides of the Court, or Parterre, are bounded
by deep Thickets of Trees, Hedges, and various Evergreens and Shrubs, ascending
in a wild, but delightful Slope, beginning with these of the humblest Growth, and[,]
gradually rising, end with lofty Elms and other Forest Trees. This Grass plot is
join'd to the Garden by a subterraneous Passage, or Cavern; which entering the
House below the Middle of the Front, and passing cross under the high Road, opens
into a Wilderness Part of the Garden. Over the Front Entrance into this Grotto lies a
balustraded Platform, and serves the Building both as a Vestible and Portico; for
a Balcony projecting from the middle Window of the second Story, and supported
by Pillars resting upon the Platform, makes so much of it resemble a Portico; but the
Platform extending without these Pillars, becomes more a Vestible: Add to this,

the Window opening into the Balcony being crowned with a Pediment, gives the several Parts an Air of one Figure, or whole, and adds an inexpressible Grace to the Front.* Mr *Pope*, you may observe, in a Letter to Mr *Blount*, says, that in forming the subterraneous Way and Grotto, he there found a Spring of the clearest Water, which fell in a perpetual Rill that eccho'd thro' the Cavern Day and Night: The Discovery of this rilling Fountain was a fortunate Accident to Mr *Pope*, whose Taste was so admirably suited to give a Thing of that kind the happiest Turn of poetical Improvement; as you will presently see. The Grotto is an irregular Vault and Passage, open at both Extremities, and further illuminated by two Windows to the Front: In passing it along [along it?], we are presented with many Openings and Cells, which owe their Forms to a Diversity of Pillars and Jambs, ranged after no set Order or Rule, but aptly favouring the particular Designs of the Place: They seem as roughly hew'd out of Rocks and Beds of mineral Strata, discovering in the Fissures and angular Breaches, Variety of Flints, Spar, Ores, Shells, &c. among which the Stream issuing from the Spring of Water is distributed to a Diversity of Purposes: Here it gurgles in a gushing Rill thro' fractur'd Ores and Flints; there it drips from depending Moss and Shells; here again, washing Beds of Sand and Pebbles, it rolls in Silver Streamlets; and there it rushes out in Jets and Fountains; while the Caverns of the Grot incessantly echo with a soothing Murmur of aquatick Sounds. To multiply this Diversity, and still more increase the Delight, Mr *Pope*'s poetick Genius has introduced a kind of Machinery, which performs the same Part in the Grotto that supernal Powers and incorporeal Beings act in the heroick Species of Poetry: This is effected by disposing Plates of Looking glass in the obscure Parts of the Roof and Sides of the Cave, where a sufficient Force of Light is wanting to discover the Deception, while the other Parts, the Rills, Fountains, Flints, Pebbles, &c. being duly illuminated, are so reflected by the various posited Mirrors, as, without exposing the Cause, every Object is multiplied, and its Position represented in a surprizing Diversity. Cast your Eyes upward, and you half shudder to see Cataracts of Water precipitating over your Head, from impending Stones and Rocks, while saliant Spouts rise in rapid Streams at your Feet: Around, you are equally surprized with flowing Rivulets and rolling Waters, that rush over airey Precipices, and break amongst Heaps of ideal Flints and Spar. Thus, by a fine Taste and happy Management of Nature, you are presented with an undistinguishable Mixture of Realities and Imagery. In passing out of the Grotto we enter into a Wilderness, and have in view directly before us a Rotundo, or kind of Temple, entirely compos'd of Shells, and consisting wholly of a Cupola, or Dome, supported upon rustick Columns, so as

---

*See the Frontispiece of this Magazine [i.e. Plate 12].

to leave it open every Way to the surrounding Garden. From the Grotto to the Temple we ascend along a Walk in the natural Taste, being rather strew'd than pav'd with Flints and Pebbles, inclos'd with Thickets, and over-arch'd with wild and interwoven Branches of Trees. From the Temple, this sylvan Arcade, together with the Passage of the Grotto, makes a sort of continued Tube, thro' which a small Expanse of the *Thames* is beheld as in a Perspective, making a beautiful remote Appearance; where Vessels that pass up and down the River, suddenly glance on the Eye, and again vanish from it in a Moment. Before I lose Sight of the Grotto, I must not omit taking Notice of an Inscription from *Horace*, placed over the Entrance from the Garden.

—*Secretum iter, et fallentis semita vitae.*

An *English* Translation of this, equally poetical, elegant, and concise, I think is hardly possible: By attempting it, I have greatly fallen short in the last respect,

> A hid Recess, where Life's revolving Day,
> In sweet Delusion gently steals away.

I would next give you some particular Idea of the Garden, but am afraid I shall fail most of all in this Part of my Attempt: for that free natural Taste, and unaffected Simplicity, which presides every where in the Plan, wanders so much from all common Forms and stated Fashions, that a Wood or a Forest doth not deviate much more from Rule: It is not here,

That—Grove nods at Grove, each Alley has a Brother,
   And half the Platform just reflects the other,
But—Pleasing Intricacies intervene,
   And artful Wildness to perplex the Scene.

Near the Bounds of the Garden, the Trees unite themselves more closely together, and cover the Hedges with a thick Shade, which prevents all prying from without, and preserves the Privacy of the interior Parts. These Wilderness Groves are either Quincunces, or cut thro' by many narrow serpentine Walks; and as we recede from the Boundary and approach towards the Center, the Scene opens and becomes less entangled; the Alleys widen, the Walks grow broader, and either terminate in small green Plots of the finest Turf, or lead to the Shell Temple. The Middle of the Garden approaches nearest to a Lawn or open Green, but is delightfully diversified with Banks and Hillocks; which are entirely cover'd with Thickets of Lawrel, Bay, Holly, and many other Evergreens and Shrubs, rising one above another in beautiful Slopes and Intermixtures, where Nature freely lays forth the Branches, and disports uncontroul'd; except what may be entirely prun'd away for more Decency and Convenience to the surrounding Grass-plots, for no Shear-work or Tonsure is to be found in all the Scene. Towards the South side of the Garden is a Plantation of Vines curiously disposed and dress'd; it adjoins the Wilderness, and is in the same Taste, but opener to the Sun, and with more numerous interveening Paths. Among the Hillocks on the upper Part of the open Area, rises a Mount much higher than the rest, and is composed of more rude and indigested Materials; it is covered with Bushes and Trees of a wilder Growth, and more confused Order, rising as it were out of Clefts of Rocks, and Heaps of rugged and mossy Stones; among which a narrow intricate Path leads in an irregular Spiral to the Top; where is placed a Forest Seat or Chair, that may hold three or four Persons at once, overshaded with the Branches of a spreading Tree. From this Seat we face the Temple, and over-look the various Distribution of the Thickets, Grass-plots, Alleys, Banks, &c. Near this Mount lies the broadest Walk of the Garden, leading from the Center to the uppermost Verge; where, upon the gentle Eminence of a green Bank, stands an Obelisk, erected by Mr *Pope* to the Memory of his Mother: It is a plain Stone Pillar resting upon a Pedestal; and the Plynth of the Pillar bears this Inscription on its four Sides, beginning with that which faces the Walk.

AH EDITHA!

MATRUM OPTIMA.

MULIERUM AMANTISSIMA.

VALE.

As this Obelisk terminates the longest Prospect of Mr *Pope*'s Garden, it shall also put a Period to my Description; which is not of a Place that bears the high Air of State and Grandeur, and surprizes you with the vastness of Expence and Magnificence; but an elegant Retreat of a Poet strongly inspired with the Love of Nature and Retirement; and shews you, with respect to these Works, what was the Taste of the finest Genius that this or any other Age has produced. I cannot conclude my Epistle better, than with a few Lines from the great Master himself, which contain his own Remarks upon his Situation at *Twit'nam*.

> To Virtue only and her Friends a Friend,
> The World besides may murmur or commend.
> Know, all the distant Din that World can keep,
> Rolls o'er my Grotto and but soothes my Sleep.
> There my Retreat, the best Companions grace,
> Chiefs out of War, and Statesmen out of Place.

There ST JOHN mingles with my friendly Bowl,
The Feast of Reason, and the Flow of Soul.
And *HE, whose Lightning pierc'd th' *Iberian* Lines,
Now forms my Quincunx, and now ranks my Vines:
Or tames the Genius of the stubborn Plain,
Almost as quickly as he conquer'd *Spain*.
Envy must own, I live among the Great,
No Pimp of Pleasure, and no Spy of State;
With Eyes that pry not, Tongue that ne'er repeats,
Fond to spread Friendships, but to cover Heats;
To help who want, to forward who excel,
This all who know me, know; who love me, tell;
And who unknown defame me, let them be
Scribblers or Peers, alike are Mob to me.

In South Sea Days not happier, when surmis'd
The Lord of Thousands, than if now excis'd:
In Forests planted by a Father's Hand,
Than in five Acres now of rented Land;
Content with little, I can piddle here
On Brocoli and Mutton round the Year;
But ancient Friends (tho' poor, or out of Play)
That touch my Bell, I cannot turn away.
'Tis true no Turbots dignify my Boards,
But Gudgeons, Flounders, what my *Thames* affords.
To *Hounslow-Heath* I point, and *Bansted-Down*,
Thence comes your Mutton, and these Chicks my own:
From yon old Walnut Tree a Shower shall fall,
And Grapes, long-lingring on my only Wall.
Fortune not much of humbling me can boast,
Tho' double-tax'd, how little have I lost?
My Life's Amusements have been just the same,
Before and after standing Armies came.
My Lands are sold, my Father's House is gone;
I'll hire another's; is not that my own?

Earl of Peterborough

And yours, my Friends? thro' whose free opening Gate
None comes too early, none departs too late.
For I (who hold sage *Homer*'s Rule the best)
Welcome the coming, speed the going Guest.
"Pray Heav'n it last! (cries *Swift*) as you go on!
"I wish to God this House had been your own:
"Pity! to build without a Son or Wife:
"Why, you'll enjoy it only all your Life."—
Well, if the Use be mine, can it concern one,
Whether the Name belong to *Pope* or *Vernon*?
What's Property? dear *Swift!* You see it alter
From you to me, from me to *Peter Walter*.—
Shades that to *Ba——n* could Retreat afford
Are now the Portion of a booby Lord:
And *Hemsley*, once proud *Buckingham*'s Delight,
Slides to a Scriv'ner, or a City Knight.
Let Lands and Houses have what Lords they will,
Let us be fix'd, and our own Masters still.

                                                          T.

Appendix B

"Inventory of Pope's Goods Taken after his Death"

THIS "INVENTORY" was contributed to *Notes and Queries*, 6th Series, v (1882), pp. 363–65, by "F. G." (Colonel Francis Grant). Grant states that the original was then at Mapledurham and guesses that it had been drawn up after Pope's death "for the purpose of valuation for probate duty." Plainly the most striking category of Pope's goods was its fifty-six or more portraits, mainly of his personal friends. In other furnishings it was extremely modest save for a very small number of items, and in certain matters, such as china, one is tempted to suppose that for some reason or other less was entered in this inventory than Pope actually had. Perhaps certain items came with the house and were not his property, like the harpsichord he was prevented from lending Lady Mary Wortley Montagu (15 September 1721: *Correspondence*, II 82).

INVENTORY OF POPE'S GOODS TAKEN AFTER HIS DEATH.

Among the interesting papers at Mapledurham is an inventory of Alexander Pope's furniture, probably drawn up for the purpose of valuation for probate duty. It has, I believe, never been published, and, although a lengthy document, it seems of sufficient importance to be published in the columns of "N. & Q."

A Catalogue of the Goods at Twickenham.

IN THE GARRETS.

The room next the leads 17 drawings by Mr Pope.

A picture of a goos with Gulls.

four Prints in black frames.

THE ROOM NEXT YE THAMES

a grate fire Shoull tongs & Popker.

I.e. shovel, tongs, and poker.

Mr Scraggs Pictture in a gold frame.

Actually James Craggs (TE IV 356). This was possibly a copy of a portrait by Kneller; a portrait of him from the studio (*c.* 1708, National Portrait Gallery no. 1134) may be seen in Piper, plate 30 *i*. See also Piper, pp. 88–89.

Mr Digby in Ditto.

Doubtless Robert Digby, younger son of the fifth Baron Digby. A letter from Bethel to Pope,

25 March 1744 (IV 512), speaks of Pope's having had "your friend Mr. Digby drawn after his death" and this portrait is perhaps the one in question. "Drawn" was often used to mean painted: see below, p. 246 (Wycherley).

Lord Shrousbury in Ditto.

Charles Talbot, twelfth Earl and only Duke of Shrewsbury (TE IV 388), who had succeeded Oxford as Lord Treasurer just before Queen Anne's death in 1714. He was painted by both Lely and Kneller. One may suppose that Pope's portrait was a copy of the latter's work, since he and Kneller were friends and neighbors for some years. A copy after Kneller (c. 1685) is NPG no. 1424 (Plate 19c in Piper).

Duches Buckingham in Black frame.

Katherine Darnley Sheffield (1682?–1743), natural daughter of James II, 3rd wife of John Sheffield, Duke of Buckinghamshire (TE IV 385), whose posthumous *Works* Pope had edited in 1723. She is the supposed original of Atossa in the *Epistle to a Lady* (TE III ii 57–60, 155–64). Horace Walpole had what was apparently a miniature of her "in enamel by Zinke" (*A Description of the Villa of Mr. Horace Walpole ... With An Inventory of the Furniture, Pictures, Curiosities, &c.* (1784), p. 22. The Zincke miniature is reproduced in J. L. Propert, *History of Miniature Art* (London, 1887), p. 96.

Mr Wallsh in Ditto.

William Walsh (TE IV 392), one of Pope's earliest literary friends, praised in *Essay on Criticism*, 729. Kneller's unfinished portrait of Walsh (NPG no. 3232) may be seen in Piper, Plate 26d. Another portrait, perhaps earlier (by an unknown artist), was engraved for T. R. Nash, *Worcestershire* (London, 1781), I 5. See also Piper, pp. 370–71. Again, Pope's picture is likeliest to have been a copy of Kneller's work.

A Large Flower Poice in Ditto.

I.e. Piece. This was no doubt one of the multitudinous Dutch compositions in this vein, often designed to fill the role of *memento mori*.

Three prints in Ditto.

a Glass and Black Table.

I.e. a wall mirror above (or a standing mirror on) a table that was painted black or, possibly, japanned.

five Brack Chaires.

This may be the inventoryist's error for "Black," or he may refer to the type of chair (introduced around 1700) having cabriole legs reinforced against the frame by curved brackets of various sizes and sorts. The *OED* does not, however, record the term bracket-chair.

A Small carpet to ly by the bead [i.e. bed] Side.

THE ROOM NEXT Ye ROAD.

A Bead Bolstor [i.e. bolster] Beadstods with bleu wolsen hangings.

Probably linsey-woolsey, but perhaps woollen.

Three Blankets and a Quilt.

Fiveteen Prints in a black frame.

Mr Honee in a Gold Frame.

This man is unidentified.

a Lady's pictture in d°.

a black table three black Chaires.

THE GAROT [i.e. garret] STAIRE CASE.
The Model of Burlington House.
Two large Pictures.

IN THE CHINESE ROOM FRONTING THE THAMES.
Chince Curtains Valent [i.e. valance] and Counterpane.
A Etherdown Quilt.

I.e. eiderdown. The bed itself, if not already removed at the time of the inventory, goes unnoticed here, though there are bed-curtains, valance, counterpane, eiderdown, and a carpet to lie beside it. This may simply mean that it was unpretentious, though I find this unlikely. Perhaps the bed ordinarily found in the room is the "Camp Bead" that has migrated in the inventory to "the Best Room fronting ye Thames," where it seems curiously out of place in a chamber otherwise furnished more like a sitting room than a bedroom. Or perhaps the bed was furnished with the house as rented and so was not subject to inventory.

a carpet for the Bead side.
a Walnut tree [i.e. walnut-wood] Dressing table and Comb Box.
a Dressing Glass Black Frame.

This is probably a swiveling toilet mirror (introduced around 1700) on a black frame, which stood on the walnut dressing table (next item above).

An Octagun Inlaid Table.
A Closstole [i.e. close-stool].
Two Walnut tree Arm Chaires & Scarlet Camblet.

I.e. camlet, an upholstering plush.

a Grate fire Shoule toungs poker & fender.
Mrs Blounts Pictture in Crane [i.e. crayon, pastel] in Gold frame.

Martha Blount, presumably, since Pope's relations with Teresa were severed before "crayon-painting" became widely popular (Wimsatt, p. 280) and since the unspecific "Mrs Blount" is more likely at this time to point to Martha than to her sister, especially in an inventory being taken in part for her as Pope's chief heir. It seems likely that this pastel, like that of Pope shown in Plate 1, was by William Hoare.

The "Mapledurham" portrait of the Misses Blount together appears in Spence, 1 160. Of this portrait Robert Carruthers (*The Poetical Works of Alexander Pope* [London, 1858], 1 xi) says "In the original picture, on the riband binding the flowers, is inscribed, in very small characters, *Sic positæ quoniam suaves*—an allusion to the young ladies being represented as in a garden gathering flowers. The names of 'Martha' and 'Teresa' are also given, and the date '1716.' " See Wimsatt, p. 10.

Individual drawings of Martha and Teresa taken by W. N. Gardiner from the Mapledurham portrait may be seen in Edith Sitwell, *Alexander Pope* (London, 1930), opposite p. 68. A picture by Charles Jervas (NPG no. 112) shows (presumably) Martha Blount with Pope. Wimsatt, fig. 3, 2, is a reproduction of this; see *ibid.*, p. 23.

Another alleged likeness of Martha—almost unrecognizable—is shown in William Ayre, *Memoirs of the Life and Writings of Alexander Pope, Esq.* (London, 1745), II, opposite p. 17.

Mr Wicherleys Pictture in a Gold Frame.

Spence says (no. 97) "The picture Mr. Pope has of him [Wycherley] was drawn when he was very old. As Sir Godfrey (?) said he would make a very fine head without a wig, it was drawn at first with his little straggling grey hair. He could not bear it when done, and Sir Godfrey was forced to draw a wig to it." The portrait ascribed to Kneller (reproduced in Killinan opposite p. 11 and dated by him 1715) shows no wig. James M. Osborn suggests (Spence, 1 41) that Pope's portrait of Wycherley may have looked more like the one by Thomas Murray which he reproduces opposite 1 41.

Wycherley was also painted by Lely *c.* 1668. (NPG no. 880 is a copy of this; see Piper, Plate 12*c* and p. 388.)

Mr Betterton's Ditto.

Kneller painted Betterton in 1703 (reproduced in John Doran, *"Their Majesties' Servants"*: *Annals of the English Stage* (London, 1888), 1 opposite p. 184); the portrait was copied by many—including Pope in 1713 (Pope to Caryll, 31 August 1713: 1 189). According to Norman Ault (*New Light on Pope* [above, p. 46], pp. 73–74) this portrait—possibly the only one of Pope's still extant—is in good condition in the collection of the Earl of Mansfield, contrary to rumors of its damage by fire. For the origin of these rumors see William T. Whitley, *Artists and their Friends in England*, 2 vols. (London [1928]), 1 42–43. This portrait is reproduced as frontispiece by Benjamin Boyce, *The Character-Sketches in Pope's Poems* (Duke University Press, 1962); see also pp. 131–32.

Other versions of Kneller's portrait include one by R. Williams (1703, reproduced in Killinan, opposite p. 58); one by an unknown artist (*c.* 1690–1700, NPG no. 752); and others cited by Piper, 27–28.

Earle of Peterborough Ditto.

Charles Mordaunt, third Earl of Peterborough and 1st Earl of Monmouth (TE IV 374), Tory hero of the Spanish campaigns, ardent gardener like his friend Pope. Peterborough was painted by Kneller, Michael Dahl (1708), and an unknown artist. Pope's portrait may be guessed to have been a copy of the Kneller, which is reproduced in Thomas Birch, *Heads of Illustrious Persons* (London, 1813), opposite p. 151. For Dahl's portrait, see Spence 1, opposite p. 112.

a Chimney Glass Black Frame.

Two peices Cutt Paper in Ditto.

a Drawing of Mrs Pope in Ditto.

Probably one of the drawings made of Pope's mother by Jonathan Richardson (Wimsatt, pp. 80–81, 150–51). See below, p. 252.

Two Picture' in Ivory in Ditto

Evidently a superior "s" mistranscribed as an apostrophe.

Two Indians in Ditto.

Just possibly the "two Turkish heads" that Spence (no. 108) tells us he has seen "of Mr. Pope's drawing."

one Head of a Woman Ditto.

two Pictures of Boys in Ditto.

Seven Prints of the Cartones in Ditto.

These would be Raphael's seven cartoons for tapestries, commissioned by Pope Leo x and purchased by James 1 after the tapestries had been made. In Pope's time they occupied a special gallery at Hampton Court. Engravings of them are advertised in *Tatler*, no. 69 (17 September 1709), and it may be a set of these that is in question here.

Seven Other Prints in Ditto.

a Large Peire Glass with Six Squares in Ditto.

A mirror designed to go on a "pier" wall, i.e. between windows or doors. The "Six Squares" indicates that it was exceptionally large.

four Beach Chaires.

I.e. beech. Beech chairs went out of fashion during William III's reign and were always for modest incomes. Their presence even in this "Chince Room" and in the "Great Parlor" and library indicates the comparative simplicity of Pope's material surroundings, as does the conspicuous absence of mahogany, save for three pieces shared between the library and his own room.

Window Curtaines.

IN THE NEXT ROOME FRONTING THE THAMES.

Lord Bolingbrokes Pictture in Gold Frame.

Henry St. John, Viscount Bolingbroke (TE IV 383). Portraits of Bolingbroke are mentioned in the *Correspondence* at III 326, IV 119, 123, 148, 400. One of the pictures referred to in this inventory was possibly a drawing by Jonathan Richardson which later passed into the hands of Horace Walpole. See Wimsatt, pp. 150–51, 173–75.

There is an oil portrait of Bolingbroke attributed to Richardson in the National Portrait Gallery (no. 1493). Other portraits include one by T. Murray (*c.* 1705?, engraving reproduced in George Paston, *Mr. Pope and His Times* (New York, 1909) II, opposite p. 578); one attributed to Alexis Simon Belle (1712?, NPG no. 593; Piper, Plate 18d); and one by Kneller (1715, reproduced in Gilbert Burnet, *History of His Own Time* (London, 1838) II, opposite p. 854). See Piper, pp. 29–31. See also below, pp. 250, 254.

Dean Swift / Bishop Rochester / Mr Gay / Doctor Arbuthnot / Mr Parnell / in ditto.

Evidently a group of small portraits (engravings and/or drawings?) framed together. All the men pictured had been members of the Scriblerus Club, which may account for the arrangement of their portraits here. We know that a Swift portrait by Jervas was engraved by George Vertue (Jervas to Pope [October, 1714?]: I 269). A portrait by Jervas that is probably later than this one is NPG no. 278 (reproduced in Harold Williams, ed., *The Correspondence of Jonathan Swift* [Clarendon Press, 1963], III, frontispiece). See Piper, pp. 336–38 and Richard W. Goulding and C. K. Adams, *Catalogue of the Pictures Belonging to his Grace the Duke of Portland* (Cambridge University Press, 1936) pp. 394–95.

Edmond Malone was told by Horace Walpole that "Pope had an original picture of Bishop Atterbury painted by Kneller. Of this picture he used to make Worsdale the painter make copies for three or four guineas; and whenever he wished to pay a particular compliment to one of his friends, he gave him an *original* picture of Atterbury. Of these *originals*, Worsdale had painted five or six" (James Prior, *Life of Edmond Malone* [London, 1860] p. 385; see Wimsatt, p. 42). C. H. Collins Baker (*Lely and the Stuart Portrait Painters* [2 vols. London, 1912] II 174) dates the Kneller painting 1718. A reproduction may be seen in George Paston, *Mr. Pope His Life and Times* (above, I, opposite p. 282).

The portrait of Gay in the group was probably the engraving by F. Milvins (i.e. F. Kyte) of the portrait by William Aikman. The engraver's plate, now the property of W. K. Wimsatt, has the inscription: "To Alexander Pope Esqr. this Plate is most humbly inscrib'd."

Pope writes to Arbuthnot's son George, 6 August 1735 (III 480) that he is having a copy taken of "your picture"—i.e. presumably of the Kneller portrait of Arbuthnot, which, according to C. H. Collins Baker (*Lely and the Stuart Portrait Painters* [see above] II 89) bears the inscription: "Opus ultimus G. Kneller. A. Pope D. [onum] D. [edit] to George Arbuthnot."

But Arbuthnot had also been painted by Jervas (Wimsatt, p. 10) and William Robinson. The latter is reproduced as frontispiece in Lester M. Beattie, *John Arbuthnot Mathematician and Satirist* (Harvard University Press, 1935). See also George A. Aitken, *Life and Works of John Arbuthnot* (Clarendon Press, 1892) pp. 162–63.

A Drawing Oliver Cromwell black frame.

I suppose this to be a copy of the likeness by Pope's uncle, Samuel Cooper, the miniaturist, which was copied again and again during the seventeenth and eighteenth centuries. Possibly it was an original by Cooper, but if so, one would expect the name to be attached, in view of Cooper's early fame and high market value. One suspects that Pope came by it through inheritance, as it is difficult to imagine his seeking out the portrait of one whom he calls (in the *Essay on Man*, IV 284) "damn'd to everlasting fame."

Drawing Mr Prior in Ditto.

Pope asks Oxford, 29 September 1723, for the loan of his portrait of Prior by Rigault "to my house to be copied. ... Or else the Painter may do it where you please" (II 204). The Rigault portrait is reproduced in *Historic Gallery of Portraits and Paintings* (London, 1812), IV Plate 25. Prior was painted many times; for fuller information see Wimsatt, p. 76; Piper, pp. 286–88; and Goulding and Adams, Portland *Catalogue* (above, p. 248), pp. 382–83.

a Drawing of Lord Burlington Black Frame.

Richard Boyle, third Earl of Burlington (1695–1753), leader of the English Palladians. Burlington was painted by Kneller, Knapton, and an anonymous artist. Knapton's portrait is reproduced as frontispiece in Lees-Milne; see also pp. 121–22. Kneller's may be seen in Walpole's *Anecdotes of Painting*, ed. James Dallaway (London, 1828), IV opposite p. 216.

a Drawing of Homer in Ditto.

Possibly the drawing by Jervas of the Farnese bust of Homer which was engraved for the frontispiece of the *Iliad* translation (*Correspondence*, I 262). The item just below might well be the drawing of the Arundel bust from which the *Odyssey* frontispiece was engraved. See below, however, p. 253, where "a Drawing of Homer" is listed.

a Nother Drawing in Ditto.

a Walnut tree Book Case with Glas Dores.

a Chimney Glass with a White Frame.

a Delph Jarr.

I.e. Probably this need not have been Dutch Delft. Delftware was made in Lambeth from about 1650 on.

IN THE BEST ROOM FRONTING YE THAMES.

Mrs Blounts [above, p. 246] Pictture in a Gold Frame.

Lord Bathurst Ditto.

Allen, first Earl Bathurst (TE IV 345), with whom at Riskins and Cirencester Pope often stayed. Bathurst was painted twice by Kneller (1714, 1719), and once (with his wife) by Dahl (*c.* 1705). There is a bust by Nollekens. The 1719 Kneller portrait is reproduced in Lees-Milne, opposite p. 32.

Lady Harvey Ditto.

Mary Lepell, one of Pope's liveliest friends among the Maids of Honor during his early years in London, after 1720 wife to John Hervey. Pope seems to have remained on amicable terms with her despite his hostility to her husband.

A reproduction of a portrait of Lady Hervey by Allan Ramsay (1762) is in Walpole, XXXI, opposite p. 82. A portrait by Enoch Seeman is reproduced in *Lord Hervey and his Friends* (Earl of Ilchester, ed., London, 1950), opposite p. 36. Another unidentified portrait faces p. 58 in Lewis Melville, *Lady Suffolk and her Circle* (London, 1924).

Doc^t Garth Ditto.

Samuel Garth (TE IV 361) was painted *c.* 1710 by Kneller for the Kit-Cat Club (NPG no. 3208, reproduced in Piper Plate 23b). Another painting by Kneller is at Knole. Garth was also painted *c.* 1705–10 by an unknown artist (NPG no. 1076); see Piper, pp. 133–34. A supposed likeness of Garth shown with Pope at Button's Coffee House, obviously in several senses a pastiche or forgery, is reproduced and described in Wimsatt, pp. 330–32.

Lady Suffolk Ditto.

Henrietta Howard, mistress for many years of George II, Countess of Suffolk from 1731. She was Pope's near neighbor at Marble Hill from 1724. A portrait of her by Jervas is reproduced in *Memoirs of Horace Walpole* (2 vols., London, 1851) I, opposite p. 169, with the inscription: "From the picture in the poet Pope's collection, bought by the Countess of Suffolk at Martha Blount's sale and presented by her to Horace Walpole." A younger portrait by an unknown painter may be seen in Lees-Milne, opposite p. 80.

Lord Boolingbroke Ditto.

See above, p. 248; below, p. 254.

Lady Mary W. Mountague Ditto.

Lady Mary Wortley Montagu (TE IV 373). Pope commissioned Kneller to paint Lady Mary in 1719 (*Correspondence* II 22–23). It seems very likely that this picture is the one referred to here. A reproduction may be seen in Robert Halsband, *Life of Lady Mary Wortley Montagu* (above, p. 172), opposite p. 100. Kneller had painted Lady Mary twice before, in 1710 and 1715. She was also painted by Charles Jervas, Carolus De Rusca, Jonathan Richardson, and J. E. Liotard. Reproductions of various likenesses of her may be seen in Halsband's *Life*, his edition of her letters (Clarendon Press, 1965), and Edith Sitwell, *Alexander Pope* (above, p. 246).

a Pink and Silver Sette.

Both colors are probably those of the upholstery fabric, though wood was sometime silvered and then varnished over to keep the surface from tarnishing.

Six Walnut tree Chaires.

two Vrns.

three Marboll Tabels with Wood Brackets.

a Large Piere Glass with a Gold Frame.

two flower Peises for the Chimney Blinds.

two Small Piere Glasses.

a Large French Carpet.

4 Glass Sconces.

Johnson defines sconce as "a pensile candlestick, generally with a looking-glass [as here] to reflect light."

a Camp Bead.

two Small Land Skips.

Window Curtains.

IN THE LIB^y.

We may perhaps infer from the absence of pictures in this room that its walls were occupied by bookcases.

a Large Writing Table with Draw^s.

a Small Writing Table Walnut tree.

a Small Mahogany Table.

a Cane Squab with fower Cushings.

A rattan settee with four cushions. Cane furniture was mainly in vogue under William III and Anne.

two Arm Chaires covered with green Bays [i.e. baize].

two Arm Chaires Beach (above, p. 248).

a Indian Screen a Canvas Screen.

Doubtless in the library these were fire-screens for warding heat from the face, one of them having eastern motifs in its design.

A Stove fire Shoule Toungs & Poker.

a Marvoll Globe and Stand.

Either a terrestial or celestial globe. Probably not marble in fact but made of two heavy spheres of wood or pasteboard bound together, plastered over, and then incised or painted.

BUSTOS MARVOLL.

Homer / Sr Isack Newton / Spencer / Shakespear / Milton / Dryden.

(*a*) Homer. Conceivably, this is the bust pictured in Jervas's portrait of Pope sitting (Wimsatt, fig. 3.2). If so, it rather strongly resembled the Farnese bust in Naples, which Jervas drew and Vertue engraved for the frontispiece of Pope's quarto *Iliad*, 1. On the other hand, the only bust of Homer mentioned in Pope's will (bequeathed to William Murray, the later Lord Mansfield) he describes as a "*Marble Head of* Homer *by* Bernini." There is no record of Bernini's ever having made a Homer and Pope was doubtless wrong in the ascription. But the fact that he attributes the bust to Bernini suggests that it was not a copy of the Farnese, which he obviously knew. In an article on Pope in *Apollo* (LVII[1953]6), G. W. Beard reproduces a portrait of Murray by David Martin in which a bust of Homer is depicted that he believes to be this one. I find it impossible to be sure.

(*b*) Newton. This must be the "*Marble Head of Sir* Isaac Newton, *by* Guelfi" which Pope's will also bequeathed to Murray, and which is now at Scone Palace. Giovanni Baptista Guelfi came to England about 1714–15, was patronized especially by Burlington, and worked under Kent (M. I. Webb, *Michael Rysbrack Sculptor* [below, p. 307], pp. 153–54).

(*c*) Spenser, Shakespeare, Milton, Dryden. Pope's will says: "*I desire Mr.* Lyttelton *to accept of the Busts of* Spencer, Shakespear, Milton, *and* Dryden, *in Marble, which his Royal* Master *the Prince was pleased to give me.*" Mr. Lyttelton was his young friend, George Lyttelton, at this period secretary to Frederick Prince of Wales, and subsequently first Baron Lyttelton. Though unsigned, the busts are attributed on early authority to Peter Scheemakers, whose best-known work is the monument to Shakespeare (designed by Kent) in Westminster Abbey (1741), and are now preserved at Hagley, the Lyttelton family seat in Worcestershire. They are pictured in the *Apollo* article by Beard, cited above.

IN PLASTER OF PARIS.

Shakespear / Poladio / Indigo Jones

Palladio and Inigo Jones here were probably copies of the busts made by Michael Rysbrack for Burlington's Chiswick House, as noted at Plate 45n. (M. I. Webb [below, p. 307], figs. 36–37). So many contemporary sculptors made one or more busts of Shakespeare that it is idle to speculate about the origin of Pope's plaster copy.

two Boxses Spar and Gilt.

Materials acquired, one supposes, for the grotto.

Mr Pope^s Traveling Box.

UPON THE BEST STAIRE CASE.

29 Prints in Black Frames.

The presence of 29 prints in this staircase and of 26 pictures in the great parlor, not to mention 19 in the little parlor, makes it clear that Pope's walls were simply paved with pictures, like Walpole's at Strawberry Hill.

a Eight Day Clock.

a Small Mercury Bronse.

a Pire Glass in two Squares in Black Frame.

IN THE GREAT PARLOR.

a Large Glass in a gold Frame.

a Marble Table and Brackets.

a Marble Table Iron Brakets.

one Large Ovoll Table.

The oval shape was commonly for dining. Presumably the chairs listed just below were dining chairs.

Six Beach Chaires 4 Windsor Arm Chaires.

Mr Pope^s pictture in Gold Frame.

Inasmuch as his father is distinguished below (p. 253) as "M^r. Pope Sen[i]or," this is evidently a portrait of the poet himself. It is impossible to identify Pope's portraits, since they are so numerous as to fill an entire volume—here designated "Wimsatt."

two Mrs Blounts [above, p. 246] in Ditto.

Mr Priors in Ditto.

Rable in Ditto.

Probably a phonetic rendering of Rabelais. A popular seventeenth-century portrait of Rabelais (based on an earlier likeness with some claim to authenticity) may be seen as frontispiece in Albert J. Nock and C. R. Wilson, *Francis Rabelais* (New York, 1929); see also pp. xvi–xvii.

a Duck Peice in Ditto / Duches Hamilton in Ditto.

Elizabeth Gerard Hamilton (d. 1744), second wife of James Douglas, fourth Duke of Hamilton. Pope writes from London, October 1717 (1 437) that he is having her portrait made, presumably by Jervas.

Mr Pope when a boy in a Black and Gilt Frame.

Probably the portrait now in the collection of Mr. and Mrs. James M. Osborn of New Haven, Connecticut. (Wimsatt, fig. 1.)

His Aunts in Ditto being three of them.

Pope's mother Editha Turner is said to have had fourteen sisters (George Sherburn, *Early Career of Alexander Pope* [above, p. 10, n. 3], p. 33). We hear mostly of three—Elizabeth, who taught Pope to read; Alice, who married Richard Mawhood; Christiana, who married Samuel Cooper the miniaturist (*ibid.*)—and these may be the three here pictured, though this remains guesswork. It is quite possible that some of the other portraits in this room came to Pope from Christiana, who willed to him (following the death of her sister Elizabeth) "all my bookes, pictures, and meddalls, sett in gold or otherwise" (Whitwell Elwin and William J. Courthope, eds., *The Works of Alexander Pope* [10 vols., London, 1871–89], v 6), and it is equally possible that some were Cooper's work. On this item and the two following, see Pope's will, below, p. 264.

Mr Pope Senor in Ditto.

Only one portrait of Pope's father is known today—a drawing with pen and watercolor, taken by Jonathan Richardson at his deathbed (Wimsatt, p. 81). The portrait in question may be this one, but could just as easily be a family portrait dating from an earlier time.

Mrs Pope in Ditto.

Probably again a family portrait dating from an earlier time.

A Frute Peice in Ditto.

a Small Frute Peice with a Dog in Ditto.

a Landskip by Titeman.

This is apparently Peter Tillemans (1684–1734), a well-known landscape painter. Spence (no. 109) reports Pope as saying that "Tillemans and Wootton [are] the two best landscape painters in England. 'Twas the former's landscape at Mr. Robartes' (Lord Radnor's uncle?) that Mr. Pope stole some strokes in; the side look [when he spoke about it], and smile after."

a Vew of Sr John St Aubins House & Landskip.

Sir John St. Aubyn, third Baronet, was an MP for Cornwall (1722–44) who had joined the Opposition. He was a friend of Allen's and Borlase's. There are records of at least two visits to Pope in *Correspondence* IV 245n and 520n. The view in question, though it belongs to a familiar genre, has not been identified.

a drawing of Mr Betterton [above, p. 247] in a Black Frame.

a drawing of Mr Pope in Ditto.

Very probably one of the Richardson drawings reproduced in Wimsatt, pp. 137–222.

a Drawing of the Duches of Mountague in Ditto.

Lady Mary Churchill (1689–51), youngest daughter of the first Duke of Marlborough, one of the reigning beauties of the 1710–20 decade, complimented in Pope's *Epistle to Jervas*, 59. She married John Montagu, second Duke of Montagu, in 1705. During his studies with Jervas, Pope tells us (31 August 1713: I 189) that he threw away several efforts to picture the Duchess, probably after an original by Jervas, who had painted members of the Marlborough family. See Walpole's *Anecdotes of Painting* (above, p. 249) IV 19–20 and E. K. Waterhouse, *Painting in Britain 1530–1790* (Pelican History of Art, 1953), p. 107. A portrait of Lady Mary by Kneller may be seen in David Green, *Sarah Duchess of Marlborough* (London, 1967), opposite p. 256. According to C. H. Collins Baker, *Lely and the Stuart Portrait Painters* (above, p. 248, Lady Mary was also painted by Jonathan Richardson (II 229) and Michael Dahl (*c.* 1709, II 179). Pope's portrait of her may have been made by Richardson, Kneller, or Jervas; or it may have been his own sketch of a portrait by one of these.

a Drawing of Homer [above, p. 249] in Ditto.

a Drawing of Mrs Maden in Ditto.

Judith Cowper (aunt of the poet William Cowper), who married Captain Martin Madan in December, 1723, having corresponded for some time before that with Pope. In a letter to her husband of 4 August 1744 Mrs. Madan notes that "Mrs Blount wh[o is] Mr Popes chief Heir, has given me that Picture Jervas did in Craons for L^{dy} P. so long agoe." "As late as 1932, this drawing still survived in the Madan family" (Falconer Madan, *The Madan Family* [Oxford, 1933; printed for Subscribers], p. 97).

a Drawing of Lady Mary W. Mountague [above, 250] in Ditto.

a Picture of our Savor &c. in Ditto.

Pope tells us that in his early efforts as draughtsman and painter he "crucify'd *Christ* over-again in effigie" (23 August 1713: 1 187). Possibly this entry alludes to some such sketch of the crucifixion.

Venuc & Cupet [i.e. Venus and Cupid] in Ditto &c.

a Nother Picture in Ditto.

a Land Skepe of Twickenham in Ditto.

Any or all of these local landscape views may have been sketches by Pope himself. For one such sketch which has survived, see Plate 4. Perhaps it is worth remarking that three of these landscapes show Pope bringing his exterior environment so far as possible within doors.

a Settee Chaire.

I.e. a chair-back settee, with separate backs for each sitter.

IN THE LITTLE PARLOR.

Lord Bolingbroke [above, pp. 248, 250] in a Gold frame.

Shakespear in Ditto.

In a letter to Caryll, 11 June 1711 (1 120), while still at Binfield, Pope mentions having "pictures of Dryden, Milton, Shakespear, &c. in my chamber." His edition of Shakespeare (1725) has an engraving by Vertue of a miniature supposed to represent the playwright, which had been acquired by his friend the second Earl of Oxford about 1719. The portrait is certainly not of Shakespeare, but possibly Drake. See David Piper's *O Sweet Mr. Shakespeare: The Changing Image of Shakespeare's Person, 1600–1800* (London, 1964).

the Earle of Oxford in Ditto.

This could be either Robert Harley, first Earl of Oxford, to whom Pope addressed his poem entitled *Epistle to Robert Earl of Oxford, and Earl Mortimer* (1722) or his son Edward, second Earl, the poet's very close friend. Robert Harley was painted often, most notably perhaps by Kneller (1714, NPG no. 4011; reproduced in David Green, *Sarah Duchess of Marlborough* [above, p. 253] opposite p. 128); Edward by Kneller (1716) and Michael Dahl (*c.* 1720, reproduced in Lees-Milne, opposite p. 176). For fuller information on portraits of these two men see Goulding and Adams, *Portland Catalogue* (above, p. 248), pp. 370–72.

a Ruen by Wooton in Ditto.

John Wootton (1686–1765), painter of hunting scenes and occasionally of landscapes. M. H. Grant, in *The Old English Landscape Painters*, (2 vols. London, 1926) 1 26, says of him: "when for relaxation he deserted his rural sports, [he] often deserted also the countryside which owned them, to enter a region of temple and villa-crowned heights, of umbrageous lakes and broken architecture." Grant also says that at Duncombe Park there is a painting by Wootton of "Pope's Villa," but I have been assured by J. J. Paterson of the Duncombe Park Estate office that the painting is not now there, and I have been unable to trace it elsewhere.

a Chausor in a black frame.

This may be the "grave old Chaucer ... from Occleve" that Spence (no. 108) mentions among the drawings by Pope that he has seen.

a fine Landskip in Ditto.

a Landskip of Richmond Ferry in Ditto.

See n. above on Land Skepe of Twickenham.

a Landskip of the feilds Opposite of Mr Popes House in Ditto.

See n. above on Land Skepe of Twickenham.

a Colour in Ditto.

Six Prints in Ditto.

a Small frute Pece in Ditto.

a Oldman without a frame.

a Little Pictture in a black frame.

a Picture of the Shell Temple in Ditto.

Conceivably, this was a version of William Kent's "fantasy," for which see Plate 16.

a Marvoll Table with a Wood Pedestall.

three Chaires.

IN Mr POPES ROOME.

a Bead Pillow & Bolster & Bedsted &c. with Hariten

Harrateen was a native all-worsted fabric. The presence of two beds (see next entry) in this room may be accounted for by the poet's need for special care during his last illness.

Hangens / three Blankets & White Quilt.

a Sette Bed three Blankets & Calicoe Quilt Hariten Curtains.

"A bed that can be folded so as to form a settee"—*OED*. The inventory use of this term is earlier than any in the *OED*.

a Chest of Draw^s Walnut tree.

a Stove fireshoule poker.

Mr Bethels Picture in a Gold Frame.

Bethel and Pope exchanged portraits in early 1744 shortly before Pope's death. Pope acknowledges the receipt of Bethel's in a letter of 20 February (IV 500) and tells his friend that "it shall be before my eyes, in my Bedchamber, where I now pass much of my time." At the time of the inventory, it was obviously still there, the only portrait in the room.

a Mahogany Night Table.

This is the "pot-cupboard" which was replacing the close-stool.

a Mah^y Table.

a Large Crimson Damas Arm Chaire.

Pope describes this amusingly in a letter to the Countess of Denbigh ([?1742]: IV 397–98), telling her of his "Golden apartment at Twitnam: where I sit like Apollo, incompassed with my own Gilding, under four Pillars of the Doric order, on a Throne of flame-colourd Damask." This may be the chair which he refers to as given to him by the Duchess of Marlborough ([June 1743] IV 457).

three Black Chaires.

ON THE BACK STAIRES AND PASSAGE.

20 Prints in Black frames.

a Print of Constantinople.

Constantinople and other eastern sites were beginning at this time to become a popular subject for "views." Pope may have had his view from Lady Mary Wortley Montagu during or after her sojourn there in 1716–18, when her husband was ambassador.

a Corner Cubord.

a picture of a Man without a frame.

a picture of a Woman without a frame.

a bass Viall.

By Pope's day this term usually applied to the violincello rather than to the true bass viol. On the other hand, the instrument may have been inherited from an older time and the inventory term may be precise.

PLATE

a Large Silver Cup and Cover.

a Small Ditto.

one pare of Silver Candlesticks and Snufers.

two handel Cups & Salvers D S.

These may well be the cups for which Pope thanks Swift on 22 August 1726 (II 388): "Indeed you are engraved elsewhere than on the Cups you sent me, (with so kind an inscription). ..." In that case, "D S" perhaps stands for Dean Swift. The salvers were flat trays.

two Silver Tumblers.

two Silver Salts.

a Silver Strainee.

Perhaps a lemon strainer for punch.

three Silver Casters [i.e. sugar-casters].

twelve Silver Knives and forks.

If these are the forks referred to by Swift (to Gay, 10 November 1730; III 148), they were "bidential"—two-pronged which is once again in keeping with the somewhat old-fashioned character of Pope's goods. Two-pronged forks had largely been superseded by three-pronged ones in Pope's day. Referring to a *faux pas* he had committed at table, Swift tells Gay that "the ill management of forks is not to be helpt when they are only bidential, which happens in all poor houses, especially those of Poets."

twelve China Knives and forks two blades broke.

twenty fower Spoons and three tea spoons.

a Silver Writing Stand Inkhorn Sand Dish.

Candlestick & Bell [for calling a servant].

A Coffee Pot.

FRENCH PLATE

4 Candlesticks two Suce Boats.

two Saltsellers two Kettle and Salver.

a Small Coffee Pot.

IN ONE ROOME.

a Bed Bedsteds Bolster &c.

three Blankets and Quilt.

two Chaires.

a half tester and Linee [linen? lined?] Curtaines.

IN THE KITCHEN

Six Puter Covers.

I.e. domed covers of pewter for keeping food warm on a plate.

11 Puter Dishes.

36 Plates.

a Jack [clockwork spit-turner] &c.

two Spitts and Racks.

one Round Table three Chaires.

3 Sacepans [i.e. saucepans].

a Soop pott with a Copper Cover.

a Large Boyling Pott with a Cover.

a Small Ditto.

a Bras tea ketell and Lamp.

6 Brass Candelsticks.

a Brass Morter [i.e. mortar].

a Old Copper tea kettle.

a brass Ladle and Skimer.

I.e. skimmer (large, usually perforated, spoon).

a Iron Driping pan.

4 Stewpans with Copper Covers.

fire shoule Toungs poker & Salemander.

I.e. salamander (a circular iron plate to be heated and then placed just over a pudding or cake to brown it).

the Kitchen Grates.

I.e. fireplace grates. There were usually two fireplaces in a kitchen such as this with a low grate in one, above which pots were hung to boil, a higher grate in the other, for roasting joints on the spit.

a Iron Culender & Copper Grates.

I.e. A colander and grating tools.

a Grid Iron.

CHINA

It will be noticed that no glassware is listed, only the silver "Cups" and "Tumblers" (on p. 256 and these "Coffe Cups." The absence of a tea set is surprising (there is a "Slop basson" and "Shuger Dish") and may again suggest that some living equipment came with the leased house.

a Soop dish and 12 plates.

a frute Dish and 6 enamold plates.

Six bleu and White plates.

fower Coffe Cups fower disshes and Saucers & teaspon.

Slop basson and Shuger Dish.

IN THE GARDING.

See the note on Plate 45. Many of Pope's garden ornaments would perhaps be by Henry or John Cheere, who kept a sculptor's yard at Hyde Park Corner. A number of his urns were certainly made by two stone masons named Biggs, whose services Pope acquired through Ralph Allen. See Pope to Allen, 18 May 1739, 23 July 1741, 28 August 1741 (IV 18, 353, 360). Pope's Mercury and Venus are likely to have been copies, like his Palladio and Inigo Jones, of originals at Chiswick House, made for Lord Burlington by Guelfi.

4 Lead Vrns.

16 Stone Vrns and Pedestals.

a Venus with Stone Pedestall.

a Mercury with a Wood Pedestall.

a Stone Statue with a Wood Pedestall.

10 Wood Chaires & two Arm Windsor Chaires.

4 Bussto^s Antike with Stone Termes.

IN THE HALL.

4 Busto^s Mod^n with Wood Termes.

6 Windsor Arm Chaires.

a Glass Globe.

A terrestial or celestial globe with the figures of the earth or of the constellations painted on it.

LINEN

one fine Damask Table Cloath.

one Ditto Diaper.

OED: "The name of a textile fabric; now and since the 15th c. applied to a linen fabric ... woven with a small and simple pattern, formed by the different directions of the thread, with the different reflexions of light from its surface, and consisting of lines crossing diamond-wise, with the spaces variously filled up by parallel lines, a central leaf, or a dot."

ten fine Damask Napkins.

six fine Diaper Ditto.

five tables Cloaths 23 Napkins.

five pare of Holand Sheets.

two pare Flax.

two fine Damask table Cloaths.

and one Dus [dozen] Napkins un Made.

three fine pieces of Chince wth a pattern of paper.

F. G.

Appendix C

"AN Account of the MATERIALS which compose the GROTTO."

THIS ACCOUNT was published by Pope's gardener John Searle in 1745, on pp. 5–10 of *A Plan of Mr. Pope's Garden, As it was left at his Death*. The Roman numerals I–X designate chambers or sections in the grotto. See Plate 17. The less familiar terms in Searle's list are defined below in the Index, *q.v.*

AN
Account of the MATERIALS
which compose the GROTTO.

—Secretum iter et fallentis semita vitæ. HOR.

Numb. I.

AT the Entrance of the Grotto, next the Garden, are various sorts of Stones thrown promiscuously together, in imitation of an old Ruine; some full of Holes, others like Honey-combs, which came from *Ralph Allen's*, Esq; at *Widcomb* near *Bath*. Several fine Fossils and Snake-stones, with petrified Wood, and Moss in various Shapes, from the petrifying Spring at *Nasborough* in *Yorkshire*, by the Reverend Doctor *Key*. Fine Verd Antique from *Egypt*, with several sorts of *Italian* sparry Marble of diverse Colours. Amethysts, several Clumps of different Forms, with some fine Pieces of White Spar, from her Grace the Duchess of *Cleveland* at *Rabey-*Castle in *Westmoreland*. Some fine Pieces of *German* Spar intermixt with Yellow Mundic, with Moss, and some *English* Pebbles. In the Center is a fine Spring.

Numb. II.

Are Flints, Moss of many sorts, many Pieces of *Plymouth* Marble of different Colours, from Mr. *Cooper* of that Place; several Pieces of well-chosen things from the Glass-House; several fine Flakes of Gold Clift, from Mr. *Cambridge*; with several fine Pieces of White Spar, from the Duchess of *Cleveland*.

The Motto over the Enterance from the Garden.

Numb. III.

Many small Dice of Mundic and Tin Oar; two sorts of yellow flaky Copper; one shewing, by the different Strata of Metal, that different Masses of Copper will, tho' concreted at different times, unite close into one Globe or Lump. Several Groups of *Cornish* Diamonds incrusted, semipellucid, and shot round a Globe of Yellow Copper. Many thick Incrustations of shot Spar of a Yellowish Cast, sprinkled with small Cubes of Mundic, Lead Ore, Kallan, or Wild Iron. Many fine Pieces of Yellow Mundic, several small *Cornish* Diamonds tinged with a blackish Water, and others with a green Water. Several large Groups of *Cornish* Diamond, very transparent, from the Rev. Dr. *William Borlace* of *Ludgvan* in *Cornwall.* Many fine large Pieces of Red Spar out of Colonel *Stapleton*'s Lead-Mine, from *George Littleton*, Esq; Fine Petrifactions from *Gilbert West*, Esq; at *West Wickham* in *Kent*; fine Incrustations from Mr. *Allen*'s Quarries; and several Pieces of sparry Marble of different Colours from *Plymouth*; with many large *Cornish* Diamonds and other Petrifactions, which form two fine Rocks with Water distilling from them.

Numb. IV.

Fine sparry Marble from Lord *Edgcumb*'s Quarry, with different sorts of Moss. Several fine Pieces of the Eruptions from Mount *Vesuvius*, and a fine Piece of Marble from the Grotto of *Egeria* near *Rome*, from the Reverend Mr. *Spence*; with several fine Petrifactions and *Plymouth* Marble, from Mr. *Cooper.* Gold Clift from Mr. *Cambridge* in *Gloucestershire*; and several fine Brain-Stones from Mr. *Miller* of *Chelsea.*

Numb. V.

Many Pieces of sparry Marble of diverse Colours; and between each Course of Marble, many kinds of Ores, such as Tin Ore, Copper Ore, Lead Ore, Soapy Rock, Kallan, and Wild Lead intermixed, with large Clumps of *Cornish* Diamonds, and several small ones of different Degrees of Transparency. The several sorts of figur'd Stones are rich white Spars, interlaced with black Cockle, or Spars shot into Prisms of different Degrees of Waters. Some very particular sorts of Fossils, of different Sizes and Colours; Copper Ore of a fine Purple Colour; several fine Pieces of granated white Mundic, intermixed with plain Spar in a Copper Bed. A very uncommon sort of Mundic mix'd, or rather inclos'd in Wild Lead; several thin Crusts or Films of bright Spar, form'd on a Surface before shot into Protuberances; a Lump of Yellow Copper, that has a very singular Crust of Spar; some Grains of Mundic interspers'd, of different Colours, some Yellow, some Purple, and others of a deep

Blue inclining to Black; all from the Reverend Dr. *William Borlace*. Several fine *Bristol* Stones of different Colours, some of a dark Brown, others of a Yellow Cast, &c. from Mrs. *Broxholme*; and several fine Incrustations from Mr. *Allen*.

Numb. VI.

Several large Pieces of fine Crystal intermix'd with Yellow Mundic; a fine Piece of Spar interwoven like many Oyster-shells, and intermix'd with White Mundic; a fine Piece of Spar with a Mixture of Copper interwoven like a fine Lace; several Pieces of Crystal with brown Incrustation and a Mixture of Mundic, from the *Hartz* Mines in *Germany*; a fine Piece of Gold Ore from the *Peruvian* Mines; Silver Ore from the Mines of *Mexico*; several Pieces of Silver Ore from *Old Spain*; some large Pieces of Gold Clift, from Mr. *Cambridge* in *Gloucestershire*. Lead Ore, Copper Ore, white Spar, petrified Wood, *Brazil* Pebbles, *Egyptian* Pebbles and Blood-stones, from Mr. *Brinsden*. Some large Clumps of Amethyst, and several Pieces of White Spar, from the Duchess of *Cleveland*. Some fine Pieces of Red Spar, several fine Isicles, and several sorts of Fossils, from *George Littleton*, Esq; Many Pieces of Coral and petrified Moss, and many other curious Stones from the Island of *St. Christopher* in the *West Indies*; with several Humming Birds and their Nests, from *Antony Brown*, Esq; of *Abbs-Court* in *Surrey*. *Plymouth* Marble of different Colours, one fine *Cornish* Diamond from the Prince's Mine in *Cornwall*, near a Hundred Weight, from the Reverend Dr. *Askew*. Several fine Pieces of Yellow Mundic; some Purple Copper stained by Mineral Water; two Stones from the *Giants Causeway* in *Ireland*, from Sir *Hans Sloan*; some Pieces of petrified Wood, with Coral and petrified Moss round a Bason of Water.

Numb. VII.

Different Kinds of *Italian* Marble, many fine *Kerry* Stones of different Waters, with several fine Fossils from *Ireland*, from the Earl of *Orrery*. Many Flakes of White Spar and Mother-Amethyst, from the Duchess of *Cleveland*. The Roof of small Stones incrusted over, out of the River *Thames*. Some square Dice of Mundic, several Pieces of Silver Ore from *Old Spain*, with several sorts of Moss.

Numb. VIII.

Different sorts of Sparry Marble from *Italy*; several large Stones interwoven like Honey-combs, and others like old broken Pillars; many large Pieces of *Plymouth* Marble, *German* Spar, and Spar from *Norway*, by Mr. *Afterloney*. The Roof of Purple Spar, and some Yellow Spar, and several fine square Dice of Mundic, from

Mr. *Ord*'s Mines in *Yorkshire*. And round a Piece of Water are fixed different Plants, such as Maidenhair, Hartstongue, Fern, and several other Plants, intermix'd with many Petrifactions, and some uncommon *Cornish* Diamonds, from Lord *Godolphin*'s great Copper-works in *Ludgvan*.

Numb. ix.

Some very natural Rock-work, compiled of Flints and Cinders, from the Glasshouses, Furnaces, *&c.* with some Grains of Mundic artfully mixed with White Spar.

Numb. x.

A fine and very uncommon Petrifaction from *Okey-Hole* in *Somersetshire*, from Mr. *Bruce*.

Appendix D

"A True Copy of the Last Will and Testament of Alexander Pope, Esq."

I INCLUDE Pope's will here as one of the documents which shed light on his possessions at Twickenham. I have used for copy the text given on pp. 55–64 of *The Life of Alexander Pope, Esq.; With a True Copy of His Last Will and Testament* (London, 1744), published by Charles Corbett. In a different slightly inferior printing, this work was also published by Weaver Bickerton.

A
TRUE COPY, &c.

IN THE NAME OF GOD, AMEN. *I* Alexander Pope, *of* Twickenham, *in the County of* Middlesex, *make this my last Will and Testament. I resign my Soul to it's Creator in all humble Hope of it's future Happiness, as in the Disposal of a Being infinitely Good. As to my Body, my Will is, That it be buried near the Monument of my dear Parents at* Twickenham, *with the Addition, after the Words* filius feci—*of these only,* Et sibi: Qui obiit Anno 17. AEtatis———*and that it be carried to the Grave by six of the poorest Men of the Parish, to each of whom I order a Suit of Grey course Cloth, as Mourning. If I happen to die at any inconvenient Distance, let the same be done in any other Parish, and the Inscription be added on the Monument at* Twickenham. *I hereby make and appoint my particular Friends,* Allen *Lord* Bathurst; Hugh *Earl of* Marchmont, *the Honourable* William Murray, *his Majesty's Solicitor General; and* George Arbuthnott, *of the Court of* Exchequer, *Esq; the Survivors or Survivor of them, Executors of this my last Will and Testament.*

But all the Manuscript and unprinted Papers which I shall leave at my Decease, I desire may be delivered to my Noble Friend, Henry St. John, *Lord* Bolingbroke, *to whose sole Care and Judgment I commit them, either to be preserved or destroyed; or in case he shall not survive me, to the abovesaid Earl of* Marchmont. *These, who in the Course of my Life have done me all other good Offices, will not refuse me this last after my Death: I leave them therefore this Trouble, as a Mark of my Trust and Friendship; only desiring them each to accept of some small Memorial of me: That my Lord* Bolingbroke *will add to his Library all the Volumes of my Works and Translations of* Homer, *bound in red Morocco, and the Eleven Volumes of those of* Erasmus: *That my Lord* Marchmont *will take the large Paper Edition of* Thuanus, *by* Buckley; *or that Portrait of Lord* Bolingbroke, *by* Richardson; *which he shall prefer: That my Lord* Bathurst *will find a Place for the three Statues of the* Hercules *of* Furnese [Farnese], *the* Venus *of* Medicis, *and the* Apollo *in* Chiaro oscuro, *done by* Kneller: *That Mr.* Murray *will accept of the Marble Head of* Homer, *by* Bernini; *and of Sir* Isaac Newton, *by* Guelfi; *and that Mr.* Arbuthnot *will take the Watch I commonly wore, which the King of* Sardinia *gave to the late Earl of* Peterborow, *and he to me on his Death-Bed, together with one of the Pictures of Lord* Bolingbroke.

Item, *I desire Mr.* Lyttelton *to accept of the Busts of* Spencer, Shakespear, Milton, *and* Dryden, *in Marble, which his Royal Master the Prince, was pleased to give me. I give and devise my Library of printed Books to* Ralph Allen, *of* Widcombe, *Esq; and to the Reverend Mr.* William Warburton, *or to the Survivor of them (when those belonging to Lord* Bolingbroke *are taken out, and when Mrs.* Martha Blount *has chosen Threescore out of the Number) I also give and bequeath to the said Mr.* Warburton *the Property of all such of my Works already printed, as he hath written, or shall write Commentaries or Notes upon, and which I have not otherwise disposed of, or alienated; and all the Profits which shall arise after my Death from such Editions as he shall publish without future Alterations.*

Item, *In case* Ralph Allen, *Esq; abovesaid, shall survive me, I order my Executors to pay him the Sum of One hundred and fifty Pounds; being to the best of my Calculation, the Account of what I have received from him; partly for my own, and partly for Charitable Uses. If he refuse to take this himself, I desire him to employ it in a Way I am persuaded he will not dislike, to the Benefit of the* Bath-Hospital.

I give and devise to my Sister-in-law, Mrs. Magdalen Racket, *the Sum of Three hundred Pounds; and to her Sons,* Henry *and* Robert Racket, *One hundred Pounds each. I also release, and give to her all my Right and Interest in and upon a Bond of Five hundred Pounds due to me from her Son* Michael. *I also give her the Family Pictures of my Father, Mother and Aunts, and the Diamond Ring my Mother wore, and her Golden Watch. I give to* Erasmus Lewis, Gilbert West, *Sir* Clement Cotterell, William Rollinson, Nathaniel Hook, *Esqrs. and to Mrs* Anne Arbuthnot, *to each the Sum of Five Pounds, to be laid out in a Ring, or any Memorial of me; and to my Servant* John Searle, *who has faithfully and ably served me many Years, I give, and devise the Sum of One hundred Pounds over and above a Year's Wages to himself, and his Wife; and to the Poor of the Parish of* Twickenham, *Twenty Pounds to be divided among them by the said* John Searl[e]; *and it is my Will, if the said* John Searl[e], *die before me, that the same Sum of One hundred Pounds go to his Wife or Children.*

Item, *I give, and devise to Mrs.* Martha Blount, *younger Daughter of Mrs.* Martha Blount, *late of* Welbeck-Street, Cavendish-Square, *the Sum of One thousand Pounds immediately on my Decease*; *and all the Furniture of my Grotto, Urns in my Garden, Household Goods, Chattels, Plate, or whatever is not otherwise disposed of in this my Will, I give and devise to the said Mrs.* Martha Blount, *out of a sincere Regard, and long Friendship for her*: *And it is my Will, that my abovesaid Executors, the Survivors or Survivor of them, shall take an Account of all my Estates Money, or Bonds, &c. and after paying my Debts and Legacies, shall place out all my Residue upon Government, or other Securities, according to their best Judgments, and pay the Produce thereof, half-yearly, to the said Mrs.* Martha Blount, *during her natural Life*: *And after her Decease, I give the Sum of One thousand Pounds to Mrs.* Magdalen Racket, *and her Sons* Robert, Henry *and* John, *to be divided equally among them, or to the Survivors or Survivor of them*; *and after the Decease of the said Mrs.* Martha Blount, *I give the Sum of Two hundred Pounds to the abovesaid* Gilbert West; *two hundred to Mr.* George Arbuthnot; *two hundred to his Sister, Mrs.* Anne Arbuthnot; *and One hundred to my Servant,* John Searle, *to which so ever of these shall be then living*: *And all the Residue and Remainder to be considered as undisposed of, and go to my next of Kin. This is my last Will and Testament, written with my own Hand, and sealed with my Seal, this Twelfth Day of* December, *in the Year of our Lord, One thousand, seven hundred and forty-three.*

ALEX. POPE

Signed, Sealed and Declared
     by the Testator as his
     last Will and Testament,
     in Presence of us,
Radnor,
Stephen Hales, Minister of *Teddington,*
Joseph Spence, Professor of History, in the
     University of *Oxford.*

N.B. The above Will was proved at *London,* before the Worshipful *George Lee,* Doctor of Laws and Surrogate, on the 14th Day of *June* 1744, by the Oaths of the Right Hon. *Allen* Lord *Bathurst,* the Right Hon. *Hugh* Earl of *Marchmont,* the Hon. *William Murray,* Esq; his Majesty's Sollicitor General, and *George Arbuthnot,* Esq; the Executors to whom Administration was granted, being first sworn duly to administer.

Appendix E

The Legendary Poet

1. Robert Dodsley, *The Cave of Pope. A Prophecy* (1743)
2. *Horti Popiani: Ode Sapphica* (1743)
3. Pope's Willow: "the Muses' fav'rite tree" (1792)
4. Jacques Delille: Part of "Chant III" of *Les Jardins* (1801)

I give here four samples of the sub-species of poetry which fostered something like a Pope-and-Twickenham legend during the first sixty-odd years after his death, till his villa was torn down and his grotto dismantled by the Baroness Howe. Numbers 1 and 2 appeared with the first separate publication of Pope's *Verses on the Grotto* in a pamphlet published by Robert Dodsley. *The Cave of Pope* is item VI in this pamphlet and is signed "By R. Dodsley." *Horti Popiani: Ode Sapphica* is item V and is unsigned. Number 3 is quoted without a title (but attributed to the year 1792) in R. Ackermann's *Microcosm of London* (3 vols., London, 1808), III 276–77. A footnote by Ackermann declares that the fall of the willow foretold in the poem has by the time of his writing taken place. For Pope's "willow," or willows (the evidence is ambiguous), see also Plates 6, 8, 9, 27, and nn; and passage IV below. The passage quoted from Delille was added for the first time to his *Les Jardins* (Paris, 1782) in the 1801 edition.

I

The Cave of POPE. A Prophecy (1743)

By R. DODSLEY.

WHEN dark Oblivion in her sable Cloak
    Shall wrap the Names of Heroes and of Kings;
And their high Deeds, submitting to the Stroke
    Of Time, shall fall amongst forgotten Things;

Then (for the Muse that distant Day can see)
    On *Thames*'s Bank the Stranger shall arrive,
With curious Wish thy sacred Grott to see,
    Thy sacred Grott shall with thy Name survive.

Grateful Posterity, from Age to Age,
   With pious Hand the Ruin shall repair:
Some good old Man, to each enquiring Sage
   Pointing the Place, shall cry, the Bard liv'd there,

Whose Song was Music to the listening Ear,
   Yet taught audacious Vice and Folly, Shame;
Easy his Manners, but his Life severe;
   His Word alone gave Infamy or Fame.

Sequester'd from the Fool, and Coxcomb-Wit,
   Beneath this silent Roof the Muse he found;
'Twas here he slept inspir'd, or sate and writ,
   Here with his Friends the social Glass went round.

With aweful Veneration shall they trace
   The Steps which thou so long before hast trod;
With reverend Wonder view the solemn Place,
   From whence thy Genius soar'd to Nature's God.

Then, some small Gem, or Moss, or shining Oar,
   Departing, each shall pilfer, in fond hope
To please their Friends, on every distant Shore,
   Boasting a Relick from the Cave of POPE.

II

Horti Popiani: Ode Sapphica (1743)

Popii fas sit nemus & penates
Ingredi; quamvis strepitum malignæ
Plebis hic grato vacuus sub Antro
                Spernit & arcet.

Ipse, Musarum comes ac virentis
Hortuli cultor, per amoena Vatis
Rura vicini pede non profano,
                Dum licet, errem.

Quo duces, quo me rapitis, Camoenae,
Saxeis laetum latebris, & arctae
Calle Speluncae, Thamisisque fluctu
                Praetereuntis?

Me levis Lymphae trepidante rivo
Sparge; muscosi mihi, Naï, venas
Fontis & sacros penitus Cavernae
               Pande recessus:

Est tuum fessi recreare nervos
Ingenî: nec vos, Lemures, coruscis
Dedecet Conchis Domino Coronam
               Nectere vestro.

Quis procul summo Lapis in vireto
Candet? agnosco memoris Querelae
Signa, & incisam meritâ Parentis
               Laude Columnam.

Quo vagor? magnis simulata cernam
Tecta, Apum sedes? Caveamne, lentis
Quà Salix ramis, tremulâque moerens
               Imminet Umbrâ?

An Toros Herbae magis? an comantis
Copiam Sylvae, nitidaeque Lauri
Plurimum mirer Decus? an patentis
               Laeve Palaestrae

Gramen? O! quis Me in speculâ reponet
Frondei Collis, juga qui decorae
Villulis Shenae, vitreumque latè
               Prospicit Amnem!

Illius ritu ferar O! perenni
Fonte decurrens; nec iners, nec acer;
Plenus, at ripae patiens, profundo
               Flumine purus.

Quid novâ posco prece? Me procacis
Barbiti solers leviore Cantu
Musa, Me nugis voluit Jocisque
               Fallere curas.

Littore hoc saltèm viridante tecum
Considens, Flaccum videar tueri;
Dicta depascar tua, sub Cavernae
               Tegmine Popi.

III

Pope's Willow: "the Muses' fav'rite tree" (1792)

Weep, verdant Willow, ever weep,
And spread thy pendent branches round:
Oh! may no gaudy flow'ret creep
Along the consecrated ground!
Thou art the Muses' fav'rite tree;
They lov'd the bard who planted thee.

The wintry blast assails in vain;
The forked lightning passes by,
To stretch the oak upon the plain,
Whose tow'ring branches brav'd the sky:
The Muses guard their fav'rite tree;
They lov'd the bard who planted thee.

And oft, 'tis said, at evening hour,
To Fancy's eye bright forms appear
To glide beneath the leafy bower,
While music steals on Fancy's ear:
The Muses haunt their fav'rite tree;
They lov'd the bard who planted thee.

But all the Muses' tender care
Cannot prolong the final date:
Rude time will strip thy branches bare,
And thou must feel the stroke of Fate;
E'en thou, the Muses' fav'rite tree,
Must fall like him who planted thee.

But still the Muse shall hover near;
And, planted there by hands unseen,
Another willow shall appear,
Of pensive form, upon the green;
To grace the spot, when thou no more
Shalt overarch the hallow'd shore.

IV

Jacques Delille: Part of Chant III of *Les Jardins* (1801)

Gardez donc d'attenter à ces lieux révérés;
Leurs débris sont divins, leurs défauts sont sacrés.
Conservez leurs enclos, leurs jardins, leurs murailles :
Tel on laisse sa rouille au bronze des médailles :
Tel j'ai vu ce Twicknham, dont Pope est créateur;
Le goût le défendit d'un art profanateur;
Et ses maîtres nouveaux, révérant sa mémoire,
Dans l'œuvre de ses mains ont respecté sa gloire.
Ciel! avec quel transport j'ai visité ce lieu
Dont Mindipe[1] est le maître, et dont Pope est le dieu!
Le plus humble réduit avoit pour moi des charmes.
Le voilà ce musée où, l'œil trempé de larmes,
De la tendre Héloïse il soupiroit le nom;
Là, sa muse évoquoit Achille, Agamemnon,
Célébroit Dieu, le monde, et ses lois éternelles,
Ou les régles du goût, ou les cheveux des belles;
Je reconnois l'alcove où, jusqu'à son réveil,
Les doux rêves du sage amusoient son sommeil;
Voici le bois secret, voici l'obscure allée
Où s'échauffoit sa verve en beaux vers exhalée :
Approchez, contemplez ce monument pieux
Où pleuroit en silence un fils religieux :
Là, repose sa mere, et des touffes plus sombres
Sur ce saint mausolée ont redoublé leurs ombres;
Là, du Parnasse anglais le chantre favori
Se fit porter mourant sous son bosquet chéri;
Et son œil, que déja couvroit l'ombre éternelle,
Vint saluer encor la tombe maternelle.
Salut, saule fameux que ses mains ont planté !
Helás ! tes vieux rameaux dans leur caducité
En vain sur leurs appuis reposent leur vieillesse,
Un jour tu périras; ses vers vivront sans cesse.
Console-toi pourtant; celui qui dans ses vers

---

1   I.e. Stanhope's son-in-law, Lord Mendip.

D'Homère le premier fit ouïr les concerts,
Bienfaiteur des jardins ainsi que du langage,
Le premier sur les eaux suspendit ton ombrage :
A peine le passant voit ce tronc respecté,
La rame est suspendue, et l'esquif arrêté ;
Et même en s'éloignant, vers ce lieu qu'il adore
Ses regards prolongés se retournent encore.
Mon sort est plus heureux ; par un secret amour
Près de ces bois sacrés j'ai fixé mon séjour.
Eh! comment résister au charme qui m'entraîne ?
Par plus d'un doux rapport mon penchant m'y raméne.
Le chantre d'Ilion fut embelli par toi ;
Virgile, moins heureux, fut imité par moi.
Comme toi, je chéris ma noble indépendance ;
Comme toi, des forêts je cherche le silence.
Aussi, dans ces bosquets par ta muse habités,
Viennent errer souvent mes regards enchantés :
J'y crois entendre encor ta voix mélodieuse ;
J'interroge tes bois, ta grotte harmonieuse ;
Je plonge sous sa voûte avec un saint effroi,
Et viens lui demander des vers dignes de toi.
Protége donc ma muse ; et si ma main fidéle
Jadis à nos Français te montra pour modéle,
Inspire encor mes chants ; c'est toi dont le flambeau
Guida l'art des jardins dans un chemin nouveau :
Ma voix t'en fait l'hommage, et dans ce lieu champêtre,
Je viens t'offrir les fleurs que toi-même as fait naïtre.

Appendix F

Sir Robert Walpole and Houghton as "Timon" and His Villa

SINCE MISS MAHAFFEY's article was published, I have stumbled on the following further points, all perhaps tending in some way or degree to confirm her argument.

I. The name Timon was applicable to Walpole not only as spendthrift, or in Miss Mahaffey's terms (p. 196), "prodigal tyrant ... hosting lavish entertainments attended by crowds of sycophants," but also as rich patron whose fall was inevitable and would leave him stripped of all his purchased friends. This is a continual theme of the *Craftsman*: see, for example, the issue of 14 September 1728, ostensibly devoted to the fall of Sejanus.

II. Some features of the portrait of Timon's villa that might strike understanders of the current political argot as allusions to Walpole, in addition to those given by Miss Mahaffey, are these:

(1) Reference to the meal as a "sacrifice" in a "Temple" (155–58). These were familiar contemporary terms for Walpole's entertainments at Houghton. The issue of the *Craftsman* mentioned just above, while purporting to speak of other historical royal favorites like Sejanus under Tiberius and Buckingham under James I, describes Walpole's "*sumptuous Feasts,* as if they had been *Sacrifices*" and his "Pallaces, guilded as if they had been *Temples*"; and in "A new Norfolk Ballad" (Percival, p. 38) we are told with reference to one of his entertainments at Houghton: "And *Custards* compleated the whole Sacrifice."

(2) Reference to "Sancho's dread Doctor and his Wand" (160). Pope alludes here to *Don Quixote*, pt. II, ch. xlvii, where a doctor touches with a wand he carries each dish spread before the hungry Sancho with the result that it is whisked away before he can touch it, like the successive courses at Timon's dinner. The "Wand" is of course itself suggestive, being a possible allusion to the Lord Treasurer's staff of office, as in Swift's Sir Hamet's "Rod" (*Poems*, ed. Sir Harold Williams, pp. 131–35) and the "white Wand" attributed to Harlequin-Walpole in *Craftsman*, 2 December 1727. The "dread Doctor" could conceivably have reference to the frequent presentation of Walpole (e.g. Stephens, nos. 1931, 2420) as a quack doctor, a sorcerer, and a "Sir Sidrophel"

out of *Hudibras* (*Fog's Weekly Journal* 28 July 1733; see also *The Quack Triumphant: Or, The N[o]r[wi]ch Cavalcade*, 1733). The Sancho reference seems to be especially pointed, and not merely because of Walpole's corpulence. The issue of *Fog's Weekly Journal* cited immediately above carries a long parodic account of Walpole's triumphant "Cavalcade" through Norfolk in July 1733, where Walpole is described under the name Sir Sidrophel and his brother Horatio as Sir Sidrophel's zany Whachum. Toward the close, "Whaccum ... makes a Speech in Praise of himself and Sir *Sidrophel*; Sir *Sidrophel* he extoll'd as the greatest Doctor, and himself as the most finish'd *Zani* in the World. ... The Evening concluded with a magnificent Feast, for Sir *Sidrophel* spared no Cost, and indeed he need not, for he was only treating the Fools with their own Money. ... Next Day they departed ..., Sir *Sidrophel* appearing as full of Glory as *Sancho* when he was made a Governor, and *Whaccum* as proud as Sancho's Ass drest up in new Trappings to accompany his Master to his Government. ..." This passage is later than Pope's reference to Sancho in the portrait of Timon, by which just possibly its comparison of Sir Sidrophel to Sancho was inspired. But satire of Walpole as both Don Quixote and Sancho was already circulating as early as September 1731, some months before the *Epistle to Burlington* was published. See *The Statesman's Fall or Sir Bob in the Dust* (Percival, p. 56):

> His Person, Parts, and Wit proclaim
> Him of *La Mancha*'s Breed,
> With all of *Sancho* in his Frame,
> And *Quixot* in his Head.
> From native Bronze, and starch'd Grimace,
> Surnam'd the *Knight of Rueful Face*.

In a mock citation in n. 24 of his *Vernoniad* (1741), Fielding also associates Walpole with Sancho.

(3) Reference to the Wall in Houghton gardens: "On ev'ry side you look, behold the Wall!" (114). There seems no conclusive evidence that Houghton gardens were walled, nor would this allusion, even if they were, guarantee that Pope had Houghton in mind. But Walpole was widely thought of by his supporters as the "Wall" and much was made of one or both syllables in his name by friend and foe alike. An engraved "glorification" of Walpole (11 June 1730: Stephens, no. 1842, here Plate 34) showing him, within Corinthian arches on the summit of a great rock, as the support and defender of his people, contains a

scroll whose anagram of the name Walpole and Latin epigram upon it are eluci-
dated in "The Explanation" as follows: "WALPOLE. WALL AND POLE, WALPOLE,
Anagr. VALLUM, POLUS.) with the Explanation of it in the two Latin Verses.

> Nil metuens terris, tuto potes ire per Altum,
> Anglia, qui VALLum WALPOLUS, ipse POLUS.

Thou England that fears nothing by Land may boldly sail yᵉ Seas, WALPOLE who
is the Strong WALL that guards thee shall be thy POLE at SEA." The *Craftsman*,
13 June 1730, translates the Latin statement into an English query, at the close
of some ironic comments on the print as a whole:

> WALL, POLE.
> How great, O *England*, may thy Greatness be,
> Whilst He's thy WALL by Land, Thy POLE by Sea?

The idea appears again in *Sir Robert Brass: or, The Intriegues, Serious and
Amorous, of the Knight of the Blazing Star* (1731), ll. 569–70:

> To all a constant *Guard* I'll be,
> Your *Wall* by Land, Your *Pole* by Sea.

Earlier (19 October 1728), in a tale about two Eastern princes who cunningly
stole from their father's royal treasury, the paper had commented on how vain
it was for a king to amass treasure since so often the very persons assigned to
guard it would become its despoilers. "An *Hole*, you see, in our WAL——*of the
Court*, that was to guard this Treasure was of very great Convenience as it
helped the Person to creep in at it and rob the King, and then to creep out of
it again to save Himself." For evidence of the continuing currency of the play on
Walpole's name, see Stephens, nos. 2453, 2454 (July 1740).

   We shall never know whether Pope intended by Timon's "Wall" anything
more than a landscaping reference, but there were certainly contemporary
readers educated to see in it a little private joke.

III. Two comments by contemporaries may be evidence that they, at least, understood Timon to be Walpole.

   (1) Welsted, in *Dulness and Scandal. Occasioned by the Character of Lord
Timon, in Mr. Pope's Epistle to the Earl of Burlington* (above, pp. 122–25 and
nn.), refers to Pope as "The Friend of Catiline, and Tully's Foe." Catiline here
can only be Bolingbroke. This being so, Tully has to be Walpole. Yet, what evi-

dence existed in 1732 when Welsted's poem was published, apart from the Timon portrait, that Pope *was* Walpole's "Foe"? Welsted seems to be aware of something that so far as we can tell had to come to him from special understanding, not from any overtly published avowal by Pope. This special understanding need not have consisted in the awareness that Timon was Walpole, but it may have.

(2) The anonymous author of *Yes, They are* (above, p. 197, n. 5) gives his own portrait of the profusion at Houghton, which he then imagines to be defended by a Walpole supporter in the following words:

> How many indigent and needy poor
> Have liv'd in riot at his open door?
> How many needy families supply'd,
> With only keeping up this *decent Pride*?
> This dignity, this show and pomp of state,
> This just distinction 'twixt the mean and great,
> Not for Himself he lives, his cares extend,
> To be to ev'ry *worthy* Friend—a *Friend*.   (p. 12)

It is a little hard to believe that there is no allusion here to Pope's lines about Timon:

> Yet hence the Poor are cloath'd, the Hungry fed;
> Health to himself, and to his Infants bread
> The Lab'rer bears: What his hard Heart denies,
> His charitable Vanity supplies.   (169–72)

Decent Pride, stressed, reminds one of Pope's "civil Pride": "Sick of his civil Pride" (166). "Not for *Himself* he lives" reminds one of the prodigal with whom, in anticipation of Timon, Pope begins his epistle:

> Not for himself he sees, or hears, or eats;
> Artists must chuse his Pictures, Music, Meats;

Even "To be to ev'ry *worthy* Friend—a *Friend*" carries possibly an echo of an important line from another of Pope's poems that is concerned with Walpole: "To VIRTUE ONLY and HER FRIENDS, A FRIEND (*Imit. Hor.*, *Sat.* II i 121). It strikes me that the author of *Yes, They are* has Pope and Walpole much on his mind in these verses and that they were likely to convey to any knowledgeable reader's consciousness an implication that his Walpole at Houghton and Pope's

"Timon" at Timon's villa are one and the same. By 1740, the date of *Yes, They are*, such knowledge *may* have been, in Opposition circles, an open secret.

IV.   Pope's letter under the name of Cleland in *The Daily Post-Boy*, 22 December 1731. In the letter, Pope all but asserts outright that the comments mistakenly applied to Chandos are intended to be personal but have become attached to the wrong person. He then says (*Correspondence*, III 257): " I really cannot help smiling at this stupidity—while I lament the slanderous Temper of the Town. I thought no Mortal singly could claim that Character of *Timon*, any more than any Man pretend to be Sir *John Falstaff*." Why Sir John Falstaff, culled from all the possible instances Pope might have used? It may be that for the knowing an answer had been supplied in the *Craftsman* of 19 June 1731, about six months before, when the career and appearance of Verres (ever one of the Opposition's favorite analogues for Walpole) were likened to the career and appearance of Falstaff in these terms:

He was, as Sir *John Falstaff* is described, '*a whoreson round Man, of a brazen Complexion, which, when he was about Fifty, became fixed and turned into a high Copper.*' He was a very *pleasant, laughing Creature*; and to make out his Story, or when it tally'd with his Interest, he would not stick at a *Fib* now and then. Like the *fat Knight* too, *tho' he was not witty Himself, he was most certainly the Occasion that Wit was in other Men.* His great Delight was, where Sir *John*'s Joy seems chiefly to lye, in *robbing the Exchequer. Verres* always chuckled at a Proposal of that Kind, and actually put it in Practice more than once. You see the *Roman Orator* calls him *Depeculatorem Ærarii; Robber of the Exchequer. Shakespeare* makes Sir *John* declare that he *would do it with unwash'd Hands*; and *Verres* is mention'd, in this Manuscript, to have had *turpiculas Palmas; little, dirty, unwash'd Hands. Verres*, we see, in the heighth of his Wealth, grew so audaciously familiar with *Authority* as to attempt to *bribe the Senate*, who were his *Judges*; and *Falstaff* publickly invites his *Prince* to take Share of the Plunder. *Verres* robbed in *good Company*. He plundered under the Character of a *Preserver of Property*, and always distributed a Share of the Booty among his *chief Officers* and *Projectors of his Jobs*. The *pleasant, fat Knight*, I think, says "*that He was joined with no Foot Land Rakers; no long-staff, sixpenny Strikers*; (That is, with no *little, footpad Villains*) *but with Nobility and Tranquility; People* (says He) *that do not PRAY to their Saint the Commonwealth, but PREY on her.*" This, we see, is exactly the Case of *Verres*. Tho' I did not think of a Parallel between *these two Heroes of the Highway*, when I first began to read my Manuscript; yet, upon re-considering *those Charac-*

ters together, I find they may be compared very justly. Sir *John* delighted always in *low, dull Drudges* about his Person and his Pleasures. *Poins* and *Bardolph*, and *Peto* are his Creatures. They suffer his Jokes, and eat. They swallow greedily the Scraps of his Generosity.—*Sociis servilibus, & de plebeculo, depeculatoribus gaudebat*, says my Author; That is, He chose *dirty Companions*, who had large Stomachs and a quick Digestion of publick Plunder. Sir *John*, we know, especially when he talk'd of his Courage, would *lye* most abominably; and not trouble himself how to get off, when detected. *Verres* would *shoot flying*, as the vulgar Phrase has it, in the Face of a *full Senate*. He would affirm to the *Fathers* that a Fact was true one Day, and on the very next Day, without the least Blush, without the flattening of one Muscle, deny before the same Assembly what he had affirm'd. *Fat Jack* cries out, in a penitential Fit, '*would I knew where a Commodity of* good Names *was to be bought!*'— *Verres* actually attempted to buy *this Commodity*, and hired great Numbers of *dull Scribes* with Money, to write *weekly Letters*, and to declare to all the World that He was a *wise*, a *righteous*, and a *just Man*. *Falstaff* in a Fit of Vanity, in another Place, declares, '*there are not three good Men unhang'd in* England, *and one of them is fat, and grows old.*' *Verres* affirms, with the same Vanity, that he was summoned by the *Necessity of Affairs to take Care of the Commonwealth*; and that he was the only Man capable of doing it. *Rerum Necessitudine ad tuendam Rempublicam arcessitus*, says the Manuscript. Sir *John*, we all know, was a *Braggadochio*; an unreasonable Boaster of himself and his Parts. In his Dialogue with the *Prince of Wales*, he says, '*there is a goodly, portly Man and corpulent, (innuendo Himself) of a chearful Look, a pleasing Eye, and a most noble Carriage; his Age some fifty; or, by your Lady, inclining to threescore; there is Virtue in that Man.*'—Exactly in these Words did *Verres*, and his *Dunces*, use to laud him. Every one has heard of the *famous Statue*, (mentioned by *Dion* the *Syracusian*) which was raised to the perpetual Infamy of *this corrupt Minister*, and the *little, blind Image*, called *Plutus*, placed before him, pouring Money into his Lap, and endeavouring to screen him from *Justice*; which *Goddess* appears in a threatning Attitude at a very little Distance, under the Character of the *Genius of Rome*. *Falstaff* places his *little Page* before him, to cover him from the Sight of my Lord Chief Justice. The Allusion is clear; the Moral is just; and the Parallel runs on all Four.

It would be a remarkable concidence if Pope were unaware of this and fell upon the reference to Falstaff by pure accident. Similar but briefer allusions occur in the *Craftsman* for 25 July 1727 and 23 March 1734.

All things considered, the case for supposing that Walpole was intended to be seen as chief among the leading originals of the Timon portrait (*primus inter pares*, or even *maximus inter magnos*) strikes me as convincing.[1]

1/The one piece of evidence that might seem to stand in the way is the name written above the cue phrase at the foot of the second and final leaf of the extant manuscript in the Pierpont Morgan Library. Here, I take it, Pope first entered the cue "Thro' &c," intending to place next some version of lines 89–98 ("Thro' his young Woods how pleas'd Sabinus stray'd"). Just to the left of "Thro' &c" Pope has written the word "At," just below "Thro' &c" the word "Timon's," and just above "Thro' &c" a word not easily deciphered that is probably, as Mr. Bateson has noted (TE III ii, pp. xxvii, 171), "Vatia's." As the name of a Roman who retired to the obscurity of his Cumaean villa to be safe during the regime of Sejanus, Vatia doubtless points at some one who had withdrawn from politics under Walpole—possibly, Mr. Bateson thinks, Chandos, though the resemblance seems less than compelling. Whomever the name was meant for, it cannot, one suppose, have been intended for Walpole himself.

Does this mean that the portrait of Timon cannot in any respect have been intended for Walpole? I think not. In the first place, we have no way of inferring with certainty what sort of "portrait" was planned to follow the cue "At Vatia's": we do not know, in short, that the lines to follow this cue were the lines that in the published poem follow the cue "At Timon's." In the second place, at this stage in the composition of the poem, it is clear that the portrait of Timon, as we now have it, had not yet taken final shape. Parts of it—notably lines 169–76—are already set down in the Morgan manuscript in quite another connection. This being so, it remains possible that *our* "Timon" did not yet exist, that a character based on bad taste and ostentatious wealth was taking or had taken form in Pope's mind, but with application to some one who had buried himself on his country estate rather than to some one who was at the heart of government. The name "Timon" may have occurred to the poet only after he had begun to color this (or another) portrait with certain details from Houghton and veiled allusions to its master. It may even be that the insertion of "Timon's" in the manuscript took place well after the poem had been completed in a manuscript or series of manuscripts that has not come down to us, perhaps many weeks or even months after the poet had first toyed with the notion of a "Vatia." To sum up, nothing that we know seems to me to require us to believe that Timon has *no* application to Sir Robert Walpole, while certain things we know seem rather unmistakably to point toward such an application.

Notes to the Plates

1 This is a pastel, or "crayon-painting," 22 1/2" × 17", made by William Hoare of Bath, probably in 1743, the year of the final *Dunciad*, when the poet was fifty-five. An inscription on the back of the canvas indicates that it once belonged to Martha Blount. The inscription, in faded red chalk, reads: "For Mrs Blount to be left at the Lady Gerard's in Welbeck Street by Oxford Chappel" —where from about November 1743, Martha was living. In a letter of 23 November to Slingsby Bethel acknowledging a hamper of Madeira that Bethel has procured for Martha, Pope tells him (as if it were a recent change of address): "She is now at Lady Gerard's house ... in Welbeck Street, Oxford Chappel" (*Correspondence*, IV 485).

Pope and Hoare doubtless first met at Bath on one of Pope's several trips there during the later 30's and early 40's, when he was the guest of Ralph Allen (Wimsatt, p. 282). Pope's last visit to Allen was made in July of 1743, in the company of Martha, and it seems reasonable to suppose that the portrait was made at that time, perhaps especially for her, though it may of course date from an earlier visit and have been sent to Martha in late 1743 or early 1744 as Pope became increasingly aware that he had not long to live. Pope seems to have first sat for Hoare in December 1739, or January 1740 (Wimsatt, 63. 1–2).

This pastel resembles one in the National Portrait Gallery, no. 299; Wimsatt, 63.3*a*. That, however, is dated 1784, and differs also in the coloring, arrangement of clothing, and somewhat in the angle of the head. Behind the cap in the present portrait are the faint outlines of an earlier disposition of the cap, and beside the cheek to the viewer's left there is some repainting which suggests that the placement of the head was also slightly altered. Both features suggest, though they do not prove, that this version was made from life. Its resemblance to the Hoare oil described in Wimsatt 63.4 is very close.

This pastel is pictured (badly), together with the NPG version, in *Country Life*, 15 September 1966, p. 618. It belonged at that time to John Hickman of Roughton House, Bridgnorth, Shropshire. Mr. Hickman has informed me that it came to him via an intermediary from a Worcester dealer, now dead, in whose possession it had been for some considerable time.

2 Line engraving, 16 1/2" × 22 1/8", by John Green, who seems to have been active in the late 50's, from a sketch by J. H. Müntz, dated 1756. The names

engraved at the foot of the plate identifying the houses read, from left to right: "Lord Radnor's," "Mr Hudson's," "Mr Pope's/Now S^r Wm. Stanhope's," "Lady Ferrer's," "Mrs. Backwell's."

The house of Henry Robartes, third Earl of Radnor, is the one with Gothic windows in the foreground, its right boundary marked by a grotto edifice. The house of Thomas Hudson, the portrait painter, to the immediate right, was built after Pope's time. Pope's house is recognizable by the notably pitched roof of its central block rising from lower wings. Beyond it, to the right (actually at a far greater distance than the engraving indicates), the dome of Lady Ferrers' summerhouse is visible, a notable landmark in many "views" of the river; and beyond it, "Cross Deep," a house belonging at this date to the widow of Barnaby Backwell whose occupant during Pope's residence at Twickenham remains unidentified. Lady Ferrers was the widow of Sir Robert Shirley, first Earl Ferrers, whose daughter Fanny was a friend of Martha Blount's and the subject of Pope's poem "On receiving from the Right Hon. the Lady *Frances Shirley* A Standish and Two Pens" (TE, VI 378–80). A house this side of Cross Deep is not visible in Müntz's sketch. Its predecessor belonged in Pope's day to William Feilding, fifth Earl of Denbigh, but was lent to the French ambassador and burned down during his occupancy on 14 June 1734.

According to M. H. Grant's *The Old English Landscape Painters* (London, 1926), I 62–63, John Henry Müntz was chiefly a protégé and general artistic handyman of Horace Walpole, "performing every kind of pictorial service for his employer," though undoubtedly "behind his times in art."

3   Ink, with grey-green wash, on paper, $7'' \times 4\,1/2''$. The identifying hand is confirmed by W. S. Lewis to be that of Horace Walpole. The houses identified are "Mrs. Hathaway's," "Edwards's Fisherman," "Pope's," and one whose identification can no longer be read, owing to the mutilation of the drawing at some earlier time. The name, however, is almost certainly that of Barnaby Backwell (Plate 2n). From the resemblance of this view to the Heckell-Mason print of 1749 (Plate 13: see in each sketch the similar spread of the two small trees in the left foreground on either side of the road coming down to the river), one would guess at a like date but perhaps a little later, since the hedge on the right seems now to be a wall, the busts and terms in the hedge have been replaced by globes surmounting short pillars, and the supplemental windows of the grotto porch are round.

In view of the role of J. H. Müntz vis-à-vis Horace Walpole (Plate 2n), it is possible that he is the author of this sketch.

4   This pencil sketch is on the verso of a blank flyleaf in Pope's copy of *Homeri Opera quae exstant omnia, Graeca et Latina*, ed. Stephanus Berglerus (2 vols., Amsterdam, 1707), now in the library of Major S. V. Christie Miller, Clarendon Park, Salisbury. The facing recto of a second flyleaf bears the following inscription in Pope's hand: "E. Libris A. Pope / Donum Dñi Pellet, M.D. / 1714 / E. Libris A. Pope / 1714 / Finish'd ye Translation / In Feb. 1719–20. /—A Pope." Below this Horace Walpole has written: "This book belonged to Mr. Pope, / and the Drawing is by him, / Horace Walpole / 1766. / It is a View of Twickenham Church / from his own garden."

Walpole's last statement must, I think, be in error, for such a view of St. Mary's can hardly have been taken from Pope's garden. A letter from the Borough Librarian of Richmond, Mr. Gilbert Turner, confirms me in this skepticism, and adds: "Furthermore, there has never been a bridge anywhere near Twickenham Parish Church and the Church itself does not appear to conform to reality." There the puzzle presently must rest.

The Pellet who gave Pope the book is evidently Thomas Pellett (1671[?]–1744), a London physician who lived in Henrietta Street, Covent Garden, and was a friend of Pope's friend Richard Mead.

5   Pencil and grey wash on paper, 9 1/2″ × 15″. Signed and dated: "AH 1748". Augustin Heckell (1690–1770), a German engineer living in Richmond, made a series of such sketches at about this period, which were engraved by James Mason and sold with the imprint of "John Bowles at the Black Horse in Cornhill" and the date "22 Apr. 1749" (see below, Plate 13). St. Mary's Church, where Pope is buried, is seen at left and at the far right the Palladian house that in Pope's time belonged to his friend Lord Strafford. This sketch was shown at Marble Hill house in 1967; it is no. 15 in the catalogue mentioned below, Plate 7n.

6   Watercolor, 20″ × 14 3/4″, on paper, 22 1/4″ × 17″. On the back there is an inscription by Horace Walpole which reads: "View of Richmond Hill, Twickenham, and Mr Pope's House, from the Terrace at Strawberry Hill—by Mr. Pars 1772." The special virtue of this painting for our purposes lies in its revelation of the elegant rural character of Twickenham's surroundings. Pope's house after Stanhope's renovations (below, Plates 8, 9), and with a large willow in front of it, is visible between the first and second trees at the extreme left. Between the second and third trees, Twickenham village with the square tower of St. Mary's may be faintly seen.

William Pars (1742–82) is known especially for his Oriental scenes and portraits, which from about 1776 he exhibited at the Royal Academy. He traveled as draughtsman for several patrons in France and Italy, and died at Rome.

7   Oil on canvas, 25″ × 47″. This view was formerly in the Ionides collection and is now the property of the Borough of Twickenham. It was exhibited at Marble Hill house in Twickenham during the summer of 1967 and is listed in the catalogue of that exhibition published by the Greater London Council: *Richmond and Twickenham Riverside: An Exhibition of 18th and 19th Century Pictures from the Ionides Bequest* (1967), no. 5.

At right centre, with detached octagon room, is a large house built by James in 1710 for James Johnston, Pope's "Scoto" (above, p. 15). After Johnson's death in 1737, the property belonged to George Pitt, former Governor of Fort St. George, and in the early nineteenth century was the residence for a time of Louis Philippe, then Duke of Orleans. The house has been variously known, therefore, as Governor Pitt's house and Orleans House. In both centuries, with its fine grove, it supplied a favorite subject for landscape painters. The village of Twickenham may be seen in the distance beyond. On the far southwest side of the village, as we view it here from Richmond Hill, was situated Pope's house.

Antonio Joli, a pupil of Pannini, was at work in England from about 1744. He did a well-known series of Thames views for the London engravers, of which this is one. Characteristic of his landscape paintings is the elongated shape in Neapolitan style designed to fit over doorways.

8   Oil on canvas, 36″ × 18 1/2″. The picture is difficult to date. The striking changes that appear in the structure of the house and in the parterre and waterfront, including especially the large willow (?) to the left of the boathouse in the middle foreground, point to a date considerably later than that of the engraving of 1749 based on one of Heckell's sketches of 1748 (below, Plate 13). In a letter to Mann of 20 June 1760 (Walpole, xxx 417), Horace Walpole speaks of alterations to Pope's house by Stanhope that may be as extensive as those pictured here. Probably, then, the painting dates between 1760 and 1772, when Scott died. The earliest dated view of the villa showing these alterations (Pars's sketch apart: Plate 6) is that drawn, engraved, and published by W. Watts, "Octo. 1ˢᵗ. 1782." A view very like this one, also attributed to Scott, is in the Ionides Collection, now the property of the Greater London Council, and was pictured in the *Country Life Annual* (1963), p. 74. The present view is described in *Burlington Magazine*, LXXVII (1940), 170.

9   Joseph Farington's view of Pope's house (engraved by Joseph Constantine Stadler) shows it with Stanhope's enlargement of the wings, and two willows which were later reputed, on no very reliable authority, to have been of Pope's planting. The trees of the garden behind the house have now shot up to unprecedented heights and the villa appears to sit alone in a wide park. A Palladian staircase, not visible in the Scott painting, but perhaps merely because of the angle of the view, is here plainly to be seen. By this date the house belonged to Welbore Ellis, Stanhope's son-in-law, who had been created first Baron Mendip the year before.

  In 1807 the house was torn down by Baroness Sophia Charlotte Howe, who had purchased the property from Welbore Ellis's heir, and who is said to have been intensely displeased by the visits of tourists and trippers who came to pay tribute to Pope. Her "vandalism," as it was called (she was also believed to have stripped the grotto of many of its minerals so as to destroy its attraction for visitors: *Gentleman's Magazine*, N.S. XVIII [1842], 44; *Notes and Queries*, 8th series, x [1896], 21–22) aroused considerable resentment. Mary Berry records in her journal, 21 November 1807: "Went into Pope's back garden, and saw the devastation going on upon his quincunx by its now [*sic*] possessor Baroness Howe. The anger and ill humour expressed against her for pulling down his house and destroying his grounds, much greater than one would have imagined" (*Extracts from the Journals and Correspondence of Miss Berry from the Year 1783 to 1852*, ed. Lady Theresa Lewis [London (1866], II 334). Others called her "Queen of the Goths," and contrasted her performance with that of Alexander the Great, who spared Pindar's house in sacking Thebes because it had been Pindar's (R. S. Cobbett, *Memorials of Twickenham* [London, 1872], p. 288).

10   In John Vardy's *Some Designs of Inigo Jones and M^r. W^m. Kent* (London, 1744), two engraved plates (together numbered 25) show the two garden vases illustrated here, each with the inscription "W. Kent Inv^t.", "J. Vardy Delin. et Sculp." No other information is given on or below the plates, but in the "Table" at the beginning of the book, Plate 25 is entitled: "Two Vases with Pedestals for M^r. Pope." Whether these vases were ever actually made and set up in Pope's garden remains of course uncertain. For what is known about the urns in his garden, see the text, p. 28 and n. 6.

11   This plate shows the poet's obelisk to his mother as it appears in an engraving in Edward Ironside's *History and Antiquities of Twickenham* (London, 1797), Plate v. The engraving distorts the first line of Pope's inscription, which

reads "Ah Editha." Above, p. 51. Even in the engraving, however, the effect of "painting" with various shades of greenery can be noticed. Below, p. 285, Spence, no. 610.

12   This engraving of Pope's house appeared in the first issue of the *Newcastle General Magazine, or Monthly Intelligencer,* January 1748, in company with a letter signed "T"—"To Mr. P——T—— in Newcastle"—describing Pope's house and gardens (above, pp. 42, 46–47, 52–53, and Appendix A). The closest and most detailed view that I know of, it is obviously based on the view by Rysbrack (Plate 45). The line of newly planted trees within Pope's boundary hedge at left may (or may not) signify that an actual visit was made by the artist of 1747 to the scene. No name of artist is indicated, but "T Smith sculp." in the right-hand corner preserves the name of the engraver.

13   An engraving by James Mason of Heckell's (1748?) sketch of Pope's house, published by John Bowles in 1749 (see above, Plate 5n). This is the first view of the villa to mention its new owner Sir William Stanhope, to whom some of the changes at the river-front (e.g. the shifted opening to the river, the new river house, the low waterside hedge, and the wall extending from the right wing of the villa with niched curving hedge reaching down from it) are possibly owing, though they may of course have occurred between 1735, the date of the Rysbrack view (Plate 45), and Pope's death. If it were possible to be certain that the *Newcastle Magazine* illustration represented the actual state of affairs in 1747, one could date these novelties between 1747 and 1749.

14   Oil on canvas, 17 1/2″ × 22″. The painting is a forgery, or perhaps simply a *capriccio*, based on the sketch by Heckell (above, Plate 13n), but incorporating extraneous "picturesque" elements such as the Pantheon-like building between Pope's house and Lady Ferrers' summerhouse in the right background, and the obelisk (intended to represent Pope's obelisk to his mother?) in the far right foreground. For a fuller account of this work, see a forthcoming article by John Walker, "Engraved Views of the Thames in English and Chinese Painting." Mr. Walker suggests that the Pantheon-like building is copied from the Shakespearean temple that Garrick built on his estate at Hampton about 1755. He also gives such evidence as there is for the identity of the painter, who was probably a certain Joseph Nickolls (or Nicholls). The painting is unsigned and undated, but a companion painting of Secretary Johnston's house is signed "J. Nickolls" and dated (impossibly) 1726.

15   A pen and ink and wash drawing, 3 1/2″ × 5″, by William Kent or Lady Burlington, of Pope meditating or writing in the central chamber of the grotto. At his left above the table hangs, presumably, the alabaster lamp mentioned in his letter to Edward Blount (p. 44). Wimsatt, 15.

16   William Kent's drawing of Pope's garden, though obviously whimsical, is the only visual clue we have to its appearance. One may be properly incredulous about the dolphin (emblem of poetry?) in the foreground, the theophany and rainbow—not to mention the curious shape of the urn—at left, the size of the bust of Homer on the right, and possibly the size and elaboration of the shell temple— housing, presumably, an unquenched flame (emblem of immortality?). Yet the three arched openings suit with the three walks shown on Searle's "Plan"; the design of the shell temple is at least authentic in its obvious instability (the actual temple fell down in December 1735 and had to be rebuilt the following summer: *Correspondence*, III 512, IV 22); and through the grotto arch, between two "pillars" of the temple, a boat on the Thames may be seen—as seems to have been possible in fact. The figure with palette would doubtless be Kent; the short slightly humped figure, Pope.

17   John Searle's "A Plan of the Grotto" (Plate 21n) suggests that there were no important structural changes subsequent to the sketch of 29 December 1740 (Plate 23). The design corresponds almost exactly with that drawn for Oliver. The numberings of the rooms and passages in Searle's diagram are intended to cue them to his account of the minerals to be seen in each. This may be consulted in Appendix C.

18   Searle's "Perspective View" of the grotto (see Plate 25) is useful in conveying its general rough-hewn triple-arched construction and the perspective-glass view of a part of the garden obtainable through the central arch. (For a similar view in the opposite direction, see above, Plate 16.) The object in the roof (represented here as an oval formed of parallel horizontal lines) is probably the mirror of which Pope speaks in his letter to Blount (above, p. 44).

19   Pope mentions the "building" of the obelisk in a letter to Fortescue of 22 March 1735 (III 453) and it appears again briefly in a conversation with Spence (no. 610) in the summer (?) of 1739, when he speaks of creating effects of distance in landscaping by darkening the greens used "and by narrowing the plantation more and more toward the end, in the same manner as they do in

painting, and as 'tis executed in the little cypress walk to that obelisk." Horace
Walpole speaks of the "solemnity" of the same cypress walk (above, p. 26) and
William Kent in his description of a picture he had just seen at Richardson's
tells Burlington that it contains Pope in mourning for his mother, together "with
a strange view of ye garden to show the obelisk" (above, p. 129). The monument's later history can only be inferred. By the mid-nineteenth century, it is at
Gopsell in Leicestershire, seat of the Howes (Carruthers, *Life of Pope*, 2nd ed.
[1858], p. 304n). Probably it came there in 1835 on the death of the Baroness
(above, Plate 9n), who, after destroying Pope's house, had built her own close by
and continued to live there till she died. Gopsell was sold in 1922. The obelisk
is now to be seen in the park of the present Lord Howe at Penn House, Amersham, Leicestershire. For information leading to its present whereabouts, and
generous help in obtaining the photograph reproduced here, I am much indebted
to Professor A. R. Humphries of the University, Leicester.

20   The illustration shows a section (considerably enlarged) of John Rocque's
*An Exact Survey of the City's of London, Westminster, ye borough of South-
wark and the country near ten miles round begun in 1741 and ended in 1745*
(1746). Pope's property is to be seen just opposite the central curve of the
Thames marked by the single large "ait." Against a very black background the
white lines of his garden walks may be seen, together with the positions of shell
temple, orangery, large mount, bowling green, and obelisk. In the white space
of the bowling green there is an inscription, easily legible on the map itself but less
so in the illustration, reading: "Mr. Popes Gardens." It is perhaps revealing that
of all the fine gardens in and about Twickenham, Pope's is the only garden to be
named on Rocque's map.

21   In 1745 Pope's gardener John Searle (the "good John" of the opening lines
of the *Epistle to Dr. Arbuthnot*) published a 30-page quarto pamphlet containing sketches of the grotto (see Plates 17, 18), an account of its contents (see
Appendix c), together with a fold-out diagram of the poet's garden, illustrated
here. Though necessarily much reduced, the cue numbers on the diagram can be
seen in the illustration, and the "Explanation" is given in the caption. The
intricate arrangement of walks, open spaces, grove, mounts, wildernesses, urns,
statues, glimpses, and vistas is notable.

22   This drawing of Pope's grotto, now in the Penzance Library, in Cornwall,
was first published by Benjamin Boyce in "Mr. Pope, in Bath, Improves the

Design of His Grotto," *Restoration and Eighteenth Century Literature: Essays in Honor of A. D. McKillop* (University of Chicago Press, 1963), Plates I and III, opposite p. 148 and p. 149. It was sketched by Pope in a letter of 14 January 1740 that Dr. Oliver was sending to the Rev. William Borlase, Oliver's kinsman, who lived at Ludgvan, Cornwall. No other record gives us as much information about the dimensions of the grotto at this time (50 feet in length, 7 feet high increasing to 10 in the middle portion, 6 feet in the passages) and about the strong effects of light and shadow it supplied, effects (above, p. 46) always congenial to Pope. The sketch also shows one arrangement of Pope's "waterworks," flowing here from a "Spring" to a "Waterfall" to a "Bagnio" and so to the Thames.

23   This second sketch by Pope of his grotto, drawn, as the inscription indicates, for Dr. Oliver on the poet's next visit to Bath in December 1740, shows some of the striking "improvements" of that year. The waterfall, according to the *Correspondence* (IV 267), had now become three falls; the bagnio had been shifted sharply to the right as the drawing shows; a passage-way and stair to the house had been constructed laterally off the central chamber; two "rooms" had been added on either side of this chamber, and a "porch" in front of it. Characteristically, spring and bagnio are now named for Dr. Oliver and Ralph Allen, according to Pope's letters (IV 278–79), and the names of other friends who had helped with materials or plans are inscribed on the porch. Sir John St. Aubyn of Cornwall, visiting the grotto in December 1741, writes back to Borlase that "Borlase" is to be seen there in letters of gold (Benjamin Boyce [cited above, Plate 22n], p. 150).

24   A view of the *arma Christi* at the entrance to Pope's grotto, the crown of thorns above, the five wounds (feet, hands, and heart) below. The interesting inscription above the five wounds, which (so far as I could tell on close inspection in 1965) is incised on a stone distinct from that carrying the five wounds, reads "JR 1696," which I suspect stands for "James Rex 1696." If so, 1696 may allude to the year when James II's natural son by Arabella Churchill, the Duke of Berwick, crossed from France to raise a Jacobite insurrection, and a small band of James' guardsmen under Sir George Barclay plotted to assassinate William III. The discovery of these plots rallied to William many whom his rule had begun to alienate and led to clauses in the Peace of Ryswick (1697) whereby Louis agreed to withhold support in future from any Stuart attempt at Restoration and to remove the Stuart court from St. Germains to Avignon.

Thus 1696 was a critical year for the Jacobite cause. From then on, James II turned his attention increasingly away from the world and toward religious retreat, and, conceivably, Pope had this in mind in placing the inscription at the entrance to his grotto. It must be stressed, however, that this is pure speculation, as must be also any effort to guess whence Pope had these stones or what, exactly, they meant to him. It is even possible that they were added after Pope's time, though my own examination of the structure round about them makes this seem unlikely.

25   Kent's headpiece for Book V in Pope's subscribers' quarto of the translation of the Odyssey (vol. II, 1725) shows the grotto of Calypso with Hermes visible in the distance as he descends to instruct her to let Odysseus go, and, in the round medallion, Odysseus cutting down trees to make his raft. The triple-arched rough-hewn design, decorated with shells, is interesting in its resemblance to Pope's own grotto, both possibly exhibiting a common literary inspiration from the ancient and Renaissance celebrators of grottoes, and expressing a shared sense, playful, though perhaps not merely playful, of numinous place. See TE, VII ccxxiv–ccxxvi; above, pp. 77–79.

26   A second version of Pope writing or meditating in his grotto. Pen and ink and wash drawing, 8 5/8″ × 7 3/8″, by William Kent or Lady Burlington (see above, Plate 15). In this version, the lamp, differently suspended, is on the poet's right. The grotesques above the archway seem to have been a favorite form of doodling with Lady Burlington and may not (or may) be intended as a comment upon the scene (Wimsatt, 16).

27   An anonymous sketch in pen and ink and wash, 8 3/16″ × 10 3/4″ , undated, looking from what seems to be the porch of Pope's grotto, past the iron gate mentioned at Plate 30n, past one of the statues introduced by Stanhope (Plate 31), toward an aging (willow?) tree with the Thames beyond. The tree is probably the ailing one shown in Samuel Scott's painting of Pope's house (Plate 8). Since in an engraving of Pope's house by William Watts, dated 1782, there is no evidence of such a tree and the parterre seems to flourish with foliage more abundantly even than in the Farington view of 1795 (Plate 9), the drawing must like Scott's painting predate 1782 by a number of years. It is preserved in a grangerized copy of the Foulis edition of Pope's works (Glasgow, 1785) now in the Pierpont Morgan Library, vol. IV, at p. 79.

28 Pope's grotto today is a poor remnant indeed. Most of the minerals described in Searle's pamphlet have long ago disappeared in the hands of curio-hunters or under the hammers of Baroness Howe's workmen (above, Plate 9n), as Robert Dodsley's poem predicted (Appendix E); many of the rest are tarnished and oxidized beyond recognition. The porch shown in 23, 27, 30, 31 has gone. Above the archway may still be seen, however, the inset sculpture of the five wounds and the crown of thorns, shown in a closer view in Plate 24.

29 The sleeping nymph in the grotto of Henry Hoare's garden at Stourhead as it appears today. Pope's verses (above, p. 78) are inscribed on the marble rim of the pool and are barely visible in the photograph. The letter to Blount containing the verses was first published in 1735. How soon thereafter they were incised at Stourhead it is impossible to say. Probably not soon, since Hoare did not begin serious work on his gardens till the 1740's. The lines were definitely in place by 1766, when they were published in *The Festoon* with the title: *Under the Statue of a Water-Nymph at Stourhead, Somersetshire. By Mr. Pope. From the Latin.* See TE, VI 248–49.

30 This plan of the grotto, found in Edward Ironside's *History and Antiquities of Twickenham* (London, 1797), reprinted in John Nichols, *Miscellaneous Antiquities In Continuation of the Bibliotheca Topographica Britannica*, vol. x., is dated 1785 and shows the alterations in the grotto made by Stanhope. It is now sixty-four feet long; statues have been added in the porch (Plate 31) and an iron gate at the entrance (Plate 27); and the left-hand room first added in 1740 (Plates 17, 23) has become—probably in response to Dodsley's poem (below, Appendix E) and I suspect quite mistakenly—"the Cave of Pope."

31 A "perspective view" of the grotto forty years later than Searle's, showing the changes introduced by Stanhope, including, if the engraving may be believed, a paved floor. At the end of the long vista, the engraver *may* intend us to make out the shape of Pope's obelisk to his mother, but this would be impossible without a shift in its original position. This engraving, like the foregoing, appears in Ironside's *History and Antiquities of Twickenham.*

32 Copper medal, dated "M. DCC. XLI." on reverse. Diameter 2.15 inches. By Jacques Antoine Dassier. Wimsatt, 62.1 *a* and *b*. George Vertue (*Note Books*, III : Walpole Society, XXII, 1934, p. 104) speaks of this medal as "done from the life and ... free and boldly cut." The cloak Pope wears is probably the furred

scarlet one seen in some of Richardson's portraits of him (e.g. Wimsatt, 52.1),
but Dassier's handling of the fur gives it an ermine-like appearance and the
whole costume a slightly Renaissance cast. Pope is now realized in a "living
medal," as he had dreamed that Britain's great men might one day be in his *To
Mr Addison, Occasioned by his Dialogues on Medals* (1720), 53–62:

> Oh when shall Britain, conscious of her claim,
> Stand emulous of Greek and Roman fame?
> In living medals see her wars unroll'd,
> And vanquish'd realms supply recording gold?
> Here, rising bold, the Patriot's honest face;
> There Warriors Frowning in historic brass:
> Then future ages with delight shall see
> How Plato's, Bacon's, Newton's looks agree;
> Or in fair series laurell'd Bards be shown,
> A Virgil there, and here an Addison.

33   Lead pencil on vellum, 6 3/8″ × 5 1/8″. By Jonathan Richardson. Dated:
"31 Jan 1733/4." Department of Prints and Drawings, British Museum. Wimsatt, 23 *a–b.*

This is one of the most attractive of Richardson's laureated heads of Pope,
drawn in the poet's forty-sixth year with friendship for its special theme.
Jonathan Richardson, Jr., has inscribed on the back: "The Verses were my
Fathers, M^r. Pope made the Little/alteration, perhaps they were better before./
J. R. jun^r." Richardson frequently laureated Pope: see Wimsatt, 26a, 27, 36,
38a, 54.

34   Engraving 13 1/4″ × 18 1/2″. This print (Stephens, no. 1832) was
issued to glorify Walpole in 1730, probably in May or earlier, since in May appeared a parody of it glorifying Colonel Chartres on his pardon by the king
(Stephens, no. 1841). "The Explanation" reads as follows:

A. Great Britt. *alluding to ye Motto of S. R. W. Arms.* ["FARI QUAE SENTIAT"]
   He procures me all the advantages wch he Speaks & thinks. (Quot sentit, quot
   fatur, tot mihi commoda curat.)
B. Fame. *Sounding.* (Tantam ad gloriam non sufficit una.) *One Trumpet Suffice's
   not to publish so much Glory.*
C. Minerva. *aiding S. R. W. to mount to the top of ye Rock, and Holding a Dukes
   Corronet to him.* (Nec par sudoribus.) *It equals not his labours.*

D. Policy. *with her attributes mounting the Rock with S. R. W.*

E. The Hydra. *Crush'd under the Rock, from whose trunk Spring four Serpents Representing.*

1. Envy. (Candidiora denigro.) *I blacken the most Innocent Actions.*

2. Detraction. (Semper sibilo.) *I hiss perpetually.*

3. Impudence. (Nil erubesco.) *I blush at nothing.*

4. Disquiet. (Cunctis et mihi gravis.) *I am a burthen to the World & to my self.*

F. *S. R. W. Saying.* (Tam cautis ductoribus, inter tot aspera firmor.) *such prudent guides secure me in ye most rugged paths.*

G. *An Anagram of the Name. WALPOLE. WALL & POLE* (WALPOLE, Anagr. VALLUM POLUS.) *wth. the Explanation of it in two Latin Verses.*

> (Nil metuens terris, tuto potes ire per Altum.
> Anglia. qui VALLum WALPOLUS. ipse POLUS.)

Thou England that fears nothing by Land may boldly sail ye Seas; WALPOLE who is the Strong WALL that guards thee there shall be thy POLE at SEA.

H. *Six latin verses in Praise of S. R. W.*

> Sit celeber jugulans ferro vetus HERCULES Hydram!
>   Ingenio plures atterit iste novus.
> Concilians pacem proprio sudore paratam,
>   Suadet quam patrius non suus urget amor.
> Invidus improperet! strideat, vel garriat amens!
>   Hunc qui tanta patrat docta MINERVA regit.

Let them praise that Ancient HERCULES, who wth. his Sword Vanquish'd the Hydra! but much more this modern one, who having Vanquish'd several by his Wisdom, & procur'd the peace through his painful management, proves himself to be conducted by the love of his Country, more than self love. Let ye envious detract! Let the senseless Chatter or gnash his Teeth! he who does such great deeds, is Conducted by the Wise MINERVA.

The four medallions are:

I. Great Britt. *between the Empire and Spain, taking Spain by ye hand* (Utile primo). *I prefer the usefull.*

K. *The Fable of the Ox & Frogs.* (Coaxsantes Crepunt.) *They burst wth quacking.*

L. *S. R. W. leading Great Britt. to ye Temple of Felicity along a narrow Plank wch serves as a bridge over a Torrent in which several Crocodil's strive to oppose their passage.* (Lente sed tutó.) *Slowly but Securely.*

M. *The Emblem of Trade.* (Hic scopus laborum.) *This is ye Aim of my labours.*

The print is satirically commented on in a verse epigram printed in the *Grub-street Journal*, 16 July 1730, as follow:

> Three Frenchmen, grateful in their way,
> Sir R——'s Glory would display;
> Studious, by Sister-Arts, t' advance
> The Honour of a *Friend of France*:
> They consecrate to W——'s Fame,
> Picture, and Verse, and Anagram.
> With Mottos quaint the Print they dress,
> With Snakes, with Rocks, with Goddesses.
> The Lines beneath the Subject fit,
> As well for Quantities, as wit.
> Thy Glory, W——, thus enroll'd,
> E'en Foes delighted may behold.
> For ever sacred be to Thee,
> Such *Sculpture,* and such *Poetry*!

In the meantime, the plate had fallen into the hands of the Opposition and was reissued accompanied by a long letter of commentary, dated 11 June and signed "W——polius," which had appeared in the *Craftsman* on 13 June. This letter follows:

To CALEB D'ANVERS, *Esq;*

Mr. D'ANVERS,

I have such an Opinion of your Candour and Impartiality, that I hope you will not neglect an Opportunity, which now presents itself, of doing Honour to a *certain, great Personage,* whom you have often been accused of calumniating. Nay, I am confident you will do it; though you should be obliged, at the same Time, *to take a little Shame to your self.*

I presume you must have observed that a *Curious Piece* hath been lately advertised in the News-Papers, and is now exhibited to Sale in the Print-Shops, entitled, *the Draught of a Print,* most humbly inscrib'd *to the* GLORY *of the right honourable Sir* R——T W——LE.

The Authors of this beautiful Piece are Messieurs *Faget, Dumouchel,* and *Fourdri-nier,* (three *loyal Frenchmen*), who having observed, with equal Resentment and Concern, the licentious Manner, in which several restless Scribblers have bespat-tered that *great Man,* on Account of his close Conjunction with *France,* very generously club'd their Wits together, and have defeated his Adversaries in so masterly a Manner, that I think they deserve the Thanks of every good *Englishman*, who hath any Regard for that *illustrious Family.*

The Design of our *foreign Patriots*, in this Piece, is to represent a *triumphal Arch,* supported by four Pillars of the *corynthian* Order, and embellished with a Multitude of ingenious Devices, which they have taken Care to explain by *marginal Notes* and *Labels* from the Mouths of their principal Figures; but as this *fine, emblematical Panegyrick* (to the Honour and Glory of that *great Man*) may not have yet reached all Parts of the Kingdom, I hope you will contribute your Endeavours to the Propagation of it; and am very sure that your Readers will think themselves obliged to you for anticipating their Pleasure by a short Account and Description of it.

On the Top of the *Arch* stands the Figure of *Britannia* on a large Pedestal, with a Wreath upon her Head, leaning upon her Spear with her right Hand, and holding an *Olive Branch* in her left; from whence comes a Label with this Motto; *Quot sentit, quot* fatur, *tot mihi Commoda curat*; that is, as the Authors tell us *He procures me all the Advantages, which He speaks or thinks*; in Allusion to his *Honour's* Arms; *Fari quæ sentiat*; *He speaks what He thinks.*

I am inform'd that, in the first Draught of this Piece, the Figure of his Majesty King *George* supply'd the Place of *Britannia*; but that the *Authors* were prevail'd upon to alter it as it stands at present, lest the Appearance of the *Prince* should eclipse the *Glory* of the *Minister*; for though Cardinal *Wolsey* was modestly contented with only placing Himself *before his Master*; yet it is certainly more glorious for a *Minister* to appear *singly* in a Panegyrick, without any visible *Dependance*, or *Support*; and instead of writing, as the *Cardinal* did, *Ego & Rex meus*; *I and my King*; it would run much better thus; *Ego sine Rege meo*; *I, by myself, I.*

Just beneath this Figure the Goddess of *Fame* is represented in a flying Posture under the *Arch,* with this Motto, *tantam ad Gloriam non sufficit una*; that is, *one Trumpet suffices not to publish so much Glory*; (though Sir *James Thornhill* thought *one* sufficient to sound the Duke of *Marlborough's* Exploits in *Blenheim Hall*) and therefore our Authors have very wisely equipp'd her Ladyship with a Trumpet in *each Hand*, though she is not able to blow them both at once, as the famous *Herodorus Megarensis* was said to do of old; and as I have seen a *modern Artist* wind a Pair of *hunting Horns*; which, perhaps, might have been more properly put into the Hands of the *Goddess*, upon this Occasion, to represent that the *Hero,* whose Praise she sounds, is a *great Sportsman,* as well as a *consummate Minister.*

The next Figure, *Gentlemen,* that presents itself to you, is the Goddess *Minerva,*

sitting upon a Cloud; who supports Sir *R. W.* with one Hand, in mounting the
S·ummit of a *Rock*, and holds a *Ducal Coronet* in the other, with this Device, *nec
par sudoribus; it equals not his Labours*; artfully insinuating that she ought to give
Him the *East-Indies* with one Hand, and the *West-Indies* with the other; or, at least,
that He deserves an *Imperial Crown*, instead of a *Duke's Coronet.* I think This a
sufficient Warning to a *certain Emperor* to alter his Conduct.

Behind *this Gentleman* upon the Rock (who appears in a rich, *flowing Robe*, and
a great, *full-bottom'd Perriwigg*, with a *French Air*) stands another odd Kind of a
Figure, which the *Annotator* informs us is *Policy, with her Attributes, mounting the
Rock with Sir* R. W. She is drawn with a large *Spying-glass* in her Hand, to express
Foresight, or *Penetration*; and a *Serpent* twisting round it, to denote *Wisdom.* She
likewise holds one of her Fingers upon her Lips, to represent *Secrecy*; and hath a
vizard Mask on her Breast, typifying, as I suppose, *Dissimulation*; which in this
Particular, seems to clash a little with the *Motto* before-mention'd, *He speaks what
He thinks*; unless it ought to be understood *what He thinks* proper *or* convenient.

I must indeed be so free as to give my Opinion, that this Part of the Design is not
so well executed as it ought to be; for the *Rock* itself seems to resemble the *Tarpæian
Rock* at *Rome*, as it hath been described to us by Travellers and Historians; and the
Gentleman is represented in such a Posture upon it, that He seems in the utmost
Danger of pitching headlong down the *Precipice*, if *Minerva* (who is known to be a
Queen of great Wisdom) did not graciously stretch forth her Hand to support Him.

The *Gentleman*, on the Rock, is represented speaking thus in Gratitude to his
*Conductors; tam cautis Ductoribus inter tot aspera firmor; such prudent Guides
secure me in the most rugged Paths*; alluding to that unreasonable Opposition to his
Measures, which He hath lately met with both at *home* and *abroad.*

At the Bottom of this *Rock*, We see *four Serpents*, of an enormous Size, issuing
from the Trunk of the *Hydra*, which We must suppose to be crush'd under it, as the
Annotator informs us. These *four Serpents* represents the *Quadruple Allyance of
Grub-street*, who have lately given the *Gentleman* so much Disturbance in his
Ascent; and therefore We must not suppose them to be any of your *wise Serpents*,
like That which twists round the Hand of Madam *Policy*, but a Sort of mischievous
Hedge-snakes, or *Vipers*, whose only Talents are *stinging* and *biting.*

The *Annotator* hath explain'd these four *serpentine Allies* in the following
Manner.

The *first*, says He, is *Envy*, and bears this Motto; *Candidiora denigro; I blacken
the most innocent Actions*; in Allusion, perhaps, to the *Hessian Troops*, the *Pension
Bill*, the present State of *Dunkirk*, and the Contract in Favour of *Don Carlos.*

The *second* is *Detraction*, with this Motto; *semper sibilo*; *I am continually hissing.*

The *third*, which is *Impudence*, hath this Device; *nil erubesco*; *I blush at nothing.* It is observable that this *shameless Snake* looks the *great Man* full in the Face, and hath almost got hold of one Part of his Robes.

The *fourth*, we are told, is *Disquiet*; whose Motto is, *cunctis et mihi gravis*; *I am troublesome to all the World, as well as myself.*

I wonder indeed that our *ingenious Artists* should not mark out these *four libelling hissing Snakes* in a still plainer Manner, and that instead of the Figures 1, 2, 3 and 4, or the Words *Envy, Detraction, Impudence* and *Disquet*, They did not give them their *proper Names*, and call them, without any Disguise, *D'Anvers, Fog*, B——dg——ll and C——x——l.

I cannot forbear observing that this Representation of our *Libellers* under the Figure of *Snakes*, or *Serpents*, is very artful and satyrical; for the *Devil* Himself tempted our *first Parents* into Disobedience, under this Shape; as their *diabolical Successors* endeavour to beguile us into *Sedition* and *Patriotism*—But as the *first crooked Serpent* fell, so shall They fall; upon their Bellies shall They go, (just as They do in *this Piece*) and *Dust* shall They eat (even the *Dust*, which They have rais'd) all the Days of their Lives.

These are the *principal Figures* within the *Arch*; but there are several other, *hierogliphical Devices* hung round it, like Trinkets to a Lady's Watch; of which I must also give some Account.

In one of them, *Britannia* appears between a Man with a Crown upon his Head, signifying the *Empire*, and a vixonish Sort of a Woman, who represents *Spain*. *Britannia* takes this Lady by the Hand, in Token of Friendship, with these Words, *utile primo*; *I prefer the most useful, or profitable.*

Just opposite to This, We see another little Emblem; in which the Fable of the *Ox* and the *Frogs* is delineated, with this Device at the Bottom; *coaxsantes crepunt*; *They burst with croaking*; meaning again those *graceless Libellers*, who endeavour to vye with that incomparable *great Man*, to whose *Honour* and *Glory* this Piece is inscrib'd.

In the next Piece, a *Gentleman* appears leading a *Lady* by the Hand cross a long, narrow Plank, over a large River, or Body of Water; which, at first Sight, seems to be a typical Representation of *Don Carlos*'s transmarine Expedition into *Italy*; but the *Annotator* sets us right in This, by telling us, that it represents Sir *R. W.* conducting *Britannia* to the *Temple of Felicity*, which appears at a *great Distance*; and indeed we should have been at a Loss to judge, without his Information, whether They were *going to it*, or *coming from it*—The *same envious. detracting Writers*, who were before described under the Types of *hissing Snakes* and *croaking Frogs*, are stigmatiz'd, in this Place, under the Shape of *false, deceitful Crocodiles*, who endeavour to oppose our *Fellow-Travellers* in their Passage to the *Temple*; and yet affect, at the same Time, to weep over their *Misfortunes*. The *Motto* to this Emblem is very apposite to the *Design* of it; *viz. lente sed tuto*; SLOWLY *but securely*.

The *fourth* ingenious Conceit is an *Harbour*, full of Ships, and a Groupe of People unlading them, to represent *Trade*, with this Device; *hic scopus Laborum*; *This is the End of my Labours*; alluding to the Obligations, which We lye under to that *great Man*, for the Improvement of our *Commerce*; the flourishing Condition of our *Colonies* and *Plantations*; and the Reparation, which He hath procured to our *Merchants* for all their Losses and Depredations.

There is another Device, at the Base of the *Arch*, in the Shape of a *Coat of Arms*, which is bound round with a *Garter*, and hath these Words inscribed upon it; *Honi soit qui Mal y pense*; *Evil be to Him, that Evil thinks*. What is most remarkable in this *Coat* is that it bears *three Axes*, on one Side; and that the *Crest* is a *Man's Head*, with a strange Sort of a *Cap and Bells*, which hath a *Ducal Coronet* at the Bottom, by way of Border.

Besides all these ingenious, emblematical Devices there are likewise two Staves of *Latin Metre*, to the Praise and Glory of that *great Man*; which I have attempted in *English*, for the Use of my unlearned Readers; though I cannot have the Vanity to think they come up to the Beauty of the *Original*. The *first* runs thus in the *Latin*.

> *Sit celeber jugulans Ferro vetus Hercules* Hydram.
> *Ingenio Plures atterit Iste novus.*
> *Concilians* Pacem *proprio sudore paratam*;
> *Suadet quam Patrius, non suus urget Amor.*
> *Invidus improperet, strideat, vel garriat amens!*
> *Hunc, qui tanta patrat, Docta* MINERVA *regit.*

In *English* thus.

> Let Bards with Honour *old Alcides* dub,
> Who slew the *Hydra* with his *Sword*—or *Club*.
> Our *English Hercules* is greater far;
> Whose Toils for *Peace* exceed his Toils in *War*;
> He slew *one Hydra*; ours hath many slain;
> Preferring publick good to private Gain.
> Let *Envy* gnash her Teeth; let *Craftsmen* rail;
> Whilst *Pallas* is his Guide, He cannot fail.

The other is an *Anagram* on the *great Man*'s Name; which is thus in the *Original*.

VAL*lum*, PoL*us*.

Nil metuens Terris, *tuto potes ire per* altum,
Anglia, *Qui* VAL*lum*, WALPOLUS, *ipse* PoL*us*.

Englished thus.

WALL, POLE.

How great, O *England*, may thy Greatness be,
Whilst He's thy WALL by Land, thy Pole by Sea?

Having given a particular Account of this *typical, panegyrical Arch*, I beg Leave to add a general Observation or two upon it.

I think This is a fresh Instance that the *French Nation keep their Fidelity even to a Nicety*; for as the *Cardinal* was graciously pleased to demonstrate his good Will to *England*, by supporting a *certain Minister*, with his Recommendation, in a very critical Juncture; so *Three* of his loyal Countrymen have now compleated our Happiness, by destroying that *malignant Cabal*, which hath so long endeavoured to obstruct it.

What a Mortification must it be to you, Mr. *D'Anvers*, and to all the Enemies of that *great Man*, to see all your Arguments answer'd and all your Designs defeated upon a single Sheet of Paper?

I am glad to hear that it hath already met with the Approbation and Encouragement of a *very great Family*; and I hope shortly to see it display'd in the richest Colours upon *Fans* and wrought into *Screens* and *Hangings* for the Use and Ornament of the Palace of N——k.

<table>
<tr><td>St. James's, June
11th, 1730.</td><td align="right">I am, SIR, &c.
W——POLIUS.</td></tr>
</table>

35   Engraving, 9″ × 5 7/8″, dated 1737. Stephens (no. 2326) gives the following description:

This print shows a ship in a storm, raised by young Winds, who are among the clouds; one of them is kicking a hat, another contumeliously salutes the ship. Neptune rises to allay the tumult. On the shore is Britannia, pointing to the ship, with these lines engraved before her feet:—

"She, *While yᵉ Outragious Winds yᵉ Deep deform*
Smiles on yᵉ Tumult, & enjoys yᵉ Storm."

Under the engraving is:—

"Tanta hæc Mulier *potuit Suadere* Malorum."

In December, 1736, the king determined to return from Hanover to England, and embarked on the 14th at Helveotsluys; soon afterwards a most violent storm arose, which lasted four days, during which time there were no tidings of his Majesty. After having been in extreme peril, his yacht put back to Helveotsluys, where he was detained by contrary winds for five weeks, and did not arrive in England until January 7, when he reached Lowestoft. The king was notoriously of a very impatient disposition, liable to sudden bursts of passion, and vented his feelings in actions which were not a little ludicrous. It was a frequent practice with him in these ebullitions to kick his hat about the room, and in one of his paroxysms during the storm he is supposed to have kicked his hat overboard, an action imitated in ridicule by a young Wind. The smiles of Britannia, referred to in this inscription, probably allude to the unpopularity of the king.

See also above, pp. 138–39.

36   Engraving, 7 1/8″ × 8 3/4″, dated 19 December 1738. Stephens (no. 2348) gives the following account:

This engraving shows the interior of a room where a King (George II.) is seated in a chair, and dallying with a lady (Madame Walmoden); while the sceptre is falling from his hand. On a side table are wine-glasses, a bottle, sausages in a plate, and a sheet of paper which is inscribed "*The Black Goat*".[1] On the ground lie the King's gloves, hat, and some papers bearing "*A Whimwam* [i.e. whim-wham] *new come over*" and "*Cabinet of Love*". A pug dog plays with a mourning hatband. Against the wall hangs a portrait of Queen Caroline, and a suit of mourning for that lady, who died Dec. 1, 1737.

Below the design is engraved "Come let us take our Fill of love untill the Morning let us Solace ourselves with Love; For the Good Man is not at Home, He is gone a

---

1/"The Black Goat" refers to the form in which Satan was reputed to appear before his devotees at the Black Mass, where they first danced about him and then kissed his backside. (See M. A. Murray, *The Witch-Cult in Western Europe: A Study in Anthropology* (Clarendon Press, 1921), pp. 68–69, 129, 144–46, 159–60, 180, 183.) The allusion seems to carry approximately the same implications about the King as the "Festival of the Golden Rump" (Plate 37), or as "Idol Worship" (Plate 38) about Walpole. Notable too is the position of the King's leg, a motif used in sixteenth- and seventeenth-century paintings to symbolize sexual possession. On its interesting history see Leo Steinberg, "Michel-Angelo's Florentine Pietà: The Missing Leg," in *Art Bulletin*, L (1968), 343–53.

Long Journey, He hath taken A Bag of Money with him & will come home at the Day Appointed. Proverbs, 7 18 19 20."

37   Described in the text, pp. 143ff.

38   Engraving, 9 7/8″ × 13 3/4″. Described in the text, p. 149.

39   Engraving, 9 1/2″ × 12″, dated 3 December 1743—nearly two years after Walpole's fall and twenty-one months after the *New Dunciad*, where the great yawn was first celebrated. Below the portrait are engraved *Dunciad*, IV 605–18 (with a slight adaptation of l. 605).

40   Engraving, 12 3/4″ × 9 1/4″, dated 1 October 1743. The print shows clearly, like the *Dunciad* mythology in *Common Sense* (see pp. 160–61), how Pope's poetical inventions were adapted to political satire during his later years. Stephens (no. 2604) gives the following explanation of this print:

An engraving showing the court of a royal palace, used as a farmyard, in which stands "*A*", George II., as proprietor of herds of swine, holding a whip, "*B*", in one hand, and a branding iron, "*C*", inscribed "*D——t——g——n*", in the other, and remarking, "*They groul dam'ly—I fear they wont feed.*" "*D*", Lord Carteret, replies, "*Not feed—Ill answer for 'em, tis yᵉ Nature of yᵉ Beast.*" On the ground is his hat, marked, "Worms 1743". In his left hand he holds "*F*", "*Comissiays*", "*Colonels*", "*Ambassadors*", "*Pay Off*"—, "*Navy Off*"—, "*Post Office*". With his right he is feeding "*G*", a pig, "*Sussex*", with garbage, "*E*", which is marked "*Chaʳ of Exche-quer*", "*First Comʳ. of yᵉ T——y*," "*Lᵈ. of the T——y*". The "*Paymaster*" which "*G*" discharges is eaten by a second pig, "*G*", named "*Worcester*", who voids the "*Cofferer*", which is devoured by a third pig, "*Worcester.*" The two former "*Gs*" have "H-A-N-R" rings in their noses. The third voids "*Lᵈ. of Treasury*" to a fourth pig "*G*" "*Windsor*", who voids "*Board of Works*" on the ground, where this last emission lies accompanied by dung bearing the names of officers, "*Comissionars of Salt Customs*," "*Excise*," and "*Stamps*", the ordure is swept up by "*I*" the Duke of Newcastle, who keeps a Chamberlain's key between his feet, inscribed "*For my Brother*". Near him is "*K*", a swineherd, feeding "*L*", "*L*", "*L*", "*L*", a group of hogs with "*M*" "*M*" "*M*", garbage marked with the names of places, "*Comissary Genˡˡ.*", "*A Ribbon*", "*A Regiment*", "*Genᵗ. of Bed Chamber.*", "*Remembrancer*", "*Joint Recever*", "*Pay Master of Pensions*", "*Kˢ Councel.*" The swineherd, "*K*", is desiring the Duke to "*Take it up Clean or they wont eat it.*" The Duke replies, "*Not eat it—damn 'em there's nothing two nasty for 'em.*" Other hogs are in a sty, which is marked "271", and they are feeding out of a trough full of places. On the other side is a shed, in which are hung flitches marked, "*Q*", "*Orford Flitch*", "*Bath*

Flitch", *"Ilchester Flitch"*, *"Edgecombe Hoek"*, *"Ombersley measly"*. These are new peers to be cured in the smoke of the burning scrolls, *"S"*, *"Mag*(na) *Char*(t)*er"*, *"Habeas Corpus"*, and *"Bill of Rights"*.

Above the design the following is engraved: —

> *"Let Courtley Wits to Wits afford Supply,*
> *As Hog to Hog in Hutts of Westphaly;*
> *If one, thro' Nature's Bounty or his Lord's,*
> *Has what the frugal, dirty Soil affords,*
> *From him the next receives it, thick or thin,*
> *As pure a Mess almost as it came in;*
> *The blessed Benefit not there's confin'd,*
> *Drop's to the third, who nuzzles close behind;*
> *From Tail to Mouth they feed, and the*[y] *carouse*
> *The last full fairly gives it to the House."*

Below the design is engraved the following "Explanation. A. The Patentee. B. mark of Authority. C. marking Iron or Brand. Vide Faction Detected Page 113 first Edi^n. D. Foreman or Swine-Herd, in his Hand. E. a Pudding properly prepar'd, in ye other F materials for ye Compost. G G G G. 4 of ye Principal Hoggs in ye Course of Feeding. H. Being measly, was despatch'd to ye Smoking House but for ye sake of ye Scheem &c. keep's his place. I. Bacon Face 1st Hogg-man gleaning ye Garbage K. But ye Tub-man carrying it from one Tire to another. L L. Some very unruly ——Swine Broke out of ye Stye. M M. Something to stop their Mouths. N N. The great Feeding Trough with food for ye Herd. O. the Bacon or Smoking House. P. The Inside or Section. Q Q. the Flitches properly mark'd & Rang'd. R R. Hooks on which They ought to be Hang'd. S. the Materials for Smoking, which unless managed with ye utmost Nicety & discretion, will go off in Explosion to ye Utter destruction of ye House & Undertaker."

The number "271" on the sty was that of the M.PS. who voted for retaining the Hanoverian troops in the British service.

Placemen are here compared to a herd of swine, feeding on filth of every kind, one devouring what another had discharged, as one placeman accepts of an office which another had just resigned. When Mr. Pelham was made Chancellor of the Exchequer, Aug. 25, 1743, he resigned the Paymastership of the Forces, which post was taken by Sir Thomas Winnington. Pelham was Member of Parliament for Sussex, Winnington for Worcester; Sandys, the other member for Worcester, had been Cofferer and Lord of the Treasury, in which latter office he was succeeded by Henry Fox, member for Windsor.

As Stephens notes, the specific references in the hanging bacon flitches are to Sir Robert Walpole, Earl of Orford; William Pulteney, Earl of Bath; Richard Edgecombe, Lord Edgecombe; Stephen Fox, Earl of Ilchester; Samuel Sandys, Baron of Ombersley. The lines quoted from Pope (on which the design is based) are 171–80 of *One Thousand Seven Hundred and Thirty-Eight*, Dialogue II (1738). Above, p. 218.

41   Engraving, 14 1/4″ × 11 1/4″, dated 13 September 1740. This is one of several prints in which a quotation from Pope is used to strengthen or sharpen the point. Stephens (no. 2420) explains the design as follows:

This print represents a landscape, with a road passing through it, from the front to the distance, where is a fortress, the Castle of Edinburgh, on a hill. In the foreground, on our right, is the Exchequer, London, an ancient building with dormers in the roof, bay windows on the first floor, and a single square-headed doorway on the ground floor. All the windows are latticed, *i.e.* they form chequers. At the door of this edifice stands Sir Robert Walpole, attended by two men, one of whom appears in his shirt sleeves. Sir Robert gives a paper to a gentleman, who is loaded with bags of money and Exchequer tallies. On the paper is "£5000 *You are hereby impower'd to quest y*ᵉ *North*." On the ground near this group lie a group of Exchequer tallies, or notched sticks, a bag of money, marked "1000", and a paper, on which is "*Ready Money*". Near this stands a pack-horse, feeding from a large basket. A thistle has fallen from the basket, a rose still lies in it. A scroll, with a label, on which is "*Nemo me impune lacessit.*" hangs from the basket. The horse is loaded with Exchequer tallies, scrolls, rods or whips, and bags of money. On some of the scrolls are inscriptions, thus—"*Court Promis*"(es), "*By me Kings Reign*", "*Riches and Honours*," and "*Ribbons of all Sorts*". The last alludes to the re-establishment of the Order of the Bath by Sir Robert Walpole, which had been done not long before the publication of this print. An itinerant musician, who is performing on a bladder and string, seems to be singing. A long scroll, like those on which popular songs are printed, is twined about his arm. On this is:—

> "*Good People all I pray take heed*
> *Behold an humble Slave*
> *Who changes his shape from Man to Beast*
> *Oh what more would you have*".

Another man, with his finger at his lips, stands near, and watches the horse feeding.

Behind this group, nearly in the middle-distance of the engraving, is a wizard, who has drawn a magical circle on the earth; near him are "*Doomsday Book*", and a large bottle, marked "*The Cordial Julip*". A toad and two serpents are outside this circle, but seem unable to pass its margin. The wizard points with his wand to one part of the circle, where is written "*Deuid o' th' Prize*". At his girdle is a paper, inscribed "*Transmigrati*" (on). With his left hand he points to where, in the air, the Devil is flying on a broomstick, with a whip in one hand, and in the other the bridle, by means of which he guides the broomstick. On the bridle is "*Qui Capit ille facit.*" He is hasting towards the north, as if he had left the Exchequer building for that purpose.

On our left of the road which leads to Edinburgh is a milestone, inscribed "300 *Ms to Edinborough*". Close to this is a Scotchman, standing and holding a picture, which represents the appearance of the angel to Balaam's ass. Before he speaks to the rider, Balaam beats the animal with a stick. The angel holds a scroll, on which is "*The Duke of Argyl speech.*" Over the picture is written : —

> "*The Ape of Balaam through oppression Spoke*
> *Our Pack Horse of Oppression brings the Yoke.*"

This refers to the journey of the horse, before described, to Scotland.

In the distance, and at the foot of the rock on which the Castle of Edinburgh stands, the Devil appears, as if just alighted on the earth; he is still astride of the broomstick. The pack-saddle of the horse which, as before described, stands at the door of the Exchequer building, lies on the ground as if it had reached Scotland; the load has been removed, and is arranged in a circle on the earth. On the saddle the rods, or whips, and some of the scrolls remain. The objects which have been placed on the ground comprise Exchequer tallies, coins, bags, "*Commissions*", papers with seals appended to them, and probably intended for patents of nobility, a "*Petition*", &c. The rider, or gentleman who is talking with Walpole at the door of the Exchequer building, seems to be in the act of removing articles from the horse's load to the ground; he stoops to place two bags, one of which is marked "*Lottery Ticket.*" Two groups of Scotchmen, consisting of four persons each, are placed near the circle of gifts, or bribes; the individuals of one of these groups turn away in disgust and contempt, rejecting the bribes; those of the other group gather eagerly near the money bags and seem about to take possession of them; to these the Devil points, as if he offered them.

A gentleman, the Duke of Argyll, leans against a pedestal or table, which was probably intended for the front of a rostrum, and, pointing towards the circle of bribes, says, "*Remember your Country*". On the front of the pedestal is "*When impious Men bear Sway the Post of Honour is a private Station*". On our right of this the Duke appears again, in the act of receiving a deputation of gentlemen, the leader of whom, kneeling, presents an address, on the scroll of which is "*May it please y^r Grace.*" The Duke replies, "*I have only done my Duty Merit I have none.*" A pole is placed on the ground behind the group of gentlemen; on a pennon which flies from this is:—

> "*Argyll! a Nation's Thunder born to Wield*
> *And Shake alike the Senate and the field.*"   (POPE.) ...

This print may be explained thus; Sir Robert Walpole, finding that the Duke of Argyll, after resigning his appointments, had gone to Scotland, and being apprehensive of the effects of his grace's eloquence and personal influence on the Scotch, and on the people of Edinburgh in particular, is supposed to have despatched after the Duke an agent, who was empowered to pacify malcontents by means of bribes or force; on this account the pack-horse is laden with bribes and rods. In the air, the Devil, obedient to the order of the wizard, flies towards Edinburgh, where the agent and the pack-horse likewise proceed. The Devil and the agent appear in the distance of the design as at their arrival; the former bestows part of the load on the corruptible Scotchmen, while the latter sets forth the other articles on the ground, in order to tempt those who might be induced to support Walpole; the virtuous Scotchmen reject the bribes with disdain.

Below the print these lines are engraved:—

> "In this Mysterious Mythologic Time,
> Picture much plainer Speaks than Prose or Rime;
> Let Lights and Shades before your Eyes Depaint,
> His Country's Hero—and a Devil's Saint
> Of Metamorphoses you've oft been told,
> Here, a North-British-One you may behold!
> His Venal Soul his Errand does foretell,
> For Gold, his Faith and Liberty he'll Sell"

It may be worth noticing that the Devil's bridle carries the same legend here that is applied to Walpole elsewhere (see p. 198): *Qui Capit ille facit.* The couplet from Pope praising Argyll is a slightly altered version of ll. 86–87 of *One Thousand Seven Hundred and Thirty-Eight,* Dialogue II (1738). For the inscription on the pedestal on which Argyll leans, see above, p. 212.

42   Engraving, 14″ × 11 3/8″, issued before 26 September 1740, at which time it is advertised in the *Daily Post*, as follows: "A Political Medley; or, The Champion loaded with his Honour's Creed, or Political Faith: Being a curious Print, or Deceptio Visus; with the King and—[Whore?] of Diamonds, the Curse of Scotland [i.e. Walpole], the Knave of Diamonds. With a Letter to the Electors of Great Britain on the Importance of an uncorrupted Parliament."

Stephens (no. 2453) gives the following elucidation:

This print is a medley or representation of many papers, with engravings and letter-press, lying one over the other, and all placed on a page of the above-named newspaper, the ornament of its title being the British Eagle, bearing three crowns, pouncing on a prostrate figure of Cardinal Fleury, who grasps a label inscribed "*Dunkirk*", and emits a "*F——t for Trea*" (ties). By the Treaty of Utretch, fortified by subsequent conventions, France stipulated not to have a fortified town, nor a fortified port, at or near Dunkirk. Cardinal Fleury, relying on the apathy of Walpole, despised these treaties and repaired the harbour at this place. Over "The Champion" lies "*HIS POLITICAL CREED.*" a blasphemous parody of the "Creed" in rebusses, expressing belief in George II. and his minister Walpole.

The other represented prints and letterpress texts comprise several playing cards, one of which is George II., as the King of Diamonds, with, inscribed on a paper beneath, "*Give not thy Strength unto Women, nor thy Ways to that which destroyeth Kings. Prov.* 31: 3." This alludes to the king's attachment to Amelia Sophia Walmoden, who at this time (March 24, 1740) was created Countess of Yarmouth, and is here represented as the Queen of Diamonds, with a scroll at the side, inscribed "*With her much fair speech she caused him to Yield, with the flatt'ring of her lips she forced him. Prov.* 7 21". On the other side lies a pair of spectacles, on the spring of which is "*O Lord! Open our Eyes,*" *i.e.* that we may see the true features of this man who now deludes us, one of the glasses being placed over the face of the Knave of Diamonds, Sir Robert Walpole; on a scroll below this card are engraved the following lines:—

> "*Who wickedly is wise, or madly brave,*
> *Is but the more a Fool, the more a Knave.*
> *Stuck o'er wth Titles, & hung round wth Strings*
> *That thou may'st be, by Kings, or Wh——es of Kings.*
>   Pope's Essay."

Under the Knave lies a portrait of the Duke of Argyll, who at this time was a vehement opposer of Walpole and had indignantly resigned all his employments. ...

A burlesque tournament is engraved at the foot, between a mouse mounted on a leopard and a frog mounted on a lobster.

Under the portrait of the Duke of Argyll, and probably intended for a speech by him, is an inscription on a scroll, which is engraved—

> "By Heaven he shall not have a Scot of them;
> No, if a Scot would save his Soul, he shall not!"
>
> Shak:" [speare]

Over this, in the upper corner of the assemblage of represented prints, is a letter directed thus:—"To Mr. Geo: Wickham jun' Engraver & Drawing Ma': at His House in May's Buildings Covent Garden." ... In the opposite corner to this is a scrap of paper, with parts of three lines of music, and "Spain". Over this lies another fragment of paper, being part of a public journal, with the following engraved in imitation of letterpress:—

(Ri)"ght Honourable Sir

Edinburgh, July 5, 1740

Sir, A Crisis of Time is now approaching, the most important to the British Nation, and the most deserving of your serious Attention, that perhaps was ever known in this Country; a Crisis, on the Events of which not only our Trade, our Honour and our Safety from foreign Enemies will depend, but the Preservation of that Liberty at home, which is the first Support of the others, and by which only they become valuable to us. The War we are now engag'd in must convince you of the one, as must the Sta [te] of our domestic affairs (if consider'd) of the other."

Stephens suggests (no. 2452) that the mouse on the leopard is the Spanish Admiral and the frog on the lobster the British Admiral Nicholas Haddock. The Spanish admiral had been too timorous to risk battle, the British too dilatory in his blockading of the Spanish fleet.

The use of Pope's lines in *Essay on Man*, IV 231–32, 205–6 is noteworthy. Whether or not 205–6 were intended for Walpole (see p. 135) they are here used against him. The "Creed"—which Stephens found too distasteful to transcribe—reads as follows:

*I Believe in King [George] y*ᵉ *2*ᵈ*, y*ᵉ *[grate] -est [cap]-tain, & ye [Wis]-est Mon[ark], [bee]-tween [heaven] & [earth], And in S*ʳ*. Rob*ᵗ*. [Wall]-[pole], his only [son] our [Lord], who was [bee]-gotten by barrel [=Burwell]*[1] *y*ᵉ *At[tor]ney,*

1/Walpole's mother was Mary Burwell, daughter of Sir Jeffrey Burwell, an attorney of Rougham in Suffolk. This allusion appears to insinuate that Walpole was incestuously begotten

born of M^{rs}*. [Wall][pole] of Hough-[town] [axe=ac]-cused of corrup[eye=ti]on,
exp-[L=ell]-ed & im-[prison]-'d he went down into Nor-[fork=folk] y*^{e} *[3rd]
[ear=year] he came up again, he [ass]-sended into y*^{e} *Ad[minis]tra[eye=ti]on, &
[sit]eth at y*^{e} *[head] of y*^{e} *Treas-[yew]-ry, from thence he shall pay [awl=all] those
who Vote [ass=as] they are [comb=com] manded.
....[Eye=I] [bee]-[leaf=leave] in Horras's [=Horatio Walpole's] [tree]-ties y*^{e}
Sanc[eye=ti]ty of y^e *[bishops]'s, y*^{e} *Inde-[pen]-dancy of y*^{e} *[Lord]s, y*^{e} *Integ[eye=
ri]ty of y*^{e} *[Comb=Com]mons, a Res[eye=ti] tu-[eye=ti]on from the [guard=
guarda-costas], & a [discharge] of the Pub-[leek=lic] Debts A-[men].
NB. Who ever would be in Office should above all things Profess this Political Faith.*

43   Pope was presented several times by Roubiliac in the manner of the Roman
portrait bust (Wimsatt, 227). One of these (Wimsatt, 58a, dated "1738"), now
at Milton, Peterborough, bears the inscription *Qui nil molitur inepte,* which may
be very freely translated: "He touches nothing that he does not adorn." This is
Horace's elegant praise for Homer (*Ars Poetica,* 140) and a reminder of Pope's
achievements as the British Homer. The bust pictured here (Wimsatt, 59.1,
dated "1740") associates Pope with the traditions of Roman satire and specifically with Horace and Lucilius. The inscription cut into its base—UNI AEQUUS
VIRTUTI ATQUE EJVS AMICIS—is Horace's well-known phrase for his predecessor
Lucilius in his first satire of the second book (1. 70) and Pope's for himself in his
imitation of that poem (1. 121): "TO VIRTUE ONLY and HER FRIENDS, A FRIEND".

Rudolf Wittkower, speaking of the eighteenth century's "idealized portraiture
of great men" as "a new genre" in British sculpture, observes of the bust mentioned above what may be said of Roubiliac's portraits of Pope as a group: "The
penetrating head, ... entirely modern in spirit, recalls Roman busts of the
Augustan age translated into a philosophical mood" (F. Säxl and R. Wittkower,
British Art and the Mediterranean [Oxford University Press, 1948], p. 68).

44   Rysbrack's terra cotta bust of Walpole admirably catches the power of his
personality, his keen sense of "the specialty of rule" (to use Ulysses' phrase for the
proper management of authority in Shakespeare's *Troilus and Cressida*), and
perhaps, in the glimmer of the smile about the mouth, his pleasure in it. See also
Plate 49.

by his maternal grandfather. (There is no doubt a glance too at Walpole's alleged partiality
for the scrivener and attorney class, the money-men.) Apparently the obscure joke persisted.
The *Craftsman* more than once refers to Walpole as having been "bred an *Attorney*" (5 July
1729, 9 June 1733, 25 October 1735).

45   My description of the exterior of Pope's house in Chapter I is based on the engraving shown here. It is entitled "An Exact Draught and View of Mr. Pope's House at Twickenham" and signed "Rysbrack delin. & pinx.," "Parr Sculp." It depicts Pope's house and a few neighboring buildings from across the river, several swans and boats in the river, a party of visitors landing on Pope's greensward with two small dogs scampering before them, and, in front of the grotto opening, a figure with a dog that plainly belongs to Pope's long line of Bounces. Below the picture are printed (without separation, as if they belonged to the same poem) *Imit. Hor., Sat.* II i 123–24 and II ii 137–50. The artist in question is probably Peter Andreas Rysbrack, brother of the more famous Michael, who is known to have specialized in landscape and topographical views for engraving. (See M. I. Webb, *Michael Rysbrack, Sculptor* [London, 1954], pp. 19–20.) The engraver is probably Nathaniel Parr, who was active in London in work of this kind between 1730 and 1760.

This view of Pope's villa is apparently to be identified with the "Prospect *of Mr.* Pope's House, *from the* Surrey Side," which, according to his own account (*Mr. Pope's Literary Correspondence*, II [London, 1735], "To the Reader"), Edmund Curll had Rysbrack make for him on 12 June 1735, when he visited the villa in company with the artist, Pope himself being then in London:

> Mr. CURLL *is the sole Editor of this Volume, and it* Is, *what the former* WAS, *a* Collection *of what has been printed, and a* Compilation *from* Original Manuscripts; *but not stollen, either from* Twickenham, Wimpole, *or* Dover-street; *but at the last Place, while Mr.* Pope *was dangling, and making* Gilliver *and* Cooper *his Cabinet-Counsel, away goes Mr.* CURLL, *on the* 12th *Day of* June, *in the Year of our Lord God* 1735, *and, by the Assistance of that Celebrated Artist Mr.* Riisbrack, *takes a full View of our Bard's Grotto, Subterraneous Way, Gardens, Statues, Inscriptions, and his Dog* BOUNCE. *An Account of some of them are hereunto subjoined. And a* Prospect *of Mr.* Pope's House, *from the Surrey Side*, *will be shortly exhibited, in a very curious Print, engraven by the best Hands.*

The gardens, statues, and inscriptions that Curll refers to do not appear in the extant Rysbrack "Draught and View." But Curll is not known for accuracy. He may have regarded Pope's parterre and hedges as sufficient to justify the term "*Gardens,*" since no view of the front of the house could possibly include the garden proper. He may during his visit have seen "Statues" with "*Inscriptions*" niched into the parterre hedge, which Rysbrack did not record in the painting. In the description of the house to which Curll refers as "*hereunto subjoined,*" he makes it clear that he has penetrated the actual garden:

Mr. POPE'*s* HOUSE,

It must be allow'd, by all who have seen this Place, that the Owner's Description of it is very just; and every Spectator must bear Testimony how little it owes to Art, either the Place itself, or the Image he has given of it. But, since that Time, he has been annually improving the Gardens, to the Amount of above Five Thousand Pounds, as Mr. *Serle* his Gardener assured us. He has lived with Mr. *Pope* above Eleven Years, and in the Hortulan Dialect told us, that, *there were not Ten Sticks in the Ground when his Master took the House*; so that all the Embellishments to this natural Situation have been at the sole Expence of Mr. *Pope*. There is now in the Ground a fine Statue of the *Grecian Venus* Dancing (but it is in the leaden Taste); at the End of one Walk, is a *Busto* of Sir *Isaac Newton*. And in a little Summer-House, another of Mr. *Dryden*. He has likewise, as a very commendable Act of Filial Respect, raised an Obelisk to the Memory of his Mother, with this Inscription round the Verge;

AH EDITHA

MATRVM OPTVMA

MVLIERVM AMANTISSIMA

VALE.

Over the Entrance of the Grotto, or Subterraneous Way, is this Inscription;

SECRETVM ITER

ET FALLENTIS

SEMITA VITAE.

The Rysbrack "Draught and View" is the earliest view of Pope's house, and the only one published in his lifetime with which I am familiar. How far Gibbs, if it was Gibbs, brought the villa to this appearance during the early alterations, how far it was modified by later ones, is perhaps now impossible to determine. In a letter to Digby that Pope dates 1 May 1720 (II 44), he refers to "my Tuscan Porticos, or Ionic Pilasters." This accords well with the Tuscan order featured by his portico and the Ionic order featured by his bow windows, as we see them in the Rysbrack "Draught and View." But there are references in 1732–33 to the building of a "portico," evidently designed by Kent and approved by Burlington; to his need of Burlington's counsel "about the Upper Cornish of my house, & the Moldings & Members of the Entablature" before going on with "Stuccoing"; and to a "New Room" (III 322–23, 329, 341, 353, 356, 406). A letter to Fortescue in 1736 (13 April: IV 10) indicates that "improvement" is still going on.

The design of Pope's portico as depicted in the "Draught and View" stems from a formula found with some frequency in facades of Palladian inspiration. The seventeenth-century Villa Contarini near Padua shows an application of the formula that closely resembles Pope's (Guiseppe Mazzotti, *Ville Venete*, 2nd ed. [Rome, 1958], Plate 291. So does the T. C. Simon house at 128 Bull Street, Charleston, South Carolina.

A shorter version of the foregoing note will be found opposite the reproduction of this view of Pope's house in the earlier version of Chapter 1 of this book published in *From Sensibility to Romanticism: Essays Presented to Frederick A. Pottle*, ed. F. W. Hilles and Harold Bloom (Yale University Press, 1965).

46   Good views of Houghton are rare. That published by Horace Walpole in his *Aedes Walpolianae* (1742), being rather an elevation than a view, gives little idea of its grandeur and no idea of its luxury. For this, one must turn to the engraving by William Watts here reproduced and to the description that accompanies it in the Boydell volume:

HOUGHTON, one of the most celebrated Edifices in *England*, was begun by Sir *Robert Walpole*, in the Year 1722, and completed in 1735, as appears from the following Inscription over the South-end Door, which is the common Approach to the House. "*Robertus Walpole, Has Aedes, Anno S.* MDCCXXII. *Inchoavit, Anno* MDCCXXXV. *Perfecit.*" It stands about five Miles from *Fakenham*, in a fine Park, and is surrounded by magnificent and extensive Plantations, which form a Circumference of about eight Miles. The whole Building is of Stone, and though not strictly conformable to the present Taste in some Particulars, is, nevertheless, a superb and elegant Structure. It extends, including the Wings, which contain the Offices, five hundred Feet. The Center is one hundred and sixty-five Feet by one hundred, and consists of a rustic, principal, and attic Story, terminated at the four Angles by Cupolas; the West Front is ornamented with a Pediment, containing the Arms of the Family supported by four *Ionic* three-quarter Columns, and is crowned with Statues. The Entrance was originally in the principal Story, by a grand Flight of Steps in each Front, but is now confined to the Basement (similar to *Holkham*) the Steps having been lately pulled down, in Consequence of their being considerably decayed.

The principal Apartments at *Houghton* are the following: The Saloon, forty Feet long, forty high, and thirty wide; the Hangings of crimson flowered Velvet; the Ceiling by Kent, who designed all the Ornaments throughout the House; the Chimney-piece, as well as the Tables, are of black and Gold Marble; The Hall is a

Cube of forty feet, with a Stone Gallery round three Sides; the Ceiling and Frieze by *Altari*; the Figures over the Doors by *Rysbrack*: The Drawing Room is thirty Feet by twenty-one, hung with yellow Caffoy, and adorned with some fine Carving by *Gibbons*: The *Carlo Maratt* Room (so called from its being formerly hung with Pictures by that Master) is of the same Dimensions; the Hanging[s] are green Velvet; the Tables of Lapis Lazuli; at each End are Sconces of massive Silver; The common Parlour is also thirty Feet by twenty-one, and contains some carving by *Gibbons*: The Marble Parlour is thirty Feet by twenty-four; one entire Side of the Room is Marble, with Alcoves for Sideboards, supported by Columns of *Plymouth* Marble; over the Chimney is a fine Piece of Alto Relievo, by *Rysbrack*: The Library is twenty-one Feet by twenty-two, as is also the Cabinet: The Gallery (which is in the right-hand Wing) is seventy-one Feet long, twenty-one wide, and twenty-one high; the Hangings of *Norwich* Damask;—it was originally intended for a Green-House, but on Sir *Robert Walpole's* Resignation in 1742, it was fitted up for the Pictures which were in *Downing* Street.

The capital Paintings which formerly ornamented these Apartments, and which unquestionably formed the finest Collection in the Kingdom, except the Royal One, we are sorry to observe, are now in the Possession of the Empress of *Russia*, who, it is said, has lately purchased them for 40,000l.

47   This is the title-page vignette by Francis Hayam and C. Guignion in William Mason's *Musaeus: A Monody to the Memory of Mr. Pope, In Imitation of Milton's Lycidas* (London, 1747). In a scene notably "grottesque," a figure representing immortal fame and wearing the creative sunburst of Apollo (see Plate 48) supports and receives the dying Poet, while Milton, Spenser, and Chaucer (left to right) look on. There is a similar scene in the poem itself, though there the female figure is called "Virtue" and the three attending poets each speak some lines that vaguely evoke their poetic styles. Wimsatt, Appendix, 4.8.

48   This is the "ornament" by Gravelot which accompanies Pope's portrait at the end of the second volume of Birch's *Heads of Illustrious Persons of Great Britain. Engraven by Mr. Houbraken and Mr. Vertue* (1751). Beneath the traditional sunburst of creative light and energy and within sight of a temple that is possibly meant to represent a temple of fame, Apollo attended by nine muses stretches out a laurel (?) wreath toward a vaguely Popean figure in a loose gown who spurns some misshapen figures in the dark right-hand corner as

he is led forward by Homer and another to receive his emblem of poetic immortality (Wimsatt, 66.16).

49 A modern photograph of the Stone Hall at Houghton. The bust seen in the center of the mantel in this plate is a marble version by Rysbrack of the terra cotta shown in Plate 44. To quote once more from Rudolf Wittkower, it "stands over the mantel piece in the Stone Hall at Houghton, surrounded by a number of ancient busts, as an equal among equals" (F. Saxl and R. Wittkower, *British Art and the Mediterranean* [Oxford University Press, 1948], 68).

50 Pope is here represented by his friend Jonathan Richardson in a Chaucerian dress based on the so-called Hoccleve image, which was several times engraved during his lifetime. The "Chausor in a black frame" noted by the inventory on the wall of his "Little Parlor" was probably an engraving of the Hoccleve type or his own copy of such a likeness. Richardson's repeated experiments in drawing heads of Pope makes it impossible to assign any clear significance to the representation, but it is certainly in keeping with the assimilation of Pope to his predecessor poets which is seen in Plates 43, 47, 48. Below the drawing runs an inscription, partly torn away, reading: "Pope as a c [?]. ..." If this letter is "c," it may be the first letter of some form of the word Chaucer or Canterbury. Wimsatt, 19 (12).

51 Another of Richardson's experiments in drawing Pope's head, with, in this case, an unmistakable intent to assimilate his admired contemporary to the image of a great predecessor and vice versa. Wimsatt, 37 (1), 38, 38 bx. A Greek transliteration of Milton's name (ΜΙΛΤΩ) is inscribed on the plate; the legend below, "A. Pope, as Milton," seems to be in the hand of Jonathan Richardson, Jr., the painter's son.

52 Pope and the *Iliad*. Oil on canvas. 35″ × 26″. By Sir Godfrey Kneller, signed and dated 1719 ("G. Kneller / 1719"). The Baron Barnard, Raby Castle, Durham. Wimsatt, 5.1.

This is one of the many images of Pope which seems to present him as a version of "the Poet." The book he holds is unmistakably shown to be the *Iliad*. That it is no less unmistakably shown to be an *Iliad* in the original Greek may be a tacit rejoinder to critics who had accused him of having none, but failed to convict him. The Greek reference is surprisingly specific. The leaf Pope is about to turn to contains the opening of Book IX (i.e. Book Iota: the "I" may be seen at the top of the leaf), and the initial letters of its first five or six lines are clearly visible:

> Ὣς οἱ μὲν Τρῶες φυλακὰς ἔχον· αὐτὰρ Ἀχαιούς
> Θεσπεσίη ἔχε φύζα, φόβου κρυόεντος ἑταίρη,
> Πένθεϊ δ᾿ ἀτλήτῳ βεβολήατο πάντες ἄριστοι.
> Ὣς δ᾿ ἄνεμοι δύο πόντον ὀρίνετον ἰχθυόεντα,
> Βερεῆς καὶ Ζέφυρος, τώ τε Θρήκηθεν ἄητον
> Ἐλθόντ᾿ ἐξαπίνης·

This Pope had translated:

> Thus joyful *Troy* maintain'd the Watch of Night,
> While Fear, pale Comrade of inglorious Flight,
> And heav'n-bred Horror, on the *Grecian* part,
> Sate on each Face, and sadden'd ev'ry heart.
> As from its cloudy Dungeon issuing forth,
> A double Tempest of the West and North
> Swells o'er the Sea, from Thracia's frozen Shore. ...

I know of no reason for Pope's choosing this passage. Possibly the intent was to indicate the point he had reached in the translation (i.e. vol. III, containing Books IX–XII) at the time when the earliest picture of this type (1716, according to the mezzotint of 1717) was painted.

I have borrowed here my own note accompanying this portrait in TE, VIII xiv.

53   Pope at thirty-three, wearing the "Critick's Ivy." Oil on canvas. 24 1/2″ × 22 1/2″. By Sir Godfrey Kneller, in or about 1721. Sir Alexander Douglas-Home, the Hirsel, Coldstream, Roxburghshire. Wimsatt, 6.2.

In his *Essay on Criticism*, Pope assigns to his predecessor Vida both the "Poet's Bays" and the "Critick's Ivy." Though the association of ivy with learning and art (and poetry) was of course ancient, Pope seems to have been the first to associate it so flatly and crisply with the art and learning of critics, and was censured for doing so by Concanen. (See the note on the *Essay*, 1.706, in TE, I, and J. B. Trapp, "The Owl's Ivy and the Poet's Bays. An Enquiry into Poetic Garlands," *Journal of the Warburg and Courtauld Institutes*, XXI [1958] 227–55.)

The profile view and toga seemingly invite the beholder to think of ancient medals and the famed men on them. See above, Plate 32. I have drawn part of this note from that which accompanies this portrait in TE, x xii.

54/55   Pope at thirty-four. Oil on canvas. 28 1/2″ × 24″. By Sir Godfrey
Kneller, signed and dated 1722 ("G. Kneller /1722"). The Viscount Harcourt,
Stanton Harcourt, Oxfordshire. Wimsatt, 7.1.

The poet is here shown resting (as it were, literally, with a volume of his *Iliad*
under his elbow) on his achievements, eyes thoughtful and far away. The
"poetic" character of the pose is very clear in the detail (Plate 55), which somewhat resembles in attitude and gaze Severn's miniature of Keats.

Index

This index is the work of Annetta Bynum and the author, the latter of whom is responsible for its shortcomings. For the most part, it aims to identify as precisely as possible the persons and places referred to in the text, giving full names, titles, dates, and sometimes other particulars, thus to inform the reader in advance of the general content of the references he will find when he consults the page(s) referred to. The letters AP and RW are used throughout to refer to Pope and Walpole. Plates are referred to by *P*.

Aaron: RW staff of office compared to his rod, 145

Abs-court, Surrey: in AP poem, 110; source of materials for AP grotto, 261

Ackermann, R.: *Microcosm of London* (1808), 266, q269

Acrisius father of Danaë: in Horace's *Ode III xvi*, 88

Adams, C. K.; *see* Goulding, R. W.

Addams, Charles, *New Yorker* cartoonist, 24

Addison, Joseph, 1672–1719, essayist and critic: *Spectator*, q22, 22n, q24, 24n, q36, 36n; *Cato* (1713), 134, q134n, q212; *see also* AP poem *To Mr Addison, Occasioned by his Dialogues on Medals*

Adonis, gardens of, 24

Aegisthus: *see* RW

Aeneas: and Evander, 72; and the Sybil, 221; *see also* George II

Aeolus, god of winds, 93, 145n

Africa: contentment on little better than riches of, in Horace, *Ode III xvi* 86–87

Afterloney, Mr. (unidentified): contributes materials for AP grotto, 261

Agamemnon; *see* George II

Aikman, William, 1682–1731, portrait painter, 248

Aitken, George A.: *Life and Works of John Arbuthnot* (1892), 249

Alcinous, gardens of, 24, 52

Alexander the Great: spares Pindar's house, 283

Alfred, 849–901, King of England: in AP poem, 139; contrasted with George II, 140

Allen, B. Sprague: *Tides in English Taste* (1937), 21n

Allen, D. C.: *Image and Meaning: Meta-phoric Traditions in Renaissance Poetry* (1960), 23n

Allen, Ralph, 1694–1764, friend of AP: his residence at Prior Park, 16n; commemorated in AP poems, 31; friend of St. Aubyn, 253; recommends stone masons to AP, 258; contributes materials for AP grotto, 259, 260, 261; legatee of AP will, 264; AP guest of 279; AP bagnio named for, 287; *see also* AP, correspondence

Altick, R. D.: article on AP grotto, 42n

Amelia, Sophia Eleonora, 1710–86, Princess Royal: in AP poem, 164, 178

Amersham, Leicestershire: present site of AP obelisk, xvi, 286

Amhurst, Nicholas, 1697–1742 (pseud. Caleb d'Anvers), editor of *Craftsman*, 158, 159, 295, 297; *see also Craftsman*.

Anglicanism: AP solicited to convert to, 63, 65

Animism: in AP treatment of nature, 8

Anne, 1665–1714, Queen of England: in *Windsor Forest*, 5, 95; death of, 154 and n, 234, 245; prodigies lacking at death of, 154n; furniture in vogue during reign of, 251

Apollinax, Mr.; *see* Eliot, T. S.

Apollo: god of poetry, *P* 47, *P* 48, xviii, 310; AP compares himself to, 255; repre-sented by Kneller, 264

Appius; *see* RW

Apulia: famous for rich farms, 86–87

Arbuthnot, Anne, d. 1751, daughter of Dr. Arbuthnot: legatee in AP will, 264, 265

Arbuthnot, George, 1703–79, son of Dr. Arbuthnot: executor of AP will, 263, 265; legatee in AP will, 264, 265; *see also* AP, correspondence

Arbuthnot, Dr. John, 1667–1735, friend of

This book

was designed by

ALLAN FLEMING

with the assistance of

ELLEN HUTCHISON

University of

Toronto

Press